AF754710

# Rights and Their Limits

# Rights and Their Limits

## *In Theory, Cases, and Pandemics*

F. M. KAMM

OXFORD
UNIVERSITY PRESS

OXFORD
UNIVERSITY PRESS

Oxford University Press is a department of the University of Oxford. It furthers the University's objective of excellence in research, scholarship, and education by publishing worldwide. Oxford is a registered trade mark of Oxford University Press in the UK and certain other countries.

Published in the United States of America by Oxford University Press
198 Madison Avenue, New York, NY 10016, United States of America.

© Oxford University Press 2022

All rights reserved. No part of this publication may be reproduced, stored in a retrieval system, or transmitted, in any form or by any means, without the prior permission in writing of Oxford University Press, or as expressly permitted by law, by license, or under terms agreed with the appropriate reproduction rights organization. Inquiries concerning reproduction outside the scope of the above should be sent to the Rights Department, Oxford University Press, at the address above.

You must not circulate this work in any other form
and you must impose this same condition on any acquirer.

CIP data is on file at the Library of Congress
ISBN 978–0–19–756773–9

DOI: 10.1093/oso/9780197567739.001.0001

The manufacturer's authorised representative in the EU for product safety is Oxford University Press España S.A. of El Parque Empresarial San Fernando de Henares, Avenida de Castilla, 2 – 28830 Madrid (www.oup.es/en or product.safety@oup.com). OUP España S.A. also acts as importer into Spain of products made by the manufacturer.

*In memory of my dear parents, Mala and Solomon,*
*who survived the trampling of their rights.*

# Table of Contents

# Acknowledgments

I am grateful for the invitations to write on the topics of several of the chapters in this book. These include invitations from groups at Harvard, New York, Oxford, and Rutgers Universities; the University of Arizona; the University of California, at Berkeley and Irvine; and Boston University and Yale University Law Schools. Many of the chapters were written while I was the Littauer Professor of Philosophy and Public Policy at the Harvard Kennedy School and Professor of Philosophy at Harvard University. I am grateful for the support provided by Harvard and by the Edmund J. Safra Center for Ethics at Harvard. Other chapters were written during my first few years as the Henry Rutgers University Professor of Philosophy and Distinguished Professor of Philosophy at Rutgers University and I am grateful for the support I have received from the Rutgers Philosophy Department and Rutgers University.

Material in many of the chapters benefited from discussion with Shelly Kagan, Jeff McMahan, and Larry Temkin. More detailed acknowledgments are to be found in each chapter.

This book was composed during the frightening COVID-19 spring of 2020 while on a leave from teaching at Rutgers University. I began the spring as a visiting fellow at Columbia Law School and thank Prof. Bert Huang for facilitating the visit. Subsequently sheltered in a beloved but technologically challenged home, I received important technical help from Agnes Mosejczuk even while she also worked online as a dedicated teacher. I am also grateful for the other help and encouragement during difficult times that she, Hubert Mosejczuk, and Maria Twarog provided. Lauren Lyons, Rutgers philosophy graduate student, made some much appreciated deliveries. I thank Peter Ohlin, philosophy editor at Oxford University Press, New York, for helping me acquire a contract for this book in the midst of the pandemic. The index was composed by Audrey Powers. Jennifer Valois and Margaret Collins did invaluable typing and editing on the book especially when help was needed quickly given the uncertainty of future events (and even survival).

# Introduction

Overall this is a book about some theories of moral rights and other elements of nonconsequentialist morality, the use of case-based reasoning to decide about these theories, and their implications for some practical issues.[1] Nonconsequentialism does not deny that consequences matter morally only that they are not all that matter; the other parts that matter are typically referred to as deontological (though some use nonconsequentialism and deontology interchangeably). The book begins by considering moral status and its relation to having rights including whether animals have them and what rights future persons have. It considers whether rights are grounded in duties to oneself, which duties are correlative to rights, and whether neuroscientific and psychological studies can help determine what rights we have. The possible limits of the right not to be harmed are investigated by considering Derek Parfit's case-based critique of deontological distinctions and "moral inertia," the costs required to avoid harming, and a proposal for understanding the permissibility of harming and resisting harm in the Trolley Problem. Different approaches to limits on rights are distinguished based on whether or not they allow that such limits involve losing something of moral value or leave a "negative residue" (such as wronging someone). The possibility that the Trolley Problem can help determine what rights are involved in programming self-driving cars, providing medical treatments, and redistributive economic policy is considered. The book concludes by comparing the use of case-based judgments about extreme cases in moral versus aesthetic theory, and by exploring the significance of the right not to be harmed for morally correct policies in the extreme cases of torture and a pandemic. When pertinent, the views on these issues of C. Korsgaard, R. Dworkin, D. Parfit, J. Thomson, A. Sen, A. Gibbard, J. Greene, and A. Danto, among others, are considered.

The book is divided into three parts. The first focuses on the idea of rights and their correlative duties in the light of some theories and judgments about real and hypothetical cases. Its emphasis is on what I call "rightsousness" (to be contrasted with righteousness). This is a new word by which I mean to communicate rights-respecting attitudes and behavior.[2] The second part focuses on the

*Rights and Their Limits: In Theory, Cases, and Pandemics*. F. M. Kamm, Oxford University Press.
© Oxford University Press 2022. DOI: 10.1093/oso/9780197567739.001.0001

limits of rights to constrain our conduct by considering the moral significance of differences in *how* we come to harm and not aid others. Limits that have this source are consistent with rightsousness since they do not involve violating a right and may also have to be distinguished from what is known as "threshold deontology." This part considers whether we may be involved in infringing rights and wronging others even when we do not act wrongly, whether this licenses others to resist our actions, and also whether what we would permissibly do to someone could make some other act that would otherwise violate a right be "secondarily permissible." The third part focuses on some other reasons someone's rights can fail to constrain us. These include someone's being a threat (even a morally innocent one) which leaves him open to being harmed or constrained, as well as extraordinary bad consequences of not overriding another's rights.

In particular, Chapter 1 is about senses and levels of moral status and their significance for having rights and being the object of different types of duties. It also considers what is known as "person-affectingness" and whether it has a role in connecting different levels of moral status. The chapter introduces a new form of person-affectingness, examines its connection with rights, and considers its implications for the Non-Identity Problem and the No-Difference View with which Derek Parfit is identified.

Associated with Chapter 1 are two appendices. The first deals with the ideas of claiming and waiving rights. The second examines the views of three different philosophers about the moral status and rights of nonhuman animals.

Chapter 2 continues the discussion of rights by considering the grounds and content of rights and duties, in particular duties to aid and rights not to be harmed. The chapter critically examines Ronald Dworkin's view that rights that persons have not to be harmed and to be aided, as well as other elements of interpersonal morality, derive from ethical duties one has to oneself as a matter of personal dignity. Dworkin presented this theory, arguably very different from his earlier views of rights, in his *Justice for Hedgehogs,* where he also claims that his view about personal responsibility explains moral distinctions between intended and merely foreseen harm as drawn by the Doctrine of Double Effect. The chapter considers this claim and its connection with Dworkin's views about the Trolley Problem and the possible use of ex ante agreements.

Chapter 3 focuses on the roles for theory and case-based reasoning in answering questions in practical ethics including what rights we have. It situates the discussion in Chapter 2 within the broader context of Dworkin's views (presented in his *Balzan Lecture* and in *Justice for Hedgehogs*) about the need for theory and the limited usefulness of intuitive judgments about cases in deciding about practical issues concerning rights. The chapter critically examines Dworkin's view that one must first arrive at theories of value, metaphysics, and interpretation and then use these to answer practical ethical, political, and legal questions. The chapter also considers his claim that there are no true conflicts of values and apparent conflicts can be avoided by interpreting values in the light of each other as if one were solving simultaneous equations. This is his distinctive way of dealing with the issue of limits on rights, claiming that there is both nothing of moral value lost and no "negative residue" remaining when we fashion rights in the light of each other and other values. There is a seamless fit between all aspects of morality. Dworkin's view contrasts with the view that rights may be overridden by other more important rights or values so that something of lesser moral significance is lost and some negative residue remains, possibly requiring compensation.

Chapter 4 continues the discussion of the need for theory to answer practical questions by considering whether one needs an ideal theory of justice to identify particular injustices. It considers Amartya Sen's views on this issue in his *The Idea of Justice,* as well as whether his view of rights and the duties correlative to them involves a conception of rights and justice that distinguishes them from other moral notions. The particular implications of his views for practical issues such as international obligations to provide aid and international human rights are also examined.

Chapter 5 continues the discussions about the legitimacy of relying on intuitive judgments in reaching moral conclusions and the use of veil of ignorance reasoning. It then considers the role of strains of commitment in deciding between a consequentialist and nonconsequentialist moral theory. It discusses these issues by considering Allan Gibbard's views in his *Thinking How to Live with Each Other.* Gibbard's way of justifying the use of intuitive judgments is examined and the views of Gibbard and Scanlon on the point of morality and the use of the veil of ignorance are contrasted. Finally, the chapter contrasts Gibbard's views with those of nonconsequentialists about acting from a personal rather than an impartial perspective,, taking rights as constraints on action, and the explanatory role of strains of commitment.

Chapter 6 continues the discussion of intuitive judgments about cases and whether we should rely on them in moral theorizing by considering empirical work by psychologists about the Trolley Problem. Using functional magnetic resonance imaging (fMRI), philosopher/psychologist Joshua Greene tried to locate the parts of the brain that result in consequentialist and nonconsequentialist intuitive judgments about trolley problem cases. The chapter considers whether his work and that of some other psychologists correctly identify responses as consequentialist and offer adequate explanations of nonconsequentialist responses. It proposes additional possible experiments to see if any would undermine nonconsequentialist views about rights not to be harmed and the worth of case-based judgments to support moral views.

Chapter 7 considers whether intuitive judgments about cases can undermine (rather than support) the moral significance of deontological distinctions and "moral inertia" as Derek Parfit attempts to show in volume 3 of his *On What Matters*. The chapter first examines Parfit's concern that commitment to "common sense" deontological (nonconsequentialist) morality may be undermined because it conflicts with practical reason (that determines what we ought to do overall). The chapter examines his attempt to show that morality is not essentially deontological and so does not conflict with practical reason. This involves comparing his views about different measures of the stringency of both rights and duties with my own. Further discussion examines and argues against how he uses intuitive judgments about trolley problem cases to try to undermine the significance of "moral inertia," moral distinctions between harming and not aiding, harming as a side effect and harming as a mere means, and redirecting existing threats versus creating new ones.

Chapter 8 examines further issues that arise as a result of there being different measures of the stringency of both rights and duties. For example, one can have a duty to make personal sacrifices rather than harm others even though harming others would be permissible for the sake of a greater good were it necessary. This can be true even though it is beyond the call of duty for an individual to impose the harm on himself for the sake of that greater good. The different measures of stringency also raise the question of whether, if it were possible, one would have a duty to sacrifice oneself to achieve a greater good rather than not fulfill a duty to aid or not harm another person to achieve that good. Alternatively, might what would ordinarily be a duty to sacrifice oneself rather than fail to aid or not harm others become supererogatory (i.e., beyond the call of duty) even in nonconsequentialist morality? The chapter explores the relevance of these issues to Judith Thomson's later view that a bystander may not turn a trolley from killing five people when it will kill one other person and her argument for this based on cases in which one might harm oneself rather than another to save the five. Like Gibbard, Parfit seeks to justify acting from a common rather than a personal perspective that he takes to be characteristic of nonconsequentialism. The chapter ends by considering Parfit's claim that this personal perspective on action can incorrectly forbid what would ordinarily be one person's nonconsequentialist permission to harm others for the greater good when someone else could permissibly achieve that good by causing greater harm.

Chapter 9 continues the discussion of the Trolley Problem that was a focus of Chapters 6 through 8. It first distinguishes the Trolley Problem from cases in which it is possible to harm some of those already under a threat to save others from the threat. It then considers the views of some other philosophers about the Trolley Problem and presents six principles that together make up a principle of permissible harm that I refer to as the Doctrine of Productive Purity (DPP). It is a nonconsequentialist approach to sometimes justifying harming innocent non-threatening people in order to help other people even given that persons have a right not to be harmed. The DPP as presented in this chapter, which revises and adds to my earlier characterization of it and the Principle of Permissible Harm (PPH) on which it is based, is a non–state of mind principle that focuses on *how* harm is brought about. According to the DPP, harms may be justified by what produces them, as opposed to the goods they produce as in consequentialist views. Hence, I say it is a "downstreamish" theory. However, it is argued that even when causing harm is justified, one may not be required to bring it about because it can still wrong those harmed who may permissibly resist the harm. Its account of the limit of the right not to be harmed is contrasted with that of "threshold deontology" that justifies overriding a right because of a conflict between it and avoiding grave consequences. On the other hand, by contrast to Dworkin's view about a seamless fit between all parts of morality, the DPP allows that a negative residue can occur due to permissible harming, involving wronging of the person harmed and/or their permissible resistance. The chapter closes by considering the limits of the DPP (due in part to a Principle of Secondary Permissibility), its relation to nonconsequentialist views about relations between people, and how a new type of trolley problem bears on the moral distinction between killing and letting die.

Chapter 10 discusses what many have seen as the relevance of the Trolley Problem to several practical issues. These include programming self-driving cars and other artificial intelligence (AI) devices, deciding on medical treatments, and more generally the rights and duties people have when harm must be distributed to some rather than others. It critically examines discussions of these issues intended both for the general public and for professional audiences. It then offers positive proposals for factors to be considered in dealing morally with partially and completely self-driving cars.

Chapter 11 considers the relevance of the Trolley Problem to an issue important in libertarian political theory: what the role of the state should be in economic policy insofar as this relates to individual rights. In particular, does the permissibility of turning a runaway trolley from killing five toward killing one other person undermine the libertarian argument that we may not harm some people, by way of taxation policies, in order to help others to a greater degree. Guido Pincione has argued that the conditions that make it permissible to turn the trolley are also satisfied in the taxation case. The chapter examines Pincione's account and raises three concerns with it, noting that (i) there may be morally significant differences between killing and imposing economic harm, (ii) accepting Pincione's analogy may have counterintuitive implications, and (iii) the conditions that make it permissible to turn the trolley may not be satisfied in the taxation case. The chapter closes by considering how more recent work on the Trolley Problem (discussed in Chapters 8 and 9) bears on Pincione's discussion.

Chapter 12 considers the use of case-based judgments in theorizing about the concept of art and how it compares with the use of such judgments in moral theorizing. The use of thought experiments (another term for hypothetical cases) played an important role in Arthur Danto's work on the concept of art and in a debate between him and Richard Wollheim about that concept especially in "extreme" cases. I consider this debate and try to show that when Danto dealt with the ethical issue of torture, he adopted a view about case judgments in extreme cases similar to the one Wollheim employed in criticizing Danto's work on the concept of art. Questions are also raised about the correctness of Danto's substantive views on torture, an ethical issue discussed in more detail in the following chapter.

Chapter 13 examines the moral status of torture from a nonconsequentialist perspective. It first considers the conceptual issue of what torture is and then examines the possible violation of moral rights involved in torture and torture-like treatment in several different contexts. The first context involves such treatment being done to a perpetrator either during or after his threatening act in order to rescue his own identifiable intended victim(s). The second context involves such treatment being done to prevent perpetrators from exposing large numbers of people to risk of harm that will result in several future victims who are not currently identifiable. The third context involves such treatment being done to a perpetrator as punishment in order to deter other perpetrators from harming people. When the perpetrator is the focus, one issue is whether there are intrinsic limits to the right not to be harmed such that someone who has threatened to harm others is no longer protected against harm insofar as harm to him would be necessary to prevent the threat he poses. The right having such "contours" or even being forfeited is by contrast to his intact right being overridden and thus limited by factors extrinsic to it. Also considered from the perspective of moral rights are cases in which it might be proposed that those who are not perpetrators be tortured or treated in torture-like ways for the sake of avoiding extremely bad outcomes.

Chapter 14 first deals with what libertarian and libertarian-like views held by ordinary U.S. citizens about individual rights imply about a moral duty to wear masks that prevent transmission of COVID-19, and about the permissibility of self-defensive actions in a pandemic. The chapter then examines the policy of lockdowns to prevent transmission of the COVID-19 virus. It considers different ways of weighing the costs and benefits of such a policy by examining different approaches to interpersonal aggregation. It ultimately connects libertarian and libertarian-like views about rights and duties, discussed in the first part of the chapter, with theories of aggregation to reach a conclusion about the moral status of lockdowns.

Chapter 15 considers the comparison that was made in February 2021 when the numbers of U.S. deaths due to the pandemic of 2020 were said to have reached the level of deaths of U.S. soldiers in several wars in the twentieth century. It argues that equal numbers may conceal other crucial differences among these deaths. These include the amount of harm done to each of the people who died in war or due to COVID-19, the degree to which they were wronged (as distinct from harmed) and by whom, and the extent to which their deaths were meaningful.

## Notes

1. I can illustrate some of the famous hypothetical cases that have played a prominent role in recent philosophical ethics by compressing several of these cases (owed to Peter Singer, John Taurek, Judith Thomson, and Michael Tooley) into one story: People seeds were coming into a house despite protective drapes and taking root in a carpet. One of these seeds is the result of a kitten seed having been given a serum that gave it the potential to become a person in cat form. Though this seed could have permissibly been given an antidote, the cat baby is now growing at a rapid rate, threatening to crush the woman in whose house it is growing. She manages to eject it but it lands in a pond and is drowning. Someone who cares nothing for starving cat people far away is willing to wade into the near pond to save it. However, he notices five other developing cat persons in another pond. Deciding that numbers don't count, he tosses a coin and saves the one cat baby. But his aim is only to use it to escape his enemies by strapping the cat baby to his tank to inhibit his enemies' fire. Despite this hard beginning in life, the cat baby grows up to become a famous violinist. Alas, a cat's kidneys frequently fail and to save this one the Society for Musical Cats attaches him to a woman without her consent to use her kidneys. This same woman who ejected him from her house now wants him disconnected from her body. Suffice it to say that her gain was music's loss.
2. My original proposal for the title of this book was *RIGHTSOUSNESS: In Theory, Cases, and Pandemics.* It was replaced because there was concern that the new term wouldn't be understood without explanation or might even be perceived as a typographical error. I think it would be worth making the term a separate part of our moral vocabulary.

# PART I

# RIGHTS BY THEORY AND CASES

# 1

# Moral Status, Rights, and Parfit's No-Difference View

## A. Senses of Moral Status and Ways of Mattering Morally

1. In one broad sense the moral status of an entity is about how it is morally permissible or impermissible to treat it by contrast to how it is actually treated.[1] This should not be interpreted to imply that every change in how it is permissible to treat an entity (at least in the case of persons) is a change in moral status. Rather, at least in the case of persons, that their decisions about what to do or how we should treat them can affect the permissibility of treating them in certain ways (e.g., punishment for wrong conduct) just is part of their moral status. In the broad sense in which its status is about what it is permissible or impermissible to do to an entity, rocks are entities whose moral status may permit anything to be done to them. If your moral status makes it impermissible for someone to kill you, you do not lose that status merely because you are actually impermissibly killed. One way to ensure that no morally impermissible things happen in the world is to simply populate it with entities whose status is such that it is permissible to treat them in any way. Yet most would not think that such a world—for example, one with only rocks in it—would be morally preferable to one with entities whose moral status makes treating them in certain ways impermissible, even if they are sometimes mistreated. This might be because the more morally important or valuable an entity is, in itself, the more it matters how one treats it, and it is better to have a world populated by more important or valuable entities.

2. There is a different sense of moral status where the contrast is not between how it is permissible to treat something and how it is actually treated but between entities that do and do not "count" morally in their own right. Call this about having Level 1 moral status.

When we say that something counts morally in its own right, we are often thinking of its intrinsic rather than instrumental value. Christine Korsgaard has argued that the true contrast to mere instrumental value is value as an end,[2] and some things may be ends in virtue of their extrinsic rather than intrinsic properties. But it is also possible to distinguish intrinsic properties from intrinsic value, which then might also be based on extrinsic as well as intrinsic properties. The intrinsic properties are all of an entity's nonrelational properties;[3] the extrinsic

*Rights and Their Limits: In Theory, Cases, and Pandemics*. F. M. Kamm, Oxford University Press.
© Oxford University Press 2022. DOI: 10.1093/oso/9780197567739.003.0001

properties are those it has in virtue of its relation to other things. An entity's ability to produce an effect (i.e., be instrumental to it) is a relational property between it and the effect. It is possible, given what Korsgaard has said, that something could have value as an end or alternatively have intrinsic value because of its extrinsic properties such as causing or being capable of causing an effect even if it never does.

3a. A work of art or a tree may count morally in its own right in the sense that it gives us reason to constrain our behavior toward it (e.g., to not destroy it) just because of what it is.[4] (This need not mean that its value can never be trumped, nor that it should never be treated as a mere means.) But this is still to be distinguished from constraining ourselves *for the sake of* the work of art or the tree, which depends on its getting something good for it out of (benefiting from) what we do for it. We could say that sunlight is good for a tree, meaning that the tree needs it to live. However, this does not mean that it is good for the tree to live in the sense that it gets something good for it out of being alive. The tree is not capable of getting anything out of its continued existence. Hence, it is not something that in its own right *and* for its own sake has value as an end. By contrast, we can save a bird for its own sake if it will get something good for it out of continuing to exist.

When moral status is ordinarily attributed to an entity, what is meant, I think, is that the entity can provide a reason to treat it in certain ways *in its own right and for its own sake.* I shall say that such entities have moral status at Level 2 and are a subclass of those at Level 1, all of which have moral significance in their own right. In the case of entities at both these levels we could have what I call "direct duties" that require us to treat them in certain ways only because of their properties.[5] This is to be contrasted with having indirect duties with regard to them because of duties we have to others, as when we must take care of something because we promised another person to do so.

It may seem that something must have or have had the capacity for, or exercise of, sentience or consciousness in order for it to have Level 2 moral status. This is because having (or having had) the capacity for, or exercise of, subjectivity seems necessary for an entity to have a "sake" (and so be a beneficiary or a victim).[6] (I say "had" because someone now dead may have desired, for example, that their book be published. If by fulfilling this past desire we would be adding value to the life they lived, then doing so could be good for them even if they do not experience it.) Having a subjective life in the sense of "there being something it is like to be that entity" does not necessarily involve being a continuing subject. So it might be morally wrong to cause pain to a being that had only momentary existence. Further, the capacity for, or exercise of, both sentience (physical sensations) and consciousness (awareness) is not necessary to be able to act for the sake of the entity; either alone could suffice. For example, an entity with consciousness and without sentience could still have preferences and agency for the sake of which others could act (to satisfy its preferences or not interfere with its agency).[7] (I think we conceive of angels as such beings.) Agency requires a capacity to act usually on beliefs and desires (not merely having them), yet in the case of conscious nonagents others could act for their sake by satisfying their desires.

Whether Level 2 moral status (or agency) really requires either sentience or consciousness is a question raised in the first instance by the existence in conscious entities of unconscious desires, intentions, or acts and the possible moral significance of unconscious satisfaction of such desires and intentions and noninterference with such acts. Suppose one should sometimes act for the sake of satisfying a conscious entity's unconscious desires or intentions even if this had no effect on their conscious states. Then could nonconscious desires in nonsentient and nonconscious entities (e.g., certain robots) have the same moral significance as unconscious desires in conscious beings and also ground Level 2 moral status? Or is sentience or consciousness necessary to establish Level 2 moral status, which in turn could be necessary to endow unconscious desires, intentions, and acts with moral significance?

Importantly, conscious beings could prefer outcomes and will acts that have nothing to do with their own good. If it could be wrong to interfere with these acts and right to help them achieve these goals, how can we say that we refrain or act "for their sake" when this commonly is taken to mean "for their own good"? I will henceforth assume that "for their sake" goes beyond "for their own good" and includes satisfying their preferences and willings more generally.

3b. That something's sentience or consciousness should affect how we treat it for its sake does not yet mean that making it nonsentient or nonconscious henceforth would be in itself morally wrong. For example, a reason not to engage in factory farming is that it causes pain to animals involved. Another way to avoid such pain is to eliminate the animals' capacity for pain, which might be good for them. However, suppose the capacity for painful sensations were connected with their capacity to experience appropriate unhappiness, such as feeling "pained" at separation from other animals.[8] It might be wrong to do what reduces their capacity for appropriate responses to relationships as that seems to lessen their worth as beings. Similarly, being conscious might be a good in itself that outweighs low-level pain even if it were the only content of consciousness. Furthermore, eliminating an animal's consciousness would not be good for it if this would eliminate overall good states of consciousness.

That it would be bad for an entity to lose its capacity for consciousness does not yet imply that it has a right not to lose it: Having rights might require more than being an entity with (or the capacity for) consciousness or sentience. We shall consider this further later on.

3c. Entities with Level 2 status have characteristics (e.g., they can suffer) that speak in favor of any type of being and even natural events such as tornadoes not harming them. However, many sentient and conscious beings cannot see that these qualities in a being (including in themselves) should affect how they are acted upon. Entities that are not moral agents strictly do no moral wrong when, for example, they interfere with the agency of other Level 2 beings (e.g., by eating them); these other beings themselves may dislike such treatment without comprehending what factors count morally against its being done to them. Human persons typically constrain the behavior of both animals and those among us, such as sociopaths, who are incapable of seeing reasons not to harm or interfere with the agency of others, even when they would harm those who are not moral agents (e.g., human babies). Hence, we need a justification for not similarly constraining such behavior in some nonhuman Level 2 beings even when it affects only other nonhumans at Level 2.

One possibility is that the moral duty not to harm is more stringent than the duty to aid, and in not stopping much harm that animals do to nonhuman Level 2 beings, we would fail to aid the latter rather than harm them. Nevertheless, in the case of humans we think that we have a reason to stop harm that we did not cause as well as a reason not to cause harm. Then we still seem to need a justification for not stopping at least some harm caused by nonhuman Level 2 beings to other such beings.

3d. On the account given, a nonsentient, never-conscious human embryo (that lacks preferences and will) lacks moral status at Level 2. But the embryo could count morally in itself and be at Level 1 (e.g., give us reason in its own right not to destroy it) because of intrinsic and/or extrinsic properties such as its potential. This is different from its having instrumental value since even if an embryo deprived of an environment in which to develop is not instrumental to there being a person, it could have properties that contribute to its potential to develop, and these could give it greater value than an embryo that lacks these properties.[9] That an embryo may have such value in virtue of its intrinsic and/or extrinsic properties could account for why it might be wrong to use it for frivolous purposes.[10] Notice that an embryo that will not develop could have greater value in its own right if it has the properties for becoming an extraordinary person (e.g., Beethoven) even if that person would have the same moral status as an ordinary person if he were to exist. Indeed, this Level 1 embryo that could have become Beethoven may be more morally significant (e.g., give us stronger reasons to preserve it) than a Level 2 bird.

Given that it is only at Level 1, we cannot be acting for the embryo's sake in saving its life, and the person who would arise from the embryo cannot be harmed by never coming to exist if the embryo is not saved. Still, we can protect an embryo for the sake of a person who will definitely arise from it when that embryo will be allowed to develop. See Section B for more on this.

3e. There are other examples where we may not have as much reason to save beings for whose sake we can act as to save entities that matter in their own right but whose existence cannot be extended for their own sake. If we had to choose whether to destroy the Level 1 Grand Canyon that matters in its own right but gets nothing from its continued existence or a Level 2 bird that can get something out of life, it could be morally wrong to choose to destroy the Grand Canyon. This further supports distinguishing the *moral significance* of an entity and its *moral status* as commonly understood, which involves being at Level 2. Value and moral significance can vary independently of such moral status. This could even be true of things that do not matter in their own right but only instrumentally. Suppose the Grand Canyon should be preserved rather than a bird and a certain tool is necessary and sufficient to save the Grand Canyon. Then saving the tool should take precedence over saving the bird.

3f. What if the contents of one bird's life are more valuable than another's (e.g., it lives a longer and more pleasant life)? This need not imply that it has a higher moral status; as the "containers" of content the birds may have the same moral status. An indication of this is that we might seek to give to the second bird contents as valuable as the first bird's. If we couldn't accomplish this, might we decide which bird to save on the basis of the value of the contents of its life if it would continue? But in light of their equal moral status we might also consider what each bird will have had in its life by the time it dies, letting die the one who will have gotten more out of its life already so that the other bird can still acquire more in its life.

Suppose there is a difference between an entity's moral status and the value of the actual content of its life. This leaves it open that differences in the capacities to have value in its life (due to an entity's own properties rather than its environment) could ground different sublevels of moral status at Level 2 and ground levels beyond Level 2. That is, suppose we could rate activities and products of activities in a non-species-relative way as objectively more and less valuable. Then the entities that have the capacity to engage with the more valuable activities and products in a way that makes their own lives good for them by way of this engagement might have higher moral status. When their own good "tracks" objective value in this way, they are not merely instruments for the existence of these valuable activities and products in the world.

4a. We can have "direct" duties concerning entities that count in their own right just because they count in their own right, including those at Level 2. However, I suggest, there is a difference between having such a duty and having a *duty to that specific entity*. The latter is known as a "directed duty"; typically the entity to whom the duty is owed has a correlative right or claim against whoever owes the duty. (Note that one may have a directed duty to many entities simultaneously as when one has a directed duty to everyone not to kill each one of them.[11]) Correspondingly, there is a difference between doing the wrong thing (e.g., in not fulfilling a nondirected duty) and *wronging* some entity in failing to perform the duty owed to her. I shall say that entities who are the bearers of such rights and to whom directed duties are owed have Level 3 moral status. This includes persons and possibly other beings who are sufficiently subjects to whom things can be owed.[12] One would need to be a subject (not merely have subjective experiences) to have rights, though perhaps not a subject for whose own welfare anything could be done.[13] For example, we could imagine persons whose well-being remained constant no matter what they did or what others did to them. Yet these persons could have reasons for actions (e.g., a duty to acquire knowledge, preferences concerning others) and a right to noninterference with their actions.

The entity to whom a duty is owed is not necessarily the entity to be affected by the duty. For example, if you owe it to me to save my mother, it is ordinarily thought that I am the right holder, not my mother, even though she is the object of the duty.[14] Does this imply that in acting to fulfill directed duties we may not be acting for the sake of the right holder and so some right holders need not have Level 2 moral status (i.e., be entities for whose sake we can act)? "Acting for something's sake" (as noted earlier) can be broad enough to include aiming to satisfy what some entity wants for another entity. So it should also include "fulfilling duties owed to" and "not wronging" someone whose rights concern something to be done for another entity. (So those at Level 3 are part of those at Levels 1 and 2.)

Part of the significance of having a right is the added protection for interests it should provide so that the duty owed to right holders could take precedence over satisfying the equal interests of those without rights. Further, whereas the interests of some entity at only Level 2 may be outweighed by the somewhat greater interests of another individual, outweighing rights could require that much greater interests be at stake for another individual.

It is possible that some of those with rights to whom correlative duties are owed do not themselves have duties correlative to the rights of others since they are moral patients but not moral agents. This has been claimed about some animals and is true of persons who are infants. By contrast, persons who can appreciate and govern themselves in the light of reasons can mutually obligate each other. Only in the case of such persons can what is owed depend on what a person authorizes (e.g., whether she waives her right and releases us from a claim she has against us) or whether she acts in a way that results in her forfeiting rights. One hypothesis is that only such persons are full-fledged subjects (e.g., self-conscious, self-reflective, and self-governing) and that only they can have what is called "self-ownership" of their lives. That is, even if entities at only Level

2 have lives and we can act for their sake, they (and perhaps even some animals at Level 3 to whom we can owe things) may not have "ownership" claims over their lives. Their lives are theirs in the sense that they live them but, the suggestion is, not in the sense that their lives belong to them so that the strongest prohibitions exist on harming them for the good of others and on paternalistic acts done for their own good but against their will.[15]

It seems reasonable to think that (at least many) Level 3 entities have a *higher* moral status than those only at Levels 1 or 2 and possibly that some Level 3 entities have a higher moral status than others at that level. But this need not mean that beings at Level 3 should have a higher chance of having their interests as sentient or conscious beings satisfied. The good *of* them can be greater even if occasionally not the significance of the good *for* them. This might be true because what grounds an interest (or right) makes the interest or right just as strong in a being with lower moral status as in a being with higher moral status. For example, suppose a capacity and desire to communicate grounded (or most clearly pertained to) an entity's having a protected interest (or right) in communicating. That the entity lacked other properties necessary for higher moral status may not mean that the protection provided this interest should be weaker than the protection (or right) accorded the interest in the higher status being. In general, if property x grounded (or most clearly pertained to) a protected interest in or right to m, the failure to have properties y and z that could raise one's moral status (and ground other rights) may not affect the importance of according m to those with only x relative to those with x, y, and z.

Another reason those with Level 3 moral status need not have a higher chance of having their interests satisfied is illustrated by a case where we would have to kill one person to save five other people from being killed. Each person's chances that his interests as a sentient and conscious being would be satisfied would increase ex ante if there were a policy of killing one to save five. However, the one person's moral status (including his self-ownership) may prohibit us from killing him without his consent. By contrast, we might sacrifice a Level 1 or 2 entity (e.g., a painting or a chicken) that lacks self-ownership to save more entities (even) of the same type.[16] As with those at Level 2 but not 3, we should distinguish between having Level 3 moral status and the value of things in a Level 3 being's life. One person may have wealth, beauty, and physical adeptness that another lacks (with no compensating goods). But if these goods do not ground Level 3 moral status, the two persons would have the same status.[17] Might even having and exercising the capacity for a better or more worthwhile life when what is good for one tracks objectively valuable pursuits (that might raise the moral status of some beings) have no role in raising the moral status of those who are already persons? Then the morally important characteristics that make one a person would preempt or silence an additional factor that might raise another entity's moral status in their absence.[18]

4b. The possibility of wronging some entities could imply that moral status in the broad sense (discussed in subsection 1) may not be completely defined by how it is permissible and impermissible to treat an entity. This would be so if it were possible to wrong an entity in the course of acting permissibly.[19] For example, it might be permissible to bomb a military target with side effect harm to civilians but still wrong them in doing this. The permissibility of their resisting our permissible act could be evidence that we still wrong them in acting permissibly.[20] It is tempting to think that those we could wrong in the course of a permissible act would have a higher moral status than those not so wronged by the same permissible act, even if some of those with respect to whom such an act would be impermissible would have a still higher moral status.

## B. Moral Status, Affecting a Definite Future Person, and Parfit's No-Difference View

1a. In Section A, I considered different senses and levels of moral status. Now I want to consider whether an embryo at Level 1 that *will in fact* develop into (or give rise to)[21] a person at Level 3 is protected against nonlethal interventions that will negatively affect the future person it will develop into in the same way that those who are already persons are protected.[22]

According to what I call "the View," we have as strong a duty not to do things to an embryo that will result in harm (or failure to prevent harm) to the person who the embryo will definitely develop into as we have to that person when he exists.[23] One way to understand the View is that it assigns protections that ordinarily belong to a Level 3 person to what is only a Level 1 entity because we can affect the Level 3 person by acting on the Level 1 entity from which it develops (or arises). (One can deny the View while still believing we have duties, though perhaps weaker ones, with regard to an embryo at Level 1 only because of the person into whom it will develop.)

I will present hypothetical (unrealistic) examples that show the View is wrong by showing it can be permissible to affect a definite future person by doing something to the embryo, egg, or sperm from which the person will arise though it is impermissible to affect the person in the same way by doing similar things to him once he exists (in the sense that he then has the capacities that are distinctive of being a person).[24]

Suppose a woman discovers her egg or embryo has genes that will result in a person with a 160 IQ. She decides this is too smart, not for that person's good but for the good of the family. So, she takes a drug that affects her egg or embryo to reduce the future person's IQ to 140. (Call this the 160 IQ Case.)[25] I assume that lowering IQ to this degree does not change the identity of a person and so this is a case of causing a definite future person to be worse off than he would otherwise have been. (Similarly, an adult who has an accident that reduces his IQ from 160 to 140 is not a different person; this is why we say of the person after the accident that something bad has happened to *him.*)[26] Derek Parfit would call what happens to the person who arises from the egg or embryo a Narrow Person-Affecting change. It contrasts with what he calls a Wide Person-Affecting change in which we create one person with a 140 IQ rather than another person with a 160 IQ.[27] Doing the latter would result in what is called a nonidentity case in which no person who exists is worse or better off than he would otherwise have been since someone else, not he, would otherwise have existed.

Could a person with a 140 IQ from birth not be worse off than if he had a 160 IQ because things it is in his interest to do and have would not be served by his having had the higher IQ?[28] I do not think so. First, many things that would be in the interest of someone with the 140 IQ could be more easily achieved if he had a 160 IQ. Second, at the time when an egg or embryo would be modified to give a person a lower IQ the person does not yet exist who would be wedded to the life had by someone with a 140 IQ. So even if what is in the interest of someone with a 140 IQ differed radically from what is in the interest of someone with a 160 IQ, there are no pre-existing 140 IQ interests that would conflict with or not be served by having had the higher IQ.

Third, suppose that a child with a 160 IQ would be no problem for the family twenty years hence and the woman has the option of affecting her egg or embryo so that the definite person to whom it will give rise has a 140 IQ for the first twenty years of life and 160 after. This would be a change over time within the person's actual life by contrast to a comparison between two possible diverging types of lives. (The intra-life change could be gradual or sudden.) It could be better for the person created if the woman chooses for him to have a life with the change in it rather than a life with 140 IQ throughout, other things equal (i.e., no overriding negative side effects). This could be true even if what is in the interests of a person with a 140 IQ differs from what is in the interests of the same person with a 160 IQ so long as the change leads to a better future for that person. One might say that a person has a meta-interest in better things being in his interest.[29]

1b. I believe that the woman's causing a definite person to be worse off than he would have been by affecting her egg or embryo so that the eventual person has a 140 instead of a 160 IQ is permissible (for reasons to be given later). Though she harms the person, she does not do so wrongfully or wrong him. But once her child (assumed to be a Level 3 person) exists (in the sense that he has the properties distinctive of persons), it would not be similarly permissible (were it possible) for the woman to give him a pill that reduces his IQ from 160 to 140 or that alters his genes so that the child will have an IQ of 140 rather than 160 in the further future. This would wrongfully harm him, thus wronging him. (This is so even if the alteration occurs before the child has experienced living with a 160 IQ.) The woman would be significantly affecting a Level 3 person for the worse by doing something to his body once he already exists. I will call this a Super Narrow Person-Affecting change. This is a sense of person-affecting that Parfit did not distinguish as a separate category. I think it should be distinguished for moral reasons.[30]

What is the difference between (1) affecting the person by affecting the egg or embryo from which he arises and (2) affecting the person himself by giving him the pill? An egg or embryo is not the sort of entity that is entitled to keep a characteristic that it has, such as the genetic makeup for a 160 IQ. It lacks moral status in the sense of mattering for its own sake (it is not at Level 2) and lacks additional properties that would make it a rights bearer (it is not at Level 3). Also, the person who will develop from the egg or embryo will have an acceptable level of intelligence at 140 IQ, so he (as a person) is not owed a 160 IQ by his parent. These two facts are crucial to the permissibility of not giving to, or taking back from, the egg or embryo IQ points that the parent originally gave it. By contrast, since a child is already a person, he has a right to keep a beneficial characteristic even if doing so raises him beyond the level he is owed by the parent(s) who created him. In particular, I believe it is a violation of his rights to give the IQ-reducing pill to the child even if his IQ would not fall below the minimum a creator should provide to her child.[31]

Because the egg or embryo is not a person (or has other properties that make it an entity entitled to keep what is given to it), taking away its characteristics (which will impact the person who will arise from it) is no different from not giving the egg or embryo those characteristics to begin with. And one would have a right not to give genes sufficient for a 160 IQ in a future person to one's egg or embryo that will give rise to the person. Analogously, suppose that a parent puts money she need not give into a bank account that will belong to her offspring only when he is an adult. Even if the child will definitely become an adult and the parent's removing the money makes him significantly worse off, it is permissible and does not wrong the child for the parent to take back the money before her offspring reaches the age at which he has a right to his bank account.[32]

Now consider a case I call Delayed Change. Suppose the woman is not able to remove the genetic material at the embryo or egg stage and (as I have argued) is not permitted to give the pill that would remove IQ points from the Level 3 child. May she give to the embryo or egg a drug that will have a delayed action in childhood, altering the child's genes so that he will have a 140 rather than a 160 IQ? I believe this is impermissible for it involves doing something at time $t_1$ that will remove something good at time $t_2$ from the person who then exists and to whom the good item already belongs at $t_2$ (whether or not he has already experienced, come to rely on, or formed expectations based on its effects).[33]

1c. Now imagine (unrealistically) that the woman in the 160 IQ Case could take back genetic material from her egg or embryo and transfer it into two other eggs or embryos—hers or someone else's—thereby raising the IQs of the people to whom the other eggs or embryos give rise from 100 to 110 each. What I have said earlier implies that this would be permissible and would not wrong the person from whose egg or embryo the material is taken even though he is worse off than he would otherwise have been. The woman would be morally free to equalize beneficial traits among future persons by affecting the embryos or the eggs from which the people arise. This is so even though she thereby makes the future person from whose egg or embryo the genetic material is taken worse off than he would otherwise be for the sake of other future persons. However, I do not think it would be permissible for her to take genetic material from a child (already a person), lowering his IQ from 160 to 140, in order to transfer the material into two other children (or the eggs or embryos from which they arise) to raise their IQs from 100 to 110. The moral importance of the "separateness of persons" can apply to the child, but there is no comparable moral "separateness of eggs" or "separateness of embryos" of persons who will definitely exist.[34]

If what I have said is correct, there is a sense of person-affectingness that is crucial in dealing with those who have Level 3 moral status and which is not captured by either of Parfit's senses of person-affectingness but only by what I have called Super Narrow Person-Affectingness.

What if it were permissible to make the changes I have described only to the egg but not to the embryo? Then Narrow Person-Affecting changes made by changing an egg would still have to be distinguished from Super Narrow Person-Affecting changes. However, Super Narrow Person-Affecting changes would no longer be defined as affecting a person who already exists by changing his or her body. This is because changes to an embryo would not involve this and yet they would also be morally distinguished from mere Narrow Person-Affecting changes that occur by way of egg alteration. Either way it will be morally important to distinguish *how* we come to make a definite future person worse off than he or she would otherwise have been, not merely that we do so.

2. Derek Parfit famously argued that sometimes it seems not to matter morally whether we are affecting the same person for the worse or bringing someone into existence who is worse off than some different person would have been had they been brought into existence instead. He called this the No-Difference View about the so-called Non-Identity Problem.[35] (Wide Person-Affectingness is present in nonidentity cases since it is still persons who ultimately experience lives. To simplify matters, I will here assume that "person-affectingness" involves its narrow form.) What I have said against the View may bear on the No-Difference View about the Non-Identity Problem. This is because I have argued that sometimes *the way in which* we affect someone for the worse can make a moral difference,

not just the fact *that* we affect the person for the worse. If we affect someone in a Super Narrow Person-Affecting way, this can have greater moral significance than achieving a similar change in a mere Narrow Person-Affecting way. Often affecting people for the worse involves Super Narrow Person-Affectingness since we standardly interact with those who are already Level 3 persons. Hence, mere Narrow Person-Affecting cases involving a nonstandard way of affecting people (such as through the egg that gives rise to them) may not be morally different from Wide Person-Affecting cases involving nonidentity This would support the No-Difference View for these cases. By contrast, Super Narrow Person-Affecting cases may be morally more significant than Wide Person-Affecting cases involving nonidentity and so undermine the No-Difference View for these cases. Performing easily avoidable acts (including omissions) that affect an egg or embryo and lead to a given offspring having fewer good traits may have the same moral significance as performing easily avoidable acts that lead to creating a worse-off person rather than a different better-off person. And both sorts of acts may be less morally problematic (other things equal) than performing an act that will take from someone what he is entitled to keep (or not provide him help to which he is entitled in order to keep) something resulting in his having fewer good traits.

The person-affecting cases that Parfit used to help generate the No-Difference View of the Non-Identity Problem do not involve rights based on a person's possession of personal properties. Hence, they do not compare the strongest, super narrow form of Person-Affectingness with Wide Person-Affectingness. This means that Parfit's argument for the No-Difference View (i.e., moral equivalence of Wide and Narrow Person-Affecting actions) is crucially incomplete since it uses the weaker form of Narrow Person-Affecting cases. For example, he compares (1) a case in which a pregnant woman omits to take an easy-to-use drug at an early stage of pregnancy and therefore her child will have a defect in a life still worth living with (2) a case in which someone gets pregnant with a child who will have the same defect rather than waiting a short, nonburdensome time and having a different child who lacks it. If these cases were morally alike, this would not show that the Wide Person-Affecting case (2) is morally equivalent to (3) a Super Narrow Person-Affecting case in which someone omits to do something easy for her child who is already a person and therefore he will have that same defect. It may also be significant that Parfit uses cases involving omissions to prevent a natural harm rather than commissions that cause a harm since the moral difference between Wide Person-Affectingness and Super Narrow Person-Affectingness may be greater in cases of commission (such as I used in B.1).

3. This analysis in terms of Super Narrow Person-Affectingness may also bear on the rights of future generations and our duties to them. Suppose (contrary to fact) that we knew that certain particular people will definitely exist 100 years in

the future but no such person will exist before 100 years. These are people whose existence does not depend on what we do.[36] Suppose we have a choice between doing what will reduce an existing person's IQ from 160 to 140 by affecting his body or doing what will reduce one of these future people's IQ from 160 to 140 by affecting the egg that will be used to create him. Arguably, we morally should do the latter rather than the former. The particular people who will exist in 100 years could also be affected for the worse by how our behavior affects the environment 100 years hence. What has been argued earlier implies that if no person now exists who will then exist and whose environment that future environment will be, then we may now permissibly do what reduces the superior environment they would otherwise have even when this is Narrow Person-Affecting. This is so as long as we do not reduce it below the acceptable level that they are owed and the reduction does not come to what they already have once they exist. It also implies that it could be morally right to favor not worsening by a certain amount the environment that currently existing people have over not reducing by the same amount the environment into which future people will be born (holding constant the level to which each would fall).[37] By contrast, we may not be permitted to have the same negative effect on the environment if the effect is delayed so that it affects the superior environment that already "belongs" to those particular people once they exist. Hence, in order not to wrong the pre-determined people in this future generation it will be important to know the sort of environment to which they have a right independently of what they would be entitled to keep once they have it. It will also be important to know when the effects of our behavior will affect the environment relative to when the persons affected by our behavior exist.[38]

Of course, it may be unlikely that our effect on future people will be of the Narrow Person-Affecting sort. If it actually involves nonidentity depending on what we do, then there may be an even greater contrast between affecting the future generation and affecting those who are already persons in a Super Narrow Person-Affecting way.

Determining the rights of a future generation to an environment is also complicated by the possibility of tradeoffs between goods since having a good environment is not all that matters. It has been surmised (by the philosopher John Broome) that unless the current generation alters its behavior by a certain amount, its effect on climate will be such that people 100 years hence will not have (on average) 7.5 months of life they could otherwise have had.[39] However, suppose that due to other effects we and intervening generations have on people 100 years hence (through public health, medical advances, etc.), those people will live on average 20 years longer than we do now with a higher quality of life. It is an open question how much effort we should make to avoid changes to the climate when the loss of 7.5 months still leaves them with somewhat over 19 years more life than we have. Indeed, if what we and others do that extends their lives by so much is itself what has a big effect on climate, it seems they are overall benefited by what is done that changes the climate. There are tradeoffs between different goods.

It is said that between 1920 and 2020, average human life expectancy doubled. Suppose it was 40 in 1920 and 80 in 2020. Also suppose that without bad effects on the environment caused by industrialization (including climate change) during that period, life expectancy in 2020 would have been 81. Would those in 2020 be justified in complaining that those who could live on average to only 40 did not alter their behavior if it would have lowered the quality of their shorter lives, so that we who live twice as long as they do and at higher quality could live even longer? This complaint would be particularly misplaced if industrialization was necessary to lengthen the human life span so dramatically. Those who live 100 years hence may be in a similar position relative to those in 2020 as those who live in 2020 are to those alive in 1920.

These points (as well as Broome's) make use of average gains and average losses. However, averages can hide severely bad conditions that would occur to some if, for example, they are affected negatively by climate change. Hence, arguments about the moral significance of effects on future people would need to consider more than just data about average effects.

## Notes

1. This chapter draws, in part, on ideas in my *Creation and Abortion* (New York: Oxford University Press, 1992); "Moral Status," "Rights Beyond Interests," and "Owing, Justifying, and Rejecting," reprinted in my *Intricate Ethics* (New York: Oxford University Press, 2007); "Moral Status, Personal Identity, and Substitutability: Clones, Embryos, and Future Generations," reprinted in my *Bioethical Prescriptions* (New York: Oxford University Press, 2013); and "Affecting Definite Future People," *American Philosophical Association Newsletter on Philosophy and Medicine*, Spring 2010. An earlier version of this chapter was published as "Moral Status, Person-Affectingness, and Parfit's No Difference View," in *Rethinking Moral Status*, ed. Stephen Clarke et al (Oxford: Oxford University Press, 2021). For comments I am grateful to members of the audience at the Oxford University Conference on Rethinking Moral Status, June 2019, and to Alex Guerrero, Stephen Clarke, and Daniel Cohen.
2. See her "Two Distinctions in Goodness," *Philosophical Review* 2, no. 481 (April 1983): 169–95.
3. Except, perhaps, relations between its parts.
4. Its mattering in its own right means that even if no beings existed to positively interact with the artwork or tree, the world would be a better place if these things existed in it rather than if the world were empty. (This is like G. E. Moore's famous thought

experiment.) Further, if one were the last person to ever live, it would be better not to do what destroys the work of art or tree even if no one has yet or will ever interact positively with it.

5. Note that I distinguish between direct duties (in my sense) and "directed duties," which I discuss later.
6. Having the capacity for sentience or consciousness is not the same as actually being, for example, sentient. It is also not the same as merely having the potential to be sentient or conscious, which would be consistent with merely having the potential to have the capacity for sentience or consciousness.
7. In my "Rights Beyond Interests" I gave the example of beings whom we conceive to lack sentience but are still conscious agents.
8. Christine Korsgaard claims that being "in pain" and "being pained" are both constituted by wanting a state to end. But there is a difference between painful sensations, nausea, and unhappiness even if one wants them all to end. See her *Fellow Creatures* (Oxford: Oxford University Press, 2018), Chapter 10.
9. Having these properties is different from its having been possible that it had these properties. For example, suppose an embryo could have had these properties had not radiation eliminated the basis for them in the egg from which the embryo developed. Then the embryo's moral status may not differ from an embryo that could never have had those properties.
10. I first argued for this in my "Embryonic Stem Cell Research: A Moral Defense" in *The Boston Review*, November 2002, reprinted in *Bioethical Prescriptions*.
11. See Appendix 1 for criticism of the view that directed duties (to everyone) would require agreements (with everyone).
12. Tom Regan argues for animal rights in his *The Case for Animal Rights* (Los Angeles: University of California Press, 1984), focusing on animals who are agents with continuing selves. However, he moves from having duties that are direct to having duties whose correlative is a right. This is so even though there may be beings simpler than those on which he focuses with respect to which we can have direct duties (in the sense that nothing but what they are accounts for duties to do or not do things to them) but they lack sufficient degree of selfhood to be subjects who are rights bearers. Hence, a problem in Regan's derivation of rights in more complex animals from duties stems from his taking direct duties in the sense given earlier to also be *duties to a being*, implying they are directed duties that have rights as their correlative. But there may be no immediate connection between duties not being indirect and their being directed (rather than merely direct) duties, and so correlative to rights. For further discussion of some views about the rights and moral status of animals see Appendix 2.
13. I described such beings in my "Rights Beyond Interests," 248.
14. H. L. A. Hart first noted this in his "Bentham on Legal Rights," in *Oxford Essays in Jurisprudence*, 2nd series, ed. A. W. B. Simpson (Oxford: Oxford University Press, 1973), 171–201.
15. See Appendix 1 for some additional issues concerning the claiming and waiving of rights.

16. However, it is possible that in the case of a creature sufficiently simple and short lived, it is not worth engaging in a destructive act even to one of its kind to save many of its kind.
17. Furthermore, suppose we had a choice between (i) saving these good things in the life of a person who is not at risk of losing his life and (ii) saving the life of another person who has not and would not have these good things in his life. Presumably we should save the life. Suppose this is so and we now have a choice between saving the first or second person's life. A life will be lost no matter what, and additionally, many valuable things in a life will be lost only if we do not save the first person. If it was worth losing the valuable things in order to save the second person's life, can saving them along with the life in which they exist be enough to deprive the second person of an equal chance to be saved (other things equal)? Should having (what might be considered) the benefit of the possibility of more goods in his life give the first person the additional benefit of having his life saved in a forced-choice situation? We may answer differently depending on whether we are concerned with proper treatment of persons, each of whom wants to be the one to survive, or with producing best outcomes. Our decision in this case may be different from what it would be if the choice was between birds whose pasts were the same but whose futures would contain different amounts of goods.
18. This is different from there being a threshold on the amount or degree of characteristics that could be relevant for increasing moral status.
19. As I suggested in *Intricate Ethics*, Chapter 5.
20. I have suggested that though one may redirect a lethal threat from five people toward one different person, he could resist our permissible act by sending the threat back because he is wronged by the act. See my *Intricate Ethics*, *The Trolley Problem Mysteries* (New York: Oxford University Press, 2016), and Chapter 9 in this volume.
21. Though "develop into" and "give rise to" are different notions, I will use them interchangeably here.
22. Some think that an embryo is not a being in its own right but a stage in the life of a human being. On this view being a person is also a stage in the life of a human being. Others think an embryo is a stage in the life of a person and that stages of people do not have different moral status from the people whose stages they are even though the properties that distinctively identify something as a person are not yet present. Some (e.g., Korsgaard in her *Fellow Creatures*) hold that a person who will definitely exist is an atemporal entity. Its well-being should be considered even before its early stages exist in the same way as the well-being of the person once its distinctive person-properties are present during its time alive. The view I shall present may give us reason to doubt this last position. Though I will conceive of the embryo as an entity in its own right, I think my moral positions are compatible with a "stage view."
23. Such an argument is made in Allen Buchanan, Dan W. Brock, Norman Daniels, and Daniel Wikler, *From Chance to Choice: Genetics and Justice* (Cambridge: Cambridge University Press, 2000).
24. For this discussion I will assume the egg and sperm's moral status to be Level 1, though they may be below that (i.e., in their own right it is permissible to do anything

to them). A revised version of the View would then assign protections owed to Level 3 persons to entities below Level 1 from which persons arise. An egg or sperm is not a stage of that person. It is a means to the person's existence that can also affect the person's well-being and so is relevant to the View and those whose positions were described in note 22.

25. I first discussed the 160 IQ Case in *Creation and Abortion*. I here combine it with the 160 IQ Egg Case, which I first discussed in "Affecting Definite Future People." It could also be the father who affects his sperm or alters an embryo in a lab to lower the IQ of his offspring to 140. In all these examples, I assume that both prospective parents are in agreement about what is done.
26. This is on the assumption I will make here that it is better for the person himself to have the higher IQ.
27. See Parfit's *Reasons and Persons* (Oxford: Oxford University Press, 1984).
28. Jeff McMahan refers to what he calls the Divergent Lives Problem (in his third Rutgers Philosophy Lecture, November 2019) as occurring when it would have been better to have created one type of person rather than another for the sake of a person himself (e.g., a 160 IQ person rather than a different 140 IQ person), but once created to the less choice-worthy life, it could no longer be in a person's interest to have had the more choice-worthy life if that life would not have served what are now his actual interests.
29. A case that clearly makes this point involves someone who has lived a life worth living for twenty years with Down syndrome. This person may be happy doing activities that make it be in his interest to acquire vocational training and prepare for the Special Olympics. Suppose he could be cured of Down syndrome at age twenty. Being cured would not serve any of the things that are in his interest as a person with Down syndrome and it would make new things (such as going to college) be in his interest. Presumably he should be cured and a sudden cure might even be better than a gradual one other things equal (i.e., no overriding negative side effects). The same point can be made by considering a father-to-be whose only options are using a sperm that would create someone to a life worth living with permanent Down syndrome or another sperm that would create a different person who would have the syndrome for twenty years and then gradually or suddenly be cured. Presumably, the father-to-be should create the person who would be cured at twenty (other things equal).
30. Not all ways of affecting for the worse a person who already exists (i.e., a being with the properties distinctive of persons) are ruled out. Suppose (hypothetically) a parent having another child would limit her existing child's intellectual development (because resources were spread thinner) so that he had a 140 IQ rather than a 160 IQ. (I owe this case to Francesca Minerva.) It need not be impermissible to have the other child. I am here only concerned with the impermissibility of affecting someone by doing something to his body (e.g., giving the pill for the purpose of lowering his IQ). It is consistent with nonconsequentialist moral theory to distinguish morally among different ways of bringing about the same consequences.
31. I discuss what parents owe to the offspring they create in *Creation and Abortion*.

32. This analogy may help in dealing with the view that the embryo is not a being but a stage in the life of a person or human being. Childhood is a stage in the life of a person. Nevertheless, the person would not be wronged by the parent not putting money in the bank account nor by her removing money from it during the person's childhood. This is so even if the person will eventually be at an adult stage where he has control over the account.
33. Suppose the delayed change would remove ten IQ points and a child with a 150 IQ would not present problems for the family. The only alternative is acting on the egg to remove twenty IQ points without delay. Though it is better for the person to lose fewer points, this may not be enough to justify the delayed change. Nevertheless, I present an argument for doing so in "Genes, Justice, and Obligations in Creating People," in *Bioethical Prescriptions*, Endnote 47, 289–90.
34. The moral importance of the separateness of persons refers to the moral importance of recognizing that imposing a sacrifice on one person that will only benefit another person is not morally the same as imposing the same sacrifice on one person that will benefit that same person.
35. See his *Reasons and Persons*.
36. This could happen if a particular egg and sperm combination determined the identity (if not all the characteristics) of a particular person and it was stored for a long time before being triggered to begin developing 100 years hence.
37. These points concern affecting for the worse people already existing by contrast to definite future people. Hence, it is different from and goes beyond the claim that we should favor (a) not making a person already in existence at level y worse off by amount x rather than (b) doing what will produce a person who will have a life at level y rather than a different person who will have a life at level y – x. Option (b) involves nonidentity and so non-person-affectingness. (I believe that Jeff McMahan in a paper presented at the Rutgers Conference in Memory of Derek Parfit [2018] has discussed such a case and criticized Parfit for thinking there is no moral difference between [a] and [b].) Parfit's No-Difference View would imply both that there is no moral difference between what is morally at stake in (a) and (b) and that what is at stake in (b) is no different from a choice that would determine whether a definite future person will be at level y or at level y – x (a person-affecting case).
38. I also discuss these implications of arguments against the View for obligations to future generations in "Moral Status, Personal Identity, and Substitutability," reprinted in *Bioethical Prescriptions*.
39. Presentation by Broome on May 8, 2021, at a University of North Carolina conference in honor of Douglas MacLean. I here leave it undetermined whether the "they" are the same people who would otherwise have lived longer lives or there is a nonidentity between those who would have lived longer and those who would live shorter lives.

# 2

# Rights That Ethical Responsibility Cannot Justify and Agreements May Not Undermine

In Chapter 1 we considered the relation between moral status and rights. In this chapter we will consider what rights not to be harmed and to be aided (and their correlative duties) are had by persons and why. Ronald Dworkin is famous for his defense of individual rights as "trumps" that constrain the pursuit of the greater good. In his later work he argued that a principle of dignity implies that we have a duty to ourselves that grounds rights. In this chapter we will investigate his arguments for this claim and consider some alternatives.[1]

## I. Ethics and Morality

Ronald Dworkin argues in *Justice for Hedgehogs* that ethics of personal life (to be distinguished from interpersonal morality)[2] is based on dignity that requires, first, that one think of oneself and how one's life goes as objectively and intrinsically important (principle of self-respect) and, second, that one has a special responsibility for choosing values that make one's life a good one (principles of authenticity and ethical independence).[3] I will refer to these elements as "importance" and "responsibility." This responsibility to try to have a good life involves seeking to live a successful life well, including within moral constraints that have to do with relations with others.[4] According to Dworkin, a good life includes pursuing success according to one's independently chosen goals and values (authenticity). Doing this is an objective responsibility, not a mere personal preference for self-chosen goals.[5] Further, a person must choose goals and values in response to what he views as having objective value apart from his choice.[6] This view implies that one could choose the wrong goals and values, and then one would not have lived successfully. (A question this possibility raises is whether one could still have lived with dignity because one took one's life seriously and lived according to one's own, albeit mistaken, views of objective value.[7])

Dworkin emphasizes that one can live well even if one's life is not a success due to bad luck or because one abides by moral constraints when they conflict with

*Rights and Their Limits: In Theory, Cases, and Pandemics.* F. M. Kamm, Oxford University Press.
© Oxford University Press 2022. DOI: 10.1093/oso/9780197567739.003.0002

success.[8] He also (reluctantly) concedes that one's life could still be successful if one violated moral constraints. So, if the only route to success involves corruption, one lives well by not being corrupt, though one does not have success.

Dworkin argues that these two ethical principles, which I refer to as importance and responsibility, can help us to derive the content and explain the attraction of morality (understood as obligations to others such as to aid or not to harm). In his view, it is important that morality not be merely a component of an ethical life where the content of the component is derived independently of ethics. Dworkin wants ethics when described *independently of morality* to play a role in deriving the content of morality (which may then play a role in characterizing the ethical life). This is connected with his interpretative view of normative concepts, according to which our understanding of each concept should be formed in the light of others. This is Dworkin's way to eliminate conflicts between the different normative components.[9]

He thinks we can derive morality from ethics because first, one cannot correctly believe that one's life and how it goes has objective importance unless this is true of other people too, as it is only in virtue of the properties making one a person that one shares with others that one has importance.[10] Call this Importance-Moral. Dworkin thinks that morality requires us to respect others for their own sake, not merely instrumentally for our sake;[11] and we could not correctly believe that others ought to respect us for *our own sake* if we did not think the same of them. In this way, Dworkin thinks that our attraction to morality can be explained by the threat to our own dignity if we do not treat others as important in their own right.

A problem would arise for this first component in the account of the relation between morality and ethics if there were moral obligations to entities whose importance is not grounded in the properties that ground a person's own importance. For example, the moral importance of animals might be grounded differently from that of human persons. If one's own importance were not implicated in denying direct moral duties concerning these beings, one would have to find some account other than the coherence of morality and an ethical ideal to explain our attraction to the part of morality dealing with animals.[12] Dworkin's account of the relation of morality and ethics may underestimate our capacity simply to act for reasons such as the importance of others independent of there being a connection between their importance and our own importance. Indeed, some might say it is this capacity that is one source of our own dignity.

The second component of dignity—responsibility—he thinks also helps isolate the content of morality, for if one has a special responsibility for one's own life going well, this will be true of every other person and will affect what is morally expected of each person. Call this Responsibility-Moral.

## II. Responsibilities to Self and Helping Others

A.(i) One of Dworkin's aims is to show that our importance implies moral duties to aid other persons. He speaks in terms of duties (or obligations) but says that "we might have standard morality through the idea of rights. We might have asked, for example, what aid we all have a right to have."[13] Hence, we will here assume that the duties that Dworkin derives are owed to others and are correlative to rights that others have. (This is so even though it might be suggested that at least some duties to aid by contrast to duties not to harm are not correlative to rights. Dworkin does not deal with this issue in *Justice for Hedgehogs*.) But despite everyone having equal importance, he thinks we are not required to show as much concern for others as for ourselves.[14] Indeed, he says, "I cannot treat someone else's life with the same attention and concern as I treat my own without trespassing on and so denying his personal responsibility as well as neglecting my own."[15] This statement suggests that showing equal concern for ourselves and others is not only not required but also generally wrong. Dworkin says that in deciding how much one owes others (a matter of morality), "The test is interpretive. Which acts, in which circumstances, show a failure to respect the objective and equal importance of human life? . . . It is a matter of the right distribution of self-concern and concern for others."[16] It is the responsibility of each person to decide what the right answer is, but one could independently decide and get the *wrong* answer. That is, there was something one should have done for oneself or others that one did not do. He further argues that we owe aid only when not giving it shows disrespect for human life because it shows indifference,[17] and this does not occur if we refuse to aid when it would involve either neglecting responsibilities to ourselves[18] or interfering with responsibilities others have for themselves.[19]

Dworkin's initial view was that this weighing of self versus others to determine one's moral obligations to others occurs *after* one has decided what constitutes a successful life for oneself. That view allows that one could consider the interests of others in deciding what constitutes success in one's own life but not because one morally owes them this.[20] For example, one might consider whether helping others would make one happier and so more successful. The view that it is only reasonable to decide among life projects by in the first instance taking account of moral considerations would be an objection to his initial view.[21] However, Dworkin ultimately holds that anyone who embraces projects that require him to ignore the suffering of others altogether lacks self-respect. This is because those projects are inconsistent with the right regard for the objective importance of the lives of others and therefore of his own.

(ii) One worry about these views of Dworkin's is that showing equal concern for oneself and others need not involve neglecting one's special responsibility for one's own life if such equal concern comes from choosing projects and values (independently of thinking of them as morally required) that involve equal concern for oneself and others. If one chooses such projects and values, one will have taken one's life seriously and fulfilled the responsibility to choose projects and values autonomously, but success will involve showing equal concern. A second worry arises when we consider a different case in which equal concern for oneself and others *would* interfere with success in one's chosen goals. Dworkin himself says that it could be admirable, saintly, or generous to give up one's success to save others from disaster, though it does not show disrespect for them not to do so.[22] And while he says that a person must not "aim to make [others'] lives more successful overall because it is their responsibility to choose goals that they can manage,"[23] this seems inconsistent with his claim that it would be generous—and thus not wrong—to give up a trip on behalf of someone who could not otherwise manage to fulfill a lifelong goal of taking such a trip.[24]

It seems to me that those who act nobly in helping another person in an unforeseen disaster may do no wrong because they will still have fulfilled their *responsibility to live well.* This could be so even if they give up their own success not because it conflicts with moral constraints but because it conflicts with doing a *supererogatory* act (whose nonperformance would not be disrespectful of others). Suppose this is so. Then other people who do not act similarly but choose instead to make a success (as they have identified it) of their life cannot claim, contrary to what Dworkin argues, that it would have been wrong of them to aid because they would have neglected their responsibility to themselves (or to their chosen goals). It may indeed be permissible for them to pursue their success, but it would be self-deceptive and self-serving for them to think that they can cloak this morally permissible choice as a requirement not to do something ethically wrong.

Therefore, it is important to argue, as Dworkin *does not*, that even when there would be *no* improper neglect of individuals' ethical responsibility for themselves if they sacrifice success in order to aid others, the equal objective importance and respectful treatment of each person does *not* imply that one must provide such aid or be equally concerned for each person. It need not be the presence of overriding ethical *responsibilities* that makes *un*equal concern permissible but rather a *moral right* to attend to one's own concerns. Dworkin seems to lack confidence that a right on its own could stand up to the objective importance of other people and their needs if it is not accompanied by an overriding *ethical responsibility* to oneself. I think his lack of confidence in the power of such a right on its own, as well as his confidence that an ethical responsibility can fill the gap, is unwarranted.[25] This also means that we should inquire into some other ground for the right rather than its usefulness for fulfilling one's ethical responsibilities.

Suppose that responsibilities to self need not constrain one from making big sacrifices for others. This need not imply that there is no responsibility to make something good of one's life but merely a personal preference for one's own success. As I have argued in earlier work, it is not true that one must always fulfill a responsibility (e.g., to give a presentation) rather than do a supererogatory act (e.g., risk one's own life to save a drowning person).[26] We can agree with Dworkin that we have a responsibility, not a mere preference, to make something good of our lives so long as (1) we think that we really should be doing this when we have not chosen to do something else more important from an impartial point of view (such as saving many others) and (2) we may not choose to abandon our ethical responsibility just because we prefer to do something unimportant for someone else.[27]

Still, suppose we choose to fulfill our responsibility to ourselves because it is a responsibility, when it would not be ethically wrong to do a noble act instead. Sticking with one's responsibility to oneself may still reveal self-preference rather than a concern for fulfilling responsibilities in general. This would be so if someone would abandon a responsibility he has accepted for the success of other people's lives but not his responsibility for the success of his own life in order, for example, to save strangers from a disaster.

B.(i) One particular factor that Dworkin thinks may bear on whether we have a duty to aid others is what he calls "confrontation."[28] For Dworkin, this is in part a question of whether we are physically near to, rather than far from, someone who needs help.[29] However, he also seems to include under confrontation psychological interaction with a victim who, in the cases he discusses, likely knows that we could help.[30] Dworkin says that it is hard to explain why confrontation should matter morally, but he thinks it does to a limited extent.[31] However, when a terrible disaster would occur if we do not provide easy aid (his example is African famine), he thinks the absence of confrontation does not matter morally.[32]

(ii) I am inclined to agree with this part of Dworkin's discussion and am interested in it, in part, because of my own discussion of the possible moral relevance of physical distance to a duty to aid.[33] In that discussion, I argued that being physically near rather than far could be shown to be of some moral significance if the size of the effort one would be morally required to make varied with distance to the person in need.[34] For example, if one were near the person needing aid, one might be required to make a larger effort than if one were far, other things equal.

Nevertheless, I have reservations about Dworkin's discussion. First, he does not distinguish the role of distance per se from psychological interaction carefully enough. In my view, it could be that the person who needs aid is not aware of us and does not know we are able to aid, we do not identify him (say, a bush is between us), and yet our being near him and knowing this could be morally relevant to our having a duty to aid him.

Second, I have argued that, surprisingly, we could have as strong a duty to help people who are distant from us as those who are near, even at large cost, on account of nearness being morally relevant.[35] This is because we may be *near* to (rather than far from) a *threat* that is now far from but will soon be near people if we do not act, or because our *means* with which to help someone are near to that person even though we are far both from our means (e.g., our boat) and the person who could be helped. Other discussions of the moral relevance of physical distance (including Dworkin's) have not considered all these factors that could be near or far from each other but have only focused on the aider being near or far from the recipient of the aid.[36]

My third concern is with Dworkin's view that not providing easy aid to someone in desperate need at one's feet must reflect indifference to, and lack of respect for, the objective value of a person.[37] Suppose that one is on one's way to save 1,000 people who are far away and if one stops to save the person at one's feet, those others will die. It does not seem to me that one shows indifference to human life if one continues on one's way. Furthermore, suppose that the aid required by the near person is small (and so aiding her is even a *pro tanto* duty), but the aid required by those who are far is great enough so that aiding them is supererogatory. As discussed earlier, I believe that doing a supererogatory act can sometimes take precedence over performing one's duty without this showing disrespect for the person to whom one has a duty.[38] Hence, it could be permissible even in this case to abandon the person "at our feet."[39]

## III. Ethical Responsibility and Harming Others

A.(i) Dworkin's second aim is to show that ethical responsibility explains why we may not deliberately harm people.[40] First, he thinks that such responsibility grounds a right to control one's body and security over one's property, as without these one could not make a success of one's life.[41] By contrast, he thinks we do not need to deliberately harm others to make a success of our lives though we do need to do things that can lead to foreseen harm to others. It is important to emphasize that when Dworkin says, "any general transfer of control over the integrity of my body . . . would leave my dignity in shreds,"[42] it is the inability to fulfill the responsibility for the success of one's own life that he thinks explains the attack on dignity, not any inconsistency with the objective importance of the person. He says, "It cannot be the objective importance of human life that you offend when . . . you shoot the stranger [to save your own life]. The same preference for your own life is still at work and is still compatible with Kant's principle [of the objective value of persons]."[43] The same would be true if someone else shot you to save their own life. Dworkin also believes that maximizing the number of lives saved by shooting some people to save others is compatible with valuing life and showing respect for that value.[44]

(ii) My sense, contrary to Dworkin's claim, is that ethical responsibility for the success of one's life is not necessary for deriving such rights to one's body and property. Even if one had no such responsibility, other grounds would be sufficient for one's having a right to one's body or to property acquired in certain ways. Indeed, it seems dangerous to make such rights contingent on responsibilities, for suppose it is clear that someone lacks the capacity to fulfill his ethical responsibilities for the success of his life (e.g., someone is severely disabled) or either has no intention to do so or has already fulfilled these responsibilities. Such a person has no need for his body or property for the purpose of fulfilling his ethical responsibilities. Might he then lose rights to his body and property? Presumably not. And what if some types of control over one's body or property are not needed to pursue success? For example, we naturally lack control over our bodies because we cannot help falling asleep sometimes or perhaps because we suffer from paralysis, yet we can still make a success of our lives despite such lack of control. However, suppose another person were to interfere with our bodies so as to deliberately produce these exact same limitations of control. This would not interfere with our success to any greater degree than naturally occurring interference. Yet we would still have a right that the person not interfere in this way (including touching us without permission while we sleep, which would not further interfere with our success in any way).

Furthermore, having responsibilities is not sufficient, in general, for having a right to what one needs to fulfill those responsibilities, even when others do not need the same thing to fulfill *their* responsibilities. For example, if one needs a car to fulfill a promise one has made, one may still have no right to have a car. Why, then, is having a responsibility to make a success of one's life sufficient to generate rights to one's body or security over one's property even if they are needed for success? Indeed, Dworkin's assurance that one's success in life does not require deliberately interfering with others' bodies seems to depend on one's tailoring one's projects in the light of a prior recognition that one may not interfere in this way with others' bodies. If one had other projects, one might indeed need to control their bodies as much as one's own. As it is, one needs to survive in order to succeed, so one may actually need to get someone else's kidney or heart to stay alive, but this would not be sufficient to support a right to get them.

Finally, consider the analogy with artworks that Dworkin uses to support his claims about duties to aid. He says that one can recognize the equal objective value of several works of art while at the same time reasonably holding that one is responsible only for caring for those in one's collection.[45] This example works against his view that it is responsibility for the success of something of importance (like one's life) that gives one a right to control it. Rather, it is first having rights over the artworks (i.e., their being in one's collection) that makes one responsible for their care. It is also the rights that some have over the works of art, rather than their responsibility for them, that makes it impermissible for others to take responsibility for them if they wished to. Furthermore, in the case of works of art, one may sometimes lose one's right to control them (e.g., they may be transferred to another collection) if one does not take care of them properly. The same might be true if one has a right to one's own child but loses such a right if one does not provide responsible care. However, the failure to attend to one's responsibility (as Dworkin says on the last page of *Hedgehogs*) to "live a good life well" does not (except in the most extreme cases) make one lose a right to control one's own body. By contrast, as already pointed out, Dworkin's view suggests that if someone shows no willingness or ability to fulfill his ethical responsibility to live a good life well, he would also have no special grounds for claiming a right to control his body.

Hence, while I do think one's dignity would be threatened if one did not have rights over one's body, I do not think these rights derive from any responsibility one has to make something of one's life. Such responsibility, I have argued, is neither necessary nor sufficient to justify the right. This suggests that the right to control one's body is antecedent to, rather than derived from or contingent on, anyone's responsibility for making a success of his life or living well. Given that one has this right, one would be the only person who could take on these responsibilities (if they exist) insofar as they require controlling one's body.[46]

Suppose neither the objective importance of human life nor the responsibility to make a success of one's life accounted for a right to noninterference with one's body and yet such a right is crucial for the dignity of the person. This would suggest that Dworkin's conception of dignity is seriously incomplete. (However, it is possible, contrary to Dworkin, that it is the objective value of human life in the sense of the worth of each individual person that grounds a right to one's body. For example, the value of each life would be lower if it were permissible to kill some to minimize the number of others killed; more would live but the value of each would be lower.[47])

B.(i) One of Dworkin's concerns is to justify a moral distinction between harming and not aiding, which he seems to think involves the act/omission distinction.[48] Dworkin tries to show that deliberate harm (but not harm that comes to others as a side effect [e.g., because we compete with them]) is morally worse than denying aid (even given the same motive and aim).[49] He thinks this is because of the connection between dignity and bodily control and that deliberate harm (which interferes with bodily control) but not refusing aid usurps a person's *responsibility* to control his own life.[50]

(ii) One problem with this account is that harming per se seems to be morally worse than not aiding per se even if one has no responsibility for controlling one's own life but only a *right* to control one's own life independent of such a responsibility. We must keep separate two different types of arguments: (1) deliberate intrusion on another's body is wrong because it interferes with his right to control his own life (not derived from his responsibility to control his life), and (2) deliberate intrusion on another's body is wrong because it interferes with his responsibility to control his own life. The latter is Dworkin's position.

A second problem is that nondeliberate harm also seems to be worse than not aiding other things equal. For example, suppose someone had to get to an important meeting and therefore refused to slow down his car to avoid foreseeably but not deliberately (i.e., not aiming at) hitting someone on the road. This seems more serious than someone who had to get to an important meeting and therefore refused to stop to avoid foreseeably but not deliberately (i.e., not aiming at) letting someone die by the side of the road.

Third, does Dworkin's claim that deliberate harm is wrong because it usurps someone else's responsibility for his own life[51] conflict with the distinction that he himself draws between the impermissibility of ethical paternalistic interference and the permissibility of some other sorts of interference? If Dworkin were attempting to connect the wrongness of deliberate interference with usurping another's ethical responsibility for making a success of his life and living well, this would suggest that those who harm us for their own benefit are trying to lead our lives for us, but this does not seem to be true. They are ignoring whether what they do helps us live successfully or well and just thinking about what will help themselves.

He says:

> Coercion justified on economic, moral or aesthetic grounds does not invade the personal responsibility of anyone to identify and find value in his own life. Government may forbid people to discriminate. . . . [I]t may tax people for funds to protect . . . treasures. . . . However personal value is different from both impersonal and moral value. Government may not force people to live lives that conform with the views of those in power about which lives are worthy and which unworthy.[52]

According to this statement, government coercion does not usurp a person's ethical responsibility for controlling his own life when it is *not* done to make him lead a life the government thinks is right for him but for some other reason such as protecting treasures. Further, its doing this can be permissible even when the government's coercing for this reason affects the person's ability to pursue his goals (e.g., discriminate against some people if that is his goal, support something other than art if that is his goal). If this is so in the case of the government, it is not clear why an individual who deliberately harms someone in order *to help herself*, not in order to make the person harmed lead a successful life, also does *not* usurp that person's ethical responsibility and so might also act permissibly despite interfering with the person's ability to pursue his goals.[53] With respect to property, Dworkin does claim that money doesn't belong to someone until after taxation.[54] (Even if they already possess some money because they were undertaxed, the money can be taken away from them.) So he is concerned with "normative possession" rather than physical possession. But we could have the same attitude to someone's body. You possess it physically, but normatively use of your body or its parts (perhaps at certain times) could belong to someone else. In addition, government may not only tax but also draft people and limit use of personal property for preserving its artistic value (as in landmark laws). This leaves it open that individuals might do the same to others without behaving wrongly.

Of course, a person's interference may be impermissible while the government's interference (for aesthetic, economic, etc., purposes) may be permissible. But the point is that it still has to be shown why it is impermissible, or why the interference is morally worse per se than not aiding, if it does not usurp someone's ethical responsibility for his own life.

C.(i) Having discussed cases in which an individual would harm someone else out of self-interest, Dworkin moves on to discuss an individual deliberately harming someone else to help many others.[55] His objection to harming someone to help many others against the wishes of the person harmed is here based on the idea that we would thereby usurp somebody's ethical responsibility to decide how to best lead his own life, and so act inconsistently with his dignity.[56] Dworkin says that if others decide he (Dworkin) is to be harmed to help other people:

> I suffer because others have decided that what I regard as harmful to me is nevertheless, all things considered, desirable. . . . [W]hat is forbidden in all these cases is not that someone's body be invaded or harmed but that this be done in service of a judgment about how his body *should* be used.[57]

He also says:

> I would suffer [harm] because others have usurped a decision that dignity requires me to make for myself—the decision what use is to be made of my body or my life. . . . The second principle [of dignity] does not forbid any act, like choosing a patient for a liver transplant, that saves one life and dooms another. . . . It forbids such acts only when they are based on a usurping judgment that the best use of one person's body is to save another's life.[58]

In inflicting deliberate harm, we act because we have decided there is something desirable about the victim being harmed, either as a means or as an end. By contrast, Dworkin says, when an agent causes harm nondeliberately, the agent need not decide that harm to the victim is desirable contrary to the victim's own decision.[59] Here, the agent, as much as the victim, can think it is bad that the victim is unlucky enough to be in harm's way.[60] Dworkin's additional claim is that this distinction he draws between different types of harms coincides with and even explains the importance of the distinction that the Doctrine of Double Effect (DDE) draws between intending harm as a means or an end, which the DDE holds is not permissible, and causing merely foreseen harm.[61] In the latter case, according to the DDE, proportionate (e.g., lesser) harms need not stand in the way of bringing about a greater good by necessary means, innocent in themselves.[62]

(ii) My first concern about these claims is related to the fact that Dworkin is here specifically speaking to the reasons someone's control over his body is interfered with, not merely that his control is interfered with (as in B). The reasons are about the best use of his body and Dworkin here claims that the responsibility component of dignity requires that the person himself decide about the best use of his body. However, elsewhere Dworkin claims that the distinction that is important for dignity is between interference on grounds that it would be better for someone *for his own sake* to live a certain way (ethical paternalism) and interference that is not so grounded.[63] He says the former is an attack on one's dignity (via an attack on one's ethical responsibility); the latter need not be.[64] For example, suppose the government thinks it is better that one fight in a war via the draft or be unable to destroy one's property for the sake of preserving it as an object of artistic merit. Then the government sees one's doing public service or having less control over one's property as desirable, though I see these things as undesirable. According to Dworkin's view, this does not imply that such public service and restrictions on one's use of personal property is an attack on my dignity via an attack on my ethical responsibility for my own life.[65] If the latter distinction is the crucial one, then it does not seem that what makes it impermissible to harm someone in order to *save other people's lives*—not in order to make the person harmed have a more successful, well-lived life—is that it usurps someone's ethical responsibility for his own life. That is, if drafting someone or restricting what one may do with one's property for art's sake does not involve deciding that a person will have a better life if he fights or supports art (usurping his responsibility to decide what a successful, well-lived life for himself is), then neither does harming him to save others.

In sum, (1) deciding what is the *best use* of someone's life (e.g., to be a means to saving others) is not the same as (2) deciding what makes the person's life *go best for his sake*. It may be that only the latter conflicts with Dworkin's notion of ethical responsibility for one's life.

My second concern is that Dworkin identifies the DDE's distinction between intended harm and merely foreseen harm with his own distinction between causing harm deliberately and causing merely foreseen harm. However, as Dworkin himself notes, the DDE's distinction is not meant to apply only to causing harm but also to allowing it to happen, as in not aiding with the intention that harm happen. Hence, part of the DDE could conflict with Dworkin's analysis of the relative seriousness of not aiding and harming when there is an intention that harm occur in each case. The DDE and Dworkin's views coincide insofar as neither necessarily condemns cases in which acts produce a lesser harm as a mere side effect when we are pursuing a greater good.[66] Philippa Foot argued against this part of the DDE when she claimed that it would be wrong to use a gas to save five lives if we knew the gas would kill a bystander as a mere side effect.[67] In his discussion of the Trolley Problem, Dworkin does not note that it would similarly be morally wrong to set a bomb that will redirect a trolley from killing five people when we foresee that the bomb will kill a bystander as a mere side effect.[68] Here, the fact that we do not judge a lesser harm to be in any way good and that we would merely act despite the harm in the course of saving more lives may not make causing the harm permissible.

My third concern is that sometimes it is *permissible* and does not violate someone's right for us to do something that has a bad effect on an innocent, nonthreatening person based on our judgment that it would be good if the effect occurs. Hence, the bad effect occurring gives us a reason to act contrary to the person's decision that the effect would not be good (for her). This is true, I believe, in what I call the Bad Man Trolley Case in which a bystander would not turn the trolley away from killing five people because he doesn't care about them until he realizes the person he would kill by redirecting the trolley is his enemy whom he intends to kill. (We could imagine a variant in which the bad man intends to kill the person because he can then acquire his organs, which would be useful in saving the life of the bad man's associate.) In this case it would still be permissible and not violate the victim's rights for the bad man to turn the trolley away from the five people. This is so even though he intends an innocent's death and does what would bring it about based on his judgment that it would be good if the death occurs, contrary to the innocent's own decision that it would not be good.

I also believe this is true (even in the absence of an intention to kill) in the Loop version of the Trolley Case that Dworkin discusses.[69] In this case, we would redirect the trolley headed toward killing five people only because one person immovably located on a side track will be hit, thus stopping the trolley from looping back toward the five.[70] We would not turn the trolley if he were not hit as redirecting would then not save the five, and we take it as a reason to redirect that he will be hit.

Dworkin thinks that in the Loop Case if we act on the judgment that the person's being hit is good, then we would be intending the hit as a means to save the five.[71] However, I have argued in earlier work that redirecting the trolley *because* we will bring about the hit, and so having a positive attitude to it, is not the same as redirecting the trolley intending to bring about the hit.[72] In general, acting only because one will produce an effect is not the same as either acting with the intention to produce it or acting when one merely foresees the effect. To help make this clearer, consider the Party Case.[73] I want to have a party in order for my friends to have fun but not if I have to clean up a mess afterward. I read psychological studies that show that people who have had a good time will feel indebted and clean up a mess. It is only because I believe my having the party will cause such feelings of indebtedness and this will take care of the mess that I have the party. I would not have the party if I knew the feelings would not occur. However, I do not have the party even in part in order to produce feelings of indebtedness as shown by my unwillingness to do anything else (innocent in itself) merely to produce such feelings.[74]

In the Loop Case, a willingness to turn the trolley from the five people because the one will be hit also need not imply a rational commitment to doing anything *extra* in order that the hit occur, even if the extra is not itself hard or objectionable. The absence of this commitment, which commitment should be present if one intended to hit the person, suggests that acting because one will cause the hit does not involve intending to cause it. The fact that an agent acts because the one person will be hit but not in order to hit him may play a part in some people's view of the permissibility of turning the trolley in the Loop Case. This is so even if they admit the death is not a mere foreseen side effect. Indeed, I have elsewhere argued that turning the trolley only because the hit will occur is consistent with helping the one person off the track if this becomes possible after one has redirected but before he is hit, even though the five will then die.[75] Refraining from easily removing him would indicate an intention that he be hit, and someone who turned the trolley only because the one person would be hit need not be committed to the one person remaining susceptible to being hit. By contrast, turning the trolley intending the hit is harder to make consistent with helping the one person off the track as doing this would indicate a change in intention.[76]

If what I have argued is correct, redirecting the trolley in the Loop Case need not violate the DDE because it need not involve intending to hit the one person. However, redirecting the trolley in the Loop Case still runs afoul of the distinction between harms that Dworkin wants to draw, based on whether we cause something bad to happen to someone (the hit) because we decide it is desirable all things considered for it to happen, contrary to the judgment of the person who will be harmed.[77] This shows that contrary to what Dworkin claims, the distinction he wants to draw does not overlap with the DDE even in cases of causing harm and so cannot explain or justify the DDE.[78] It also shows that we do not violate someone's ethical responsibility in the Loop Case even if we act because we consider it overall good that he will be harmed contrary to his own view of what is a good life for him.

In sum, I conclude: (1) Even intending harm to someone as a means to help others need not involve usurping his ethical responsibility; (2) Dworkin's proposed explanation of the DDE's moral distinction between intended and merely foreseen harm *does not explain it*. This is because acting on a view of the desirability of a harm to someone that the person himself rejects need not *always* indicate an *intention* that the harm occur. Therefore, (3) Dworkin's account of what is wrong with deliberate harm (whether or not it involves usurping ethical responsibility) also *does not coincide* with the DDE's account of what makes harm wrong. (4) Causing harm with the intention to harm or causing harm because it is good as an end or means contrary to the victim's own view need not make an act wrong or a violation of a victim's rights (and our correlative duties to him). (5) Violation of victims' rights can have less to do with what agents want, intend, or see as good and more with factors that are constant through agents' varying states of mind. The mind-independent factors that make an act not a violation of rights (as in the Bad Man Trolley Case) could of course ground a possible good intention if an agent acts for the sake of those factors. But the act is not permissible because of that intention since we identify the good intention by seeing that it makes reference to the mind-independent factors. It is the latter that determine that the act is permissible.[79]

## IV. Ex Ante Agreements

A.(i) Dworkin's discussion of harming someone to help other people also takes up the question of ex ante agreements (hypothetical or real) among people.[80] This is because it might be thought that harm to someone could be justified as the outcome of agreements each person could reasonably make in advance of certain events in order to maximize his own success. But Dworkin's interest in ex ante agreements is also independent of its particular relation to harm, as he first introduces them as a way of reconciling ethical responsibility with moral responsibility in general.[81] In this final part, I wish to consider his views about ex ante agreements.

Dworkin thinks that one way to derive the content of morality from ethics is to take up an ex ante perspective to one's own good from behind a veil of ignorance.[82] He thinks that seeking to make a success of one's life will lead to moral rules when one does not know what particular characteristics as a person one will actually have.[83] Yet his positive account of our duties to aid and not harm[84] that we have reviewed does not explicitly derive them from such ex ante reasoning. Indeed, it is possible that the duties that would be derived from an ex ante perspective are very different from the ones Dworkin actually endorses. He himself raises this possibility when he discusses a "spare parts lottery," in which someone will have a duty to let himself be sacrificed for his organs when this will save more people.[85] Dworkin asks: "If it would be in everyone's interest to join a spare parts lottery, then why is it wrong for us to treat people as if such a lottery had always been in place?"[86]

One reason stronger duties to aid might be derived via ex ante reasoning is that Dworkin interprets such reasoning behind a veil of ignorance as involving a single person deciding what would be good for himself. (This is also how a connection between ethics and morality in general is supposed to be established by ex ante agreements.) Many have rejected this understanding of ex ante reasoning on the ground that it threatens to ignore the morally significant separateness of persons[87] and, hence, any special responsibility one person has for his own life going well. For example, suppose it would be in *A*'s interest to sacrifice his leg in order to save his own life (an intrapersonal sacrifice). Also suppose *A* does not know, ex ante, whether he will be in the position of (1) someone who will die if another person does not give up his leg to save him or (2) someone who will have to sacrifice his leg to save another person. (These are interpersonal sacrifices). If one were to derive moral rules from a person's prudential perspective on his own life from behind a veil of ignorance, it might seem that one could derive a duty for one person to sacrifice his leg for the sake of another's life (an interpersonal sacrifice) from the fact that he would sacrifice his leg to save his own life (an intrapersonal sacrifice). This goes beyond the duty to aid that Dworkin supports.

However, Dworkin believes that one should live in accordance with dignity.[88] This means that if Dworkin uses this type of ex ante reasoning (that envisions a single person deciding what would be best for himself) to derive morality from ethics, he might try to derive morality both from an individual's concern for the success of his own life and from his accepting special responsibility for his life going well. So when a person reasons about interpersonal cases, he would be aware that his dignity is affected not only by his success (e.g., whether his life is saved) but also by who assumes responsibility for his life and decisions about how it will go.

Concern for both success and personal responsibility is consistent with a disaster victim's dignity not being sacrificed if a saintly individual sacrifices his leg to save the victim's life. It is also consistent, I argued earlier, with the saintly individual meeting his special responsibility to himself to live well (and possibly even meet his personal goal of living successfully) if he gives up his leg to save another person.[89] In that earlier discussion, I imagined that the saintly individual would voluntarily and supererogatorily sacrifice himself for someone who consents to this. The fact that the saintly person and his beneficiary each decides for himself whether to make or accept the sacrifice might mean that each would not neglect his responsibility for himself nor usurp someone else's responsibility for himself. This would satisfy the ethical independence condition Dworkin places on personal responsibility.

Nevertheless, Dworkin himself argues for *some* moral *duties* to aid that do not depend on a personal decision to aid or to accept aid.[90] For example, he thinks one would do *wrong* if one did not aid, at minimal cost to oneself, someone nearby who would otherwise be in a disastrous situation.[91] However, Dworkin does not say that anyone has a right to coerce someone to do the right and even dutiful act.[92] Even if there is a prohibition on coerced performance, knowledge of these duties could constrain an individual's independent decisions about what to do. Hence, in order to have dignity, individuals need not *always* decide what to do independently of considering what unchosen duties they have. This raises the possibility that one could satisfy the requirements of dignity to live well even if there were a *duty* to sacrifice one's leg to save someone else's life, especially if the performance of the duty could not be coerced. Hence, even ex ante reasoning that took dignity and not just success into account might still yield stronger duties to aid than Dworkin endorses.

But let us consider what Dworkin specifically says about why we should reject a spare parts lottery:

> What about the ex ante argument I made for a spare parts lottery? The lottery is a vehicle for selling yourself into a kind of slavery for what you anticipate will be your own good. If you join the plan, you give others authority, when the time comes, to make the most basic decisions about what to do with your life, decisions that the second principle requires that you make for yourself. Imagine your number has come up and others advance on you with needles and scalpels. You might think then that as you might have benefited from the scheme it is right that you now be killed in its name. But you might not: you might then think the fate too horrible or that the arrangement unjust after all or simply that your wish not to die trumps everything else. No matter: the decision is no longer yours. That is why we must not sell ourselves into slavery even for our own good. We might have longer lives but we live in indignity.[93] Volunteering for danger—volunteering for the army, for instance—is different. Volunteers have made their own decision that the best use of their lives includes accepting a heightened risk of danger. They may accept that in virtue of their

> decision someone else—an enemy soldier—has a right deliberately to try to kill them. But they do not accept that they have a duty to let him do so.[94]

Dworkin emphasizes that in a spare parts lottery others would have authority to make the "most basic decisions about what to do with your life, decisions that the second principle requires that you make for yourself."[95] Further, the agreement would give you a duty not to resist when "others advance on you" to take your organs.[96] It is important to see that this argument is intended to rule out the moral permissibility of an actual agreement ("[i]f you join the plan"), not merely treating people in accord with a plan to which they would have hypothetically agreed.[97]

(ii) I have several concerns about Dworkin's argument against ex ante agreement to a "spare parts" lottery. First, it is important to note that we can imagine forms of a spare parts lottery that filter out awareness and fear of imposition by others. In one, body parts are taken at birth (or at least once an individual is a person) and kept in reserve for those who need them later in life. Second, the most basic conclusion someone might seek to draw from an ex ante agreement argument is that one has a duty to make a sacrifice, independent of whether it should be coercively enforced. Dworkin's discussion focuses on others having the authority to enforce the agreement and one having a duty not to resist this enforcement,[98] but an argument against such authority and such a duty not to resist might not bear on whether there could be a personal duty to sacrifice.

Third, the claim that others having the authority to make the most basic decisions about what is to be done with your life conflicts with your ethical responsibility again raises the issue of the distinction between ethical paternalism and other forms of coercion.[99] If others have authority over your life not in order to make sure that *you* live your life well and successfully but in order to use you to help others, it is not clear that their act usurps your ethical responsibility. (This is especially so if you are not being coerced to join a spare parts lottery for your own good.) Similarly, the government does not usurp your ethical responsibility when it drafts you in a war or restricts use of your property to preserve art independent of thinking this is what makes your life go best.[100]

Fourth, Dworkin says that it violates one's dignity to exercise control at one time ("t1") in a way that may lead one to lose a right of control over basic decisions about one's life at a later time ("t2") when one is still competent to exercise such control.[101] In an earlier work of mine discussing ex ante agreements, I proposed such a "constant agent" view that ruled out now alienating important rights (such as to not be killed) so that one does not have control over whether to exercise or waive the right in the future.[102] I said:

> So, according to this proposal, we are taken to be *constant agents*, whose fates must be continuously determined by ourselves. The proposal is not saying that

> our chances of living must be reduced (1) for the sake of not becoming intentional killers of the innocent (the agent-focused argument), or (2) for the sake of not being mere means to the good of others, or even (3) for the sake of inviolability. It says rather that our chances of living must be reduced when only this is consistent with our being the sort of people (some of) whose constraining rights are under their own control at such time as losses are to be imposed upon them (or the nearest competent conscious period to it).[103]

This was one of the views that I said implied that "we may all lead harder lives, but our dignity is greater."[104] However, I also considered further implications of, and objections to, this view that are also relevant to Dworkin's similar view. First, I noted that it does not rule out at least an actual agreement in the second of the following cases that I discussed:

> In the first, the Disease Case, a deadly disease threatens a community. The only thing that an individual can do to significantly decrease his chance of getting the disease is to take a drug which, if it doesn't help him, will kill him *if* he is one of the *few* who are not susceptible to the disease. The death will occur some time after he learns that he is not susceptible.

Compare the Disease Case now with the Disease' Case, in which again, a deadly disease threatens a community and there is a drug that will kill those few who were not susceptible to the disease. In the Disease' Case, however, the drug itself never directly helps anyone who takes it. Rather, if you take the drug and die because you were not susceptible to the disease after all, your body parts can be used to make a serum to save others from the disease. If no one takes the drug, those who fall ill will simply die. In the Disease' Case, but not in the Disease Case, a person's death is a source of benefit to others. However, ex ante in both cases the victim takes the drug from self-interest. In the Disease Case, self-interest is served because the drug may reduce one's chances of getting the disease. In the Disease' Case, the only thing that makes it *be* in his interest to agree to take the drug is that this is the only way to ensure that others also take the drug. Then someone will die for the benefit of others when this person need not otherwise have died but his ex ante chances of survival were increased. The Disease' Case also overcomes some interpersonal, agent-focused objections insofar as the person himself, rather than anyone else, causes his death.[105]

In both cases, the person does the act that in fact kills him at a time when it could still be in his interest to do that act. The "constant agent" view implies that it is permissible for everyone to agree to take the drug in the Disease' Case. This may not be troubling to Dworkin, given his concern with someone's making his own personal decision about when to take a chance that he will die. More problematic for the "constant agent"-type view are the cases I discussed in which it seems to be *morally permissible* to make actual agreements ex ante that result in one's having a duty to make a large sacrifice when one would not volunteer it at the time and that could result in one's losing control to others over an important decision.[106] Here are two of these cases that I discussed:

(1) The Arm-for-Life Case: It seems permissible at t1 to make "an actual . . . agreement to give an arm to save five lives, when one might have been among the five in danger of dying."[107] This is so, even when the arm is given at time t2, when one knows it is not in one's interest to lose it since one is not then one of the five whose lives will be saved. In this case, a fraction of what one stood to lose (life) is paid for having gotten insurance against death. (I did *not* claim that because such an *actual* agreement could bind individuals, they would be bound in the same way based on a comparable *hypothetical* agreement.)

(2) The Two Diseases Case: There are two diseases in a community. One, the Arm Disease, causes one and only one arm to fall off and is very prevalent among a part of the population whose members we can identify beforehand. The second, the Death Disease, is very rare in a *different* part of the population that we can identify as susceptible to it. The only thing that cures the Arm Disease is a serum made from the finger of a person who was subject to the Death Disease but didn't get it, and the only cure for the Death Disease is a serum made from the arm of a person subject to the Arm Disease who did not get it.

I believe it would be in the interest, ex ante, of all involved to make an agreement to provide the resources necessary to make the serums needed at the time they are needed, and that even enforcement of this agreement ex post (i.e., once one knows who will and who will not be getting the diseases) would *not* be morally wrong. There is a high incidence of the Arm Disease; so there is a high probability that the people once susceptible to the Death Disease will lose a finger in exchange for having avoided the small risk of a big loss (death) to themselves. There is a low incidence of the Death Disease; so there is a low probability that a person once susceptible to the Arm Disease will lose an arm. That is, there is a low probability of his making a larger sacrifice for others (than those susceptible to death make) in order to lower a high probability of his suffering the loss of an arm.

Yet this is also a case (like the spare parts lottery) in which an Arm person would have to pay with the *very item* he had attempted to increase his probability of keeping (his arm), at a time when it is known to be no longer in his interest to do so (for he no longer faces the threat of the Arm Disease). He will have received only the benefit of increased probability of protection from the Arm Disease. However, a significant difference between this case and cases considered before (like the spare parts lottery) is that the arm would be sacrificed to prevent an even greater loss (death) to another person. What the person who is sacrificed loses is significantly less than what the person who is saved would lose if he were not saved. Note that the agreement is permissible even though the Arm Disease person stood no risk of getting the Death Disease.[108] It may be of moral significance in legitimating this agreement that there is (potential) reciprocal sacrifice between the Arm Disease community and the Death Disease community, even if not between an individual who must give an arm and an individual who must give a finger.

Suppose the Arm-for-Life and Two Diseases Cases are indeed examples of morally permissible *actual* agreements that generate duties and even entitle others to enforce the agreement against those resisting. Then Dworkin's explanation of why an actual ex ante agreement to kill one person in order to maximize lives saved would not be permissible does not succeed because it would also rule out these permissible agreements. Like Dworkin, I believe that even an actual agreement could not create a duty to give up one's life or create authority in others to enforce a sacrifice in the standard "spare parts" lottery. I just think Dworkin must say more in order to explain why this is so.[109]

Suppose also that only actual agreements engender duties in my Arm-for-Life Case and the Two Diseases Case. Then it would be morally wrong to act as if people had duties that could be enforced simply on grounds of imagining a comparable hypothetical agreement. This suggests that Dworkin's view that hypothetical agreements might be used to derive moral duties from ethical responsibility may also be problematic.[110]

## Notes

1. The chapter is based on my article "What Ethical Responsibility Cannot Justify," which appeared in *Boston University Law Review* 90 (2010): 691–714 (henceforth BULR).
2. I will distinguish ethics from morality in discussing Dworkin's views in both Chapters 2 and 3 in this book. However, throughout the rest of this book ethics and morality will be used interchangeably, as they typically are, unless specifically noted otherwise.
3. See Ronald Dworkin, *Justice for Hedgehogs* (Cambridge, MA: Harvard University Press, 2011). My comments are for the most part based on the manuscript as of April 17, 2009, on file with the BULR. At certain points in this chapter, I also note some instances where Dworkin's view seems to have changed from the manuscript to the published version of his book. Presumably one should think of oneself as objectively and intrinsically important only if one really is. I do not think Dworkin proves we have this importance. Rather, he indicates that we believe we have this importance by showing, for example, that we blame ourselves if we waste our lives and we think it is important to find correct values according to which to live. Ibid. (manuscript at 128–30).
4. See ibid.
5. See ibid.

6. See ibid. (manuscript at 134) ("Living well means not just designing a life, as if any design would do, but designing it in response to what one takes to be objective ethical value.").
7. Presumably, one should view things as having objective ethical value only if they have it. Is it Dworkin's view that if there were no objective ethical values and one knew this, one could not have dignity? It seems so.
8. Dworkin, supra note 3 (manuscript at 124–27). Dworkin thinks the problem of moral luck affects how good one's life is, not whether one has lived well. See ibid. (manuscript at 126) ("Someone may have a bad life in spite of living well because the goodness of his life does not depend entirely on his own decisions and efforts: it depends critically on his circumstances and luck as well.") He says that the person who faultlessly kills a child has had a less good life, but has not lived less well. Ibid. (manuscript at 127). The person may regret what happened in his life but correctly not blame himself for it. Id. Cases such as this one may, however, raise problems for Dworkin's view that living well is more important than having a successful life, for what if the person's doing something *morally wrong* would have prevented him from accidentally killing the child? For example, suppose his stopping at a bar and thus driving intoxicated would have caused him to arrive too late to get in an accident. If faultlessly harming someone can affect how good one's life is, there may be many cases in which one should prefer to have lived less well and had a better life.
9. It is also connected with his views about metaphysics. For example, Dworkin claims that moral truth is not about discovering what views *correspond* to independent moral entities (which he refers to as "morons"). Apparently, he thinks that if there were conflicts between such moral virtues as kindness and honesty that could not be eliminated by proper interpretation of each virtue, this could only be because there were such morons corresponding to each virtue. Part of his response to Richard Fallon in the BULR was pointing out that we may not be successful in being both kind and honest, but that if we were to say conflict is inevitable, "that seems to me dangerously close to believing in morons." See BULR, Ronald Dworkin, Response to Panel II 1064–66. I think Dworkin is wrong to believe that ineliminable normative conflicts have this metaphysical implication. See Chapter 3 in this volume.
10. See Dworkin, supra note 3 (manuscript at 165) (explaining the "Kant principle": the perspective of "a person who recognizes the objective importance of his life going well and therefore the equal objective importance of any life going well").
11. Ibid., 15.
12. Dworkin says that it is not out of bounds to say that one's dignity is threatened if one could not live with oneself because one did something immoral. Ibid., 122. But in such a situation, one's dignity does not help one derive the content of morality; the content of dignity is just conceived as requiring that one be moral. It thus involves incorporation of morality into dignity, not the integration of the two that Dworkin says he seeks. See ibid., 128; supra note 10.
13. Dworkin, *Justice for Hedgehogs*, 328.
14. Ibid., 165.
15. Ibid.

16. Ibid., 176.
17. Dworkin, supra note 3 (manuscript at 178) ("I show indifference to the importance of human life when I refuse aid that I could provide with no dent to the success of my own life, but not when I refuse aid that would seriously threaten my own success as I have identified it"). One might, of course, argue that being willing to give up a penny to save someone's life is sufficient to show that one is not indifferent to his life. This could be true even if one would give no more to save his life though giving more would not dent one's success. I shall assume that Dworkin is concerned with more than minimally ruling out indifference. Still, what if one has identified one's success as the accumulation of the maximal amount of money? Then even giving a penny might seriously dent one's success. Dworkin came to think that this person had made a mistake in what he identified as success because it was inconsistent with his own importance. On this see also note 21.
18. Ibid., 177.
19. Ibid., 174–75 (explaining that interfering with others' lives to attempt to make them successful would not show respect for their dignity).
20. Ibid., 175–76.
21. Both Anthony Appiah and I raised such an objection. Appiah said in his "Dignity and Global Duty," Boston University Law Review 90 (2010): 661, 669: "[Dworkin's] formulation continues to imply that the perspective of ethics permits me to utterly ignore the needs of others in *conceiving* of my success; that is, it ignores the possibility . . . that I ought to take account of the deep need of others in defining what it is for my life to go well" (though perhaps he should have said "what it is for my life to be a success" since Dworkin allows morality to affect how well one's life goes). Dworkin tries to deal with both Appiah's and my concern in *Justice for Hedgehogs* as published. See note 6, p. 468, and also p. 277 of that book where he says: "Anyone who embraces projects that require him to ignore the suffering of others altogether . . . lacks self-respect: his sense of an appropriate life is inconsistent with the right regard for the objective importance of the lives of others and therefore of his own." This locates the primary fault of selecting such projects in its being inconsistent with self-respect and derivatively with morality.
22. See ibid., 165, 174–75; ibid., 176 ("I do not show contempt for human life even when I refuse to make more admirable sacrifices. . . . I would not imply that I regarded the lives of others as intrinsically less important than my own if I refused to [make such sacrifices]").
23. Ibid., 177. Dworkin says this is true at least if there is a just distribution of resources. Although he holds that there is not currently such a distribution, he does not say whether or how our duties are different when the distribution is unjust.
24. Ibid., 176.
25. Suppose your responsibility is to someone else, not to yourself. The fact that the other person would suffer a significant loss and has not waived his right against you to fulfill the responsibility may constrain you from doing a supererogatory act for a third party. But if the person to whom you have the responsibility is willing to suffer a large loss, as you are in doing the supererogatory act, neither of you may be failing to

perform an ethical duty to yourself that should stand in the way of the supererogatory act. It might be suggested that when someone does what seems like a supererogatory act, he has simply changed the projects in his life to saintly ones and seeks success in those new projects. But this needn't be true. For example, suppose someone lives near a forest fire and feels compelled to sacrifice his belongings and risk his life to help save others. This same person may make a point subsequently of moving to some area where nearby forest fires won't occur so he won't face the need to make such sacrifices again. This shows that his projects have not changed, unlike someone who turns to live the saintly life.

26. See, e.g., F. M. Kamm, *Morality, Mortality,* vol. 2 (New York: Oxford University Press, 1996), 311–48 (hereinafter Kamm, *Morality*); F. M. Kamm, "Supererogation and Obligation," *Journal of Philosophy* 82 (1985): 118 (hereinafter Kamm, "Supererogation"). These earlier works dealt with *moral* duties in conflict with supererogation; here we are talking about what Dworkin calls an *ethical* duty and its relation to supererogation. Dworkin, supra note 3 (manuscript at 176–77).
27. Notice I have not here argued that there is no responsibility to oneself because I, to whom a duty would be owed, could always release myself from it.
28. Dworkin, supra note 3 (manuscript at 178).
29. Ibid. Anthony Appiah dismisses the idea that Dworkin thinks that physical distance in itself matters morally (and also the idea that it could matter). See Appiah, supra note 21, 669 (explaining that, "like Dworkin I think that . . . almost all of us are directly confronted with people who need help to have a chance at a life of dignity," and that "proximity of the relevant kind is epistemic, not geographical" [footnote omitted]). I think Appiah is wrong about Dworkin's view and also about whether physical distance could matter morally.
30. See Dworkin, supra note 3 (manuscript at 179).
31. See ibid., 178 ("[The confrontation scale] is more difficult to state and justify, but it is real and distinct, and we cannot make sense of much common moral understanding unless we find place for it").
32. Ibid., 179.
33. See, e.g., F. M. Kamm, "The New Problem of Distance in Morality," in *Intricate Ethics*, New York: Oxford University Press, 2007), 345–97.
34. Ibid., 347–49.
35. See ibid., 368–97.
36. Dworkin, supra note 3 (manuscript at 178).
37. Dworkin, supra note 3 (manuscript at 179).
38. For arguments that reach this conclusion, see Kamm, "Supererogation," supra note 26. An example I gave in that article involved having a duty to one's business associate that one is about to fulfill when one comes across someone drowning in shark-infested waters. The supererogatory act of diving into such dangerous waters to save someone can permissibly take precedence over fulfilling one's duty even if the associate would not have a duty to waive his right to one's performance. See also Kamm, *Morality,* supra note 26, at 304–30.
39. Dworkin, supra note 3 (manuscript at 179).

40. Ibid., 184.
41. Ibid., 185.
42. Ibid.
43. Ibid., 184.
44. See ibid., 188. The fact that Dworkin thinks that shooting someone to save others is consistent with valuing and respecting the objective value of life suggests that he takes a view about life resembling a view held by some about rights. That is, it has been argued that it is (at least) consistent with valuing rights that one deliberately transgress some rights in order to prevent the transgression of additional comparable rights, as in a case where one shoots a bystander to prevent someone else from shooting a greater number of other bystanders. (See Kamm, *Intricate Ethics*, supra note 33, at 288.) Some have even argued that if such minimizing of transgressions is impermissible, the reason cannot be concern for rights but must be concern for a duty that an agent has that *he* not transgress someone's right. Ibid., 268 (citing Jeremy Waldron [ed.], *Introduction to Theories of Rights* [Oxford: Oxford University Press, 1984]). Similarly, Dworkin argues that concern for the value of life cannot be the reason we should not take life to save others' lives; rather, an ethical duty that grounds a moral duty not to take another's life must be appealed to. See Dworkin, supra note 3 (manuscript at 187–90).
45. Dworkin, *Justice for Hedgehogs*, 274.
46. This argument is like one I used to argue that a system that allows agent-relative prerogatives to act from a personal rather than an impartial perspective should also involve rights against interference. This is because the prerogative's scope should be over what one is first decided to have a right to control, not (for example) over someone else's life. See my *Morality* , and "Nonconsequentialism," in Hugh Lafolette [ed.] *The Blackwell Guide to Moral Theory* (Oxford: Blackwell Publishers, 2004).
47. For a view like this see Kamm, *Morality*, 237–56.
48. By contrast, I think that these are two different distinctions. For example, *acting* to terminate life-saving aid that we are providing is a case of not aiding, though it does not involve an omission. Interestingly, Dworkin once denied that there was a moral distinction per se between killing and letting die, holding motive and aim constant. See Dworkin et al "Assisted Suicide: The Philosophers' Brief, " *New York Review of Books*, 44 (1997): 41–47.
49. Dworkin often uses the example of swimmers competing in different lanes as an analogy to relations between people. This implies that one is aiming to come out ahead of others as opposed to cooperating with them to the benefit of all. But it also implies that one cannot succeed unless others fail. In this case, the harm of failure to some would be a necessary side effect of someone else's success. It is somewhat surprising that he would use such a case to exemplify trying to succeed in life. By contrast, suppose an individual in one lane unintentionally affects the water level of someone swimming in another lane. It could be foreseen that this would occur and hinder another swimmer on occasion, but it wouldn't be necessary to succeed in the sport and so it would be a better example of unintended foreseen harm in general.
50. Dworkin, supra note 3 (manuscript at 185).

51. As he says on p. 289 of the published version of *Justice for Hedgehogs.*
52. Ibid., 135.
53. In the published version of *Justice for Hedgehogs* (p. 288) Dworkin added the following lines to what he had written in the manuscript version (on which I had originally made my comments): "It is important not to confuse the right of control we must have to lead our own lives with the right to ethical independence. . . . The latter is compromised when others attempt to make ethical decisions for us, the former when they interfere with our control over our bodies or property for any reason." Presumably this means that I can fail to have control over my body when I need it for my success in life because someone is controlling it for his purposes even if he does not do this for the sake of making me live according to values that he thinks will make a success of my life.
54. See his response in BULR, 1074.
55. Ibid., 188–92.
56. See ibid., 189.
57. Ibid.
58. Dworkin, *Justice for Hedgehogs* (published version), 295.
59. Ibid., 190. Such nondeliberate harm may still be the effect of a deliberate act undertaken for other reasons. Ibid. (using as an example rerouting a trolley to save five people when rerouting causes another to get killed).
60. Ibid.
61. Ibid.
62. Dworkin thinks his view explains and not merely coincides with the DDE: "Other philosophers say that it is always wrong to aim at someone's death. . . . But that explanation simply restates the problem. If someone's motives are good—to save as many people as possible—why should it matter whether he actually aims at the death of a smaller number or simply knowingly produces their death? Once again we find a more plausible answer. . . . The second principle, which requires that I take responsibility for decisions that define my living well, distinguishes between . . . bad luck . . . and cases of usurpation that do contradict it." Ibid. (manuscript at 189).
63. Ibid., 135.
64. Ibid.
65. See ibid.
66. Dworkin proposes that the impermissibility of causing harm as a side effect should depend on whether the cost to an agent of not causing the harm would be less than the cost to the victim of the side effect harm. If it is, the harm is impermissible. (This may be another way of saying that when side effect harm is less than the good that results for an agent from not refraining from action, the agent may proceed.) See Dworkin, *Justice for Hedgehogs*, 291. This ignores cases in which it seems right for an agent to suffer a greater loss to avoid causing a smaller foreseen side effect harm to someone else, as when one should suffer a broken arm and leg rather than cause someone else a broken leg.
67. See her "The Problem of Abortion and the Doctrine of Double Effect," reprinted in her *Virtues and Vices* (Oxford: Blackwell; Berkeley and Los Angeles: University of California Press, 1978).

68. Ibid., 188–92. In his comments in the BULR he denies it would be wrong to set the bomb. See ibid.,1074
69. Ibid., 191.
70. Ibid.
71. Ibid. He also thinks that whether one decides turning the trolley in the Loop Case is permissible depends on whether one sees it as involving a mere side effect death. He says, "[People's] reactions depend, I suspect, on whether they conceive of the proposed switch as a switch away from five people or a switch toward a buffer person."
72. See, e.g., Kamm, *Intricate Ethics*, supra note 33, at 91–122.
73. Ibid.
74. For more detailed discussion of the because of/intending to (or in order to) distinction and the Party Case, see generally ibid.
75. See ibid., 272–75.
76. Removing the person from the track if this becomes possible after turning the trolley is one reason I do not accept Michael Otsuka's criticism of my analysis of the Loop Case in his "Double Effect, Triple Effect, and the Trolley Problem: Squaring the Circle in Looping Cases," *Utilitas* 20(1) 92–110, 2008. He imagines that there are several tracks to which one could send the trolley and the one person starts off on one of the tracks and then moves to each of the others in turn. If one would only turn the trolley because the person would be hit, one would keep on changing the track to which one would turn the trolley so that it is the one on which the person would be hit. He thinks that this indicates that one intends to hit the person. But I think it is consistent with turning only when looping would not occur and because the one person would stop the looping. That one would help the person off the track if that became possible after turning the trolley indicates that one does not intend to hit him. To reinforce this last point, consider the following (complicated) Scarce Drugs Rescue Case. With a scarce drug for fatal disease X, I can save either persons A and B (who each need a half dose) or one other person C (who needs it all). It makes moral sense to save two instead of one, I think. However, it turns out that only in A and B will the drug have the side effect of causing fatal disease Y. Given that A and B will die soon anyway, I should give the drug to C instead. However, I also find out that if I give the scarce drug to A and B, leaving C to die, another scarce drug I would otherwise have been obligated to give C (to cure disease Z) had he lived will be available with which to save A and B from disease Y. Given all this, I think, it would be permissible to give the first scarce drug to A and B *because* C's death will make the second drug available for A and B. Nevertheless, giving the first drug to A and B only because C will die in this case is consistent with fulfilling an obligation to save C if we subsequently discovered that he could be cured of disease X by a third drug that does not work in A and B. We should save him, even though his being saved means that A and B will die for want of the second drug that will have to be given to C for disease Z when it could otherwise have cured disease Y in A and B. By contrast, it is hard to argue that saving C from disease X by the third drug is consistent with intending C's death so the second drug we would have to give to him is available to save A and B. Similarly, (as already noted) we may turn the trolley away from the five in the Loop Case only because we believe the

one person's death will block the further bad effect of its looping back to the five and yet seek to remove the one person from the track if this subsequently becomes possible, though the five will then die.

77. See Dworkin, supra note 3 (manuscript at 190). As we have seen, Dworkin also believes that causing the hit because we see it as good in relation to saving five people involves usurping a person's ethical responsibility to decide what would make his life go best. Ibid. ("The large man, in an act of near incredible heroism, might throw himself on the track [to prevent the trolley from hitting others]. He might think, as Sydney Carton did in making the same sacrifice, that that would be a far better thing than anything else he could do with his life. But no one else is permitted to make that choice for him.") Earlier, I argued against the view that even intentionally harming someone for the good of others must involve such ethical paternalism.
78. In his response to this part of my presentation at the Boston University School of Law Symposium, Dworkin said that in using his general distinction between harms that do and do not require us to override a person's own conception of what is a good use of his life, he had not aimed to solve the problem of whether it is permissible to redirect in the Loop Case. See Ronald Dworkin, BULR, p. 1074. Rather, his aim was to show that it was a problematic case just because it seemed to involve doing what is ordinarily ruled out, namely, overriding a person's own conception of his good. See id. One of my points, however, is that the Loop Case may be problematic because it is *mistakenly* taken to involve intending something bad for someone. This is because people may think, as Dworkin does, that intending the hit is entailed by acting (or omitting) on the ground that the hit would be useful. Ibid. I have tried to show that there need be no such entailment. I have also argued that redirecting the trolley because hitting the one is good for the five does not involve overriding a person's own conception of how to live successfully and well in a way that conflicts with Dworkin's notion of ethical responsibility.
79. I discuss the Trolley Problem and what may account for rights violations in many versions of it in this volume in Chapter 9. I also discuss it in *Morality, Intricate Ethics*, and *The Trolley Problem Mysteries* (New York: Oxford University Press, 2016).
80. Dworkin, supra note 3 (manuscript at 191).
81. Ibid., 169.
82. Ibid., 172.
83. See ibid. (pointing out that the veil of ignorance may serve participants' "interests because it allows them to concentrate on the crucial question of what treating everyone's life as having the same objective importance requires").
84. See supra Parts II–III.
85. Dworkin, supra note 1 (manuscript at 188).
86. Ibid., 189.
87. See T. M. Scanlon, "Contractualism and Utilitarianism," in *Utilitarianism and Beyond*, ed. Amartya Sen and Bernard Williams (Cambridge: Cambridge University Press, 1982), 127; see also F. M. Kamm, "Should You Save This Child? Gibbard on Intuitions, Contractualism, and Strains of Commitment," in *Reconciling Our Aims: In Search of the Basis of Ethics*, ed. Allan Gibbard (New York: Oxford

University Press, 2008), 120–46 (discussing interpretations and arguments for and against ex ante reasoning). Scanlon's view is that those behind a veil of ignorance should agree on a policy if one could justify that policy to each representative person beyond the veil. In this way, he thinks, the separateness of persons is respected. For more on this issue see Chapter 5 in this volume.

88. See Dworkin, supra note 3 (manuscript at 128).
89. See supra Part II.
90. See Dworkin, supra note 3 (manuscript at 176).
91. Ibid., 177.
92. See ibid., 167–68, 209. Someone might not perform his duty because he got the wrong answer when he independently decided on whether he had the duty. Alternatively, someone might not perform his duty because he independently decided not to act on his knowledge of his duty.
93. I argued against a spare parts lottery that we might live longer but our moral status would be lower (because we were more violable). See, for example, Kamm, *Morality*. Dworkin tries to explain why our being highly inviolable is important on the ground that it serves our responsibility for our own lives, which is part of our dignity.
94. Ibid., 191.
95. Ibid.
96. See ibid.
97. See ibid.
98. See ibid.
99. Ibid., 135.
100. See supra Part II.
101. Dworkin, supra note 3 (manuscript at 191).
102. See Kamm, *Morality*, supra note 26, at 297–98.
103. Ibid., 298. It is interesting to note that when I suggested the "constant agent" explanation, it was Dworkin who argued against it (at a colloquium) by pointing to many occasions when we could bind ourselves to suffer losses at a time when it was no longer in our interest to do so. An example was having to keep on paying for insurance even though we no longer needed it, as part of an agreement from which we had benefited by assuring ourselves coverage had we needed it.
104. Ibid., 294.
105. Ibid., 293–94.
106. Ibid., 300–302.
107. Ibid., 300.
108. Ibid., 301–2.
109. For a more complete discussion of my view about the right explanation, see ibid. at 290–310 (analyzing the permissibility of various agreements).
110. Johann Frick has proposed what he calls "the Decomposition Test which implies that if an ex ante rule requires us to act, at a later stage, in a manner that cannot be justified to every person at that time, then the ex ante rule as a whole cannot be justified to each person. Its justifiability to each person unravels by backward induction." He refers to the ex ante view supplemented by the Decomposition Test

as "stage-wise ex ante contractualism." See his "Contractualism and Social Risk," *Philosophy & Public Affairs* 43, no. 3 (2015): 205–6. What would the Decomposition Test imply about the Arm-for-Life and Two Diseases Cases if there had not been an actual agreement among the people involved and the loss had to be imposed by an agent on a victim? In the Arm-for-Life Case at the time the act must be done to remove the arm, it seems that the loss could not be justified to the victim since he is no longer under a threat of death. In the Two Diseases Case at the time the act must be done to remove the finger, the victim knows he is not one of those who needs an agreement with those susceptible to the Arm Disease, and at the time the act must be done to remove the arm, the victim knows that he is not one of those who needs an agreement with those susceptible to the Death Disease. So acting on the basis of a hypothetical agreement would be ruled out by the Decomposition Test. But Frick himself holds that in some cases people may permissibly alienate their rights by an actual ex ante agreement. Then even if they do not waive their rights at the time the loss would be imposed on them, they could have a duty not to resist the imposition of the loss.

# 3

# What "Must" Be Done to Answer Practical Questions?

In his unpublished Balzan Lecture, given when he received the Balzan Prize for Jurisprudence in 2012, Ronald Dworkin described what he said was his intellectual journey.[1] This description to a large extent could be read as an overview of his book *Justice for Hedgehogs,* parts of which we considered in Chapter 2.[2] Both that book and the Balzan Lecture illustrate Dworkin's view that one must have a theory (ideally, a perfect, wide-ranging theory) to answer many practical questions about rights. It would be fair to say, I think, that Dworkin was "mad about theory." Most of this chapter is concerned with whether it is true that theory is crucial in this way. This will help situate in a broader background the specific positions we examined in Chapter 2.

I will first summarize what I see as the most significant elements of Dworkin's lecture, using *Justice for Hedgehogs* to fill in some important parts of his view with which the lecture does not deal. I will comment briefly on what he says while summarizing but provide more detailed commentary on selected issues in a later section.

1. In the lecture, Dworkin describes his intellectual journey as beginning with concern about practical moral, political, and legal issues, such as whether capital punishment should be permitted under U.S. law or if it violates rights. He felt that in order to answer such practical questions he "must" answer more abstract questions. This is what he calls the "ascent." (It is like the ascent his ideal judge, whom he calls Hercules, would make before descending from the heights to decide a case.[3] Ordinary judges might have to make at least a partial ascent to decide a case, Dworkin claims.)

Dworkin says that he starts his ascent by investigating the concept of law in order to ultimately answer practical issues, arguing that law is an interpretive concept and we must decide how best to interpret it consistent with law being something of value. Given this, he thought he "must" provide a reason to believe there is a truth about what interpretation would be best and would make the law be most valuable. To do this he thinks he must first show that value judgment statements are truth-apt but not in the way empirical statements are by corresponding to things in the world. (Note that even if "law" is not an interpretive concept but what Dworkin calls a criterial concept, like "triangle," the mere idea

*Rights and Their Limits: In Theory, Cases, and Pandemics.* F. M. Kamm, Oxford University Press.
© Oxford University Press 2022. DOI: 10.1093/oso/9780197567739.003.0003

that law is something of value would be undermined if there were no true value judgments.) He thinks that he must also provide a general theory of interpretation that covers not only law but also literature and much else.

After showing that there can be value truths, he thinks he must next show what those particular truths are. These include his views examined in Chapter 2 about how an individual should live his life and how he is to relate to other people. In addition, he thinks we need to know what the community owes its members, and what liberty, equality, and democracy are. Not only does Dworkin think he must deal with all these issues, but also he thinks they must be dealt with in an interpretative manner so that the truths and concepts all cohere and do not conflict. He likens this to solving simultaneous equations. Though in his Balzan Lecture he does not specifically make the point, in *Justice for Hedgehogs* he argues that it is important to disprove the common view that fundamental values can conflict (as defended by Isaiah Berlin, Thomas Nagel, and Bernard Williams). His view (unlike the conflict view) implies that things with which some values do conflict do not themselves have value and there should not be lingering regret when they are superseded.

It may seem odd that having started with a question like whether the law should permit capital punishment, he thinks he "must" investigate all these other issues, including how best to live one's life, in order to answer it. In any case, as we have seen in Chapter 2, Dworkin's answer to the ethical question of how best to live one's life is what he calls the Principle of Dignity: The first part says that how one's life goes is intrinsically objectively important; the second part says that one has an inalienable responsibility for making a success of one's life and for living well.[4] One can live well, in part, by deciding for oneself (i.e., authentically, with ethical independence) what success is and acting on one's view even if this doesn't eventually lead to a successful life because of bad luck or poor judgment. Given that value judgments can be wrong because they are truth-apt, one's judgments about how one should live can be wrong. He admits that one might also have a good life but not have lived well because, for example, one achieved success immorally. The implication is that living well is more important than success. (As I noted in Chapter 2, I wonder whether this is always true. Suppose you kill someone having reasonably but incorrectly thought he was an aggressor. Mightn't you prefer to have unreasonably thought him innocent and so not have killed an innocent person? If so, in being unreasonable you would then not have lived well but you could, I think, have had a better life.)

It is because he believes that important concepts he is investigating must cohere and to make them cohere they must be investigated simultaneously that he fashions morality (duties to others) and ethics (duties to oneself) in each other's light, as was discussed in Chapter 2. (This must be done without being untrue to the plausibility of each area considered on its own.) Then our duties to others to recognize the intrinsic importance of their lives and their special responsibility for decisions about their lives will not conflict with our importance and responsibilities to ourselves (and vice versa).

Next, Dworkin says that the fact that persons have a special responsibility for their own lives implies that he must deal with the question of whether persons have free will in a sense that makes it possible for them to be responsible for the choices they make. (Notice the shift here between two senses of responsibility. In the first sense, one is assigned responsibility for a task [e.g., to make a success of one's life]. In the second sense, the choices one makes in carrying out the task are attributable to oneself. We might ask whether the latter sense of responsibility, if it implicates the issue of free will, is really a presupposition of one's being assigned a task.)

He uses the same two components of the Principle of Dignity to provide an interpretation of economic equality: Personal responsibility for one's life should limit social compensation for personal choices, but distributive justice among persons whose lives matter objectively involves compensating for the effects of bad luck. (In arguing that one must bear the costs of one's choices, Dworkin seems to employ a third sense of responsibility, one that Thomas Scanlon calls "substantive responsibility."[5])

No doubt for reasons of time, the Balzan Lecture I have just summarized does not discuss but only mentions some other concepts that are dealt with in *Justice for Hedgehogs*. There he claims that the freedom that has value is liberty to live one's life according to one's own conception of success and that communities that try to legislate in the light of the Principle of Dignity, even if they do not get the right answers to particular questions, at least have the right attitude. Indeed, Dworkin thinks that the fundamental right citizens have against their government is that it act with that attitude. If government tries to enforce taking personal responsibility for one's life this may be a mistake, but he thinks it does not involve the contempt involved in denying someone's personal responsibility for his life (p. 335).[6]

(But could it really be the government's attitude that is crucial? Suppose a particular governmental policy is in fact motivated by contempt for persons but it is a policy that could reasonably also be pursued by a government that had the appropriate attitude. Should we not consider the objective features of the policy rather than the framer's motivations to decide if it is what Dworkin calls "a good faith effort"? This would be consistent with Dworkin's views in his other work.)

In *Justice for Hedgehogs* Dworkin also tries to outline the degree and type of political participation that is democratic and coheres with the two components of the Principle of Dignity. In concluding his book, Dworkin comes back to deal with the law using the Principle of Dignity as a guide to how courts should decide particular cases, though he never does explicitly discuss the issue of capital punishment with which he says he began his intellectual journey.

In his discussion of all the many concepts I have mentioned, except possibly interpersonal morality, it seems that the Principle of Dignity and its components remain constant. This is so even though it appears to be an implication of Dworkin's view that personal ethics based on the Principle of Dignity should be part of a simultaneous equation involving all the other concepts that are to be interpreted. My impression is that the Principle of Dignity is foundational, the basis for interpreting most other concepts, rather than something that is equally subject to change on the basis of consideration of other concepts (with personal morality as a possible exception).

2. In my commentary on Dworkin's Balzan Lecture I will be concerned with three issues: (A) Is it true that we cannot separate practical issues from theoretical issues? (B) Is it true that all values must cohere rather than conflict? (C) Is it true that the responsibility to make a success of one's life grounds important personal rights (such as the right to one's body) (a topic considered in more detail in Chapter 2)?

A. Dworkin says in his lecture that one "can't pick apart various philosophical issues and call some practical and some of only theoretical importance. Politics and philosophy are much too closely integrated for that." As someone who often deals philosophically with practical issues, I wish to consider this claim of Dworkin's.

(i) When Dworkin says he "must" deal with various theoretical issues in order to deal with practical issues, is he just saying that this was something he personally felt he needed to do? Or rather that in order to know the answer to a certain practical issue anyone "must" deal with theoretical issues? If it is the latter, is that true? One approach (à la Dworkin) to this issue is to consider whether our best interpretation of "know" is that one cannot know the answer to a practical issue unless one knows the truth about all the assumptions on which the truth of the practical answer depends. This hardly seems so. For example, in the empirical realm if I say that I know that there is a chair in front of me, must I know what the nature of physical matter is such that there can be chairs, what the laws of optics are that support my using visual impressions to ground my claim, and what the philosophically correct understanding of knowledge is? This hardly seems to be a good interpretation of what it is to know the truth about the chair being in front of me. Something analogous may be true about knowing the truth about practical moral issues.[7]

(ii) In discussing the nature of truths about moral and value judgments in *Justice for Hedgehogs*, Dworkin concludes that the only defense of a particular value judgment is a normative argument for it. He reaches this conclusion after considering the theoretical issue of what finding truth involves in various areas of inquiry. However, if he is right about this, then someone who considers a practical issue such as the moral status of abortion only needs arguments for and against abortion, not arguments showing there is moral truth or that normative argumentation is the way to get at it. So it is not true that they "must" consider those theoretical issues. Someone of course may dispute a conclusion for or against abortion on the ground that any opinion is only a matter of feeling and there is no right or wrong answer. It might be nice to answer them with an argument for the possibility of moral truth and show that argumentation is the route to such truth. But that would be to engage in another discussion that someone who is considering the problem of abortion can legitimately decide to avoid. Nor need the person interested in abortion feel inadequate in leaving the issue of truth in the moral realm to some other philosopher and refer people to those other discussions. It is also possible that one's opponent on abortion agrees that moral claims can be straightforwardly true and so one need not convince them of this. So with respect to at least some theoretical issues there is no "must" about discussing them in order to discuss practical moral issues.

(iii) Nor need someone who is trying to find an answer to an issue in practical ethics aim to prove or even know about the second component of the Principle of Dignity. That component says that one has a responsibility to try to make a success of one's life and to live well. Someone who is trying to decide whether and why abortion is morally right or morally wrong is engaging in serious reflection and so is already satisfying a component of Dworkin's conception of living well. Knowing that she must do this (according to the Principle of Dignity) is not going to help her find the specific arguments that will yield a conclusion about the abortion issue. All the work to get that conclusion remains to be done. The second component of dignity may be helpful to a court or a government in deciding whether it or the pregnant woman should make the decision about her abortion, but whoever must decide still has to engage in argument to get to a conclusion and knowing that they have the responsibility to decide will not help them find the argument that gets them to a decision.

(iv) Is ascent and descent of the sort Dworkin describes for Hercules necessary or wise for an ordinary judge? To recall, Dworkin says: "Before Hercules sits on his first case, he could build a gigantic 'overarching' theory good for all seasons. He could decide all outstanding issues of metaphysics, epistemology, and ethics, and also of morality, including political morality. He could decide what there is in the universe, and why he is justified in thinking that is what there is; what justice and fairness require, what freedom of speech, best understood, means; and whether and why it is a freedom particularly worth protecting . . . [and]weave all that and everything else into a marvelously architectonic system. When a new case arises, he would be very well prepared. . . . From outside—beginning, perhaps, in the intergalactic stretches of his wonderful intellectual creation—he could work steadily in towards the problem at hand: finding the best available justification for law in general, for American legal and constitutional practice as a species of law, for constitutional interpretation, for tort, and then, finally for the poor woman who took too many pills."[8]

However, suppose we knew a priori that some of what Hercules knew was not relevant to making a principled decision about the practical issue. Then we could know a priori that an ordinary judge would not have to ascend to know those things in order to reach a principled decision about someone's rights in a particular case so that it cohered with other cases. It seems I can know a priori that whether there is one more or less meson in the universe is irrelevant to which legal or moral principles are correct. (This is consistent with a legal decision being based on the principle "whoever has the most arcane knowledge should win a case" and knowledge of the number of mesons is the most arcane. The truth about the numbers of mesons does not help justify this principle.) If it could be shown a priori that one can know that a normative theory is correct without first deciding which metaethical theory is correct, then one could know that metaethics will be irrelevant to legal decision-making. If "ought" judgments cannot be derived from "is" statements, then no theory about actual behavior can be relevant to a deduction of principles of political morality. (This is consistent with the correct moral principle implying that consequences are morally significant and so one will need to know empirical facts about consequences to determine what it is right to do. But this does not place the empirical knowledge in a descent to knowledge of a moral or legal principle.) If it is knowable a priori in these ways what is relevant or irrelevant to a decision, then an ordinary judge would not have to ascend to know some of the things Hercules would know in order for the ordinary judge to deduce principles with which to decide a case. Her ascent to knowledge would only mirror Hercules's most direct descent down (i.e., the descent that avoids all irrelevant issues).

If our political morality is liberal, ascent to knowledge of some other things that Hercules could know would also be irrelevant for an ordinary judge. For example, suppose Hercules determined that God and souls exist, Christianity is the one true religion, and love is the most important component in a good life, and he could deduce legal decisions from this knowledge. If ascent to knowledge of our legal system revealed it was liberal, then our judges would be committed to treating some of these truths that Hercules knows as if they were unknown since in a liberal society government may not favor any religion or view of the good life. Hence, there would be no point in these judges ascending to knowledge of which religion or view of the good life is true in order to decide about rights.

What might be called "imperfect competence" in ascending might also rule out a judge's relying on ascent in delivering a judgment. Dworkin says: "Judges will often have to make theoretical judgments that bring conviction or at least greater conviction than their rivals, even when this falls short of certainty." Having greater conviction in theoretical position A than in theoretical position B is compatible with having very little conviction in either due to incompetence in dealing with the issue. Suppose that a judge has greater conviction in A than in B but still low conviction in A and the least good outcome (recognizable independently of either theory) if a judgment based on A is wrong would be much worse than the least good outcome if a judgment based on B were wrong. Mightn't it be unreasonable both to base a decision on A and to bother to ascend to consider A versus B in detail? If so, ascending to consider theoretical issues in which conviction would be low in absolute terms might take a back seat to another way of making a decision (e.g., avoiding an outcome that would be the worst).

(v) A form of reasoning that involves neither ascent nor descent is reasoning by analogy. Dworkin denies that this is really an alternative. He said that "an analogy is a way of stating a conclusion, not a way of reaching one."[9] Analogy without theory is blind, he says. He thinks we need a theory to explain why case A is really more like case B than case C. By contrast, I think that analogy can be a way of reaching a conclusion. The relevance of another case to the initial problematic one can be clear, even if one does not have a theory that links the analogous case and the original case. While we may sometimes need a theory to *explain* why case A is more like case B than like case C, without deep theoretical justification we may still see that case A is more like B than like C and that can help us find a solution to case A. If the analogous case is a "fixed point" in which we are certain what to do, it can help us decide about the problematic case. (This was the strategy behind Judith Thomson's use of her famous Violinist Case to decide about the permissibility of some abortions.[10]) Furthermore, if one is uncertain about what one may permissibly do in the analogous case, so what one may do in *that* case is also a conclusion for which one searches, thinking of the two together can help us find a solution to both. Because analogy can be a way of reaching a conclusion, it can help us build theories that identify and explain the factors in cases that have moral or legal significance. In fact, it might be that we should test a theory by seeing whether it correctly predicts that one case is analogous to another.

(vi) Many who do practical ethics think in terms of a different kind of "ascent" from the one Dworkin describes: It goes from what they know to be true about a practical moral issue to conclusions about more theoretical issues. This may be because the conclusion about a case presupposes the truth of some more theoretical matter. (These are sometimes called "transcendental arguments.") It is also possible to "descend" by implication from a conclusion about one particular issue to a conclusion about a narrower aspect of that issue. This sort of ascent and descent are different from what Dworkin has in mind since he envisions the need to first ascend to some theory in order to then descend to a practical conclusion. Further, in his discussion of what he calls "crazy" cases (like various trolley problem cases), he insists (p. 284) that their usefulness is limited to testing theories by considering the theories' implications for cases and only clear negative responses to what they imply should lead us to reject or revise a theory. However, even if Dworkin were right about this limited role for cases, the negative response to a theory's implication in a case would prevent us from ascending to any new theory that implied the same.

Dworkin's emphasizing theory is related to his concern that relying on "intuitive judgments," such as often happens in case-based reasoning, may conflict with what he thinks is the nature of moral and value truth. He worries that when one makes an intuitive judgment about what is morally correct in a real-life case, one might attribute that judgment to somehow being able to accurately perceive some morally charged state of affairs in the external world. He calls such a state of affairs a "moron" (p. 283). He doesn't believe that we perceive or need to perceive morons in order to seek truth about moral judgments. Since he denies that we perceive (or need to perceive) morons in the real world to engage in truth-seeking moral judgment, he does not oppose use of merely hypothetical cases. However, given this, he should also realize that those who defend a large role for intuitive judgment about a real (as well as hypothetical) case need not be committed to a belief in morons. A moron-free interpretation of intuiting the permissibility of an act is that though the act seems or even is known to be permissible, one does not yet know what makes it permissible and one must investigate further to pin down the properties of the act that make it permissible. That means that the intuitive judgment is not derived from conscious judgments about those properties. These properties once found would provide the reasons in normative arguments for permissibility that Dworkin says are the basis for moral truth. Neither intuitive judgments nor beliefs about reasons are made correct by their corresponding to some metaphysically suspicious element of the external world like morons.[11] Hence, disagreeing with Dworkin about the relative importance of (i) ascent to theory from intuitive judgments about cases versus (ii) descent from theory to conclusions about cases need not involve disagreeing about the metaphysics of moral truth.

B. Internal to most discussions of practical issues is the belief that a conclusion may hold "other things equal" and that it may be "overridden" by other factors that are not up for immediate discussion. Furthermore, there is usually no attempt to solve "simultaneous equations"; one does not conclude that an answer in practical ethics has not been found until we specify how the answer relates to multiple other issues and what are the limits of its application. It is also common to think that there can be something of value lost and a "negative residue" left when, for example, a right is justifiably overridden. It might also be argued that even when we do the right act, we can still wrong someone. (For example, it may be permissible to turn a trolley away from five people toward one other innocent person. However, that the person may permissibly send the trolley away from himself [just as he need not volunteer to send it to himself] even if it goes back to the person who turned it could be an indication that he has been wronged.[12]) Dworkin himself cites the Fugitive Slave Case (p. 411) as an instance in which the institution of legitimate law (in this particular case calling for escaped enslaved people to be returned to their captors) would have continuing value even though it has to be overridden in a "moral emergency" such as returning people to slavery. He says this without saying that the institution that was overridden had no value.

These positions go contrary to the view for which Dworkin is officially arguing, namely that all things of value should cohere and support each other; there should be no conflict among them and when issues are resolved there should be no negative residue from overriding something that still has value. For example, he wants to argue that freedom to do what one wants is not a value; rather, liberty, which is the freedom one has once restrictions have been justified, is what has value. Hence, there is nothing of value lost, no negative residue, in the freedom that is not justified. But if this were so, why would we seek to alter circumstances so that a freedom that in current circumstances is not justified could become justified? For example, suppose many would like to be free to drive up a street where someone stands but the freedom to do so is not justified because it would kill the person. This does not mean that there is no value in the freedom to drive up the street that is lost, as shown by our trying to find a way to move the person so that others can drive up the street without hitting him.

Dworkin defends the coherence of values in part by insisting on the malleability (by way of interpretation) of concepts that coherence requires. Indeed, he suggests that the possibility of conflict among values would entail that moral truth is based on correspondence to external morons that, if they existed, could not be altered.[13] However, an alternative view is that conflict of values need not be tied to such a "scientistic" metaphysics of value any more than (I argued) emphasizing intuitive judgments about cases does.

C. Throughout his career, Dworkin was identified as a strong defender of individual rights. As we saw in Chapter 2, in his later work he locates the foundation of important rights such as the right to control one's body in duties to oneself given by the second component of the Principle of Dignity. That component gives one an inalienable responsibility to make a success of one's life according to what one decides are correct values. Dworkin claims that we cannot do this without having certain rights such as control over our bodies and this is what justifies our having those rights. At the time when Dworkin was originally defending individuals' rights, some argued that focusing on people's rights ignored people's responsibilities (even though rights come with correlative directed duties to those with rights). The responsibilities that were thought to be ignored were usually responsibilities to others. Nevertheless, Dworkin's focus on responsibilities to oneself might be seen as a way to satisfy those who asked that we not ignore responsibility while he at the same time strengthens the case for individual rights.

Here is a brief review of issues raised by his view of the relation between rights and responsibilities. (The issues in (iii) and (iv) were discussed in Chapter 2 and parts of those discussions are repeated here for the sake of completeness.)

(i) The first part of the Principle of Dignity claims that it matters objectively that each person's life goes well. Ordinarily when it matters objectively that something go well, we would assign the task of seeing to it that things go well to the person best qualified to accomplish this. In the case of one's life, this may not be oneself but someone else. Similarly, if someone else could not merely oversee but actually had a right to control one's body and one had a right to control theirs, each person's life might be more successful. They may also live their lives well in doing that at which they each excel (managing others' lives). Control of others' bodies would then not be contrary to morality if morality were fashioned at least in part in the light of the objective importance of one's life going well. So there may be some tension between (i) the first part of the Principle of Dignity, which focuses on the value of a life and the importance of its going well, and (ii) the second part, which focuses on one's own responsibility for deciding how one's own life goes.

One way to avoid such tension is to expand the scope of the "importance component" of the Principle of Dignity. For example, it could be that a "you-directed-your-life being successful" is what is important. Put another way, instead of there simply being a responsibility for one's life, it could just be that it is part of what is objectively important that one direct one's life.

(ii) On the other hand, suppose someone did have a responsibility to make a success of his life but he could not fulfill his responsibility without controlling someone else's body. If he needs it to make a success of his life more than the other person needs it to make a success of his own, why should he not get the right to control the body in question? If morality were formed in the light of ethical requirements (so that both cohere), taking control of someone's else's body in order to make a success of one's life (rather than to make a success of the other person's life as hypothesized in [i]) would not always violate moral constraints and hence could be consistent with living well.

Nevertheless, one is thought to ordinarily have a right to control one's own body and there are limits on interfering with others' bodies for purposes of making the best of their lives or making the best of one's own. This suggests that the right to control one's body is independent of, rather than derived from or contingent on, anyone's responsibility for making a success of his life or living well.

(It could even be independent of the objective importance of someone directing his own life.) After all, one cannot ordinarily get a right to something simply by showing one needs it to fulfill a responsibility. Given that one has the right to one's body, one would be the only person who could take on these responsibilities (if they exist) insofar as they require controlling one's body.[14]

(iii) Dworkin argues that one can recognize the equal objective importance of everyone's life and yet have responsibility only for how one lives one's own life. To support this claim he says that one can recognize the equal objective value of several works of art while at the same time reasonably holding that one is only responsible for caring for those in one's collection. But (as argued in Chapter 2) this example works against his view that it is responsibility for the success of a valuable object that gives one a right to control it. Rather, it is first having rights over the artworks (i.e., their being in one's collection) that makes one responsible for their care. It is also the rights that some have over the works of art, rather than their responsibility for them, that makes it impermissible for others to take responsibility for them if they wished to.

Furthermore, in the case of works of art one may sometimes lose one's right to control them (e.g., they may be transferred to another collection) if one does not take care of them properly. The same might be true if one has a right to one's own child but loses such a right if one does not provide responsible care. By contrast, the failure to attend to one's responsibility (as Dworkin says on the last page of *Hedgehogs*) to "live a good life well" does not (except in the most extreme cases) make one lose a right to control one's own body. Yet Dworkin's view suggests that if someone shows no willingness or ability to fulfill his ethical responsibility to live well and successfully, he would also have no special grounds for claiming a right to control his body.

(iv) One of the reasons Dworkin tries to derive rights over one's person from the second component of the Principle of Dignity is that he thinks the first component (i.e., each person's life and its going well is objectively important) cannot yield a right to noninterference by others with one's body. For example, he considers the case where we would have to kill one person in order to prevent five other people from being killed as well as the case where a person would have to kill someone else to save his own life. In both cases he thinks that killing could satisfy the condition of taking seriously the objective value of lives, either my own or many others. His alternative account of why it is impermissible to kill the one person even to save more lives is that this would usurp that person's responsibility for his life, which in this case requires him to decide about the best use of his life.

One concern about Dworkin's account (raised in Chapter 2) is that our harming someone to benefit others in these cases need not be done in order to make the person harmed live a successful life well. We do not usurp his responsibility for deciding how to make a good or well-lived life for himself. Rather, we would be ignoring that issue in order to use him, despite its effect on his life, to help others instead. A distinction should be drawn between deciding what is the best use of his life and deciding what will make his life go best. Only the latter (which Dworkin calls ethical paternalism) may interfere with responsibility for one's life and its requirements of authenticity and ethical independence.

It may also be that concern for the objective value of each person's life is not best expressed by a concern for the number of people whose lives will be saved as a result of our action. I have argued that the objective worth of an entity can sometimes give it inviolability so that the permissibility of destroying one of its kind to preserve more of its kind actually lowers the objective worth of all the entities, even those that are preserved. Consider a holy book. It would be a misunderstanding of its importance to think one should destroy a particular copy of it in order to prevent more of them from being destroyed. The same may be true of objectively important persons.

In sum, some rights crucial to one's dignity do not seem to be best argued for by way of one's ethical responsibilities for living a successful life. Since these rights are crucial to one's dignity, Dworkin's notion of dignity would be incomplete unless, perhaps, the rights stem from the first rather than the second component of the Principle of Dignity.

## Notes

1. This discussion of Dworkin's Balzan Lecture was originally prepared for the Yale University Law School Conference on Ronald Dworkin's unpublished work scheduled for February 2021. That conference was postponed due to the pandemic.
2. (Cambridge, MA: Harvard University Press, 2011.) Henceforth, *Hedgehogs,* to which all page numbers in the text refer.
3. He said, "Before Hercules sits on his first case, he could build a gigantic 'overarching' theory good for all seasons. He could decide all outstanding issues of metaphysics, epistemology, and ethics, and also of morality, including political morality. He could decide what there is in the universe, and why he is justified in thinking that is what there is; what justice and fairness require, what freedom of speech, best understood, means; and whether and why it is a freedom particularly worth protecting . . . [and] weave all that and everything else into a marvelously architectonic system. When a new case arises, he would be very well prepared" ("In Praise of Theory," *Arizona State Law Journal* 29 (1997), 358). I discussed his views about Hercules in my "Theory and Analogy in Law," *Arizona State Law Journal* 29 (1997), 405–26. reprinted in part in my *Bioethical Prescriptions* (N.Y: Oxford University Press, 2013). I will summarize some of my discussion later.

4. Though Dworkin refers to Kant's views in connection with moral obligations to others, it is interesting that he does not point to the similarity between his view about the responsibility to make a success of one's life and Kant's view that we have a duty to develop our talents. From the Categorical Imperative Kant claims to derive the imperfect duty to make something of one's life unlike the South Sea Islanders whom he says live pleasantly but without developing their talents. See his *Groundwork of the Metaphysics of Morals*, ed. M. Gregor (Cambridge: Cambridge University Press, 1998).
5. See T. M. Scanlon, *What We Owe to Each Other* (Cambridge, MA: Harvard University Press, 1999). But as we discussed in Chapter 2, Dworkin thinks that failure to perform an easy rescue of someone could show contempt for the value of human life. It seems that this could be true even when one fails to rescue someone whose mistaken choice led him to do something that could cost him his life.
6. In *Hedgehogs*, Dworkin says that even early abortions decided on too easily show a contempt for oneself, violating part of the ethics of dignity (p. 378). This is presumably because it implicates a judgment about oneself as human life. However, he thinks the law should deal with the issue as a matter of morality rather than as a matter of personal ethics, and as a matter of morality early abortion involves no harm to a person (since no person is destroyed in an early abortion). By contrast, in his *Life's Dominion* (Vintage Books, 1994), he argues for legally required waiting periods before an abortion so that the woman could be encouraged to think seriously about her decision whatever it would be. This is a type of enforcement of ethical responsibility.
7. In my "Theory and Analogy in Law" I raised concerns about his view that Hercules the judge would have to "ascend" to know about practically everything to derive a conclusion for a practical issue.
8. "In Praise of Theory," 358. My comments on a judge's ascent derive from what I said in "Theory and Analogy in Law."
9. See his "In Praise of Theory." My discussion of his views on analogy refer to that article alone. A more extensive discussion is in my "Theory and Analogy in Law."
10. See her "A Defense of Abortion," *Philosophy & Public Affairs* 1, 1971: 47–66.
11. This supports Dworkin's own view in *Hedgehogs* and T. M. Scanlon's view in *Being Realistic about Reasons* (Oxford: Oxford University Press, 2014). Neither think that one has to be a constructivist about reasons, yet one can recognize them without this implying that they are fixtures of the external world.
12. For more on this see my *The Trolley Problem Mysteries* (New York: Oxford University Press, 2016). Frank Michelman also argues for the possibility of conflict between values and for negative residues in acting. However, he claims that this cannot involve wronging someone if the act is justified all things considered. He takes this to be an axiom of a noncontradictory system. See his discussion of Dworkin in "Foxy Freedom," *Boston University Law Review* 90 (2010): 956. I disagree that a justified (nonwrong) act cannot wrong someone or that it not wronging someone is required for a noncontradictory system.
13. See his response to Richard Fallon's contribution in the *Boston University Law Review* 90 (2010), 1064–66. The issues here are reminiscent of Kantian concerns about

heteronomy versus autonomy in ethics and Kant's view that intuitionism involves heteronomy, being bound to something outside of what one could rationally will.

14. As I noted in Chapter 2, this argument is like one I used to argue that a system that allows agent-relative prerogatives should also involve rights against interference. This is because the prerogative's scope should be over what one has a right to control and not be used to decide *what* one has a right to control (e.g., someone else's life). See my *Morality, Mortality*, vol. 2 (New York: Oxford University Press, 1996), and "Nonconsequentialism," *The Blackwell Guide to Ethical Theory*, 2nd ed. Hugh Lafollette and Ingmar Persson (Hoboken, N.J.: Wiley Blackwell Publishers, 2013), 261–86.

# 4

# Rights and Their Related Duties

In Chapter 3 we considered whether a perfect "theory of everything" or even a perfect theory of morality was needed in order to reach decisions about particular moral problems. In this chapter we begin by considering whether a perfect theory of justice is needed to reach decisions about injustices.[1] Rights are thought of as important components not only of interpersonal relations but also of a theory of social justice. They are thought to help account for the priority of meeting the demands of justice over achieving many other good states of affairs in society. We will consider whether there is a conception of rights and the duties related to them involved in justice that is weaker than traditional conceptions and that affects, along with other factors, how we can tell whether rights are violated and injustices occur.

## I. Mad at Theory

In his book *The Idea of Justice*,[2] Amartya Sen argues that we do not need to know what perfect justice is to know that a particular state of affairs is unjust, and comparatively more unjust than some other state of affairs. (This is his Nontranscendental Thesis, pp. 5–7, 15–17.) Analogously, he says, we do not need to know what the perfect picture would be in order to know whether a particular Picasso is worse than a particular Van Gogh (pp. 15, 101). He also argues that we can do incomplete rankings, knowing the answers to some questions about comparative justice without being able to answer them all, and we can engage in judgments relating multiple factors without being paralyzed by incommensurability. In terms of action, he argues for eliminating particular recognizable injustices rather than pursuing perfect justice. His discussion, therefore, is about nonideal rather than ideal justice, both in claiming to do without an ideal theory and in not pursuing an ideal in action. We might say that whereas Dworkin is "mad *about* theory" (as shown by our examination of his Balzan Lecture in Chapter 3), Sen is "mad *at* theory."

As suggested by my comments on Dworkin's view of the importance of ascent to theory for deciding about a practical issue and for imaginary judge Hercules rendering judgment, I am sympathetic with many elements of Sen's position. I think I can often judge that something is right without knowing what general

*Rights and Their Limits: In Theory, Cases, and Pandemics*. F. M. Kamm, Oxford University Press.
© Oxford University Press 2022. DOI: 10.1093/oso/9780197567739.003.0004

theory or principle implies the judgment. However, unlike Sen, I think such judgments about cases can help us find a theory or principle.[3] This is a different sort of ascent from Dworkin's. Further, work on justice in "micro" contexts, such as the allocation of scarce medical resources, suggests that we can give answers about how to allocate that take account of multiple factors reducible neither to each other nor to something else (e.g., factors like how badly off someone would be without a treatment, how good an outcome we can expect from the treatment, who has a proprietary claim to the treatment, and so forth). Hence, like Sen, I think incommensurability of factors need not threaten us with paralysis. (Indeed, these medical cases are reminiscent of Sen's case involving three children and one flute when the question is who should get it: One child has worked hard to make it, another child has nothing else to play with, and a third is the only one who can really play it well.)

In addition, sometimes the answer to one medical allocation case is clear even if we are not sure about other cases, yielding the sort of incomplete ranking that Sen emphasizes. For example, imagine a case where there is no special ownership claim to a scarce resource. Suppose person A would be worse off than person B if not treated but will be either not much worse off than B or not very bad in absolute terms. Furthermore, A would get only a small improvement in his condition from the scarce resource, whereas B would get a very big improvement. We could agree that B should be helped, I think. Now imagine a case where there is something like an ownership claim (e.g., someone has paid to have a medicine delivered to him). If the scarce resource can cure a headache in the owner but a brain tumor in the nonowner, we might reasonably conclude the ownership right should be overridden to prevent a seriously bad state of affairs even if there is no rights-based argument for doing so. By contrast with these two cases there is likely to be more dispute over how to allocate an unowned scarce resource in a third case where the worse-off person's condition will be objectively very bad and much worse than others and his outcome with treatment, though significantly better than without it, will be much less good than the outcome in another person. Hence, we may only have a partial ranking of outcomes.[4]

Despite agreeing with many of Sen's claims, I have several concerns. In the first part of what follows, I shall consider how a theory of perfect justice might be needed in order to identify and decide whether to remedy particular injustices. I shall also consider the importance of distinguishing failures of justice and transgression of rights from failures in other moral duties. This last point will lead me to consider the moral duties that Sen thinks are correlative to rights. My investigation of his theory of rights and their correlative duties leads me to suggest how he may be offering a very broad and nontraditional theory of rights and justice.

The second part of what follows is also concerned with how to identify particular injustices. It first considers the role of Sen's notion of a comprehensive outcome (which includes both an end state and how it comes about) in identifying whether a state of affairs is unjust. It then considers the role of Sen's notion of open (or nonparochial) impartiality in identifying whether a state of affairs is unjust. Both these notions, I argue, complicate deciding whether an unremediated state of affairs is an injustice, though the complication is not necessarily due to lack of a theory of perfect justice.

## II. Can We Do Without a Theory of Ideal Justice?

### A. The Art Analogy

I think Sen's argument for doing without an ideal theory based on the analogy with art is problematic. This is not because there are no true judgments about what is good art but because it seems there could be no general principles that account for these judgments even ideally. That is, there are no general rules or principles such that an artwork that does not abide by them must be less good than one that does.[5] If there are no general principles, there is no temptation to think that knowing what is a perfect work of art allows us to discover principles by which to judge other works of art. For example, suppose a particular great work of art is made so by having blue in it. That does not mean that having blue moves any artwork in the direction of being good. By contrast, it is possible that by considering a truly just state of affairs, we might find general principles for perfect justice that can be used to judge other states of affairs. Sen need not deny this is possible in order to deny (as he does) that such principles are necessary to judge comparative injustice (pp. 98–102).

A better argument in support of Sen's position that does not rely on the analogy with art but is of the same general type might be: "We may not know what perfect health consists in but we can imagine that the form of such knowledge would be general principles. Yet even in the absence of such principles, we can tell that having the plague is being in worse health than having a sore throat."

### B. Effects of Piecemeal Change

My second concern is that correcting injustices without having a conception of perfect justice can raise problems in an unjust world, where correcting a clear injustice to one group may result in injustice to another group. This can happen because the injustice we correct was compensating for the effects of another injustice. For example, consider eliminating the injustice to men of having to always pay alimony. When the social system unjustly results in women not having salaries as high as men, the change in men's responsibility for alimony may result in even worse economic conditions for ex-wives.[6] Given that Sen is advocating piecemeal change without a blueprint of perfection, it would have been useful if his book had dealt more with the possible pitfalls of piecemeal change and how to avoid them. Perhaps he did not do this because it is only from the vantage point of a theory of perfect justice that we could be sure to attend to the impact of some change on *all* the factors that are relevant to justice. It may be that the theory of perfect justice will not tell us which injustice to correct and which to tolerate when we cannot eliminate all of them, but this problem might be alleviated by a theory that also ranks the importance of different elements of perfect justice.[7]

Sen associates those who want to characterize perfection with those who want to move in one step from injustice to perfect justice (p. 68). But there is no necessary connection between these views. Those who want to characterize perfect justice for the sake of the guidance it may give us can believe change should be piecemeal, achieved in small steps. Indeed, there need be no link between aiming to cure particular injustices and aiming to achieve perfect justice even among those who seek to characterize perfection.

## C. Injustice and Other Moral Faults

1. *The Role for a Limited Theory of Justice.* Most importantly, I am concerned that some of the key comparative judgments on which Sen thinks we can confidently agree without a theory of perfect justice are not really about justice (or *injustice*). We may need at least a limited theory of justice or a clear concept of justice even if not a theory of perfect justice, in order to distinguish between injustice and other moral wrongs. For example, Sen says that we can all agree about "the injustice of continuing famines in a world of prosperity" (p. 103) and about the "clear social failure involved in widespread exclusion from medical access, which calls urgently for remedying (thereby yielding an advancement of justice, even after taking note of the costs involved)" (p. 104).[8] Yet it seems to me that I can agree that famine or having no medical access is a bad thing without thinking it is *unjust* when it occurs in a world of prosperity. Let me explain.[9]

(a) Suppose a famine or no medical access were the result of a natural disaster for whose occurrence in only one part of a prosperous world no one was to blame. I think the initial existence of the famine and no medical access would not be an injustice. Sen himself agrees with this, even though the circumstance would certainly involve people lacking what he would call an important capability to have food or medical care.

(b) Now suppose that some bad people deliberately caused the famine or blocked access to medicines.[10] Then there would be injustice in the form of a violation of a perfect duty correlative to a right not to be harmed, as Sen would see it.[11] However, prosperity in the world need have nothing to do with *this* injustice. Even if (b) occurred in a world in which no one lived in prosperity, there would still be injustice.

(c) Of course, Sen also says that famine and no medical access call "urgently for remedy (thereby yielding an advancement of justice)." Certainly, if one stopped famine or denial of medical care caused by injustice as in (b), by means that involved no injustice, one would advance justice by correcting an injustice. But that is different from claiming that when a remedy is urgent (and even easy) and could even stop a clear injustice (as in [b]), failure to provide the remedy *is itself an instance of injustice*. Even if failing to provide urgent (and easy) aid to victims of clear injustice (as in [b]) is failing in a serious moral duty, it may not be failing in the duty of justice.

To support this claim, we can consider Sen's own discussions of the biblical Samaritan who helped the man attacked on the road and of the neighbors of Kitty Genovese who (it is said) did not help to save her from attack.[12] He uses these cases to speak about *neighborliness and duties of aid* arising from the capacity to aid. Sen never discusses these two personal cases as involving, respectively, satisfying and not satisfying claims of justice held by those under attack *against bystanders* with the capacity to help them. (They certainly have claims of justice against those who attacked them.) Yet these cases seem to share crucial characteristics with cases of famine and no medical access in a world where the prosperous have a capacity to aid, at least as Sen describes these cases. If not aiding in the Samaritan and Genovese Cases would not involve injustice on the part of nonaiders, even if it exhibits some other moral wrong, we need a further explanation for why not aiding famine victims or those who lack access to medical care *is* a matter of injustice. I do not think Sen provides such an explanation.[13]

This does not mean that an explanation might not be given. Some might argue, for example, that in the famine (but not the Genovese) case, the prosperous who could aid are in other countries and they interfere with the immigration of people escaping famine. Thomas Pogge and Mathias Risse argue that because there is original common ownership of the earth, those who live in territories that could provide necessary food to others could be unjust in blocking immigration or in not compensating (with food) for blocking immigration.[14] Notice, however, that this explanation of the injustice of famine and no medical access in a world of prosperity depends on *a theory of justice* based on common ownership of the earth, not merely on intuitive judgments about a world in which famine and prosperity coexist. This theory of justice is, admittedly, not a theory of perfect justice, an ideal state of affairs. It is a more limited theory of justice. Sen makes clear in his book that he is not trying to develop a new theory of perfect justice but rather arguing that we can do without one. However, he also does not offer a different, more limited theory of justice (such as Risse or Pogge seem to offer). It is this sort of limited theory of justice that we may not be able to do without if we are to settle disputes when intuitive judgments differ about injustice in particular cases.

It might also be said about Sen's cases of famine and no medical access that some of those who do not aid are in the government of the very country where famine or no medical access occurs. Presumably, a government and even co-citizens have a duty of justice (executed by taxation) to help the victims. It is also possible for people through international organizations to agree to international legal arrangements requiring help to victims that would make failure to aid a violation of a right. But here the injustice of not aiding is not simply a matter of prosperous people failing to exercise a capacity to help. It is a matter of claims against one's government and fellow citizens or against those who agreed to the international arrangements. In his original judgment that there is injustice when famine or no medical access exists in a world with prosperity, Sen was not relying on the implications of existing political relations or international legal arrangements. (Indeed, he may have been trying to present prelegal justifications for creating such arrangements.)

(d) Now suppose that those capable of aiding in (c) could have prevented an initial natural disaster that caused the famine and no medical access in (a). Suppose these people are not co-citizens or government officials but only some prosperous people somewhere who could have helped. Suppose it would not be unjust, even if morally wrong in some other way, to fail to stop a famine or no medical access due even to clear injustice (as in [b]). Then it also need not have been unjust, even if morally wrong in some other way, for the prosperous not to initially prevent the natural disaster.

The general concern that drives these remarks is that the title of Sen's book is *The Idea of Justice* and yet it is not clear that he distinguishes issues of justice from other important moral matters (such as arise in the Samaritan and Genovese Cases) or defends his placing cases in the category of injustice rather than some other important moral category.

2. *Rights, Duties, and a Conception of Perfect Justice.* However, it is also possible that Sen's analysis of the fault of observers in the Genovese Case implies that an injustice took place there, even if Sen does not specifically say so. If that were so, a similar analysis of famine/medical access cases could imply injustice there too. Dealing with this possibility will also help us to better understand Sen's view of human rights, I believe.

(a) Sen does offer an analysis of the Genovese Case in terms of rights and their correlative duties. He thinks Genovese's negative right not to be assaulted gives rise not only to a perfect duty on the part of the attacker not to attack but also an imperfect duty on the part of the observers. This imperfect duty is described as follows:

> "To consider seriously what one can reasonably do to help the realization of another person's freedom, taking note of its importance and influenceability and of one's own circumstances and likely effectiveness" (pp. 372–73).

(Presumably, there is also sometimes a duty to *act* generated by this "duty to consider.") Call this *the Genovese Duty*. It could be violated by not seriously considering another person's freedom at all or by considering it seriously but failing to weigh it properly against other factors (and, presumably, also sometimes by not acting in light of these considerations). Sen goes on to further connect the imperfect duty with rights. He says: "The presumed precision of legal rights is often contrasted with inescapable ambiguities in the ethical claims of human rights. This contrast, however, is not in itself a great embarrassment for ethical claims, including those of imperfect obligations" (p. 375).[15]

This suggests that he thinks that an imperfect obligation can be the correlative of a human right. Sen's overarching idea of a pronouncement of a human right (negative or positive) is that it is

> an assertion of the importance of the freedoms that are identified and acclaimed in the formulation of the rights in question. For example, when the human right of a person not to be tortured is acknowledged, the importance of freedom from torture is reaffirmed and acclaimed for everyone, and with this the confirmation of the need for others to consider what they can reasonably do to secure freedom from torture for all. For a would-be torturer, the demand is obviously quite straightforward: to refrain and desist (this is clearly a "perfect obligation"). For others, too, there are responsibilities, even though they are less specific and generally consist of trying to do what one reasonably can in the circumstances (this would fall in the broad category of "imperfect obligations"). (p. 376)

In sum, an imperfect duty (or obligation) may be correlative to (or at least follow from) a human right on Sen's view. It is a duty not to *ignore* the important freedom of others with respect to something in deciding what to do; others' freedom with respect to that thing is a consideration that must be added to all the other considerations, obligatory or not, that one attends to in deciding what to do. Furthermore, a reasonable weighing of all the considerations, on Sen's account, allows for nonobligatory personal interests and projects to outweigh factors that are much more important from an impartial perspective. Hence, your desire not to lose your arm can permissibly take precedence over your saving someone's life since reasonable weighing, as Sen conceives of it, takes account of someone's partial rather than the impartial perspective on losses and gains.[16]

If the Genovese Duty, introduced as an imperfect duty, is like the imperfect duties correlative to human rights, then that duty could be correlative to (or at least follow from) Genovese's human *right* not to be harmed. Suppose proper consideration involved in carrying out the Genovese Duty led to the conclusion that one should aid. Then failure to aid would violate a duty to aid that follows from her right not to be harmed.

(b) In the Genovese Case, Sen derives the imperfect duty of observers to aid from her negative right not to be assaulted. Others, of course, may deny that her right not to be assaulted gives rise to or has as its correlative any duty on the part of observers to see to it that she is not assaulted. They may think the *negative* right not to be assaulted only has as its correlative the duty not to assault and a strict positive duty on the part of the assaulter to aid his victim. It does not give rise to even an imperfect duty in those who have not performed or arranged for the assault to prevent or aid after assaults.[17] They could similarly hold that a *positive* right only has as its correlative a duty in the person directly designated to provide something. It does not give others even an imperfect duty to see to it that positive rights are met by the person directly designated to provide something. However, an imperfect duty of observers to aid a victim of attack may exist independent of its being correlative to (or following from) a negative right not to be assaulted. It would be an indication of this if the imperfect duty to aid someone is no stronger when he is attacked than when he suffers the same harm accidentally or by natural disaster without any violation to his rights.[18]

On Sen's view of rights, however, this duty to aid Genovese, freestanding from her right not to be assaulted, might still seem to be correlative to another right of hers, namely her human right to be free of losing her life. This is because Sen would, I think, view "being free from losing one's life" as an important freedom (or capability) whose realization others might be in a position to help, and this is what pronouncements of human rights are about on his view. (See earlier quote (pp. 11–12) from *The Idea of Justice*, 376.)[19] This account could also give rise to the Genovese Duty described earlier. Further, there being this duty could amount to what it is for there to be a human right to be aided on Sen's view.

(c) Yet, as noted in discussing the Genovese Case, Sen does not characterize the morally wrong failure to aid as an injustice. This suggests that violation of such a human right to be aided—call it a *Senian right*—would not give rise to injustice *as ordinarily understood*. There may be several reasons this is so. First, the duty correlative to a Senian right to be aided (or the duty to aid of nonassaulters related to a negative right not to be harmed as in 2[a] earlier) would be an imperfect duty. And while we can be at moral fault for not fulfilling an imperfect duty, this sort of failure is traditionally supposed to be contrasted with injustice. Second, some who separate perfect from imperfect duties do so specifically because they think there is *no right* to which the imperfect duty is correlative.[20] On this view the imperfect duties are supposed to be duties that are not owed to persons (though they concern persons and are "direct" in the sense that they arise just in virtue of the properties of persons that the duties concern). They are contrasted with duties owed *to* persons (including those owed to all persons) that are correlative to rights and are called "directed duties."[21] Thus, on the traditional view, no injustice can occur through violation of a right when we fail in an imperfect duty. This traditional view is clearly at odds with the view that one has a human right to be aided when there is (what can be described as) only an imperfect duty to aid on the part of others.

However, if the imperfect duty is described as a duty to consider and weigh considerations (rather than an imperfect duty to perform aid), this could be owed to everyone who has the human right and so also be a directed duty. If the consideration on some occasion leads to the view that one should act, might it be said that one owes some person to act? The issue then would be whether the act could be a directed duty with a right as correlative despite being derived from an imperfect duty whose implications for action depend on weighing factors form a personal point of view.

This brings us to the third reason that violation of a Senian right to be aided need not give rise to injustice as traditionally understood. It concerns the content of the duty. The Genovese Duty, which is like the imperfect duties Sen thinks follow from human rights in general, is weaker than the (primary) duty correlative to traditional negative rights. For example, one would not say that the primary duty correlative to the negative right not to be assaulted is a duty only to take seriously the importance to the potential victim of being free of assault and to think about how to realize the victim's freedom consistent with one's own obligatory and nonobligatory ends all weighed from a partial (not impartial) perspective. Rather, as Sen notes, the would-be assaulter has a duty not to assault and this duty is not defeasible by many obligatory and nonobligatory ends that are important from the assaulter's perspective. This is so even if the right not to be assaulted is not a trump.[22]

Similarly, traditionally the duty correlative to a positive right to be aided is the duty to provide aid, not merely a duty to take seriously the recipient's need for aid and weigh it in the balance with other things. I may have to fulfill my positive duty to give aid correlative to a positive right to be aided (e.g., if I am someone's bodyguard or was his assaulter) even if doing so interferes with my funding my child's education. But a Senian *human right* to lifesaving aid would not have the provision of aid itself as the correlative duty. The giving of aid is only a possible outcome of fulfilling one's duty to consider the presence of need along with other factors, in a reasonable weighing from a personal point of view. Hence, the giving of aid may be much more easily outweighed than the positive duty to give aid that, for example, a bodyguard has correlative to someone else's positive contracted right to receive aid.

Looked at from the other direction, suppose one has a duty to consider and properly weigh for purposes of action someone's need for some important freedom (capability), for example, to be free from lack of organs when they are needed in order to live. If human rights can give rise to imperfect duties (or can even be understood in terms of imperfect duties), there could be a correlative Senian human right not to lack organs that amounts to *a human right* to organ transplants. But this human right would not imply that anyone has a duty to provide someone with a needed organ but only that some have a duty to consider seriously the need for organs and weigh it against other factors from a partial point of view (for purposes of action).

Table 4.1 lays out comparatively the objects of the duties correlative to two types of positive rights holding other factors, such as the harm that aid prevents, constant.

Notice that because the content of the duty correlative to a Senian human right to be aided could in this way be weak (i.e., to think about the need for aid to protect important capabilities and weigh this from a partial point of view against other things in deciding how to act), the duty and the right may not be defeasible. Though Sen criticizes others for thinking of rights as trumps, it turns out that this duty and the correlative right would pretty much be trumps: One would always have to fulfill them. But this is achieved only by making the content of the right and duty that fulfills it weak.[23] Sen's conception of human rights also implies a particular view about what perfect satisfaction of human rights involves. Senian human rights to have certain things (or capabilities) and be aided in having them will often not be violated if people seriously take account of whether important capabilities are met, weigh all factors in a reasonable manner (that allows for partiality), and then act on these results. Doing this, however, could be consistent

**Table 4.1.** Traditional and Senian Positive Right

| Traditional Positive Right | Senian Positive Right |
|---|---|
| Right to be given aid (e.g., as result of promise) leads to duty [to give aid]. Giving aid may be defeated by high cost. | Human right to be given aid leads to duty [to think about need for aid and weigh giving aid against other personal and impersonal considerations]. Giving aid may be outweighed by modest cost. |

with a world in which much famine and little medical care exist. This is because no aid might turn out to be required if it is difficult to decide when the appropriate weight from a partial point of view has been given to an important matter. This is a reason it is not obvious that much of the world's being prosperous is an indication that not enough weight has been given to famine relief and access to medicine.[24]

Sen says we do not need a theory of perfect justice and he does not aim to provide one. But, it might be suggested, "all human rights being respected" *is* a description of perfect justice.[25] And if we fulfill the duties that are correlative to rights, a world of perfect rights satisfaction and perhaps perfect justice will result. It is just that given what a Senian right seems to be, the "wretched of the earth" may get less help from having more such rights (and justice in their satisfaction) than might be thought.[26]

There is, however, another construal of the sentiments underlying Sen's project. Rather than seeing him as aiming to provide an alternative view of rights whose satisfaction bears on justice, one might see his aim as criticizing the priority of justice as traditionally understood. While Sen criticizes Rawls's theory of justice on various points, he might really have meant to criticize Rawls's view that justice, at least as traditionally understood to prioritize specific and highly stringent duties and rights, is the premier virtue of a social system.[27] Instead of trying to fit many of his concerns about moral failure under the rubric of justice, by extending the idea of human rights to include the correlative of merely imperfect duties (as I have suggested he does), Sen might have argued that some other virtues of a social system are as crucial as justice.[28]

## III. How End States Come About and the Bearing of This on Eradicating Injustice

### A. Comprehensive Outcomes

Now let us consider a further important issue raised by Sen's claim that remedying exclusion from medical access will yield an advancement of justice even taking account of the costs involved (p. 104). One of the attractions of Sen's views is his idea of a "comprehensive outcome." It is supposed to include the process that leads to an end-state (or culmination outcome, as he calls it), not merely the end-state. This is a part of Sen's modification of standard consequentialism, as it will often rule out bringing about good end-states by bad means.[29] However, this modification might still lead to a moral requirement to produce a good end-state by harmful means x in order (i) to prevent a good end-state being brought about by even more harmful means y or (ii) to minimize good end-states being brought about by harmful means x. (For example, it may still lead to a requirement to severely paralyze person A to prevent someone else from killing person B in order to prevent killers from killing ten other people.) This is a conclusion most deontologists would reject. This conclusion might be blocked by another proposal Sen has made elsewhere for an agent-relative understanding of an outcome, so that from an agent's own point of view, his doing harm to produce a good end-state could be a worse comprehensive outcome than other agents' producing impartially considered worse comprehensive outcomes. This agent-relative evaluation of outcomes was intended to further restrict what an agent should do to bring about an end-state. For example, it would imply that an agent's severely paralyzing one innocent person in order to stop killers from killing ten different innocent people could be wrong because the comprehensive outcome brought about by the agent is worse from that agent's point of view.[30]

These elements of Sen's moral theory explain why Sen's concern with remedying clear injustices need not always imply minimizing or equalizing injustices among people. For example, even if substituting a lesser injustice for a greater injustice would make the end-state less unjust, Sen might be opposed to doing this if it produces a worse comprehensive outcome. How we bring about the more just end-state matters morally on Sen's view.

In this connection, Sen says that aspects of justice, such as fairness and equity, can constrain equalizing capabilities among people, even if capabilities are the correct measure of the goodness of end-states. As an example, he argues for giving equal health care to men and women, even though denying women some care and giving more to men would create more equality between men and women in their capability to live long lives.[31]

In considering the moral status of means, Sen seems to give more weight to maintaining *perfect justice in means* than he gives to achieving perfect justice overall, having rejected concern with the latter (in the Nontranscendental Thesis). But it could be part of an argument against concern with perfect justice that means used to achieve partial justice also need not be perfect or like the means that would be used in a world of perfect justice.[32] It would be interesting to know why Sen distinguishes the importance of perfection in means from that in end-states.

## B. Implications for Justice

Now consider some possible implications of Sen's concern for the way end-states come about.

1. *Means vs. Minimization.* First, suppose that famine was caused by deliberate injustice (e.g., hoarding) but prosperous noncitizens failing to give aid is not

itself an injustice (even if it is some other moral wrong). Then it is possible that extracting aid for famine relief from the prosperous could itself be an injustice. Furthermore, even if doing this were a less serious injustice than the injustice involved in the famine, Sen's concern for how an end-state comes about implies that minimizing injustice need not justify causing the lesser injustice in means in order to eradicate the more serious injustice in end-state.[33] Hence, simple weighing of injustices will not suffice for "taking account of the costs involved" in forwarding justice.

If this is true, we will need to show that the means we would have to use do not stand in the way of eliminating the famine. Likewise, until we know what means are involved, we cannot know that remedying an urgent exclusion from medical access yields "an advancement of justice" in a sense that is relevant to what we should do, rather than merely to what *non*comprehensive end-state comes about.

2. *Open Impartiality and Responsibility.* Sen's concern for the way end-states come about when combined with his discussion of "open impartiality" may have unexpected implications for the duty to aid. Open impartiality involves considering the effects that one's social organization will have on outsiders, taking into account their views and interests, as one decides on principles governing one's society.[34]

Sen imagines that the members of a society are deciding on the principles of justice to govern their society in a decision situation that, like the Rawlsian original position, is fair between all the members of the society. Such a fair situation is achieved by making the members ignorant (or imagining that they are) of their positions in society, their capacities, even their conception of the good. However, Sen thinks this veil of ignorance will result in only "parochial impartiality" on the part of the decision makers. This is not because it concerns finding principles *for* only one society. (Sen is not arguing for the use of a global veil of ignorance, for he sees such a veil as part of the attempt to pursue perfect justice, which does not concern him.) Rather, he thinks that we will not have nonparochial (open) impartiality unless the members of one society, deciding behind a veil of ignorance for their own society, consider the views of outsiders and the effect that insiders' decisions for their own society may have on outsiders. He says:

> If the institutions and policies of one country influence lives elsewhere, should not the voice of affected people elsewhere count in some way in determining what is just or unjust in the way a society is organized, typically with profound effects—direct or indirect—on people in other societies? (p. 230)

Now consider the following hypothetical case. Behind a veil of ignorance, or further along in an actual constitutional process, each member of a society accepts principles or policies that rule out using birth control or modern farming methods for reasons that make good sense to these people. According to open impartiality, in deciding to accept such principles or policies, they should consider the effect this may have on outsiders in the light of those outsiders' views. Perhaps outsiders would then find themselves with a duty to rescue the insiders from what outsiders see as morally unnecessary overpopulation or famine. They would see these effects as "morally unnecessary" if (i) they do not share the values that led the other society to live by principles that rule out birth control or modern farming and (ii) those values are not part of what any reasonable person must accept, independent of holding a particular comprehensive doctrine. This impact on outsiders, if they would come to have a duty to rescue, might have to be considered by those who practice open impartiality.

Possibly, however, the outsiders would not have a duty to rescue. Let us consider this issue in connection with Sen's views on the importance of how an end-state comes about. The overpopulation and famine that are imagined to result in our hypothetical case would be due to decisions accepted by each member of the society (by hypothesis). Sen emphasizes the importance of a person having a choice to do something or to be in a certain state, not just whether someone actually does something or is in a certain state.[35] If someone has not eaten in a month but this is because he has chosen to fast, his not having food during the month does not call for urgent aid in the way that someone's unwillingly going without food for a month calls for urgent aid. In this case, what Sen takes to be morally relevant is whether the end-state (e.g., being without food for a month) is chosen. However, there are other types of cases where the relevance of choice might be more complicated. In these cases, someone chooses to bring about a certain end-state, foreseeing but *not* choosing some further effect of the chosen end-state. For example, someone may choose to fast and foresee that she will be in pain after the fast but she need not choose to be in pain. In fact, she may wish the pain were not an effect of her chosen fast. Similarly, a society may choose no modern farming and foresee but not choose famine.

What are Sen's views on the responsibility of someone to bear the foreseen but unintended and unwanted effects of his choices? Even if Sen thinks that someone whose hunger is due to a self-imposed fast should be treated differently from someone who is unwillingly hungry, he may not think those whose unwanted pain is a foreseen effect of a chosen fast should be treated differently from those whose unwanted pain is a foreseen effect of unwilling hunger. However, it might be thought that people should sometimes be responsible for bearing the foreseen, even if unintended and unwanted, costs of their choices. Call this the *Responsibility Thesis*.

Return to our case of the society that decides in fair conditions to forgo birth control and modern farming. Suppose the Responsibility Thesis is correct. Then, *on its own*, it could imply that outsiders are relieved of, or have a diminished, responsibility to provide aid mitigating the foreseen effects of the society's choices against birth control and modern farming. Then insiders' taking the open impartial perspective when deciding on social organization could reasonably *not* expect any large potential effect on outsiders (e.g., outsiders having to aid) of the insiders' choices.

Suppose, however, that insiders' choices alone would not diminish outsiders' duty to aid. Then, from an open impartial perspective, insiders could reasonably expect that outsiders *would* have a duty to aid if famine resulted from the society's policies. Given this potential impact of insiders' choices on outsiders, open impartiality suggests that the society might be morally required to either (i) modify its reproductive and farming ways so as not to put outsiders in the position of having a duty to aid or (ii) proceed as it wishes but understand that if its chosen way of life leads to the need for aid, outsiders will be relieved of, or have a diminished, responsibility to aid.[36] On this account, open impartiality rather than the Responsibility Thesis would have a role in determining that the society faces the choices of (i) or (ii). Here I have described two possible routes to outsiders having a diminished duty to aid. One route relies simply on the Responsibility Thesis. The other route relies on Sen's open impartiality thesis, which may imply that insiders' realization that outsiders would be put in a position of having to aid should lead insiders either to modify their behavior or to accept that outsiders' duty to aid is at least diminished.

It may be hard to decide whether a society faces options (i) and (ii). For example, suppose a religious imperative makes it impossible for them in good conscience to use birth control or modern farming. In this case, it might be wrong of outsiders to deny aid that they would have given had famine resulted from a natural disaster. However, even in this case, if the conscientious believers omitted some other, not forbidden, practices that could have stopped the famine, they may face modified versions of the choice of (i) or (ii). For example, if the reason they do not use modern farming is that they all have an aesthetic preference to maintain their intimate relation to the land, they may face the choice of (i) or (ii) because they have (what Rawls might call) an "expensive taste."

Suppose these effects on the duty to provide aid are possible implications of open impartiality and/or the Responsibility Thesis. Then they will bear on deciding whether, in cases like my hypothetical one, famine or no access to medical care in a world of prosperity indicates that morally wrong failures to aid are present (whether these failures are injustices or some other moral wrong).

Sen, of course, is concerned with relieving injustices in the world as it is, and the hypothetical case does not pretend to model how famine or overpopulation comes to exist in the actual world. However, he does discuss the addition of open impartiality when a society uses the veil of ignorance to decide things fairly among its members. My hypothetical case is concerned with the implications of open impartiality (and the Responsibility Thesis) for such cases. If some real-life cases of famine or overpopulation did involve wholehearted reflection by a society on its way of life and choices comparable to the ones I have discussed about birth control and modern farming, then my hypothetical case might bear on the duty to aid in such real-life cases.

## IV. Conclusion

To review, the substantive part of my discussion of Sen's views begins by suggesting that even if we could correctly identify certain conditions as injustices without a theory of perfect justice, we might need such a theory to guide us in making piecemeal corrections. I then argued that cases Sen considers to be obvious injustices (such as famine in a world of prosperity) do not seem to differ in moral structure from cases (such as not aiding Genovese) that he does not identify as injustices. I first suggested that one might need a limited theory of justice (such as one based on common ownership of the earth) in order to distinguish these cases. Alternatively, I considered whether all these cases might involve injustices on Sen's view because they involve violation of "Senian" rights, some of whose correlatives are only imperfect duties. This could account, at once, for Sen's condemnation of some states of affairs as injustices when most would characterize them as some other moral failures and for his not referring to certain failures as injustices because they do not satisfy a more traditional conception of injustice.

I continued to investigate what factors Sen's theory requires us to consider in identifying a condition as unjust. I said that his notion of a comprehensive outcome requires that we consider whether means needed to eradicate an injustice would be ruled out by other considerations of justice. Also, his concern with how an end-state comes about combined with his notion of open impartiality requires that we consider whether choices made by some people that lead to bad end-states affect whether it is unjust for others not to improve the end-states.

In sum, I have argued that without more said about what constitutes an injustice (by contrast to other moral wrongs) and what has led to an end-state, it may not be easy to identify injustices. I have also emphasized that while our notion of justice is bound up with rights, if the duties correlative to some rights are thought of as no stronger than typical imperfect duties, we shall not have captured the distinctiveness of justice.

## Notes

1. This chapter is based on my article "Sen on Justice and Rights" published in *Philosophy & Public Affairs* 35, no. 1 (2011): 82–104. That article was based on my presentation at the Seminar on Justice and Health, Harvard Global Equity Initiative, Harvard University, December 9–10, 2009. I am grateful to Sudhir Anand for inviting me to speak. For comments on the presentation, I am indebted to Amartya Sen and others present at the seminar. I am grateful for comments on earlier written drafts of the article to Thomas Pogge, Jennifer Prah Ruger, and those attending their class at Yale University on February 22, 2010. I received helpful suggestions as well from the editors of *Philosophy & Public Affairs*. The article could be considered a companion piece to my discussion of Ronald Dworkin's theory of rights as presented in his *Justice for Hedgehogs* (Cambridge, MA: Harvard University Press, 2010). That article, "What Ethical Responsibility Cannot Justify," appears in the *Boston University Law Review* 90, no. 2 (April 2010): 691–714, and is the basis of Chapter 2 in this volume. This chapter can be considered a companion to my discussion of Dworkin in the two preceding chapters.
2. Amartya Sen, *The Idea of Justice* (Cambridge, MA: Harvard University Press, 2009). All references to Sen are to this book unless otherwise noted.
3. Sen doubts that we can get a theory of perfect justice from comparative judgments.
4. For my discussion of some allocation issues in medicine see my *Morality, Mortality*, vol. 1 (New York: Oxford University Press, 1993) and *Bioethical Prescriptions* (New York: Oxford University Press, 2013), among other places.
5. Immanuel Kant argues for this in his *The Critique of Judgment*, trans. James Creed Meredith (Oxford: Clarendon Press, 1952), as do modern aestheticians such as Mary Mothersill in her *Beauty Restored* (New York: Oxford University Press, 1984).
6. In this case, the injustice to men is a means of alleviating an effect of a different injustice to women that the man who pays alimony may not have caused (or even have benefited from). Even if the injustice to women is greater, Sen's view may rule out using an injustice to men as a means to ameliorate it. (For more on this, see section III.A later.) For another possible example of one injustice compensating for another, see my comment on Sen's discussion of equal health care for men and women (in note 31).
7. I am indebted to Esther Shubert for emphasizing these last two points.
8. Sen gives the "subjugation of women" as another example of injustice that he believes is clear. But it may only be clear because the term "subjugation" seems to imply injustice by definition. If so, while we all agree that subjugation is unjust, the debate will shift to whether unequal conditions for women constitute subjugation. Of course, Sen could go on to argue that (certain) unequal conditions for women obviously are unjust or constitute subjugation.
9. I assume Sen is not taking these cases merely to be instances of "cosmic injustice," for in that sense otherwise identical people having any unequal sets of goods due to luck (however well off they are individually) would constitute injustice. His views, described in (a) later in the text, confirm this assumption.

10. Sen has, of course, famously argued that famines arise from human actions and inactions, not merely natural disasters. See his *Poverty and Famines: An Essay on Entitlement and Deprivation* (Oxford: Clarendon Press, 1981). I am here imagining the worst of such human causes—hoarding or theft of needed food and medical supplies.
11. See p. 374.
12. See pp. 171–72, 371–75. There is now some dispute about the absence of help in the Genovese Case.
13. Thomas Pogge pointed out (in conversation) that even if the failure to aid Genovese was not an injustice itself, it would fail to promote justice because she is the victim of an unjust attack. By contrast, in the case of a naturally occurring famine or absence of medical care, Sen admits (as noted in [1(a)]) there would be no state of injustice to correct, so failure to aid could not be in the same way failure to promote justice. Failure to aid in case (b) would involve failure to promote justice.
14. See Thomas Pogge, "Eradicating Systemic Poverty: Brief for a Global Resource Dividend," in *World Poverty and Human Rights: Cosmopolitan Responsibilities and Reforms* (Cambridge: Polity, 2002), 196–215, and Mathias Risse, "Common Ownership of the Earth as a Non-Parochial Standpoint: A Contingent Derivation of Human Rights," *European Journal of Philosophy* 17, no. 2 (2009): 277–304. Pogge's and Risse's theories speak of common ownership of undeveloped resources and territory. Both theorists recognize that "asymmetrical" claims to the benefits may result from one set of people developing certain resources and territory. If the excluded seek the latter developed benefits, which another set of people has created, then the question of whether denying benefits to the excluded people is unjust will arise again. Pogge has also proposed that because the world economic order could be different, allowing for more equal distribution of wealth, the rich who impose the current order harm the poor. This would be violation of a negative right, not merely a failure to aid. My concern with this suggestion is that it may incorrectly equate failure to maximally benefit (by introducing a different economic order) with harming.
15. I assume here that the idea of obligation and duty are interchangeable though in other contexts they might not be interchangeable.
16. Similarly, we saw in Chapter 2 that Dworkin limits duties to aid so that they do not interfere with one's pursuing the success of one's life, but some projects may be ruled out because they interfere with duties to aid. However, Dworkin may think pursuing personal success is obligatory more often than does Sen.
17. Sen says (p. 384) that one cannot show that human rights do not exist simply because it is not possible to satisfy them all. By this standard, he says, we could show that there is no human right to liberty because we cannot stop all attacks on liberty. He here seems to interpret the human right to liberty as involving the right to protection from attacks on liberty and the duty of others to stop such attacks. But those whose views I have been describing (in the text) may claim there is no such human right to *protection* against attacks and no duty of others to aid correlative to (or stemming from) the human right to liberty. In particular, they would claim that such a right to protection against attacks is distinct from a "first generation" human right to liberty, which

is understood solely as a right against someone's interfering with one's liberty. That there are actually such interferences is certainly consistent with people having a right not to have their liberty interfered with, and actual interferences do not show that it is not possible to satisfy all negative rights not to have liberty interfered with.

18. Thomas Scanlon suggested that the duties to aid in these cases are the same. His view is described in Samuel Scheffler's *The Rejection of Consequentialism* (Oxford: Clarendon Press, 1982).
19. I find it odd that not losing one's life is best thought of as the object of a freedom or capability, but this is the way Sen would see matters, I think.
20. Christine Korsgaard may be an exception since she introduces the concept of an imperfect right to correspond to an imperfect duty. See her "The Claims of Animals and the Needs of Strangers: Two Cases of Imperfect Right," *Journal of Practical Ethics* 6, no. 1 (2018): 19–51.
21. The distinction between direct and directed duties (and the relation of the latter to rights) was introduced in Chapter 1.
22. Sen criticizes Dworkin's idea of a right as a trump over all other considerations. See his second footnote, pp. 360–61.
23. It might be thought that Sen's not separating out injustice from other moral failures is due to his thinking that claims to have one's rights met are more easily defeated than on traditional views about claims of justice. Our discussion comparing Senian and traditional rights suggests that this thought is not quite right. It is true that he says (p. 373) that *aiding* those who lack essential capabilities might be outweighed if the cost of aiding interferes with other obligations of aiders and even with nonobligatory pursuits in their lives. But this is not the same as saying that a *duty to aid* is outweighed. If Sen's understanding of the human *right to be aided* does not have as its correlative an ordinary duty to provide aid but only a duty to *consider* an important capability and how one might help its realization in relation to other factors in one's life (and act in accord with the conclusion one reaches), then this duty is essentially indefeasible.
24. For more on this, see discussion in Part III.
25. I owe this argument to Markus Labude. However, an editor of *Philosophy & Public Affairs* suggests that Sen might think that much of justice is not covered by the demands of human rights. I am not sure whether this is, in fact, a position open to Sen given how broad his notion of a human right is.
26. Something similar can occur with constitutional positive rights even if their apparent content is stronger. For example, suppose there is said to be a *right* to health care giving rise to a duty to provide health care (not merely to a duty to give serious consideration to the need for health care). In practice, courts may interpret this right to be only an important consideration that must be weighed against the costs of providing health care, other social needs, and other rights.
27. Others have done so, I believe. For example, Avishai Margalit argues for decency as the premier characteristic of a good society. See his *The Decent Society* (Cambridge, MA: Harvard University Press, 1998).
28. Similarly, those who reject Rawls's argument for the justice of incentives might suggest that the greater good *overrides* the injustice of introducing them.

29. See pp. 215–16.
30. See his "Rights and Agency," *Philosophy & Public Affairs* 11 (1982): 3–39. It seems odd to me to evaluate comprehensive outcomes from a partial rather than impartial perspective. But even if we do, this proposal does not seem to rule out an agent's doing harm in order to interfere with the realization of a worse end-state resulting from *his own* prior harmful acts or alternative current acts. (An example of the latter is someone who might think he should topple someone from a bridge to stop a trolley hitting five people when the only other alternative is his turning the trolley when this would kill *two* other people.) Yet, a deontological account of morality would, I think, correctly often rule this out. See my discussion in *Morality, Mortality*, vol. 2 (New York: Oxford University Press, 1996) and Chapter 9 in this volume.
31. See p. 296. I am not sure that this is a good example to support his views about what means may be used to achieve a good end-state. The problem is that his analysis of this gender case is incomplete because equalizing men's and women's capabilities for long lives might create an end-state with overall more inequality between men and women if men have other advantages over women. Hence, to complete this argument for the impermissibility of using certain means to a good end-state, we should consider how we would react if women were the ones who lived shorter lives—along with having other social disadvantages—so that they had *all* the disadvantages relative to men. Would we then think it wrong to give unequal health care to men and women, with women getting more care than men? I suspect not. A similar question can be raised for those concerned with equality of health. Michael Marmot's famous Whitehall study was said to have shown that as workplace rank went down, bad health went up. Here one group has two disadvantages: low rank and worse health. Suppose, instead, that as workplace rank went up, bad health went up. Should we be as concerned with inequality of health, per se, when those who had bad health had the advantages of high rank? After all, the combined package could make them equal to those who had good health but the disadvantage of low rank. Suppose, for argument's sake, that we should not be as concerned with inequality of health when those with high rank had worse health. This might justify our giving equal health *care* to high- and low-rank groups in our hypothetical case, even though this leaves the high-ranking people with worse health. This is consistent with its being right to give more health care to those low in rank than to those high in rank when the former *also* have poorer health. See my brief discussion of the Whitehall study in my "Health and Equity," in *Summary Measures of Population Health*, ed. Christopher J. L. Murray, Joshua Salomon, Colin Mathers, and Alan Lopez (Geneva: World Health Organization, 2002), 685–706. (I here ignore doubts that have been more recently raised about Marmot's empirical findings.)
32. This is like Jon Elster's criticism of using a Habermasian perfect discourse situation as a means to reach a world in which such a discourse situation would be an appropriate means of governance. See J. Elster, "The Market and the Forum: Three Varieties of Political Theory," in *Deliberative Democracy: Essays on Reason and Politics*, ed. James Bohman and William Rehg (Cambridge, MA: MIT Press, 1997), 3–33.
33. Notice that this could be true even if we should eradicate, by means that do not violate justice, a greater rather than a lesser injustice.

34. See Chapter 6. It is like the "all affected" principle suggested by some.
35. See Chapter 11, p. 238.
36. This assumes that outsiders do not have a duty to pay to support the insiders' choices for no birth control and modern farming simply because the costs to them of doing so would be less than the costs to insiders of giving up their preferred way of life. This seems to follow from Sen's view that minimizing or equalizing costs to different parties is not always the right way to decide what should be done.

# 5
# Intuitions, the Veil of Ignorance, and Strains of Commitment

Among the topics discussed in this chapter are (1) the nature and significance of intuitions, (2) proper use of the veil of ignorance in contractualist reasoning, and (3) whether each person's acting for a shared goal is most rational and yet something that people can reasonably reject. The examination of Allan Gibbard's treatment of these topics in his Tanner Lectures carries forward our discussions in previous chapters about the role of intuitive judgments in doing moral theory, ex ante reasoning, and whether the correct moral theory implies nonconsequentialist (or deontological) rights and moral distinctions.[1]

1.A. Gibbard begins his treatment of intuitions by discussing the views of psychologist Jonathan Haidt, who claims that we do not reason our way to moral conclusions but rather respond intuitively and then find reasons to support "preordained conclusions." Mostly, according to Haidt, reasoning constructs "justifications of intuitive judgments, causing the illusion of objective reasoning."[2] Gibbard compares this to lawyers who have to find reasons to support the side for which they are advocates.

One of my concerns with Haidt's view is his claim that finding justifications of intuitive judgments, after having the judgments, can only create an illusion of objectivity. Suppose someone has an intuitive response and then tries to find out what it is about the act or situation she is considering that accounts for her response. In one sense "accounts for" might be about what causes the judgment, but it needn't be. In having the intuitive judgment, she does not merely pick (or get assigned to defend) a position as a lawyer would; she finds it correct. Hence, if she locates the factors that causally account for her response, she should consider whether these factors "account for" it in the sense of, on reflection, justifying it. This reflective view would then yield the reasoned-to moral conclusion. If the factors do justify the initial response, that might suggest that the intuition was the result of very rapidly and unconsciously "reasoning" from these factors to a judgment. Even if factors that caused the intuitive judgment do not justify it, the intuitive judgment may still be justified on reflection by other factors. If so, the judgment is an instance of an objectively correct judgment. Hence, in these two ways the intuitive judgment is no less objectively true if awareness of the factors and reasoning that justify it comes after the judgment than if such awareness

*Rights and Their Limits: In Theory, Cases, and Pandemics.* F. M. Kamm, Oxford University Press.
© Oxford University Press 2022. DOI: 10.1093/oso/9780197567739.003.0005

comes before, contrary to what Haidt suggests. Of course, no factors may justify the judgment, in which case one might need an error theory in order to account for the original illusion of correctness. Furthermore, one should seek to avoid relying on the intuition if a tendency to believe it remains even after its inadequacy is uncovered. The willingness to admit that no factors justify an intuitive judgment can also make the conclusion not "preordained."

In this process of seeing whether there are justifications for intuitive judgments, we may move back to other intuitive judgments. For example, if we intuitively judge that we may turn a trolley away from five people and in a direction where it will hit one person, part of the ground we can subsequently uncover for this intuition may be the intuitive judgments that one person being killed is a better outcome than five people being killed and that death is bad for these people. These intuitive judgments may (or may not) have deeper grounds that can be uncovered. By contrast Gibbard thinks that intuitions are basic judgments, not based on other judgments: "An intuition . . . is a state of mind of accepting something, not on the basis of further reasoning even upon challenge."[3] My sense (exemplified by my response to Haidt and this trolley case) is that the term should not be limited to the most basic judgments for which we could uncover no further grounds. Gibbard and I can agree, however, that what I would call nonbasic intuitions can initially be had without being aware of further justifying grounds for them (though I argue that such grounds could be uncovered) and that there are some very basic intuitions that lack further grounds to be uncovered.

B. Gibbard's concern is why we should place any stock in intuitions if we accept a naturalistic picture of the world. In such a world picture, moral intuitions cannot give us insight into nonnatural facts that could support the truth of these judgments.[4] In Gibbard's view, a naturalistic picture of the world reveals that in order to survive and reproduce successfully, people must not only have accurate beliefs about the way the world is empirically but also plan what to do and feel. He says that there are no answers to these planning questions given by the natural world. However, planning what to do will involve weighing considerations such as pleasure and pain, and he holds that "weighing enjoyment in favor and suffering against, on no further ground, amounts to having an intuition about why to do things. Intuitions, then, apply to planning, and not just to thinking how things stand. If I keep challenging my thoughts about what to do and why, I end up grounding my planning in intuition."[5] But again, he notes, the question arises: "Why think we can intuit why to do things? . . . Why think we can intuit why and why not to feel certain ways about things?"[6]

According to Gibbard, "thinking of ought judgments as plans leads to an answer. . . . To say that I have this intuition is just another way of saying that I confidently weigh the chance of suffering against doing a thing, and on no further grounds even if I ask myself why."[7] So far this answer to "Why think we can intuit what to do and feel?" just seems to amount to the claims that we are capable of confidently weighing some factor positively or negatively and on no further grounds even if we ask ourselves why. This is only an empirical, de facto sense of intuition, Gibbard says. In a normative, de jure sense, "an intuition . . . is a state of mind of accepting something not on the basis of further reasoning even upon challenge, that we *ought* to place some trust in." And if we accept his account of ought judgments, according to which they are like plans to do or prefer to do something, this can yield his claim that "to think something is an intuition in this sense is to *plan* to rely on it. . . . It's a normative claim, then, that de facto intuitions are genuine intuitions—and one we need . . . for coherent planning."[8]

Any plan to rely on a nonderived judgment is subject to evaluation; we should not ultimately adopt the plan to rely on our nonderived judgment if it fails the test for being a good plan. Gibbard thinks that the test for a good plan for relying on an intuition is whether we would plan to rely on it in a situation that is ideal for making plans. This is a situation in which "what I would then *think* ought to be done *ought* to be done."[9] Some of the characteristics of such an ideal situation might be, he says, "full information vividly taken in and contemplated, and an alert, engaged, and dispassionate frame of mind."[10] But he does not think that there is yet a complete and unproblematic characterization of the conditions under which to trust one's normative judgments.

C. Here are some questions I have about Gibbard's answer to why we should place stock in our intuitions given a naturalistic worldview. In one sense, Gibbard's answer to why we should think that we can have genuine (i.e., correct) intuitions seems to imply that it is *necessary* that we have genuine intuitions. On his account, we are (naturalistically speaking) planning creatures, and we could not plan if we did not have intuitions that we thought we ought to rely on, intuitions that we thought were genuine. But, of course, these are only intuitions that we think are genuine; we could actually be planning with intuitions on which we ought not to rely (e.g., on which we would not plan to rely in an ideal planning situation). Many who think we can, in fact, have genuine intuitions are willing to accept that we might not have been able to have them, even while remaining planning creatures. Indeed, they are open to the idea that we may not, in fact, have them and we could be mistaken in thinking that we have them. The cognitive, as opposed to planning, approach to intuitions is certainly not committed to its being necessary that we have correct intuitions. On the planning approach as well it seems that we could not be sure that we had genuine intuitions unless we would form plans to rely on certain empirical intuitions in an ideal planning situation. Hence, the planning approach will not explain the genuineness of any intuitions unless we know both what the characteristics of an ideal planning situation are and that we can be sure that intuitions we rely on would be chosen in that situation. Further, intuitions relied on to characterize the ideal planning situation would, presumably, themselves be subject to evaluation (as plans).

Suppose there was no sense in which intuitions are genuine other than that we would decide, when we are in a mental state of full information, alert, dispassionate, etc., to plan to rely on them. What reason is there to think that one plan about what to do and feel in the realm of morality would be any better than another plan, or that it would pay to plan at all, unless being in an ideal mental state allowed us to be aware of reasons for doing and feeling that exist independently of what we plan to rely on in that state? (Their existing independently does not mean they are entities in the world like Dworkin's morons.) I think that the reasons for which Gibbard accepts "that normative thinking rests on intuition"[11] are not intended to, and do not, give comfort to the many who place cognitive stock in intuition, even those consequentialists who employ only very basic intuitions such as that pleasure is good and pain is bad. However, he does help to undermine the position of those who claim to be able to do ethics without any intuitions related to value.

2.A. Gibbard contrasts two approaches to morality. The first is what he calls humanistic. It approaches morality as something that has value because it is of value to humanity in a way "that can be appreciated in nonethical terms."[12] Given that Gibbard does not distinguish "moral" and "ethical," I take this to mean that it approaches morality as a way of achieving nonmoral goods for humanity. This approach, he says, may be based on the intuition (plan to accept) that humanity matters (and so it matters that they have nonmoral goods). The second approach is "intuitionistic, in one important sense of that term," he says. It relies very heavily on intuitions, seeks to systematize them, and hopes to "uncover a deep, implicit rationale for our intuitive responses" that "will turn out to be a worthy one." This hope, he thinks, implies that "the two broad styles converge."[13]

Gibbard's description of what he calls the humanistic approach suggests that it takes an instrumental approach to morality: Morality is a means to achieving nonmoral goods. Gibbard's favoring the humanistic approach may, therefore, be in some tension with his subsequent embrace of the framework of Scanlonian contractualism. Scanlon's view is that the point of morality is to act in ways that we can justify to others and that we can do this (roughly) if we act on principles that no one (who was seeking principles for living with others) could reasonably reject. Being able to live on these terms with others will require us to consider the nonmoral good of others because this good helps determine what they could and could not reasonably reject. But the goal of getting agreement and justifying one's conduct to others is not a mere means to securing nonmoral goods. Scanlon says, "It is, in a more fundamental sense, what morality is about."[14] If this is what morality is about, it seems to me that its value cannot be appreciated in nonmoral terms.

Gibbard's description of the second, intuitionist approach to morality coincides with the one I gave in 1.A in which we seek the justifying grounds of intuitions, except for his inference that "worthy" rationales for intuitions are ones that show morality to be for humanity in the sense of providing benefits that can be appreciated in nonmoral terms.

Consider in more detail what Gibbard thinks it is for morality to be for humanity. He thinks it consists in satisfying humanistic preferences, which are preferences for the benefit of all humanity. The minimal sense of this is that if one prospect will be better than a second for everyone (or even better for some and not worse for anyone), then it is morally better.[15] (This condition is put in terms of what is good for people; it does not necessarily coincide with the satisfaction of preferences people have for their own sake, for these might be mistaken.) A more robust interpretation according to Gibbard is that morality seeks the maximal good for people, understood as the maximal sum of individual utilities, and thus the maximal expected utility for each individual behind a veil of ignorance.

B. I think there are reasons to doubt, first, that morality is only for the good of persons (or sentient beings) and, second, that the parts of it that are for the good of persons take the form of arrangements that produce maximal expected utility for individuals from behind a veil of ignorance.

Consider the first point. Thomas Scanlon claims that there is a part of morality that is concerned with impersonal values, though he believes it is not the part that contractualism explains. For example, it would be morally wrong to pave over the Grand Canyon or to destroy great works of art even if this were not bad for people.[16] This is a part of morality that is not about people. Shelly Kagan and Larry Temkin[17] argue that there is a part of morality that is about people but not about doing as much good for them as possible. They argue that the Pareto condition (i.e., a state being better for some and no worse for others is simply better) is wrong: It can be morally worse if someone gets what is better for him even if his getting it is not worse for anyone else. Consider an evil person who has utility 20 and a good person who has utility 10. It could simply be morally better if people have only as much utility as they deserve in absolute terms. Hence, if the evil person deserves utility 5, it would be better if his utility were reduced, even if this does not improve anyone else's condition. It would also be better if the evil person's utility were less than the good person's, at least if this is not below the point of his absolute desert, even though this does not improve the condition of the good person (or anyone else).

C. Now consider some questions about Gibbard's view that to the extent to which morality is for people (in the sense of for people's good), it involves giving each individual his highest prospective utility from behind a veil of ignorance. Gibbard claims that this yields the system no one could reasonably reject once it is ongoing as each would be most reasonable in agreeing to it behind a veil of ignorance when deciding for his own good.

Gibbard begins by arguing that while nothing in his metaethics commits one to planning to live with others on terms of mutual respect, this seems like an intuitively plausible plan. (He does not say that anything about persons *demands* that one plan to live in this way with them.) Such mutual respect, he agrees with Scanlon, involves treating each person in ways he could not reasonably reject. This further involves, he thinks, treating people in accord with principles or arrangements they would have agreed to from an impartial point of view, that is, without their knowing what position they would actually occupy. Gibbard follows Harsanyi and Rawls, not Scanlon, in thinking that this involves treating each as he would have agreed to be treated from behind a veil of ignorance, when each chooses for his own good.[18] He follows Harsanyi but not Rawls in thinking that choosing from behind a veil of ignorance involves choosing under an assumption that one has an equal probability of being any person in any actual position in society. He follows Harsanyi in thinking that a correct choice from behind the veil of ignorance would be for a system that maximizes each person's prospective average utility, assuming that each person would adhere to what such a system requires. (Strains of commitment that would jeopardize adherence have to be considered eventually in deciding what principles to select.) If it will maximize each person's prospective average utility to risk being very poor when others are very rich, then a person who actually turns out to be poor when others are rich is being treated respectfully when called upon to remain poor, as he would have chosen such a system when deciding for his own good from behind the veil of ignorance.

In Gibbard's view,[19] the challenge for a contractualist is to derive something other than this utilitarian principle. He thinks that no one would choose a nonutilitarian principle behind a veil of ignorance when choosing for his own good (assuming adherence by all); he would only choose a nonutilitarian principle if he knew what position he would actually occupy.

(i) My first concern is whether Gibbard's intuitive endorsement of a ground-level plan to live on terms of mutual respect with others coheres with his other views about ex ante maximizing average utility. Suppose we have not yet derived his further view that treating someone with respect specifically amounts to treating him in accord with principles he would have agreed to for his own prospective good behind a veil of ignorance. Then it would remain open that taking the risk of falling into a position in which one is treated *disrespectfully* will prospectively maximize one's chances of achieving nonmoral goods. Hence, given Gibbard's view that a humanistic perspective on morality makes essential reference to achieving nonmoral goods for humanity, it is not clear why he accepts (prior to deciding what respect specifically implies) that planning how to live with others should, at its base, involve planning to live on terms of mutual respect with each person. It seems that at its base, his plan of how to live with others should involve a commitment to maximizing nonmoral goods for humanity.[20]

Of course, Gibbard does go on to give a particular interpretation of respectful treatment that involves being treated in accordance with principles to which one would have agreed on one's own behalf behind a veil of ignorance. This implies that, by definition, one *could* not, behind the veil of ignorance, agree to risk being in a *disrespectful* position as a means of maximizing one's prospective average utility. Even being treated as a mere thing for one's entire life could not, on Gibbard's view, be termed an intrinsically disrespectful position if agreeing to risk being so treated were a concomitant of choosing what would maximize one's prospective average utility. I find this an implausible implication of his view (and will comment on it further later).[21]

(ii) Gibbard is attempting to find a place for Harsanyi's utilitarian conclusion within a Scanlonian framework. So let us next consider the contrast between Scanlon and Harsanyi on contractualism. Gibbard believes that he can locate a disagreement between Scanlon and Harsanyi in the problem of identifying a conception of a person's good that can play a role in moral theory, and in particular in the choice behind the veil. While it may be true that Harsanyi and Scanlon differ in the way Gibbard thinks they do, I do not think that Scanlon's objections to Harsanyi would be limited to the problem of identifying a morally relevant conception of a person's good. In his early article "Contractualism and Utilitarianism,"[22] Scanlon directly argues against Harsanyi and the sort of reasoning behind a veil of ignorance that he proposes for purposes of moral theory, quite independently of concern about how we might conceive of a person's good. It is on this disagreement that I will focus.

Scanlon's basic objection[23] to Harsanyi's use of the veil of ignorance is with the interpretation of impartiality (and not only with what it means to decide on someone's good from an impartial point of view). He is concerned that the procedure to be used in deciding on impartial principles—both that do not favor one person over another and that one could accept independently of knowing what one's actual position is or will be—adequately respects the separateness of persons. Scanlon agrees that it can be helpful in finding such principles to use a procedure in which each imagines that he is in every other person's actual position in life (outside a veil of ignorance),[24] having that person's perspective on things, in order to see whether each person in any actual position could approve (or not reject) a proposed principle governing relations between people. While Scanlon does not make use of a veil of ignorance, his interpretation of impartiality implies that (i) if no person in any position beyond the veil could reasonably reject a principle on his own behalf, then (ii) any individual behind a veil of ignorance could agree to the principle. If someone from some position beyond the veil could reasonably reject a principle, then it could not be agreed to by any (in the sense of every) person behind the veil of ignorance. The reasonableness of rejection beyond the veil is a function of comparing the possible complaints of people in different (generic) positions to the implications of different principles.

Scanlon rejects the alternative interpretation of impartiality that Gibbard and Harsanyi accept, according to which impartiality is best exemplified by a single person deciding behind a veil of ignorance on the assumption that he has an equal probability of being in any person's position beyond the veil. The assumption of equal chances of being in any position is supposed to ensure that one does not choose principles that favor one position over another. But there is still no requirement that a decision maker behind the veil take account of whether each person actually occupying each type of position could reasonably reject a principle before he, behind the veil, decides to accept it. Rather, the order is the reverse of what it is on Scanlon's view: If any individual behind the veil of ignorance would choose a principle on his own behalf, then no person in any actual position beyond the veil could reasonably reject the principle. It is this Order Reversal, as I shall refer to it, that seems to lie at the heart of Scanlon's disagreement with the Gibbard-Harsanyi approach, for he thinks their order is the wrong way to take account of the points of view of separate persons. He says:

> Whatever rules of rational choice this single individual, concerned to advance his own interests as best he can, is said to employ, this reduction of the problem to the case of a single person's self-interested choice should arouse our suspicion. As I indicated in criticizing Harsanyi, it is important to ask whether this single individual is held to accept a principle because he judges that it is one he could not reasonably reject whatever position he turns out to occupy, or whether, on the contrary, it is supposed to be acceptable to a person in any social position because it would be the rational choice for a single self-interested person behind the veil of ignorance. I have argued above that the argument for average utilitarianism involves a covert transition from the first pattern of reasoning to the second.[25]

In Scanlon's picture, involving the first pattern of reasoning, the one person behind the veil would not conceive of the different generic positions beyond the veil as mere slots into which he might fall. He might imagine them as ones he actually occupies, as if he occupied all in order.[26] In this way, he is forced to think of the different people who will actually occupy each generic position, which is what is ultimately important. A principle may be one that a rational egoist should choose behind the veil, but this does not mean that it is a principle that nobody, regardless of their position in society, has good reason to reject. Notice also that on Scanlon's interpretation of impartiality, one does not need to assume that ex ante one has an equal chance of being in any position in society, for one would have to check whether someone who is in a particular type of position could reasonably agree to or reject a principle even if there were not ex ante an equal chance of being in that position.

Scanlon also argues by example against the conclusion that an individual's choosing behind the veil of ignorance a principle that maximizes average expected utility bears on one's ability to reasonably raise a complaint to an arrangement based on this principle. The example he employs[27] involves maximizing ex ante average utility by a principle that will allow very many people to each receive a small benefit when only a few will be very badly off. He thinks that the people who are very badly off could reasonably reject the principle by comparison to an alternative principle that could greatly improve the worse off if the small benefit does not go to each of the many. (Scanlon does not, however, commit to a maximin principle that would require improving the worse off so long as the cost to each of many others did not reduce them below the level of the worst off.)

Gibbard believes that it is only rational to sum the weight of considerations coming from each possible position into which someone may fall. Scanlon's example helps show why he rejects this idea. He considers a principle from the perspective of each type of position that will actually be occupied by someone and compares its effects on a position pairwise with every other position in order to decide whether the principle or some alternative should be adopted.[28] I believe that Scanlon's example shows that attending to the maximal sum of utilities, without considering what distribution of these is involved, would not yield the right principle.

Indeed, even when someone stands to benefit greatly, it seems implausible to think that their doing so is justified when someone else will fare very badly. For example, suppose that Ida and Jay (the characters in one of Gibbard's examples) each prefers to be a master with the other being his or her slave. Higher prospective average utility for each can occur with slavery relative to a more egalitarian system. This does not seem to justify slavery or imply that we treat whomever is a slave respectfully even if he too would have chosen such a system behind a veil of ignorance were he deciding from self-interest not knowing which position he would occupy. Another example involves two people who each face surgery knowing that one of them will come out nondisabled and the other disabled. Each will need oxygen for recovery, but there is only one tank available. The question is whether the tank should be placed in the recovery room for disabled or nondisabled people given that it cannot subsequently be moved. A single individual behind the veil of ignorance not knowing whether he will come out of surgery disabled or nondisabled person may want to maximize his chances of having a nondisabled life. He does this by deciding that the tank should be in the recovery room for nondisabled patients.[29] When someone considers his chances, he knows that if he is in the nondisabled room he is not in the disabled room. However, in the case where two people are involved, there will be someone in the disabled room—a separate person; that room is not just a slot into which one person might have fallen. Even if the disabled life is not as good as the nondisabled one, the disabled person may care as much about living his life as the nondisabled person cares about living his life. The disabled person may not be willing to give up his equal chance to live for the sake of someone else having even a better life. He could reasonably reject the principle that locates the tank in the nondisabled recovery room rather than the principle that calls for tossing a fair coin giving equal chances to each location for getting the tank.

Scanlon does believe that focusing on strains of commitment (as Gibbard eventually does) can do something to bring the results of his own and Harsanyi's versions of contractualism closer together.[30] I shall examine this issue further later.

One concern with accepting Scanlon's rather than the Gibbard-Harsanyi position on impartiality is that even Scanlon can accept that oftentimes an individual's actual (rather than hypothetical) choice to take a risk of falling into a disfavored position *does* undermine his complaint if he falls into that position; such a choice can be a substitute for considering his perspective simply as a person in a disfavored position. Scanlon would have to explain either why hypothetical choice is different or in which circumstances risks are acceptable and in which not. Let us consider this and related issues further.

To defend his view Gibbard has given the following example:[31] Many people commonly take a small risk of dying from an oncoming car in order to cross the road to get a chocolate bar (Chocolate Bar Case). They do not follow a maximin policy. They each risk a big loss in a practice that results in each of many achieving a small gain. Presumably, a person has no complaint if he loses his bet and is involved in a deadly accident (i.e., no malice or negligence is involved). However, I believe the important question is what the willingness to take such a small risk implies for risk-taking when others' not retaining but giving up the chocolate bar they successfully got could still save the accident victim from certain death. "Being willing to run a risk to have one's chocolate bar" when the risk is small that one would unavoidably die is not the same as a decision behind the veil of ignorance to run a large risk or even certainty that one will die (if *one* turns out to be the person who gets hit) in order that one (or anyone else) be able to keep a chocolate bar if one (or anyone else) turns out to be someone who successfully got the bar when giving it up could still save the accident victim's life.

There is at least one more type of case that is relevant to the question of taking risks and whether respect for persons should be understood as treating people in a way to which they would have agreed because it maximized their expected good behind a veil of ignorance. In the version of the Chocolate Bar Case we have considered, each person acquires his chocolate independent of whether another person is hit and dies in an accident. But we could imagine that it is someone's being hit and unavoidably dying that is a necessary means to others' acquiring chocolate. Behind a veil of ignorance, each must then decide whether to run the risk, perhaps small, of being hit in order to have a good chance of having chocolate, knowing that beyond the veil anyone's acquiring chocolate causally depends on someone else's being hit. On Gibbard's understanding of contractualism, and of what it is to respect people, there is nothing intrinsically disrespectful about actually using others in this way that should prevent each agreeing to treat and be treated in these ways. There is nothing in his view that distinguishes this revised case morally from the original Chocolate Bar Case. But ought we not to disagree with this view and say that the people in this case are contemplating treating each other in a disrespectful manner that rules out the agreement?

3.A. In conclusion, I shall consider in some detail Gibbard's case involving two fathers (which I shall call the Fathers Case). Gibbard uses this case to drive home his view about how to reason from behind a veil of ignorance to a common goal that both parents would share. It is also a case he uses to show that it may be reasonable to reject acting on such a common goal.

Gibbard focuses on the potential loss to each of the parents, A and B, assuming it is worse for a parent to lose two children rather than one. He ultimately imagines the case so that parent A has one child at home and another in danger in a canoe.[32] Parent B's only two children need saving in the other endangered canoe. Only A is in a position to save anyone. Given this scenario, one possible state of the world would involve A saving his one endangered child, thus winding up with two children, and B winding up with no children, having lost two. Another possible state of the world would involve A's saving B's children, in which case A winds up with one child and B with two. The second state of the world involves higher overall utility since it includes two children rather than one being saved and also higher expected utility for each parent choosing from behind a veil of ignorance (on the assumption that each has an equal chance of being in A's or B's position). Gibbard argues that an individual behind a veil of ignorance seeking to do the best he can to further his own interests would choose the utilitarian principle, which implies that A should save B's two children.

Further along, Gibbard alters this rationale somewhat. The alteration involves his speaking in terms of a parent's "goal-scale" and maximizing the chances of achieving what is on his goal-scale, rather than speaking in terms of each parent's own good conceived of as his personal utility.[33] This change reflects Gibbard's worries about identifying a person's good and the possibility that a parent is concerned to save his children for reasons other than his own good (e.g., from love or a sense of responsibility). Gibbard is also open to the idea that different parents' reasons for wanting to save their own children can differ.[34] I shall here speak in terms of personal interests in discussing the Fathers Case, but everything I say could be put in terms of goal-scales.[35]

B. Let us now consider the state of the world in the Fathers Case in which A saves B's two children. Notice that it also involves the worst-off parent (with one child at home) being better off than the worst-off parent in the alternative state of the world in which parent B winds up with no children. This leaves it open that it is the desire to pick an arrangement in which a parent who will be the worst off is as well off as he can be, rather than the desire to maximize parents' ex ante expected utility, that underlies an arrangement that results in A's being required to save B's children.

Gibbard himself says that the choice of a principle for saving people in these circumstances is predicated on a parent avoiding the greatest loss.[36] He does not say that it is predicated on maximizing utility or saving the greatest number of children. Yet, he does say that it is the utilitarian principle that would be chosen in ignorance of whom one would be. In the Fathers Case, avoiding the greatest loss to a parent and maximizing utility do overlap, but that is not sufficient reason to say that it is the utilitarian principle, rather than the principle that minimizes a parent's worst loss, that the Fathers Case could support. There might be other cases in which maximizing utility (and prospective expected utility for someone choosing behind a veil of ignorance) would require risking an outcome that is worse than the worst outcome under a non-utility-maximizing alternative. In such cases, the utilitarian principle would diverge from the principle that tells one to minimize the greatest loss that an individual can suffer and the latter principle might seem more reasonable.

C. Now consider another case. Suppose that parent B has four children, two of whom are in an endangered canoe. Parent A has only one child and she is in the other endangered canoe. In one possible state of the world, B winds up with four children and A with none when A saves B's two children. In another possible state of the world, B winds up with two children and A with one child, because A saves his one child. Arguably, ex ante expected utility of each parent is highest if there is an agreement to bring about the first possible state of the world, as in that state a parent avoids the loss of two children rather than one, and we are assuming that each parent had an equal chance of being in the position of A or B. But the worst-off parent is better off in the second possible state of the world, for he has one child instead of none, and there is also greater equality between A and B because B still has two children.

Suppose all that is relevant is how things go for A and B (as this is how Gibbard discusses his case). Then it seems that it is the state with lower expected utility behind a veil of ignorance, but in which the parent in the worst-off position is better off, that is preferable if we take seriously the good of each parent as a separate person. It seems to me (and to Scanlon as well[37]) that taking seriously the good of each person as a separate person implies that we should be concerned with the eventual condition of each person outside a veil of ignorance, not just his expected utility considered from behind a veil of ignorance. To derive this same conclusion using the veil of ignorance device may require us to conceive of the function of the veil of ignorance differently from the way Gibbard does. As noted earlier, we may have to conceive of it as a device to get us to take seriously and compare pairwise the positions occupied by actual people beyond the veil, rather than thinking of those positions as slots into which one person might fall.

Of course, this sort of "maximin" reasoning (when focusing on the parents' goal-scale rather than the fate of the children per se) could still result in the requirement that parent B, if he rather than A were the only one capable of saving anyone, save A's one child rather than his own two children in the endangered canoe. This is because B has two children at home and A stands to lose his only child. That the maximin principle has this implication is one reason to think it too is wrong.

D. Next, suppose that parent A has only one child and that child is in an endangered canoe, and parent B has only one child and that child is in the other endangered canoe along with an orphan unloved by A or B. One possible state of the world would involve A saving his one child and B winding up with no children. In another possible state of the world, A winds up with no children because he saves B's one child and the orphan. If we just focus on the parents' goal-scales. it might not seem to matter much whether a principle is chosen behind the veil of ignorance that leads to one scenario rather than the other. But, of course, the loss to the children themselves should also matter, and given that they are the only ones who stand to lose their lives, it might seem that this is what matters the most, not the suffering of the parents or even their responsibilities to their own children. And an agreement on a principle that directs A to save the two children rather than one child maximizes each child's ex ante expected utility without violating a concern for making the position of the worst-off person as good as it can be. (This is because each child would be as badly off as any other child if not helped and each parent would be as badly off as any other parent if he loses a child.) These considerations suggest that A should save the two children and let his one child die.

E. But the considerations that we have examined so far imply more. For example, in Gibbard's original Fathers Case they imply that behind a veil of ignorance, an individual seeking to maximize his expected utility would agree to a principle that requires A to kill his child if this is causally necessary in order to save B's two children. Similarly, whatever supports the view that an agreement involving a requirement for A to let his child die if this is necessary in order to save B's child and an orphan would also seem to support the view that A should kill his child if it would help save B's child and an orphan. It is notoriously difficult to see why killing and letting die should be morally different in systems that aim to maximize expected utility (whether of children or parents). And considerations that support the view that B should abandon his two children when he has two others in order to save A's only child in order to make the condition of the worst-off parent as good as it can be would also imply that he should kill his two children in the canoe if this is necessary in order to save A's only child. This is because it is also hard to see why the distinction between killing and letting die should matter in a system concerned only with making the worst-off parent as well off as he can be.

F. Gibbard, of course, offers a reason that none of these arrangements that involve a parent letting die (or, I would add, killing) his own child would be chosen, namely, the strains of commitment (i.e., the strain of committing to such duties to kill or let die).This is one part of his answer to a question he explicitly poses despite his argument for a common goal-scale: "Is it ethically permissible for any of us to give special heed to our own special concerns and our own particular responsibilities? Doubtless yes, but why?"[38] Strains of commitment imply that one will care far more for one's own child at the time her life is in danger than one will care for engaging in a reciprocal relation with others to support an arrangement that is best for everyone, and to which one would have agreed behind a veil of ignorance when seeking to maximize one's own expected good had adherence been expected. Before considering the merit of relying on these strains of commitment in an argument, let us consider some other approaches to explaining the absence of the requirements to let die or kill in the cases we have been considering.

Some might argue that a utilitarian perspective would not imply that A is required to either let die or kill his child in order to save B's children. This is because a parent who could do this could not also have the sort of strong love for his child that in most other circumstances, and overall, makes for better lives for parents and their children. So those who engage in a contractualist procedure for the sake of humanistic concerns and maximal expected utility would want the stronger form of love to exist even though it tends to lower utility on some occasions; they would reject the requirements to abandon or kill one's child. (This is a form of Motive Utilitarianism, a two-level utilitarian theory under which one chooses the motive whose presence will maximize expected utility overall, and then one acts from it even on occasions when doing so does not maximize expected utility.)

Alternatively, those who emphasize impersonal values might simply think that a greater value—superstrong love of parent for child—existing in the world could be worth even an overall loss in life and other forms of utility, by comparison to a world containing only a shallower form of love that is compatible with requirements to kill or abandon one's child.

The view that the absence of a requirement to abandon one's child could be explained by a more intrinsically valuable type of love or by love that on the whole maximizes expected utility or by the strains of commitment faces the following problem: Such explanations seem to imply that other duties that we have no trouble thinking actually exist should not exist. For example, suppose that A's child is drowning and the only way to save her is for A to kill B's child or children. A might suffer strains of commitment in living up to a principle that prohibits the killing (just as he would suffer strains of commitment in living up to a principle that required him to abandon or kill his child to save B's child or children). A's superstrong love for his child might also tempt him to kill B's child. Yet, this does not in any way diminish our pretheoretical intuitive judgment, or the tendency of a nonconsequentialist ethical theory to imply, that A is morally required not to kill the other child or children in order to save his own. The child's right not to be killed is not overridden by the strain on A of commitment to respecting the right, the value of his superstrong love, or overall good consequences of such love. (It is the child's right, not B's expected despair at his child's being killed, that is the source of A's duty not to kill.)

An even greater strain of commitment for A might arise if all of his three children will drown unless he kills just one of B's four children. This strain of commitment might be greater than the strain A would feel if he were required to let one of his three children drown in order to prevent all of B's four children from drowning. Yet, this does not diminish our pretheoretical sense, or a nonconsequentialist theory's implication, that A is morally required not to kill one of B's four children (on account of the child's right not to be killed rather than B's expected despair) to prevent his three from drowning. This is so even if we also accept that A need not abandon one of his children to save B's four.

Suppose it is true that strains of commitment do not undermine the existence of a requirement not to kill a child (whether he belongs to some other parent or is an orphan) in these cases. This suggests that it is not strains of commitment but the *content* of the supposed requirement that A let his child die in order to save B's children that makes this not actually be a requirement. Indeed, it suggests that there being no such requirement is primarily due neither to strains of commitment nor to the intrinsic or consequential good of having superstrong love that abides by no requirements conflicting with it.

However, suppose that strains of commitment were weaker in refraining from killing someone's child, when killing is necessary in order to save all of one's own children, than in letting one's child die in order to save someone else's children. I suggest that this would indicate that the strain of commitment we experience is a function of whether we antecedently think we are truly obligated to do (or refrain from doing) something. This contrasts with the obligations we have to do (or refrain from doing) something being a function of whether we would experience strains of commitment.

There is another reason, I think, that strains of commitment do not account for there being no requirement on A to save B's children and let his own die. It is often possible to coerce people into carrying out their duties, and doing so might maximize expected utility. It is not always true that utility would go down once we factor in costs of coercion. For example, suppose A knew that the state would be legally required to put his daughter to death if he failed to let her die in order to save B's two children instead. Then there would be no good reason for him not to carry out his supposed duty to save B's children. The state's killing a child who was impermissibly saved could also deter other parents from avoiding their utilitarian duties in similar circumstances, and so it could be justified in a utilitarian system.

Gibbard says that he finds it plausible to plan to live with others on terms that no one could reasonably reject. Eventually, however, he seems to change this plan somewhat. He ultimately says that, on the basis of intuitions, he takes it that we should live with others in a way to which each would have reason to *voluntarily* adhere,[39] and "the way to live with people if one can, I take it, is on a *voluntary* basis that no one could reasonably reject."[40] But why, given his other views, is voluntary adherence to a rule or principle necessary so long as people could not reasonably reject the possibility of being coerced? After all, we do not reject coercion in cases where we doubt that people would voluntarily adhere to a requirement not to kill another's child in order to save their own children. This may be a case where we think they will fail to do voluntarily what they have reason to do voluntarily, but it is not clear why on Gibbard's view the same could not be said of letting one's child die in order to save other (or others') children. Furthermore, I argued earlier that it was not clear why Gibbard should take living on terms of mutual respect with others and living in a way that no one could reasonably reject as foundational in his system, rather than maximizing each individual's expected prospective good. Hence, given Gibbard's other views, it is also not clear why living on a voluntary basis should be important when some elements of involuntariness could increase each person's expected prospective good.[41]

## Notes

1. This chapter is based on my "Should You Save This Child? Intuitions, Contractualism, and Strains of Commitment," which was my commentary on Allan Gibbard's Tanner Lectures and is part of *Reconciling Our Aims: In Search of Bases for Ethics,* ed. B. Stroud (New York: Oxford University Press, 2008), the publication containing those lectures.
2. As quoted in Gibbard, Lecture I, 11.

3. Lecture I, 23.
4. This is similar to Dworkin's rejection of "morons" that we consider in Chapter 3.
5. Ibid., 22.
6. Ibid., 22.
7. Ibid.
8. Ibid., 23.
9. Ibid., 25.
10. Ibid., 23.
11. Ibid., 22.
12. Unlike Dworkin, Gibbard does not distinguish ethics from morality. (For more on Dworkin's view, see my discussion in Chapter 2 in this volume.)
13. Here he allows that intuitions can be nonbasic. Quotes are from Lecture II, 34.
14. In his "Contractualism and Utilitarianism," in *Utilitarianism and Beyond* (ed. A. Sen and B. Williams, (Cambridge: Cambridge University Press, 1982), 128.
15. Lecture II, 42.
16. In Lecture III, 68, Gibbard himself allows that common goals that people have could involve impersonal considerations, such as species diversity. He says that "coherence requirements don't rule this out." But it seems that on his view, these considerations are a part of morality only if people are concerned about them and it is good for them that their concerns are satisfied. Scanlon thinks the impersonal considerations are independent parts of noncontractualist morality.
17. See, for example, Temkin's "Equality, Priority, and the Levelling Down Objection," in *The Ideal of Equality*, ed. Matthew Clayton and Andrew Williams (London: Palgrave Macmillan, 2000), and Kagan's *The Geometry of Desert* (New York: Oxford University Press, 2012).
18. In Lecture III, he replaces "own good" with "goal-scale," as we shall see.
19. Lecture II, 43; Lecture III, 63–65.
20. This is the sort of tension between his and Scanlon's views on the point of morality that I referred to in 2.A.
21. It is also not clear why *agreeing* to principles plays a pivotal role in Gibbard's view of respectful treatment. He allows that a utilitarian principle that maximizes prospective average utility of each person might not be adhered to due to strains of commitment. Hence, it might not be agreed to behind the veil by those who could not count on reciprocal adherence by others or by those who could not reciprocate. But, presumably, these strains of commitment could be taken account of directly in formulating a utilitarian principle to which there could be adherence, without introducing the idea of agreement.
22. In *Utilitarianism and Beyond*. When giving his Tanner Lectures, Gibbard claimed that Scanlon had never written about his objections to Harsanyi, but in his Reply to Commentators in *Reconciling Our Aims*, Gibbard acknowledged his omission of the discussion in "Contractualism and Utilitarianism," to which I alerted him.
23. As he says in "Contractualism and Utilitarianism," 124–25.
24. Scanlon uses actual generic types of positions rather than actual individual positions but for simplicity's sake I shall not distinguish these. The distinction can be important

when we do not know that a determinate individual will occupy a determinate position.

25. "Contractualism and Utilitarianism," 124–25.
26. Like the splitting-of-oneself device that Thomas Nagel suggests in his "Equality," reprinted in his *Mortal Questions* (Cambridge: Cambridge University Press, 1979).
27. "Contractualism and Utilitarianism," 125.
28. He follows Thomas Nagel, who, in "Equality," argues that pairwise comparison comes closest to being the correct way to combine people's different interests in an outcome. This raises the problem for Scanlon of whether his contractualism can ever allow the concerns of a number of individuals to outweigh the concerns of a single individual when deciding on a principle. He tries to deal with this issue in his *What We Owe to Each Other* (Cambridge, MA: Harvard University Press, 1999).
29. This example is based on the reasoning Peter Singer uses to argue for preferring to save the life of a nondisabled person rather than a disabled person, other things equal. See his "Double Jeopardy and the Use of QALYS in Health Care Allocation," reprinted in *Unsanctifying Human Life* (Oxford: Blackwell, 2002).
30. See "Contractualism and Utilitarianism," 125.
31. Gibbard raised this example in response to my oral comments on his Tanner Lectures at the University of California Berkeley, March 2, 2006.
32. Lecture II, 36.
33. Lecture III, 64–65.
34. Ibid., 66.
35. Ibid., 65. Gibbard also claims that if the parents do not choose a common goal-scale that will, from behind a veil of ignorance and assuming an equal chance of being in either position, maximize each one's chances of saving his children, then they could be involved in a prisoner's dilemma. A prisoner's dilemma involves each parent actually winding up worse off with respect to satisfying his goal-scale than he would have been if each had abided by the common goal-scale. However, it seems that a prisoner's dilemma will not result in a one-time Fathers Case. If A were to fail to save B's two children in order to save his one child, he will wind up better off than if he had abided by a common goal-scale principle that would have maximized his prospects of achieving his goal-scale ex ante. It seems that it is only if we consider multiple instances of situations like the Fathers Case that avoiding a prisoner's dilemma can be added to the rationale for each parent's choosing the principle that requires A to save B's two children in the Fathers Case.
36. Lecture II, 36–37.
37. See "Contractualism and Utilitarianism," as discussed earlier.
38. Lecture III, 79.
39. Ibid., 66.
40. Ibid., 80.
41. I am grateful to Arthur Applbaum, Ruth Chang, Shelly Kagan, Jeff McMahan, and Larry Temkin for their suggestions on my comments on Gibbard's Tanner Lectures on which this chapter is based.

# PART II

# RIGHTS AND THE TROLLEY PROBLEM

# 6
# Neuroscience, Psychology, and Moral Reasoning

In previous chapters we have both used and considered the use of intuitive judgments about hypothetical cases such as those concerning the Trolley Problem. This methodology is common in contemporary normative theory, especially in discussions of trolley problems. Experimental work in psychology has studied many persons' intuitive responses in trolley problem cases.[1] In this chapter we will consider some claims made on the basis of psychological and neuroscientific study of the Trolley Problem in advance of considering this problem again philosophically in subsequent chapters.[2]

We should keep in mind that there are differences in the philosopher's and in the psychologist's approach to studying intuitive responses. First, the philosopher considers her own intuitive judgments, not the judgments of many people gathered in psychological experiments or surveys. A philosopher is trying to find out why she intuitively thinks conduct is permissible or impermissible and whether these judgments are correct. Unlike psychologists, philosophers are not particularly interested in understanding what (they believe) are incorrect judgments. For example, suppose that psychological studies showed that most people think that pressing a switch that causes a device to topple a man into the trolley to stop it from hitting five is permissible, though pushing him over is not. If a philosopher intuitively judges both these cases impermissible, she will probably not seek an explanation that accounts for what she thinks is the wrong judgment. However, any justification she offers for other intuitive judgments may make clear why the wrong judgment is wrong. Second, many psychologists think of intuitive judgments as "gut" reactions that are not really judgments at all but mere emotional responses. By contrast, philosophers think that many intuitive reactions to moral issues are judgments as much as intuitive judgments in mathematics or metaphysics. There may be an emotional response to the intuitive judgment that something is morally wrong, but this need not mean that the judgment that something is wrong is based on the emotional response. However, even psychologists sometimes use the notion of intuitive response to apply to what they do not consider mere gut reactions. For example, like philosophers, they may think the response that it is permissible to turn a trolley from five people to one different person is properly characterized as an intuitive judgment

*Rights and Their Limits: In Theory, Cases, and Pandemics*. F. M. Kamm, Oxford University Press.
© Oxford University Press 2022. DOI: 10.1093/oso/9780197567739.003.0006

even if they also characterize it as involving cost/benefit reasoning rather than an emotional response. Furthermore, philosophers' "nongut" intuitive judgments are not derived from a theory to which they are antecedently committed; rather, they can serve as ground for developing a theory. As noted in Chapter 5, Allan Gibbard refers to them as judgments not based on any other judgment, though I have claimed that one may uncover factors that account for and justify them.[3] Finally, while psychologists think of intuitive responses as quick, by contrast to explicit reasoning that is slower, a philosophical intuitive judgment can also take time to form when it depends on fully grasping the details of a complex case.

In the first section of the following discussion, I review an objection raised by Selim Berker to the relevance of neuroscience to normative moral conclusions.[4] In the second section, I critically examine some factors that psychologists have suggested account for responses to trolley problem cases. In the third section, I first consider what a consequentialist response to experimental cases would be and argue that the data on turning the trolley do not necessarily reveal consequentialist responses (or cognitive processing associated with them) but are consistent with a form of nonconsequentialist response involving a prerogative to promote the greater good. I also suggest new experiments that would help make clear whether people's responses are consequentialist, nonconsequentialist, or prioritarian. In the remaining parts of the section, I raise additional doubts about the possibility of deriving normative conclusions directly from neuroscientific data by considering what we would think if we were confronted with certain *hypothetical* experimental data.

## I

Functional magnetic resonance imaging (fMRI) in early studies run by Joshua Greene[5] was said to show that when people judge it permissible to turn a trolley headed to five persons away from them though it will then hit and kill another person, brain centers involved in cognitive processes (and associated with rational thought) are stimulated.[6] By contrast, fMRI studies were said to show that when people judge it to be impermissible to push someone over a bridge into the trolley's path, so that his body stops it from killing the five but he dies, brain centers associated with emotion are stimulated.[7]

Some believe that these data suggest that consequentialist moral judgments involve cognitive processes to a greater degree than do deontological (or more broadly nonconsequentialist) judgments.[8]

Within the philosophical literature devoted to trolley problems, the intuitive judgment that one may not push the person over the bridge in order to maximize lives saved has been regarded by some as a reason to believe that there are deontological restrictions (or side constraints) on maximizing the good, such as duties correlative to individual rights. One way of interpreting the fMRI results just described is that they show that this intuitive judgment does not support the existence of deontological restrictions.[9] An argument for this conclusion is that if the intuitive judgments in question are the output of emotion centers of the brain, this is a sign that the judgments are morally incorrect. By contrast, insofar as the judgment that one should save the most lives is an output of the cognitive centers of the brain, this is a sign that this judgment is morally correct. Thus, the results of the fMRIs support consequentialism as opposed to deontology as a normative matter.

There are many gaps in this sketch of an argument from fMRI data to normative conclusions. The argument sounds like a pure procedural argument for rightness with the brain part substituting for a procedure: If a particular procedure (or brain part) leads to an answer, it is the right answer. Those who rely on a procedural account of rightness, however, must give an independent argument for what makes this the right procedure to use. Similarly, one would need to know why the cognitive part of the brain is better for generating moral answers than the emotion part.[10]

One strategy for answering this question is to have an independent argument for identifying the right answers and then show that one part of the brain but not another generates judgments that involve the right answers. But if one could identify what makes an answer right in some way other than by showing that it is generated by a certain center in the brain, neuroscience would not be necessary for discovering the right answer. It could only serve as a supplemental indication of the right answer.

As Selim Berker observes, the strategy of identifying in some other way what makes an answer right was used by those (e.g., Peter Singer[11]) who have argued as follows: A correct moral answer must be impersonal rather than concerned with personal factors. The emotion center of the brain responds more to personal factors, where "personal" is here taken to mean that one would have to make physical contact with a man to push him over a bridge. Hence, it gives wrong answers. (It might be that emotional responses to personal factors incorporate the results of early human evolution, concerned with regulating harm only in situations in which people come into direct personal contact with each other.) The cognitive part of the brain works with impersonal factors, where "impersonal" is here taken to mean that one merely has to press a switch to trigger a mechanical device that turns the trolley rather than have personal physical contact with the person one harms.[12] Therefore, it will yield correct answers. Berker notes that if one disagrees that such personal factors are irrelevant to correct moral conclusions, then one might reject the view that the center that ignores such personal factors gives the right answer. Hence, the emotion center could be taking account of factors that are reasons bearing on right conduct. In any case, the important point, Berker argues, is that all the normative work in this argument using neuroscience is being done by a moral theory about what factors make acts right (e.g., impersonal versus personal factors understood in the way described) and by a theory about what factors a deontologist as opposed to a consequentialist thinks are morally relevant—not by neuroscience.[13] Unless something else can be said to fill the gap in the argument from fMRI data to normative conclusions, Berker's conclusion that neuroscience data is normatively insignificant seems to follow.

## II

Those who argue from fMRI data to normative conclusions must also show that responses to what are independently deemed to be morally irrelevant factors account for the deontological responses. In this section I will consider whether they have successfully done this.

As already noted, Joshua Greene (and also Peter Singer) tried at one point to explain the difference in intuitive judgments about pushing the man over the bridge by contrast to turning the trolley, observing that someone would be up close and personal to the person he pushes in a way he would not be in turning the trolley by a switch, a mechanical means, at a distance. Subsequently, Greene argued that any "personal force" (such as using a pole to topple the man from the bridge), not just a push, would elicit the same negative response. It seemed clear that it is irrelevant morally whether we harm someone up close and/or with personal force or instead via mechanical means. Suppose deontological responses were reactions to such a morally irrelevant factor. Then, Greene argues, deontological philosophers' attempts to justify intuitive judgments about constraints on harming people by pointing to other, seemingly morally relevant factors amount to mere "confabulation" or rationalization.[14] That is, they create what seem like reasons to justify what is really an emotional response to a morally irrelevant factor.[15]

However, objections can be raised to this type of "personal versus impersonal" explanation of intuitions in trolley problem cases. For example, I have argued in earlier work that what I call the Lazy Susan Case is a counterexample to this explanation. In one version of this case, five people are on one side of a Lazy Susan turntable and the only way to save them from a trolley headed at them is to manually push the Lazy Susan. However, our doing this will push the Lazy Susan into a person standing nearby, killing him. In this case, it is intuitively permissible to use personal force to push a Lazy Susan into a person. We could also imagine a fanciful case involving only bodily contact between persons: Suppose I hold several children on one side of my body and a trolley is headed toward killing them. I am not personally threatened but to save the children I must swivel myself in such a way that I then push another person off a cliff. Intuitively, even a nonconsequentialist and supporter of individual rights might agree it is permissible to act in these two cases.[16] Greene has responded that what accounts for this (and responses in some other variants of the Lazy Susan Case) is that the significance of personal force is diminished when it interacts with only foreseen rather than intended harm (as occurs when the man is toppled from the bridge in front of the trolley to stop it hitting the five). But if this were true, it should also be permissible to turn a Lazy Susan with no one on it if doing this would stop a trolley from hitting five people though the turning Lazy Susan will hit and kill another person as a side effect. Yet intuitively I think doing this is impermissible. (What if many in psychological tests say it is permissible to use the Lazy Susan in this case? As described in my introduction, as a philosopher I am trying to explain and possibly justify intuitive responses that I [as someone who has them] have. The explanation I propose may also show why alternative intuitive responses are not correct.) Cases like the Lazy Susan Case led me to say that "nonconsequentialists are not squeamish, they are downstreamish," in the sense that they are willing to "up close" and/or with personal force harm someone when (very roughly) the person's being killed is causally downstream from the good of the greater number of people being saved.[17] In the Lazy Susan and trolley cases in which people or the trolley is turned away this is what happens, for the five are saved and the consequence is that one is killed. It is not what happens when we either push someone over the bridge as our causal means to saving the five or use means to stop the trolley that as a side effect kills a person (as in the case where a Lazy Susan with no one on it is turned). I refer to bringing about lesser harm as a consequence of greater good (itself not brought about by harming someone inappropriately) as a theory about "how" we come to kill someone. However, it should be clear that I do not mean by "how" whether someone pressed a switch or instead pushed someone, as pressing a switch to topple someone into the trolley (rather than pushing him) to save five people would also not be a case of bringing about a lesser harm as a consequence of (i.e., causally downstream from) that greater good.[18]

Furthermore, suppose that fMRI data showed that the brain's cognitive centers were as involved and the emotion centers no more involved in the judgment that it is permissible to personally push the Lazy Susan that moves people away from the trolley (or personally swivel myself to remove the children from the trolley) as in the judgment that it is permissible to turn the trolley. Then that a judgment involves an "up close" or "personal force" factor would not stand in the way of its involving the cognitive center to the same degree as judgments about turning the trolley from five to one by a pressing a switch at a distance.

On the other hand, other cases involving no personal contact or personal force could be impermissible. For example, what if it were possible to press a switch that opens a trap door under the man on the bridge so that he falls onto the trolley track and is killed when the trolley hits him, thus stopping the trolley? Or suppose it were possible to press a switch sending a second trolley onto a bridge to topple one person into the path of the trolley headed to killing five. Regardless of what fMRIs of the general population indicate, someone who objects to pushing the man over the bridge could respond in the same way to this physically impersonal way of getting the man off the bridge. Furthermore, if fMRIs of those who reject the permissibility of opening the trap door or sending this second trolley indicated an elevated emotional response to doing so, this would indicate that activity in the brain's emotion center is related to something other than personal involvement (in the sense that Greene and Singer use as described earlier). It might simply be a response to doing something judged wrong on grounds other than personal involvement.

Based on their empirical studies, psychologists have proposed other factors besides personal contact or force that are relevant to judgments of impermissibility of harm in trolley problem cases. These are action (versus omission) and intending harm as a means (versus foreseeing it as a side effect). Drawing these distinctions is not the same as offering justification for them. Such a justification is aimed at by philosophers who argue that action is important when it is a way to impose first on what someone has a prior claim to (e.g., his body); by contrast omitting aid only deprives someone of another's efforts, and getting those efforts could involve imposing first on that person.[19] However, action that ends one's provision of lifesaving aid to another who thereby loses out on only life one provides need not be impermissible. This suggests that it is the harming/not aiding distinction that may be morally important rather than the action/omission distinction. In any case, action is involved in both turning the trolley and toppling someone from the bridge so the action/omission distinction need not be playing a role in drawing a moral distinction between these cases. It also does not seem correct to always associate harm being a means with it being intended. For example, Greene thinks that harm is intended in Thomson's Loop Case in which a trolley is turned away from the five but would loop back toward them if it did not hit the person on the track. But it is arguable that in this case someone may turn the trolley only **because** it will hit the person (and thereby cause the trolley to stop) without intending that the person be hit.[20] Importantly, combining action involving personal force with intending harm as a means need not make an act impermissible. For example, consider a version of the Bad Man Trolley Case: A bad man who does not care about saving the five physically turns the trolley away from them as the switch is broken in order to kill the one person on the other track as a means to acquiring her inheritance. He would only act on his intention to kill the one person in a circumstance when the five will be saved by turning the trolley from them. Since his turning the trolley is intuitively permissible, despite personal force and intending harm as a means, these factors cannot explain (totally) why using personal force to topple someone from the bridge to stop the trolley seems impermissible. Those who use empirical studies to identify factors that are supposed to account for judgments of impermissibility should also test if there are counter cases in which these factors are present but do not intuitively render harmful actions impermissible. Searching for hypothetical counter cases is one way a philosopher checks proposals for factors that account for judgments.

Greene's subsequent proposal for why it may intuitively seem impermissible for a bystander to topple the man in front of the trolley to stop its hitting the five is "overgeneralization". That is, on most occasions pushing someone into a trolley would be contrary to maximizing utility since it would harm someone for no greater good and on those grounds should be impermissible. He thinks overgeneralization leads to a failure to judge moral permissibility on the basis of the actual cost/benefit ratio in the case where harming one person would save five other people and maximize utility. He supports this view about toppling the man from the bridge by considering a case in which someone will die in a fire unless he jumps from a building. He says that emotionally the person will resist doing this because on most occasions jumping from a building is bad for one and does not maximize utility. However, it is obviously right (prudentially speaking) to jump in the fire case.

One concern I have about this explanation of judging it wrong to topple the man from the bridge is why overgeneralization does not stand in the way of judgments of moral permissibility or prudential correctness in many other cases though it would continue to stand in the way of judging it permissible to topple the man from the bridge. In the case of jumping from the fire, initial emotional resistance would be overcome in a reasonable agent acting in his own interests. Even in inter- rather than intrapersonal cases we either do not generalize or easily overcome generalization. Here are two examples: (1) Ordinarily leaving a person to die when it is extremely easy to save them and no greater good is at stake in not saving them is intuitively judged to be impermissible. Yet when we cannot save everyone and must choose between easily saving one person or easily saving five other people, we find it intuitively permissible to leave the one person to die. We do not overgeneralize. (2) Consider someone who finds it intuitively permissible to turn the trolley from the five when it will kill one other person but impermissible to topple another person from the bridge in order to save five from the trolley not only when the person toppled would be killed but also when only his legs would be paralyzed. Nevertheless, suppose someone who judges in this way finds out that instead of turning the trolley and killing the one person, he can save the five by toppling that same person when this will only paralyze that person's legs. He could find it intuitively permissible to do that since it is better for the same person himself to be paralyzed than killed. There would be no overgeneralization from the judgment that it is wrong to topple someone, paralyzing his legs, when this was one's only way to save the five. Secondarily, as a substitute for what would have been a permissible turning of the trolley despite its killing one person, an act of toppling that would were it one's only option be impermissible can become permissible. This is an instance of what I call the Principle of Secondary Permissibility.[21] The willingness to overcome ordinary resistance to doing something in these two cases suggests that it isn't mere overgeneralization that lies behind the view that it is impermissible to topple someone when it is one's only way to save the five and that accounts for continuing resistance to doing so.

Suppose that there is a continuing higher emotional response to toppling someone, even when this satisfies secondary permissibility, than to turning the trolley on someone. The fact that one would overcome the emotional response to toppling when it satisfies secondary permissibility but not in the standard toppling case suggests that it is not the emotional response in the latter case (or not it alone) that makes one reject the act. If it were, the act would also be morally rejected in the case where secondary permissibility is satisfied. Hence, it would have been useful for psychologists who focus on resistance in the standard toppling case to have run an experiment in which this case is compared (both with respect to brain activity and intuitive judgment of permissibility) with the case involving toppling someone in order to prevent his suffering an even worse fate by redirecting the trolley toward him. I will call this Experiment Proposal 1 (as others will follow).

Suppose that people's intuitive judgments about permissible conduct in the trolley cases do not track the physically personal/impersonal distinction (as drawn earlier) or any of the other factors proposed by psychologists that I have reviewed. This raises the possibility that different factors that some philosophers offer to explain and also justify intuitive judgments in trolley cases are the factors that judgments really do track. Then these factors would not be confabulations. But could these factors explain or justify an intuitive judgment that someone reaches without being consciously aware of the factors, given that the search for explanations and justifications occurs after the judgment? As noted in Chapter 5, that one becomes consciously aware of a factor after making a judgment need not mean that it was not present unconsciously, causing the judgment. Alternatively, some shorthand heuristic that is correlated with the factor may have caused the judgment, so that the factor could be indirectly involved in causing the judgment.[22] Most importantly, that one only becomes aware of certain factors in a case after one intuitively makes a judgment does not mean that the factors cannot help justify the judgment, whether or not they causally explain the occurrence of the judgment. If they are justifying, they are not rationalizations or confabulations in the debunking sense of lacking objective merit.[23]

## III

In the remainder of this discussion, I will raise further questions about whether certain psychological and neuroscientific data reveal consequentialist or nonconsequentialist responses and whether neuroscientific data have normative implications. I will also propose some experiments that might help settle some of these questions.

### A. What Data Would Be Needed to Decide Whether People Make Consequentialist Judgments

To know whether fMRI data show that consequentialist responses involve cognitive processing to a greater degree than do deontological responses, we must know when a response is consequentialist or deontological (or something else).[24]

(i) Act consequentialism determines that the right act is always one that maximizes the good over the bad. (I will refer to this as the act that maximizes the good.) It rules out deontological side constraints (such as duties correlative to individual rights) on producing that good. It also gives one a duty to do the act that maximizes the good. Nonconsequentialists claim that there are deontological constraints on maximizing the good. Hence, they may think that it could be impermissible to bring about someone's death in some particular way though it would maximize lives saved. This leaves it open that they might think it is permissible (and even obligatory) to bring death about in another way (e.g., in a "downstreamish" way) when it would maximize lives saved. Nonconsequentialism need not deny that consequences matter; it is just claims that they are not all that matter. Hence, the nonconsequentialist need not hold that all ways of bringing about someone's death in order to maximize the good are impermissible and violate deontological constraints. This bears on whether we should say that a judgment that it is permissible for the bystander to turn the trolley from five to one is appropriately called a consequentialist judgment as has been claimed. After all, if a nonconsequentialist holds that it is permissible to save the greater number of people by killing some others *in a particular way* such as redirecting a threat, the judgment that it is permissible to turn the trolley may just as likely be a nonconsequentialist response as a consequentialist response.

This bears on the view that different parts of the brain are activated to a greater degree depending on whether we have deontological or consequentialist responses. Suppose that the intuitions about the permissibility of killing by turning the trolley and the impermissibility of killing in other cases is explained and justified by a nonconsequentialist theory about individual rights. Then if the cognitive part of the brain is activated when we decide it is permissible to turn the trolley, nonconsequentialist responses would be associated with activity in this part of the brain as much as with the emotion part of the brain. Indeed, perhaps only the killings that are impermissible from a deontological point of view involve the emotional center in those who think them impermissible.[25] Whether the perceived impermissibility of an act, whatever its content, is what is connected with an emotional response is a hypothesis that might be tested experimentally. Hence, I will call this Experiment Proposal 2.

Greene, however, describes decisions to turn the trolley as "characteristically consequentialist" in that they are easily seen to be appropriate on the basis of cost/benefit calculations but would require a more complex explanation in order to be justified by someone who supports deontological constraints. Similarly, he describes judgments as "characteristically deontological," though a consequentialist could accept them if he did "a lot of extra explaining."[26] To see that this way of categorizing responses may be problematic, consider another example in which Greene claims that a judgment is easily justified on consequentialist grounds. In his Crying Baby Dilemma, "it is wartime, and you and some of your fellow villagers are hiding from enemy soldiers. . . . Your baby starts to cry, and you cover your baby's mouth to block the sound. If you remove your hand . . . the soldiers will . . . find you and . . . kill everyone they find including you and your baby. If you do not remove your hand, your baby will smother to death. Is it okay to smother your baby to death in order to save yourself and the other villagers?"[27] Greene says that "in the crying baby case . . . a cost-benefit analysis strongly favors smothering the baby. After all, the baby is going to die no matter what, and so you have nothing to lose (in consequentialist terms) and much to gain by smothering it."[28]

Notice that while cost/benefit act consequentialism easily implies this conclusion to smother, it draws no moral distinction between killing a baby who will soon die anyway to save others and, in a different case, killing a baby who will not soon die anyway to save the others. Both killings are morally required according to act consequentialism. Furthermore, it draws no moral distinction between killing a baby whose crying makes it a threat (albeit not a morally guilty threat) to others and killing a baby who is not such a threat but whose death would save the lives of others. By contrast, a nonconsequentialist who agrees that it is permissible to kill the baby in Greene's case will emphasize the fact that the baby is no worse off than he otherwise would have been—a fact that Greene himself emphasizes—and, furthermore, that the baby was a threat. It seems wrong to describe a judgment as "characteristically consequentialist" just because a deontologist will bring in other factors besides simple cost/benefit analysis to account for and justify the judgment if those who describe the judgment as consequentialist themselves bring in such factors as Greene does when he emphasizes that the baby "is going to die anyway." This is especially true if people who endorse one judgment described as "characteristically consequentialist" would not as easily endorse other implications of a simple consequentialist approach (such as killing a nonthreatening baby who wasn't going to die anyway when it will save only two other people).

Hence, the crucial issue is whether the cost/benefit calculation takes place (i) after a side constraint or some other factor (such as "is not a threat" or "won't die anyway") is judged to be absent or (ii) independently of checking for a side constraint or such another factor being absent (as a consequentialist would do). It is not enough to check on whether there is a desire to promote a greater good rather than harm someone for its own sake in order to determine if the act is consequentialist or not. Seeking to turn the trolley from a desire to maximize lives saved but only subsequent to checking for the presence of a nonoverridden side constraint need not make that act consequentialist.[29]

(ii) In addition to denying that there are no constraints on maximizing the good, nonconsequentialists may also deny that there is a duty to maximize the good. These are separable points. Some nonconsequentialists deny both claims. That is, they claim there are constraints on maximizing the good and also that there is (what has come to be called) a "personal prerogative" not to maximize the good as impersonally conceived. This view entails that is there is no duty to maximize the impersonal good. However, some "semi-" nonconsequentialists have argued that there may be no constraints on maximizing the impersonal good but there is a personal prerogative not to do so (and so no duty to do so).[30] Others have argued that there may be constraints on maximizing the impersonal good but no such prerogative (and hence that there is a duty within constraints to maximize the good).[31] The contrast between acting from an impersonal perspective and acting on a personal prerogative that values things out of proportion to their value from an impersonal (or impartial) perspective is what is typically described as the impersonal/personal distinction in moral theory. It is not the same as the distinction (described earlier) between mechanically mediated actions and those that are physically up close and personal or use personal force that some who discuss the trolley problem have used to distinguish acting impersonally from acting personally. For example, someone might exercise a personal prerogative to mechanically turn a trolley (an impersonal act on the earlier proposal) away from five friends rather than turn another trolley away from six strangers (which would be favored from an impersonal perspective on the current and typical view of "impersonal").

Those who have run fMRI studies and discussed them have, at times, been interested simply in the supposed neurophysiological basis of the contrast between thinking it is permissible to produce the greatest good and thinking it is required to abide by constraints on producing the greatest good. Greene begins his discussion of trolley cases by saying that they raise the questions "*Ought* you to turn the trolley?" and "*Ought* you to save the five others by pushing the stranger to his death?"[32] However, in the actual experiment he ran, he says, "Participants responded to each dilemma by indicating whether they judged the action it proposes to be 'appropriate' or 'inappropriate.'"[33] If one ought to turn the trolley, this suggests that it is right to do so or that one has a duty to turn it and one ought not fail to turn it. If it is merely appropriate to turn the trolley (or push the person), this need not imply that it is inappropriate not to turn (or not push) but only that it is permissible to turn (or push) and also permissible not to turn (or push). (However, saying that it is inappropriate to push the person off the bridge implies that it is only appropriate to not push him and so one ought not to push him.) On account of the actual wording of the question, it seems that these fMRI tests have investigated only whether people think it is "permissible" to turn the trolley and whether it is "permissible" to throw the man off the bridge.

If people think it is permissible to turn the trolley or some even think it is permissible to throw the man off the bridge, this does not imply that they think there is a duty to do so or that one ought to do so. And indeed, many nonconsequentialists who think it is permissible to turn the trolley think there is no duty to do so. They think there is a personal prerogative not to turn it.[34] By contrast, act consequentialism implies that one has a duty (i.e., it is morally required) to turn the trolley and to throw the man off the bridge. Hence, it is only if respondents in surveys and in the fMRI studies held that they had a duty to push the man off the bridge and/or a duty to turn the trolley that they would be providing act consequentialist judgments strictly speaking.

The important implication of this for experimental design is that unless the questions asked are "Do you have a duty to . . . ?" or "Are you obligated to . . . ?" we shall not know the answer to the question whether their intuitive judgments are best described as act consequentialist. Call the proposal for running such an experiment Experiment Proposal 3.[35] (Of course, those who say that pushing the man over the bridge is impermissible will also deny the duty to push him, so the question of whether there is a duty to push the man over the bridge should only be asked of those who say that doing so is permissible.)

Some surveys conducted by Marc Hauser asked something like the "duty" question about turning the trolley. The respondents never claim that there is anything like a duty to turn the trolley.[36] Hauser (unlike Greene initially) used cases with a bystander not the trolley conductor turning the trolley. Notice that if respondents said there is a duty only for a conductor to turn the trolley, this is not support for the consequentialist view that both conductor and bystanders have such duties. Indeed, Judith Thomson[37] now denies that the bystander is even permitted to turn the trolley (a change from her past views) while insisting that the conductor has a duty to do so since he would otherwise kill five people (rather than merely let them die as the bystander would). Greene's original experiments used the Conductor Case and so a "duty to turn the trolley" (as well as an "appropriate" answer) would not be surprising in that case even from a nonconsequentialist responder. Nevertheless, I have argued that it would be morally impermissible even for the conductor to topple someone from the bridge and into the path of the trolley (just as it is for the bystander in the original version of that case), even by means involving no "personal force" (e.g., pressing a switch to trigger a device that pushes him off).[38]

Hence, any correlation between fMRI evidence of cognitive processing in Greene's early studies and the decision to turn the trolley seems not to show that cognitive processing is connected with consequentialism but rather that it is connected with a view that includes a prerogative to turn the trolley (or perhaps a duty for the trolley driver). That means there would be a personal prerogative to act in a physically impersonal way. If those who think it is permissible to push the man off the bridge also did not think there was a duty to do so, then evidence of cognitive processing in connection with the permission to push him and to turn the trolley would at most show that more cognitive processing is connected with a form of semi-(non)consequentialism involving the absence of constraints and the presence of a personal prerogative. In this case there would be a personal prerogative to do even something physically up close and personal that harmed someone as a means.

It would be useful if the "duty questions" were also asked in cases where there would be increasing efforts required of a bystander to turn the trolley and to push the man over the bridge. This would tell us whether respondents thought it would be permissible to refuse to turn the trolley or push the man as the sacrifice required to help the five becomes greater, though not as great as the loss of life to each of the five people that would be averted. Act consequentialism implies that it would not be permissible to refuse. The ultimate questions along these lines would involve asking whether, if one were the person to whom the trolley could be redirected, one would have a duty to turn the trolley upon oneself and so sacrifice one's life to save the five as act consequentialism implies. Alternatively, it might be asked whether, if one were the person on the bridge, one would have a duty to jump (or let oneself be pushed) to interfere with the trolley hitting the five. Saying "no" to these questions would be inconsistent with act consequentialism, which implies a duty in all these cases. Call this Experiment Proposal 4.

(iii) The greater good in the standard trolley cases—five people not being killed—is the result of aggregating the benefit of continuing life to different people. (A greater good could also be generated in this way by aggregating the benefit to two people of not being killed.) Many associate supporters of utilitarianism (and consequentialism more generally) with an interest in saving more people from death whether or not doing so involves harming others. However, some of these very same supporters of utilitarianism are committed to aggregating many small benefits to each of very many people and seeing if this aggregate is a greater good for the sake of which they could be philosophically committed to killing another person.

Hence, a different set of trolley cases might involve deciding whether it is permissible (a) to turn a trolley away from breaking a finger of each of 10,000 people when doing this will kill someone on another track or (b) to topple someone from a bridge when his being hit will kill him but also stop the trolley breaking a finger of each of 10,000 people. (We might test whether an aggregate of lesser benefits to each really is a greater good by judging whether it would be permissible to leave someone to die [rather than kill him] to prevent the same aggregate of lesser harms.) One interesting feature of such cases is that they can distinguish consequentialist responses from prioritarian responses. Roughly, prioritarianism gives priority to helping or not harming those who would be worse off if not helped or harmed as determined by comparing the expected fates of individuals as individuals. Only once the fates of those to be helped or harmed are approximately the same would it be judged permissible to interpersonally aggregate costs and benefits. Hence, another important contrast to consequentialism besides theories that embrace deontological side constraints is prioritarianism.

Suppose someone found it morally permissible (and even required) to kill a person (even by toppling him) to save 5 from the trolley but did not find it permissible to kill a person to save 10,000 from each having his finger broken. Then it is unlikely that their judgment in the first case was act consequentialist even if they do not abide by a deontological side constraint and do not recognize a nonconsequentialist personal prerogative. Rather, their judgment in the first case may have been conditioned on all potential victims facing death (or something on a par with it). This condition would have had to be satisfied before they could proceed to interpersonally aggregate; they would not proceed to a consequentialist form of cost/benefit calculation if the prior condition was not met. (This is structurally similar to checking whether a deontological constraint is present before proceeding to a cost/benefit calculation even if the content of the constraint is different.[39]) Call testing for prioritarianism by using the cases I have described Experiment Proposal 5.

## B. Using Data to Support Normative Conclusions

In III.A, we considered whether responses that had certain brain activity associated with them were consequentialist, prioritarian, or deontological. But as discussed in Section I, some have also wanted to use fMRI data to directly draw normative conclusions about which responses are morally correct. In considering this issue further, I believe it is useful to consider *hypothetical* results of possible experiments in order to test someone's commitment to drawing normative implications directly from fMRI data.

(i) Suppose that questions in Experiment Proposals 3 and 4 were phrased in terms of duties to turn the trolley or to push the man over the bridge. Further suppose that the respondents said that there are no such duties and/or that there are no such duties when the effort required for the turning or pushing goes up (but is still less than the loss that could be prevented by the effort). Suppose also that when the "no duty to turn the trolley" and "no duty to push the man" answers are given, the cognitive parts of the brain are shown by fMRIs to be functioning as much as, and the emotion parts no more than, when the "permissible to turn the trolley" and "permissible to push the man" answers are given. Then it would seem that those who think that the latter fMRI data (quite directly) support the *correctness* of the moral judgment to save the greater number in both cases should equally think the hypothetical new fMRI data support the correctness of the anti–act consequentialist view that there is no duty to save the greater number whenever this would maximize the good. They would then be using the fMRI data to support the normative claim that the correct moral view includes a prerogative not to maximize the good, even if it does not include a constraint on maximizing the good. They would be using fMRI data not to normatively support act consequentialism but rather to support one version of semi-(non)consequentialism that involves no constraint but a personal prerogative.

At this point, it is, perhaps, worth noting that the philosopher Henry Sidgwick argued that reason supports acting on self-interest (or the interests of those who bear a special relation to oneself) as much as it supports acting to produce the greatest good or doing only what is morally permissible.[40] In the light of this philosophical view, one could also test whether fMRI data show that cognitive parts of the brain are heavily involved when someone makes purely self-interested decisions (a) to turn a trolley originally headed to him in order to save himself though the trolley then kills five others (who had nothing to do with sending the trolley to him) and (b) to push five people into the trolley in order save himself from it. Call this Experiment Proposal 6. Suppose that the fMRI data showed cognitive centers were heavily involved. Then those who think it is correct to directly use the original fMRI data to argue that there are no deontological constraints and that maximizing the good is morally correct would be committed to also arguing that the new data suggest that it is morally permissible to kill five people in order to save oneself. This is clearly the wrong conclusion to reach.

Next, suppose additional fMRI data collected when asking the duty questions about turning the trolley or pushing the man (in Experiment Proposal 3) showed more activation of emotion parts of the brain in those who said (1) there is a duty to push the man over the bridge to save five, (2) there is a duty to turn the trolley to save five, or (3) there is a duty not to kill five to save oneself, by contrast to those who say there is no duty but only a permission to do these things. Then those who have argued that fMRI data on emotion-related brain activity suggest that the judgment not to push the man over the bridge is incorrect should also conclude that the fMRI data that I am now imagining suggest that the consequentialist view that there is a duty to save the greater number (or not to harm them) is incorrect.

Of course, the fMRI data in response to the duty questions or in response to the question whether there is a permission to kill five to save oneself may, in fact, be entirely different than I have imagined. The point of imagining such data is to see whether those who believe that act consequentialism is correct would be satisfied with an argument against their position based on the just hypothesized "emotion" data as imagined or on data that showed that the "cognitive" parts of the brain were involved in judgments that it is permissible to kill five to save oneself. I suspect that they would argue, as much as some nonconsequentialists do, that we cannot decide about the correctness of a moral theory on the basis of fMRI studies of which areas of the brain function when different judgments are made. (Similarly, we cannot decide whether a scientific or mathematical judgment is correct by seeing whether the cognitive area of the brain or rather the spleen is stimulated when judging.)

(ii) Another way to reach the same conclusion is to consider again what was said in Section I about how some seem to fill the argumentative gap that exists between the premise that "the emotional center is more heavily involved in generating the deontological constraint judgments" and the conclusion that "it is not correct to think there really is such a constraint." Part of their claim was that the emotional response is elicited by a physically personal rather than a physically impersonal factor and that morally correct judgments should be based only on impersonal considerations. The characterization of "personal" in this argument was limited to interacting up close or by personal force with someone rather than by mechanical intervention. However, as we have argued, there is another sense of "personal" employed in the idea of the personal prerogative. This sense of personal involves partiality by contrast to impartiality (the latter being another sense of "impersonal") and involves personal autonomy (i.e., having an option rather than a duty to maximize the impersonal good). As we have noted, it is these sorts of contrasts between personal and impersonal factors and their roles in a moral theory that are sometimes thought of as part of what distinguishes nonconsequentialist from consequentialist theories.

If cognitive centers were found to underlie responses that support a personal prerogative (a possibility imagined previously), then this would correlate the cognitive center with a personal rather than an impersonal consideration in the sense of these terms that I am now considering.[41] Suppose one thought that personal considerations allowing for partiality or personal autonomy were *truly irrelevant* to moral decisions about what to do (as, I believe, Peter Singer thinks). Given the fMRI data as I have imagined it, one would have to argue against the relevance of these personal factors to correct decisions on some ground other than that they were correlated with emotion centers, because they would not be correlated in this way. Further, if these personal factors were irrelevant to correct moral decisions, there would be no reason to think that heavier involvement of cognitive centers in the brain was a sign of a correct moral judgment. This is because these centers would be linked with irrelevant personal considerations. One would then simply have to argue independently of reference to such fMRI data about the correct moral theory.

## C. Reason and "Cognitive Centers"

Suppose the cognitive center of someone's brain were involved in the judgment that (a) it is permissible to push the man over the bridge to save the five, and also in the judgments that (b) one has no duty to push the man over and (c) one has no duty to jump (or let oneself be pushed) over if one is on the bridge. Suppose it is a requirement of rationality that we universalize our judgments. Then together the three judgments seem to rationally imply that (i) it is permissible for a third party to push one over the bridge when one does not consent. If it is permissible for a third party to do this, then presumably (ii) it is permissible for a third party to force one to push another person over the bridge though one is exercising a prerogative not to push. These two judgments are indeed implications of a semi-(non)consequentialist view that includes prerogatives but not constraints.[42]

Suppose fMRIs in a set of people showed more cognitive center involvement when they expressed judgments (a), (b), and (c). One could ask these same people whether they also hold judgments (i) and (ii). (Call this Experiment Proposal 7.) Suppose their cognitive centers are activated if they say "no" to the last question. This would indicate that exceptions to universalization involve their cognitive center. However, if universalization is truly a demand of reason, it would no longer be clear that we would be measuring the role of reason when we measured the degree of involvement of the cognitive centers. We might only be measuring the role of rational self-interest or reason when it does not conflict with rational self-interest. Of course, the actual data from fMRI studies might be very different. (For example, the emotion and not cognitive centers might be more involved in a "no" response to judgments [i] and [ii].) Perhaps it is worth doing the experiment to find out because the temptation to normatively endorse judgments that involve more cognitive processing may be reduced if they are shown to involve commitment to inconsistencies as well as if they express pure self-interest.[43]

## Notes

1. For just a few examples, see Fiery Cushman, Liane Young, and Marc D. Hauser, "The Role of Conscious Reasoning and Intuition in Moral Judgments: Testing Three Principles of Harm," *Psychological Science* 17 (2006): 1082–89, and Marc D. Hauser, Fiery Cushman, Liane Young, R. Kang-Xing Jin, and John Mikhail, "A Dissociation between Moral Judgments and Justifications," *Mind and Language* 22 (2007): 1–23.
2. This chapter is based on my "Neuroscience and Moral Reasoning: A Note on Recent Research," *Philosophy & Public Affairs* 37, no. 4 (2009): 330–45. It makes only minor changes to the earlier discussion per se. However, it adds new discussion of psychological claims beyond those discussed in the 2009 paper. Many of the additional claims are described in Joshua Greene's "Trolleyology: What It Is, Why It Matters, What It's Taught Us, and How It's Been Misunderstood," forthcoming in ed. Hallvard Lillehammer, *The Trolley Problem, Classic Philosophical Arguments Series* (Cambridge: Cambridge University Press, 2023).
3. For more on this, also see my "Understanding, Justifying, and Finding Oneself," reprinted in my *Bioethical Prescriptions* (New York: Oxford University Press, 2013), 577–84.
4. In his "The Normative Insignificance of Neuroscience," *Philosophy & Public Affairs* 37 (2009): 293–329. All references to Berker are to this article.
5. Joshua D. Greene, R. Brian Sommerville, Leigh E. Nystrom, John M. Darley, and Jonathan D. Cohen, "An fMRI Investigation of Emotional Engagement in Moral Judgment," *Science* 293 (2001): 2105–8.
6. According to Greene (in a presentation at a conference on the Philosophy and Psychology of the Doctrine of Double Effect, Princeton University, 2005), his cases involve the conductor of the trolley, who is at least causally responsible for the trolley's heading to the five, turning the trolley. For the conductor, it is thought to be a choice between killing five and killing one. In comments presented at that conference, I pointed out that this case is not what is now standardly called the Trolley Problem. The latter involves a bystander, not the conductor, who sees the trolley headed to the five and can redirect it. For the bystander, the choice is between letting five die and killing one. Judith Jarvis Thomson introduced the bystander case in her article "Killing, Letting Die, and the Trolley Problem," *The Monist* 59 (1976): 204–17. The original trolley case was presented by Philippa Foot in her "The Problem of Abortion

and the Doctrine of Double Effect," *Oxford Review* 5 (1967): 5–15. Thomson originally (in *The Monist*) referred to Foot's case as the Trolley Problem but subsequently reserved the term for her case involving a bystander (see her "The Trolley Problem" in *Yale Law Journal* 94[1985]: 1395–1415) I pointed this out in my *The Trolley Problem Mysteries* (New York: Oxford University Press, 2016). Greene subsequently changed the case in his experiments to involve the bystander. I discuss the possible relevance of this difference between cases to his subjects' responses later.

7. These results are complicated by the fact that centers involved in social cognition are also said to be stimulated in the second case. See Joshua D. Greene, "The Secret Joke of Kant's Soul," in *Moral Psychology*, vol. 3: *The Neuroscience of Morality: Emotion, Brain Disorders, and Development*, ed. Walter Sinnott-Armstrong (Cambridge, MA: MIT Press, 2008), 35–79, at 45. In addition, a center associated with emotion is also said to be stimulated in the first case. I shall ignore this complication here.
8. In using the terms "restrictions" and "side constraint" I am speaking of normative limits placed on what one may do to bring about a good state of affairs. However, I should not be understood to be implying that these constraints are absolute and can never be overridden. Greene speaks of utilitarianism rather than consequentialist views. Utilitarianism is a form of consequentialism that takes utility or well-being to be the morally relevant aspect of consequences.
9. I have in mind Peter Singer's and Joshua Greene's interpretation in work discussed later. I have also heard philosophers (and philosophy students) present such an interpretation and so it is a possible position worth considering independently of who has actually subscribed to it in print.
10. I omit discussion here of the large issue of whether there is a sensible distinction between cognition and emotion.
11. Peter Singer, "Ethics and Intuitions," *Journal of Ethics* 9 (2005): 331–52. All references to Singer are to this article.
12. This sense of the personal/impersonal contrast is different from how philosophers typically draw the contrast (to be discussed later).
13. At one time, Greene said that while he "cares" about consequentialist conclusions, he does not think that any moral theory (including consequentialism) is correct in a "realist" sense. (Remarks at Undergraduate Bioethics Conference, Harvard University, March 14, 2009. This may not represent his current view.) This view implies that it is an illusion that there are reasons that justify one moral conclusion rather than another, reasons that make some choices morally better or worse than others. This is a form of moral nihilism. Greene gave as a reason for holding this view that a Darwinian account of our evolution implies that there are no justifying reasons for moral judgments; we have just evolved to care about some things and not others. It is not clear, however, how any fact about us (e.g., how we evolved) bears on whether there are reasons that justify a moral judgment. How we evolved might explain why we have certain properties, and these properties may explain why we are capable or incapable of grasping certain reasons or are subject to illusions about reasons. This is not the same as explaining that there are or are not reasons. For example, fish cannot grasp the reasons there are to believe in evolutionary theory; that does not mean there

are no such reasons and we just evolved to believe in the theory of evolution. If there is a problem with the idea that there could be justifying reasons for moral judgments, this problem would arise quite independently of our evolution.

14. "Secret Joke," 39. We considered Gibbard's presentation of Jonathan Haidt's view that moral reasoning is often a rationalization of emotional responses in Chapter 5 and review parts of what was said there later.
15. The strategy is to show that once one accepts the permissibility of a bystander turning the trolley, there is nothing morally relevant to distinguish his doing that from his toppling the man from the bridge. As we shall see in Chapter 7, Derek Parfit follows a similar strategy though in his argument he does not focus on the moral irrelevance of the distinction between using a switch and exerting personal force.
16. See my discussion of such cases in *Intricate Ethics* (New York: Oxford University Press, 2007), 43, n. 37; 142–43, n. 34; 418, n. 46; and 421, n. 47. They are also discussed in my *The Trolley Problem Mysteries* (New York: Oxford University Press, 2016) and in Chapter 9 of this volume. Greene himself now rejects his initial personal versus impersonal way of drawing the distinction between the deontological and consequentialist intuitive judgments. See his "Secret Joke," 77, n. 2.
17. See *Intricate Ethics*, Chapter 5, and Chapter 9 in this volume.
18. Indeed, my second lecture in *The Trolley Problem Mysteries* is titled "How the Trolley Was Turned" and I there argue against Judith Thomson's acceptance of the press-a-switch-versus-push-a-person explanation of many people's intuitive responses in her "Turning the Trolley," *Philosophy & Public Affairs*, 36 (2008): 359–74. For more in this volume about a downstreamish view see Chapter 9.
19. For example, see Kamm's *Morality, Mortality*, vol. 2 (New York: Oxford University Press, 1996).
20. I discussed this issue when examining Dworkin's views about the Loop Case in Chapter 2. See also discussion of the Doctrine of Triple Effect in Chapter 9 of this volume and in Kamm, *Intricate Ethics* (Oxford: Oxford University Press, 2007).
21. I discuss this principle in *Morality, Mortality*, vol. 2; *Intricate Ethics*; and in Chapter 9 in this volume, among other places.
22. I suggested this in *Morality, Mortality*, vol. 1: *Death and Whom to Save from It* (New York: Oxford University Press, 1993), Introduction.
23. Reconsider Jonathan Haidt's claim (that we already considered in Chapter 5) that we do not reason our way to moral conclusions but rather respond intuitively and then find reasons to support "preordained conclusions." (Haidt's early article on this to which Greene and Gibbard refer is "The Emotional Dog and Its Rational Tail," *Psychological Review* 108 (4): 814–34 [2001].) Mostly, according to Haidt, reasoning constructs "justifications of intuitive judgments, causing the illusion of objective reasoning." In response one might note that someone who has an intuitive response can then try to find out what it is about the act or situation she is considering that accounts for her response. In one sense, this account might be a causal story thought it needn't involve what Ronald Dworkin calls "morons," morally charged atoms analogous to physical atoms that cause the intuitive judgment. By "what accounts for a response" we may also mean the properties of an act that would give us reason to do

it, not only cause us to think we have reason to do it. These properties may or may not have played a causal role in someone's response. In having the intuitive judgment, someone thinks the judgment is correct and so in trying to account for her response in a normative (not merely causal sense) she is trying to locate the factors that on reflection justify her response. This reflective view would then be the reasoned-to moral conclusion. The willingness to admit that no factors may justify an intuitive judgment can also make the conclusion not "preordained." Suppose the intuitive judgment is justified by factors that could not have (even unconsciously) played a causal role in accounting for her response. The intuitive judgment would still be correct.

24. Subsequent to my raising this issue and providing analyses of it in my 2009 article (repeated in parts [i] and [ii] later), others (e.g., Guy Kahane) have also pursued this issue.
25. Killings that are impermissible from a consequentialist point of view (such as turning a trolley from five to one) might also involve the emotional center in those who think them impermissible. The killings that are thought to be permissible from the deontological or consequentialist point of view would not involve the emotion center to as great a degree.
26. "Secret Joke," 37.
27. Ibid., 44.
28. Ibid., 45.
29. Psychologists have more recently focused on whether toppling someone from the bridge is a consequentialist act by seeing if it is due to a desire to promote the greater good or due to a weaker resistance to doing harm. (This is called process dissociation.) But while seeking the greater good may be a necessary condition for a consequentialist response, it isn't sufficient. An additional concern in applying the process dissociation method is that it is possible for someone to intend to abide by the consequentialist side constraint of maximizing the good in order to act on a desire to harm someone, using the opportunity to promote the greater good as a mere pretext for harming. Such a person would not harm in the absence of maximizing the good, but he would not maximize the good in the absence of the opportunity to harm.
30. Samuel Scheffler, who introduced the term "personal prerogative," describes such a view in his *The Rejection of Consequentialism* (New York: Oxford University Press, 1994). Such a view contrasts with consequentialism and so is nonconsequentialist, but it is not likely to be referred to as "deontological," as it does not emphasize duties that constrain conduct..
31. Shelly Kagan describes such a view (but does not accept it) in his *The Limits of Morality* (New York: Oxford University Press, 1991).
32. Greene et al., "An fMRI Investigation of Emotional Engagement in Moral Judgment," 2105.
33. Ibid., 2106.
34. In Chapter 9 we consider why there may be no duty but only a permission to turn the trolley.

35. In speaking of "Experiment Proposal," I am not claiming that such an experiment has not already been done. Although it would be useful to suggest experiments if they were new, it is also useful to think about the logical relation of experiments (whether already done or new) to the claims that some wish to make, for example, about evidence for the occurrence of consequentialist responses on normative matters.
36. See Cushman et al., "The Role of Conscious Reasoning," and Hauser et al., "A Dissociation between Moral Judgments and Justifications."
37. "Turning the Trolley."
38. See *The Trolley Problem Mysteries* and Chapter 9 in this volume.
39. Item (iii) is an addition to the original article on which this chapter is based. Section III.B, C, and D that follow return to the original article.
40. See Henry Sidgwick's *Methods of Ethics* (Indianapolis: Hackett Publishing Company, 1981), concluding chapter.
41. In Section II, I wondered about cognitive processing being associated with the physically up close or personal force sense of "personal" in the Lazy Susan Case.
42. Constraints might require respecting the choice someone makes when exercising her prerogative. However, if this were always true it would be impermissible to redirect a trolley from five to one person who would exercise his prerogative not to redirect the trolley to himself. For more on this issue see Lecture 1 in *The Trolley Problem Mysteries* and Chapter 9 in this volume
43. I am grateful to Selim Becker, Marc Hauser, Michael Nitsch, Alex Voorhoeve, and the editors of *Philosophy & Public Affairs* for comments on an earlier draft of the article on which this chapter is based, and to Joshua Greene and Liane Young for discussion.

# 7

# The Irrelevance of Deontological Distinctions and "Moral Inertia"?

This chapter examines whether case-based reasoning can be used to undermine "common-sense deontological" distinctions such as harming versus not aiding, harming as a mere means versus as a side effect, and redirecting threats (as in the Trolley Problem) versus starting new ones. It does this by considering Derek Parfit's discussion in his *On What Matters*, volume 3, of the irrelevance of deontological principles involving such distinctions prompted by his concern that morality will not be consistent with practical reason if it involves these principles.[1] The chapter considers how Parfit thinks one's practical reason should reconcile three issues: concerns about self-sacrifice, pursuing the greater good, and abiding by morality. It compares his views on these issues with those of the author. It then examines his use of case-based reasoning to try to undermine deontological principles and the notion of "moral inertia." In previous chapters we have considered proponents and opponents of the use and reliability of intuitive judgments about cases as a guide to normative truth. Parfit's discussion assumes that engaging in case-based reasoning is useful in this regard. Nevertheless, I will for the most part raise questions primarily about *how* he argues for his conclusions rather than their truth. I do this in an attempt to show that how we use cases, not just whether we should or should not, is crucial. My discussion will, for the most part, follow Parfit's order of discussion that first considers how to reconcile concerns about self-sacrifice, pursuing the greater good, and morality and then uses case-based reasoning involving the Trolley Problem.

## Part I

A. Parfit begins by expressing his concern that morality will be undermined because practical reason, which he thinks tells us all things considered what to do, will often conflict with what we consider to be morally right. Unlike Sidgwick, Parfit does not begin by identifying morality with a part of impartial practical reason but rather with what he considers common-sense deontology (that I have referred to as nonconsequentialism with a consequentialist and a deontological component) Also, unlike Sidgwick, he thinks it is clear that sometimes

*Rights and Their Limits: In Theory, Cases, and Pandemics.* F. M. Kamm, Oxford University Press.
© Oxford University Press 2022. DOI: 10.1093/oso/9780197567739.003.0007

self-interest (which provides some reason even impartially considered) is overridden by (other) impartial practical reasons (e.g., there is decisive reason to give one's penny to save millions of other people). In some other cases he thinks there will be sufficient reason from the point of view of one's practical reason to choose to avoid a big loss to oneself at the cost of a small loss to what is best impartially considered (e.g., saving oneself rather than someone who will have a slightly better life). Nevertheless, he says that there will always also be sufficient reason to act for what is impartially best rather than for self-interest.[2] Parfit is particularly concerned about the possible conflicts between common-sense morality and (1) one's practical reason (whose primary question is, "What do I have most reason to do?") and (2) one's self-interest.[3]

B. Parfit first tries to show how these conflicts threaten to demote morality's importance. Consider the conflict in one's practical reason between impartial reasons and morality. Parfit supposes that common-sense deontology is not absolutist. Hence, it could be wrong according to it to kill someone to save 99 other people but not wrong to do so to save 100 people. Saving 100 would then be the threshold for permissibility of killing in this version of what is called "threshold deontology." Parfit thinks that when the number you would wrongly save is only slightly different from the number you could permissibly save, your wrong act would be only "slightly morally wrong" and because it would save 99 people there would be strong impartial reason to act. Hence, he says, "this would be a case in which we had a sufficient and perhaps a decisive impartial reason to act wrongly" (p. 346). Second, he also thinks that if your self-interested reason for doing a slightly morally wrong act is strong, practical reason would permit the morally wrong act (p. 341).[4] Here the very facts (e.g., 99 people would be saved) that were taken into account in determining what was morally wrong are judged sufficient to make it reasonable for you to do the morally wrong act.

This two-step reasoning process, where the moral answer is not thought to be conclusive, may seem to involve inappropriate double counting of self-interest (in the second step of the second case) and inappropriate double counting of the 99 lives (in the second step of the first case). But this may not be so since they are counted once in the moral decision-making and once in practical reasoning that includes morality only as a part. I think a major problem with Parfit's analysis of these cases is how he decides what is "slightly wrong" in threshold deontology; the fact that we are close to acting permissibly deontologically when we act wrongly in violating a negative right does not mean our act is only slightly wrong if the consequences for the victim of our wrong act are serious (e.g., the one person is killed when he would otherwise live). Hence, our killing someone to save 99 could be seriously wrong even if killing to save 100 would be permissible.[5] If so, the issue becomes whether one's practical reason recommends doing something seriously morally wrong.

And indeed Parfit next (pp. 347–48) considers how practical reason should decide about doing what even he thinks is seriously wrong according to common-sense morality when there are strong impartial reasons to do it. He considers an American president who must choose between two policies to end a war that both involve noncombatant deaths. In the Nuclear Policy bombing a city would kill 100,000 noncombatants as a mere means to getting a government to surrender (terror bombing); in the Conventional Policy bombing military facilities would kill 300,000 completely different noncombatants only as a side effect (tactical bombing). (Call this the President Case.) Parfit assumes that deontology distinguishes morally between killing noncombatants as a mere means and killing them as a side effect, and condemns the terror bombing as seriously wrong while permitting the tactical bombing. The latter would be true only if 300,000 side effect deaths were not out of proportion to the goal of ending the war. Assume this is so. Parfit's concern is that the impartial reason to kill 200,000 fewer people overrides the serious moral wrongness of terror bombing.

In response to Parfit's analysis, it might be said that killing 200,000 more as a side effect instead of killing 100,000 different noncombatants as a mere means would meet the threshold on the significance of a deontological distinction between killing as a side effect and killing as a mere means. Hence, it wouldn't be morally wrong to kill as a means in this case. The objection Parfit raises to this response is that according to deontology, it would be wrong to kill one person as a mere means to save three other people and that is the same ratio that holds between killing 100,000 as a mere means rather than 300,000 as a side effect.

One concern about Parfit's objection is whether it is the ratio rather than absolute numbers of people killed that matters morally. Second, in Parfit's case the president's choosing to terror bomb implies that he will not otherwise kill 300,000 as a side effect. This is a two-killing-options case in which someone would kill no matter what he does because at least one of the ways of killing (as a proportional side effect) is deontologically permissible on its own. Perhaps killing as a mere means in this case is morally different from killing as a mere means in a case when one would otherwise kill no one.[6] (The similar contrast to the option in the President Case that involves killing as a side effect would involve killing as a side effect when one would otherwise kill no one.)

A third concern about Parfit's objection is that in this two-killing-options case the president would be killing 100,000 as a mere means to end the war rather than using some other means to end the war that kills 300,000 different noncombatants as a side effect. He would not be killing the 100,000 as a mere means (i.e., in a causal route) to saving the 300,000. The latter would occur if, for example, someone's bombing 100,000 people stopped a missile sent by someone else that would otherwise kill 300,000 different people as a side effect. But it is this latter scenario that is analogous to a case in which one would kill one person as a mere means to save three other people (which Parfit cites as deontologically impermissible). Hence, even if a 1:3 ratio does not justify killing some people as a mere means to saving different people, such a ratio might justify killing some as a mere means to a goal (e.g., ending a war) rather than killing three times as many different people as a side effect of doing something else that achieves the same goal. The problem here (and, as we shall see, in some other parts of his discussion of deontology) is that Parfit incorrectly equates harming fewer people to avoid harming more different people with harming fewer people as a causal means to saving more different people.[7] The latter obviously does not occur when one would end a war by means that kill 100,000 as a side effect rather than by other means that would kill 300,000 different people also as a side effect. In this case the fewer people are not killed as a mere means for any purpose merely because our reason for killing them is not to kill more different people.

I do not here say that our decision about what is morally right to do should depend on the factors cited in these three concerns, only that when using cases Parfit is not careful in attending to differences that may be morally important or at least affect some people's judgments. If this leads him to incorrectly conclude that the Nuclear Policy is morally wrong according to common-sense deontology, he will not have presented a case where practical reason seriously conflicts with morality. However, since Parfit is concerned about such conflict, assume for argument's sake it sometimes exists.

C. Parfit thinks that to deal with serious conflict between practical reason and morality, we should translate deontological wrongness into what he calls "deontic badness." For example, suppose it is morally wrong to kill one person as a mere means to prevent five people from wrongfully killing five other people. He thinks the one wrongful killing will have a certain amount of badness due to its wrongness and this is "deontic badness" that gets added to the world.[8] He argues that preventing the five wrongful killings would not prevent five times as much deontic badness from being added to the world since, he thinks, this badness has already occurred with the intention to wrongly kill the five.[9] Instead, Parfit thinks that the deontic badness of our killing one person would have to be weighed against the mere nondeontic goodness of saving five lives and the latter outweighs the former.[10] He concludes that in cases like this our practical reason directs us to want and hope that someone does the morally wrong act (p. 366).

Parfit here assumes that practical reasoning involves translating wrongness into some particular type of negative (deontic) value added to an end-state that will be weighed against any positive value (deontic or nondeontic) likewise added. This procedure presents practical reasoning as broadly consequentialist in form and concerned with how well "things will go" (p. 349). It is because of this that he can move (p. 352) from saying that "if things will go in the way that is better" it would "be better if someone acted" to make things go better. However, a nonconsequentialist form of practical reasoning would not necessarily imply that it would be better if someone acted to make things go better. His procedure also implies that moral wrongness can be reduced to the increased badness of an outcome containing it. Indeed, he says (pp. 353–54): "If there was no deontic badness it would not in itself matter whether people acted wrongly, what would matter would be only non-deontic badness of these acts and their effects." Nonconsequentialists who emphasize deontological factors would deny that the seriousness of moral wrongness depends on the badness it adds to how things go.[11] They would reject his procedure even though it does not reduce all types of disvalue to a single type and even if, as he argues, we should add the negative value of acts themselves to the calculation. It is no surprise that when translated into part of a consequentialist procedure, deontological morality would not give a reasonable answer to what should be done, but why think practical reasoning is consequentialist in form?

By contrast, an alternative form of practical reasoning might consider the impartial significance of the status of persons and not only how things will go for them or the world. If it were permissible to kill one innocent nonthreatening person as a means to save the five, no one's status would involve high inviolability even if fewer innocent people would die. If people have this status, isn't it correct to act in accordance with it? Would killing the one person despite the truth about his status and what it prohibits be analogous to what Parfit has called "motivated irrationality" (e.g., causing oneself to believe an untruth such as that 2 + 2 = 5 if one's life depended on having the belief)? But in killing the one person one would act contrary to a truth (about the status of persons) that implies how one should act in the very situation one is in (by contrast to a mathematical truth).[12]

In any case, Parfit applies his procedure involving deontic badness to the President Case in which (he assumes) there would be no deontic badness in killing the 300,000 people. According to Parfit, comparing the deontic badness that terror bombing 100,000 adds to the outcome with the nondeontic goodness of 200,000 lives spared should lead us to hope that the president terror bombs. However, Parfit accepts that it could be reasonable for the president himself not to do the morally wrong act. He cites (pp. 363–64) Thomas Nagel's view that it is incorrect to decide whether to do something seriously wrong by treating one's act as an event added to an outcome and deciding from an impartial point of view that it counts for very little by comparison to the good it does. Such a procedure, Parfit is willing to assume, incorrectly subsumes the personal perspective in acting under the impersonal perspective.

One problem with this part of Parfit's discussion of the President Case is that it tries to answer the question "What do we have most reason to hope for?" although the primary question Parfit said practical reason must answer is "What do I have most reason to do?" If Parfit accepts Nagel's view rather than his own consequentialist procedure when making decisions about one's own acts, he might conclude that each of us has most reason *not* to do seriously wrong acts. (Of course, if hoping that someone else does a wrong act is a wrong mental act, an agent might also be prohibited from hoping.) Another problem is that Nagel thought his analysis of the personal versus impersonal perspective would ground an agent-relative account of deontological prohibitions and side constraints.[13] But Parfit seems to use the account to show that doing the seriously wrong act would be a personal sacrifice and so raise a conflict between self-interest and impartial considerations in practical reason. In such conflicts, recall that Parfit claimed there was always sufficient reason to do what was best from an impartial point of view. Hence, on Parfit's account, the president might at most have a permission not a requirement not to terror bomb and there wouldn't be anything he had *most* reason to do. In any case, it seems Parfit has again failed to generate a serious conflict between one's practical reason and common-sense morality.

## Part II

Nevertheless, Parfit's next step in dealing with the supposed conflict between deontological morality and practical reason is to try to save morality by showing that it is not deontological (even as a component of nonconsequentialism) as commonly thought. This would imply that there will be little or no deontic badness to weigh against nondeontic badness in practical reason as he conceives of it. In the parts of *On What Matters* with which I am now concerned, he tries to show by way of general arguments that parts of common-sense morality are compatible with consequentialism, and by way of intuitive judgments about cases that principles embodying deontological distinctions cannot be correct. Since he is using intuitive judgments about cases in deciding about ethical theories, we can feel free to use them in considering his claims.

A. Harming versus Not Aiding. Parfit first argues against the deontological principle that there is a right not to be harmed that gives rise to a more stringent requirement not to harm than to aid others. (Call this the Harm/Not Aid Principle.) He notes there are at least two possible measures of such stringency: (a) costs one is morally required to bear in order to not harm are greater than costs one is required to bear in order to aid and (b) the priority not harming takes over aiding when these conflict. His further claim is that not harming can be more stringent than aiding by measure (a) and yet be less stringent by measure (b). That the measures of cost iand priority can come apart was one major point of my article "Supererogation and Obligation" (SO).[14] I there argued that one might, for example, have to bear greater costs to fulfill one's contractual business duty (which is a positive duty correlative to a positive contractual right) than to help save someone's life, yet one might also permissibly give priority to saving someone's life over fulfilling the contractual duty when they conflict. (Call this the Business Case.) This is true, I argued, whether saving someone's life is what is called a natural duty done at low cost to oneself or it is supererogatory because of the high cost to oneself in saving someone.[15] For example, one might miss an important business deadline to jump into shark-infested waters to save someone's life. I argued that this is true even when the person to whom the contractual duty is owed would not be morally obligated to waive it so that someone else may be saved, because of the high cost to him of doing so. However, the cases that I used to show how the two measures of stringency can come apart did not involve a choice between saving some and not physically harming someone else (a negative duty). It is the latter sort of case that concerns Parfit. Nevertheless, I did note (what Parfit emphasizes) that not harming being more stringent by the cost measure does not alone show it is more stringent by the priority measure.[16]

Parfit may emphasize the difference between these two measures of stringency because he thinks one could reject the priority within morality of not harming over aiding while not requiring great personal sacrifices for purposes of aiding. Though he does not say so, his aim seems to be to avoid the so-called Over-Demandingness Objection to consequentialism. This could be done by retaining nonconsequentialism's morally sanctioned personal prerogative not to make large personal sacrifices to achieve the greater good while jettisoning its side constraint of not harming others to achieve the greater good. This would permit those who would not sacrifice themselves for the greater good to try to sacrifice another for its sake. Parfit may think these positions are at least compatible with costly self-sacrifice being morally required to abide by a nonconsequentialist constraint to avoid harming others when only one's own interests are at stake.[17]

It might seem that if not harming has no priority over aiding, then we should not be required to bear higher personal costs to avoid harming than to aid. But I argued in SO that it is intuitively plausible that achieving greater good could sometimes take precedence over minimal positive duties of morality such as keeping promises and yet one may not avoid the personal sacrifices necessary to meet these minimal duties even if one needn't make such sacrifices to go beyond that minimum and achieve the greater good. Hence, Parfit's applying such a view to negative duties yields the same sort of seeming intransitivity that I identified in SO in the case of positive duties. To see this, combine his and my original view as follows: (1) Avoiding personal sacrifices (S) could take precedence (>) over aiding (A) (i.e., (S > A)), (2) aiding some could take precedence over not harming (N) others as well as over performing a positive (P) duty (D) for others (i.e., (A > DPN)), and yet (3) not harming others as well as performing a positive duty for them could take precedence over avoiding personal sacrifices (i.e., –(S > DPN)).[18]

I call this only a "seeming intransitivity" because different factors account for precedence relations in the different steps; there is no single relation that is shown to be intransitive. That is, the dominance of the personal in the first step is accounted for by limits on personal sacrifice to go beyond minimal requirements of morality (such as not harming or keeping promises) not because the personal involves a greater good. The greater good may be able to dominate such minimal duties, but mere personal interests (that do not involve greater good) may have to be sacrificed to achieve minimal moral requirements. It is also not because one would be doing the greater good in fulfilling a personal duty that the duty can dominate personal interests in the conclusion. Hence, the fact that personal interests can take precedence over the greater good and greater good can take precedence over personal duty need not imply that personal interests can take precedence over personal duty.

Parfit further distinguishes "differences" from "conflicts" between deontology and consequentialism (focusing on act consequentialism). He thinks that conflicts are the most serious obstacles to morality being more consequentialist and may also generate skepticism about there being moral truth. He thinks there is only difference between consequentialism and deontology regarding the personal sacrifice measure of stringency. This is because while deontology does not require the personal sacrifices for promoting overall good that consequentialism does, it does not prohibit them. There is no conflict if retaining a prerogative not to make large personal sacrifices for the greater good does not prohibit what consequentialism requires. Parfit thinks that conflicts arise on the priority measure of stringency when deontology prohibits what consequentialism requires (e.g., killing one person to save five others). Here Parfit is emphasizing his belief that the biggest stumbling block to morality being less deontological is consequentialism's omission of constraints on achieving the greater good, not its demandingness.

Unlike Parfit, I think that there can be conflicts, as he defines them, between deontology and consequentialism in the matter of personal costs rather than merely about priority among types of acts. This is because deontology might require one to suffer greater harm to prevent one's doing lesser harm to someone else, but consequentialism would prohibit this because it would make the outcome worse. (Consequentialism also prohibits the prerogative not to sacrifice [admittedly not an act] that deontology requires.) Parfit may think that there is no conflict between parties if one of them has a mere permission to act in a certain way because that party can always prevent a stalemate by acting in the way required of another party. However, it seems there is a different sense of "conflict" according to which a moral theory that merely permitted killing someone for the greater good or permitted killing anyone one wants does not merely differ but conflicts with a theory that prohibits these things. This is so even though the first theory does not require what the other theory prohibits.

B.1. Degrees of Moral Inertia. We have seen why Parfit thinks it is *possible* for there to be no priority of not harming over aiding consistent with some other aspects of nonconsequentialism. It is by considering particular cases that Parfit hopes to show that there actually is no such priority in true morality. Parfit thinks that the priority version of the Harm/Not Aid Principle is shown to be incorrect by a case he calls Side Track. It involves a bystander who may permissibly *aid* five people by redirecting a runaway trolley headed to killing them onto a track where he foresees it will *kill* one other person.[19] (Arguably this is unlike the trolley driver who in redirecting would prevent his *killing* five people by doing what he foresees will *kill* one other person.) Parfit thinks that a redirection case like Side Track can show that not harming does not have priority over aiding because it is an uncomplicated case of harming versus not aiding (p. 388). His argument for this (pp. 387–88) seems to have several steps: (i) The only reason the five people need to be aided (rather than not harmed) is that the trolley is already headed to kill them (p. 387).[20] (ii) But that something is actually going to happen to them is no reason not to change it (since there is no principle of moral inertia) (p. 387).[21] (iii) Hence, that something is actually going to happen to the five is a morally irrelevant difference between them and the one. (iv) Therefore, each of the six has an equal claim not to lose his life and so each of the five people has as much claim to have his life saved as the one other person has not to be harmed (p. 386).[22] (v) Since we should minimize lives lost, we may turn the trolley.

I agree with Parfit's step (i). However, I have questions about steps (ii) and (iii). I agree that the five do not lose a claim to be saved simply because a threat is on its way to kill them. For example, one should turn the trolley from them if one could turn it to an empty track. Nevertheless, that something is actually going to happen to them might be some reason not to change it. This would suggest that there is some form of "moral inertia" and that those toward whom a threat is already headed have less claim not to have it continue to them than others have not to have it redirected to them. Moral inertia and less claim not to be threatened is evidenced if one correctly prefers to let a trolley already headed toward one person continue in that way rather than either turn it onto a track where it will kill one person not previously threatened or toss a coin giving each person an equal chance of being the one threatened. In the case where the trolley is headed to five, suppose that a bystander has the following choice: either (a) turn the trolley away from the five toward another track where it will kill one person previously not threatened or (b) turn the trolley away from the five toward another track that loops back toward one of the five who was originally threatened. (Call this the Returning Trolley Case [not to be confused with Thomson's Loop Case].[23] Note that even though all five originally threatened would be saved if the trolley were turned toward the other track and only four of them are saved in returning the trolley, the fact that the one person on the other track would not be killed means that five people also survive in returning the trolley.) My sense is that it is morally preferable for a bystander to kill one of the people who was originally threatened rather than threaten someone new. (Indeed, it would even be permissible for the bystander to kill one of the people originally threatened by toppling him in front of the returning trolley to stop it from hitting all five.) This is not because the one killed in the returning the trolley option would die no matter what is done since he would not die if the trolley were turned to the other track. Rather, as someone already threatened he is no worse off in being killed by the returning trolley than by the trolley in its original direction; if it wasn't clear which one of the original five would be killed by the returning trolley, even the person who would be killed was benefited in getting a chance to survive that he lacked when facing the trolley from its original direction. By contrast, in option (a), the bystander would make someone worse off than he would originally have been. The significance of this factor depends on a form of moral inertia because it depends on giving weight to how things were originally going. However, in this case, it also seems true that given the presence of option (b), it may not be permissible for the bystander **not** to turn the trolley and kill someone (i.e., kill one of the five who were already threatened with death to save the other four). Hence, moral inertia can come in degrees. By contrast, it may be only permissible and not required for the bystander to turn the trolley from five to one in Side Track (which is the standard Bystander Case). If so, then the bystander in the Returning Trolley Case faces a choice between killing one or another person rather than a choice between letting five die and killing someone as occurs in Side Track.

In a second version of the Returning Trolley Case, option (a) remains the same as earlier but option (b') involves two of those originally threatened by the trolley being killed and three of those originally threatened thereby being saved. (This is Returning Trolley Case [2].) Fewer people would be killed in option (a) but someone not originally threatened would die. If it would still be morally preferable for a bystander to choose option (b'), this would show that selecting for sacrifice those already under a threat rather than affecting someone not originally threatened, and so a form of moral inertia, weighs heavily. However, suppose it would be permissible to turn a trolley headed to killing just two people toward another track where one person would be killed when this was the only option of reducing the number killed. How could it be consistent with this to refuse to turn the trolley toward one person who was not originally threatened rather than kill two of five originally threatened? (Put another way, how could it be permissible to turn from two already threatened to one not already threatened when that is one's only option if it is morally correct to choose option [b'] rather than [a]?) Could these choices be consistent because the death of the two in Returning Trolley (2) would have a worthwhile purpose of saving a greater number of others who are already under a threat along with the persons killed, something that would not be true in the case where only two were threatened by the trolley to begin with? In Returning Trolley (2) the bystander faces a choice of killing two or killing one, and because other things are not equal, it might be preferable to kill two.

An additional example that may exhibit the effect of moral inertia involves the permission that one person in Side Track may have to send back the trolley that is redirected toward him from the five (what I have called a Sending Back Case) even if he (i) would not be permitted to turn a trolley originally headed to him when it would then kill the five other people and (ii) would not be permitted to turn a trolley redirected to him so that it killed other innocent nonthreatening people than those who were originally threatened by it.[24] In one version of such a Sending Back Case, the one person on the side track who sends back a trolley turned by a driver or bystander would be putting the five back in the position they were originally in, and focusing on this factor is to give moral inertia a role. However, if he hit the driver or bystander, he would make them worse off than they would originally have been. This could be permissible not because of moral inertia but because they would infringe his right not to be harmed even if permissibly in redirecting the trolley. Suppose the five who were threatened had themselves redirected the trolley. Then in hitting the one other person they would infringe his right not to be harmed and this might make them liable to being harmed to an even greater degree than they would originally have been harmed by the trolley.

Suppose the one person would be permitted to bring about harm to the five in Sending Back Cases in only the ways in which harm to him could permissibly have been brought about to save the five. Then any principle of permissible harm would have to distinguish (a) permissible from impermissible ways of harming innocent nonthreatening persons from (b) producing greater good (or lesser harm) being what justifies use of the permissible means. This is because in Sending Back Cases it is not reducing the number who would suffer a particular harm that could play a role in justifying the one person sending back the trolley and thus harming either one other person or many other people. It remains possible that other means besides those permissible to harm the one person on the side track could permissibly be used by the one to harm the bystander or driver to stop them from permissibly infringing his right in order to save the five.[25]

Even if Parfit's rejection of moral inertia in step (ii) of his argument were correct, it would be wrong to conclude (as in step [iii]) that it is not a morally relevant difference between the one and the five that (a) respecting the five's claim to be saved involves doing what causally imposes a loss on what the one other person has (his life) independently of causally imposing a loss on the five, while

(b) respecting the one person's right not to be harmed does not involve doing what causally imposes a loss on what the five would have (their lives) independently of causally imposing a loss on the one person. It is true that this difference arises because the trolley is already headed to the five, but even if its heading to them is in itself a morally irrelevant difference between the five and one (as step [iii] claims), it is possible for (a) and (b) to be morally relevant differences that supervene on it.[26] This could block the inference to (iv) and (v). Hence, redirecting the trolley may be permissible *despite* this moral difference between the one and five, not because there is no moral difference.

I suspect that Parfit may see the Side Track Case as no different from one in which the trolley is not already on its way to the five but is at a cross point and an agent has to decide whether to send it to kill one person or kill five other people.[27] (What this comparison omits is the difference in the situation of the agent. In the Side Track Case, the bystander who would turn the trolley faces the choice of killing versus letting die, unlike the agent in the Crosspoint Case.) My own view is that there is indeed an underlying similarity between the Crosspoint Case and the Side Track Case that can help account for the permissibility of killing rather than letting die in the Side Track Case, though Parfit does not refer to it. This similarity is that the greater good of the five being alive in both cases is constituted just by the threat being away from them even though this means it has nowhere else to be but headed to the one other person.[28]

Let us assume that Side Track is a case where not harming does not take precedence over aiding. Parfit seems to believe that the Harm/Not Aid Principle implies that in all cases where not harming conflicts with aiding, not harming has priority at least when the loss to those harmed is significant. Then one case in which this is not so could disprove the Harm/Not Aid Principle. By contrast, we might understand the Harm/Not Aid Principle as nonabsolute, applying only when losses engendered in abiding by it fall below a threshold. Even so, if the potential loss in Side Track of five lives is below the threshold, that case will disprove even the nonabsolute version of the Harm/Not Aid Principle.[29]

However, deontological distinctions and deontological principles are different, and deontologists are often concerned with the first. Finding some cases in which there is priority to not harming over aiding (other things equal) could show a moral distinction between not harming and aiding per se.[30] But there being this distinction need not imply that either an absolutist or a threshold version of the Harm/Not Aid Principle is correct, since a distinction can matter morally sometimes but not always and many factors could override or silence its role besides numerical thresholds.

Parfit is trying to undermine principles, but it would be wrong for him to conclude that not harming per se does not have priority over aiding per se (i.e., thought of simply as a moral distinction) because it has no priority in the one

Side Track Case. After all, in testing for the per se difference in priority between not harming and aiding, we should hold all other factors constant. This is not done in Side Track, where one person would be killed but five would be saved. Suppose the bystander had to choose between not saving the five people and turning the trolley, thus killing five other people. If he should not be morally indifferent between these options, this would indicate at least some priority to not harming over aiding per se. Or suppose the bystander has a choice how to save the five: either (1) turn the trolley away from them toward killing one other person or (2) turn the trolley in a way that will interfere with his saving one other person. If he should do (2) rather than (1), this too would show some priority of not harming over aiding per se.[31]

So could the Harm/Not Aid Principle be saved by understanding it to apply when "other things are equal," rather than in a case involving killing one to save five? The problem is that when certain other things are equally present, they may also silence the moral significance of the distinction on which the principle is based. For example, it may not morally matter if one kills or allows to die a person in self-defense when these are the only ways to stop his certain-to-succeed attack. Nevertheless, some deontologists may try to formulate fine-grained principles that determine when the harming/not aiding distinction should imply a moral conclusion in particular cases. Who and how one comes to harm could be crucial to whether and to what degree not harming has priority over aiding, and fine-grained principles might capture this.[32] Hence, I agree with Parfit that deontologists cannot rely on a simple Harm/Not Aid Principle to yield decisions in many cases, though Parfit and I may disagree on whether successful fine-grained deontological principles might be formulated..

2. Harming as a Mere Means. Thinking he has undermined the Harm/Not Aid Principle, Parfit moves on. He notes that most believe that in what he calls the Bridge Case, a bystander may not topple a man from a bridge, making him fall in front of a trolley, thus stopping it from killing five others but instead killing the man.[33] (I will assume the bystander would use a mechanical device to topple the man as he uses such a device to kill someone in Side Track.) Parfit suggests that some may account for the difference in permissibility between Side Track and Bridge by citing a deontological principle that claims not killing someone as a side effect (as in Side Track) has no priority over aiding, but not killing someone as a mere means (as in Bridge) has priority over aiding. (He calls this the Means Principle.)[34] (Parfit distinguishes between *treating* and *harming* someone merely as a means. He thinks one would not do the former if for someone's sake one limits the amount of harm one does to him. However, one could still be harming him as a mere means when the limited harm is not in the person's interests but causally useful for others [pp. 378–80]. It is this Means Principle involving harm with which he is concerned.)

Parfit criticizes the Means Principle by revising the President Case to include a third option in which the war could also be ended by dropping a nuclear bomb on an uninhabited island in a display of power. However, as a foreseen side effect of doing this, after the war is over a third set of 200,000 completely different noncombatants would die from radiation. (Call this the Revised President Case.) Parfit thinks that doing this rather than bombing 100,000 other noncombatants as a mere means to ending the war should be ruled out either because saving 100,000 extra lives overrides morality or because the Means Principle is not part of true morality. If the Means Principle is not part of true morality, it cannot be used to distinguish morally between Bridge and Side Track.

While Parfit thinks the President Cases help us doubt that it is morally true that not harming people as a mere means (as in the Bridge Case) has priority over aiding, he ultimately rejects the Means Principle because defenses of it he examines seem inadequate. In this connection he says (p. 381), "Compared with being harmed as a means, it is neither less bad for one nor less of an objection to what other people do, if these people cause us to be equally badly harmed as a foreseen side effect."

First, consider this last point, that one has no more of an objection if one is harmed as a mere means. If Parfit thinks the president is permitted to kill noncombatants as a mere means, why should he not also think the president is permitted to prevent the 100,000 noncombatants he needs to kill from escaping his bomb or to move them into the range of his bomb? Why would also doing these things to noncombatants as a mere means to end the war be impermissible if killing them as a mere means would be permissible? While nonconsequentialists may agree with Parfit's first point, that things don't go better for people who are killed as a side effect rather than as a mere means, these additional cases may reinforce their sense that there nevertheless is "more of an objection" to being harmed as a mere means than as a side effect. This is because these cases make clear that someone who harms people as a mere means rather than as a side effect requires people's involvement to achieve his goal and therefore thinks he may simply control other people for his purposes.[35]

Now consider several problems with Parfit using the Revised President Case to raise questions about the Means Principle and any difference in permissibility of harming in Bridge and Side Track. The first problem is that the Revised President Case does not hold all other factors constant since 100,000 people would be killed as a mere means while in another option 200,000 would be killed as a side effect. By contrast, in both the Bridge and Side Track Cases one person would be killed and five saved, so any moral difference between the cases would be due to a per se difference between killing as a means and killing as a side effect. Suppose the numbers killed as a means and as a side effect in the Revised President Case were the same. Then if Parfit held that there is no moral significance to the means/side effect distinction per se, he should conclude that it would not be wrong for the president to kill the noncombatants as a mere means to end the war instead of killing the same number of different noncombatants as a side effect.

A second problem is similar to one noted in discussing the original President Case: The ratio between the 100,000 and 200,000 noncombatant deaths (or the difference in absolute numbers) in the Revised President Case might be beyond the threshold for relying on the means/side effect distinction. This could be true even if one may not kill 100,000 noncombatants as a mere causal means to save 200,000 completely different noncombatants since the same ratio could determine which alternative—killing as a means or side effect—should be chosen in order to end the war. After all, if we choose to bomb the 100,000, it would not be as a causal means to save 200,000 but as a causal means to end the war. This raises the question of why Parfit thinks the Revised President Case is relevant to deciding about principles relating to harming some as a mere means in order to aid others. Whom does Parfit think is being "aided" in this case by killing either as a means or side effect? The president is using either terror bombing or tactical bombing to end the war and this goal is not best thought of as aiding people. Parfit may think the president is aiding whichever group of people he does not kill by choosing to kill different people in a different way to end the war. However, as noted earlier, refraining from killing some people is not the same as aiding them or saving them from being killed. It is because Parfit may (mistakenly) think of terror bombing the 100,000 as a mere means to save the 200,000 that he thinks doing this would be analogous to, and support the permissibility of, killing one person as a mere means to save even two other people in a revised version of the Bridge Case where the ratio is also 2:1.

The third problem in using the Revised President Case to decide about Bridge versus Side Track is that the Revised President Case is a multiple-killing-options case, while Bridge and Side Track Cases are separate, single-killing-option cases. That is, the president will wind up killing noncombatants no matter what he does because there is at least one killing option among several that (by hypothesis) is deontologically permissible relative to not killing. This might be thought (justifiably or not) to make other ways of killing other people permissible that would not be permissible were each the only option relative to not killing. (That one will kill no matter what one does is obviously different from it being the case that more deaths will be caused if one kills in one way rather than another.) As it happens, I do not think that the fact that one will kill whatever one does alone affects what is permissible and prohibited. For example, it is commonly thought that the driver of the trolley will kill five people if he does not instead kill one person. If so, his is a multiple-killing-options case. Yet it could still be impermissible for him to topple the one person in the Bridge Case if that is the only way to stop his impermissibly killing five people. It could also be impermissible for him to topple one person as the alternative to turning the trolley and killing two people. Hence, the use of multiple-killing-options cases in itself (or combined with some difference in numbers killed in different ways) need not change what is a permissible way of killing from what it is in a single-killing-option case. Nevertheless, it can be problematic to use such multiple-options cases to draw conclusions about single-option cases because people may mistakenly focus on the agent who would have to kill (perhaps more rather than fewer people) instead of on the status of the potential victims and how their deaths would come about.

The fourth problem in using the Revised President Case to decide about the Bridge and Side Track Cases is that the president starts a new threat of a bomb (either nuclear or conventional) whatever he does. Whatever may be true in the context of war, outside of war creating a new threat may seem morally problematic by contrast to redirecting a threat already present.[36] For example, recall that Philippa Foot, a creator of the Trolley Problem, thought it was not only wrong to kill someone as a mere means to save five others but that it was wrong to save five others by introducing a gas that will as a mere side effect foreseeably kill an innocent bystander. (Call this the Gas Case.) She thought using the gas was wrong because the alternative to killing one was only not saving five. This explanation, however, would also rule out the bystander turning the trolley. An alternative possible explanation is that the gas is a new threat, whereas the trolley is a threat already facing some people in Side Track. Toppling someone off the bridge might be seen as a new threat to him (whether he is killed by the trolley or his fall). Hence, the moral difference between (i) a redirected pre-existent threat causing a side effect death in Side Track and (ii) a newly created threat causing death as a mere means in Bridge may not be due to the means/side effect distinction but to the pre-existent/new threat distinction.

3. Redirection versus New Threats. Parfit is aware that some would reject the Means Principle because they think it would be wrong to *create* a new threat when fewer are killed by it merely foreseeably even if it were permissible to *redirect* a threat so that fewer are killed by it foreseeably. (He calls this the Redirection Principle [p. 384].) He uses the following Grenade Case[37] as an example of what the Redirection Principle condemns: A grenade stops the trolley from killing five people but itself kills a bystander as a side effect. Parfit thinks that those who oppose using the grenade would support the Redirection Principle. But this need not be so. I have argued that what makes using means like the grenade wrong is not that it involves creating a new deadly threat since doing this is sometimes permissible (even outside of war). For example, in one version of my Lazy Susan Case five people who are threatened by a trolley that cannot be redirected are on a swivel table and so they can be moved away from the trolley. Their moving away will cause a new threat of rocks falling upon and killing a bystander. I think it is as permissible to move the five from the trolley in this case as it is to redirect

the trolley from the five in Side Track even though moving the five creates a new threat that will foreseeably kill someone. It is how the new threat is created that matters in my view. Hence, objecting to the Grenade Case need not imply supporting the Redirection Principle.[38]

In any case, Parfit argues against a moral distinction between someone dying from a redirected threat and his dying from a new threat. To do this he first uses a set of cases (to be considered separately rather than as three options in one case). The first is just Side Track in which redirection is assumed to be permissible. In the second, a grenade blows up the trolley before it hits the five but a piece of the trolley flies off and kills a bystander. Parfit thinks there is no moral difference between the whole trolley and a piece of it being redirected to kill one person. In the third case, a grenade blows up the trolley before it hits the five but a piece of the exploding grenade flies off, killing a bystander. Parfit thinks there is no intuitive moral difference between these three cases, while I think there is. In being killed by either a redirected trolley or its piece in Parfit's case, the one person is killed as a consequence of what in the circumstances constitutes the five being unthreatened since the elimination of the trolley threat just is their being unthreatened. Hence, the five being unthreatened, which justifies the one's death, is what causes it. This may be morally significant. Suppose that a piece of the trolley flew off and killed a bystander while the rest of the trolley still threatened the five. Then the one person would not be killed as a result of the five being unthreatened by the trolley and the piece that flew off might correctly be considered a new threat caused by a pre-existent and still existing threat. If the piece is considered a redirected, not a new, threat when it flies off as the trolley blows up, this helps show that it is not whether the threat is new but how it comes to exist (as a result of the five being free of the threat to them) that is fundamental. (This was also the point of the Lazy Susan Case.)

By contrast, a person killed by the grenade's explosion is killed by a piece of a mere causal means to, not something that constitutes, the five being unthreatened since the grenade exploding either causes the trolley to blow up or redirects it.[39] Hence, the use of a device whose importance derives from its causal role in saving the five is being valued over the one person's life. I think this involves improper subordination of the one person to the five by contrast to permissible substitution of the one for the five that occurs when the one dies as a consequence of the five being saved (as in the Side Track and Lazy Susan Cases).[40] Of course, it is not being killed by a piece of grenade versus a piece of trolley that is crucial. If a grenade will kill five people unless a trolley crushes it, a piece of the crushed grenade killing a bystander could be permissible because the grenade's being crushed constitutes the five saved. However, because in this case the trolley has only a causal relation to the five being saved, using it to crush the grenade could be impermissible if a piece of the trolley will kill a bystander.

Impermissible subordination can also occur if the means to save the five from which the one dies is a redirected threat. For example, suppose a trolley headed to kill one person can be redirected to stop another trolley from killing five, but when redirected it also causes the death of two other bystanders as a side effect. This trolley would not be redirected from one person when it will kill two people instead unless it were a causal means to stop the second trolley from killing five. Hence, the redirected trolley is a causal means to the greater good and it would kill two people instead of the original one. This makes the redirection impermissible.[41]

Parfit's second attempt to show that the Redirection Principle is wrong involves a case he calls Fire and Flood (p. 391): Ten people in a house are threatened by a fire started by lightning. One option is to save them by "using strong jets of air to redirect the fire" to a part of the house where the fire will kill five other people instead. The other option is to start a flood "which would put out the fire" but have the side effect of drowning one different person in the basement. Fire and Flood is a two-killing-options case because whatever we do to save the ten will kill others who would not otherwise die soon. It seems clear to Parfit that we should create the flood, which would be a means to saving the ten that is a newly created threat to one other person.

I have concerns about Parfit's discussion of this case. First, a case-based test for whether death by redirection differs morally per se from death by a new threat should hold constant other factors. But in Parfit's case the redirected fire would kill five and the flood would kill one. In addition, he says the flood would put out the fire, but it is not clear that redirecting the fire would also stop it. Henceforth, I will assume both stop the fire. A second concern is that Parfit may think that since the ratio is one killed (by the flood) to five killed (by redirection), deontologists who support a distinction between these ways of harming should say that saving five people from the redirected fire does not merit using a new flood threat that kills one other person as a side effect. But arguing in this way would incorrectly assume that if we may not save five people by a new means that kills one other person as a side effect (as in Foot's Gas Case), then we may not save *ten* people from the fire by a new means that kills one as a side effect rather than save them by redirecting the fire that kills five people. That is, the flood would be a means to save ten people, not five, even if we use the flood in order to avoid saving the ten by redirection that would kill five.[42] Hence, for all that has been said, it might be permissible to use a new means that kills one person as a side effect to save ten even if not to save five. This would be consistent with a per se distinction between new and redirected threats not always mattering morally and a principle based on the distinction being nonabsolute.

A third concern is that Fire and Flood is a two-killing-options case in which one option is assumed permissible. Hence, someone will be killed no matter what we do to save the ten, and this may diminish the sense that there is a moral difference between redirection and use of a new means (justifiably or not). But Parfit wants to show that there is no moral difference between redirection and use of new means when our only other option is not killing anyone, as in comparing the separate Side Track Case and Grenade Case.

Fourth, the person trapped in the basement of a house in which a fire threatens others is somewhat like a person trapped in a threat headed to others. Stopping the threat by a new means that as a side effect kills the person *in* the threat who wouldn't otherwise soon die may be permissible. A revised version of Parfit's case that eliminates this factor involves choosing between (i) starting a flood to save the ten in the house when the flood kills a person *outside* the house as a side effect and (ii) redirecting the fire from the ten in the house to the five in the house. If it were permissible to do (ii) but not (i), this would be some indication that the one person's being in the house in Parfit's original case may diminish the significance of starting a new threat.

4. Having shown, he thinks, that the Redirection Principle is incorrect, Parfit reminds us that he believes he has already shown (by the President Cases) that the Means Principle is also incorrect. Hence, he does not think that any of these principles and the distinctions they embody will make not harming (not killing) have any more priority over aiding (saving) than it has in Side Track.[43] I have tried to raise questions about the success of Parfit's arguments for this conclusion. However, in the belief he has succeeded, he proposes that true morality should include what he calls the Principle of Unintended Threats (PUT), which claims it is permissible to harm some people as a mere means or side effect if this will minimize the number of other people who die from an unintended threat such as the trolley or fire.[44] Furthermore, recall Parfit's claim that if one's self-interest is strong and doing what would serve it would be only "slightly morally wrong," practical reason would permit one to act. Since the PUT permits killing one person as a means to save two, in Parfit's view it might be only slightly wrong to kill two to save one, and so if the trolley were headed to you, it would be in accord with practical reason to topple two people in front of the trolley as a mere means to save yourself. If this is where one's practical reason and the irrelevance of deontological distinctions leads us, I do not think it is a good place to go.[45]

## Notes

1. Derek Parfit, *On What Matters,* vol. 3 (*OWM*) (Oxford: Oxford University Press, 2017) (to which all page citations refer).
2. See *OWM*, 320. Did he really believe this? I once asked him what he thought of the man who decided to give away all his organs because though he would die, several

other people would live and this was impartially best. Parfit immediately said, "I'm not talking about the crazies." I reminded him of his claim that there was always sufficient reason to do what was impartially best, so how did he know just from the man's plan that he was crazy? And even if the man had crazy motives for his act, on Parfit's view the act itself could be justified. He didn't respond but just looked at me and walked away.

3. Susan Wolf thinks that projects that provide meaning in one's life but are not self-interested in the ordinary sense present a stronger challenge to morality than does self-interest. See her *Meaning in Life and Why It Matters* (Princeton, NJ: Princeton University Press, 2010).
4. "Your very strong self interested reason to give yourself many more happy years of life would not be outweighed by your weak moral reason not to impose slightly more than this justifiable amount of harm on another making your act only slightly wrong" (p. 341).
5. Thomas Hurka argues that failing for insufficient reason to completely carry out a positive duty (e.g., to save 100 people and saving only 99) may be only slightly wrong even though someone loses his life. He thinks what matters for nonserious wrongness in the case of positive duties is that the gap between what one should have done and what one did is small, but this need not be true when one fails in a negative duty, as Parfit seems to assume. See Hurka's "More Seriously Wrong" (unpublished).
6. I actually do not think this factor makes a moral difference (for reasons I will give later), though it may sway some people's intuitive judgments.
7. For example, he says (*OWM*, 347–48), "If the President chooses the Nuclear Policy, he would kill many civilians as a means of avoiding killing . . . about three times as many others civilians. The proportions here are similar to those in Bridge . . . in which you would kill one person as a means of saving five other people" by toppling him in front of a trolley to stop it as it heads to the five.
8. There is also deontic goodness according to Parfit. According to him, both these involve the effort and intention involved in doing or omitting the wrong and right acts and so are not simply a translation of the wrongness and rightness of acts or omissions themselves. Hence, Parfit says that when doing the morally right act is easy, it has little deontic value; when it is hard (physically or psychologically), it has more deontic value. (See p. 360.) This implausibly implies that only if it is hard for someone to do the morally right act might his acting outweigh some amount of nondeontic goodness that would come to pass if he didn't act.
9. See ibid., 355–56. However, note that when Parfit first discusses (p. 351) a sheriff's act of killing one innocent to stop others from wrongly killing two other innocents, he says: "This sheriff's act would make things go better both deontologically and nondeontologically since . . . fewer people would act wrongly . . . and fewer people would be killed."
10. Note that if our wrong act of killing one person prevented five people from ever intending wrong acts of killing, on Parfit's view it would also prevent five times as much deontic badness and this could count in favor of our wrong act.

11. This is why deontologists think it is wrong to kill someone even to prevent five other wrong killings. Parfit notes that deontologists see nothing wrong in saving two people from accidental deaths rather than one person from a murder. He thinks this may show they do not think deontic badness counts for much relative to nondeontic goodness. However, since they don't determine the seriousness of wrong acts by calculating their deontic badness (as Parfit conceives of this), this needn't mean they don't take wrong acts seriously and hope they won't be done. For example, they may think that if they cannot save the two accident victims by innocent means, they should still stop the one person from being murdered to save the two even if the two will then die, and regret it if they are not able to do so. It may be hard to represent this deontologically consistent set of views by assigning a constant weight for the deontic badness of the murder that gets added to the outcome in Parfit's system.
12. I have discussed the role of status in my *Morality, Mortality*, vol. 2 (New York: Oxford University Press, 1996), among other places. Thomas Nagel tries to combine what he sees as different components of practical normative reasoning (deontological morality, consequentialist considerations, etc.) but not in a way that makes practical reasoning consequentialist. An early attempt of his is "The Fragmentation of Value," reprinted in *Mortal Questions* (Cambridge: Cambridge University Press, 1979).
13. See "The Fragmentation of Value," 133. Nagel's approach is different from the non-agent-relative account of deontological restrictions I gave that focuses on the status of each potential victim impartially considered. It is not clear why focusing on the personal view the agent has of his own acts would not imply that a driver of an out-of-control trolley who is about to kill five people may not topple one other person from a bridge so that he lands in front of the trolley, stopping it, rather than redirect the trolley, thereby killing two people instead. After all, this will cause the driver to kill one instead of five or two. Yet doing so is deontologically prohibited. For more about the contrast between agent-relative and non-agent-relative accounts of deontological restrictions see my *Morality, Mortality*, vol. 2, and Chapter 9 in this volume.
14. *Journal of Philosophy* 82 (1985): 118–38. Henceforth SO. A revised version appears as Chapter 15 in *Morality, Mortality*, vol. 2.
15. I claimed that saving at high cost to oneself remains supererogatory and not a duty even when one is willing to make the effort. Suppose it became a duty. Then one could not refuse to save at the high cost when another personal opportunity comes along if the opportunity would not override the duty to save at low cost to oneself. Yet I think an opportunity could override saving at high cost even if it could not override saving at low cost to oneself.
16. In SO footnote, p. 125. I said: "Because an act that is less stringently required by one measure may take precedence over another act that is more stringently required by that same measure, proving that negative duties are more stringently required than positive duties in the sense that we must make a greater effort to perform them, does not resolve the problem of whether we may violate a negative duty to perform a positive one. For example, Philippa Foot says that we may not kill one person to save others, because the duty not to kill is more stringent than the duty to aid (in

'The Problem of Abortion and the Doctrine of Double Effect,' reprinted in Bonnie Steinbock, ed., *Killing and Letting Die* (Englewood Cliffs, NJ: Prentice-Hall, 1980)). But that greater stringency may mean only that we would *have* to make a greater effort to avoid killing someone than to aid others, and this does not imply that if we *want* to we may not violate a negative duty in order to aid."

17. This assumes one's personal interests do not rise to the level of being an impartial greater good. However, Parfit's concern about the conflict between morality and self-interest may be an independent ground for arguing against such self-sacrifice.
18. Parfit does not consider whether one's duty to make personal sacrifices rather than harm someone else might imply having to make such sacrifices to achieve the greater good instead of harming someone else for this purpose when possible. I discuss this issue in "Can Duties Become Supererogatory or Forbidden?" in ed. J. McMahan et al, *Principles and Persons: The Legacy of Derek Parfit* (Oxford: Oxford University Press), 2021, 441–63 and in Chapter 8 of this volume.
19. The case Parfit calls Side Track is identical with the bystander version of the trolley case that Judith Thomson introduced in "Killing, Letting Die, and the Trolley Problem," *The Monist* 59 (1976): 204–17. In discussing Parfit, I shall continue to use his name for the case.
20. However, this seems to be true of all cases where the choice is between aiding the five and not harming the one. For example, the five need to be aided rather than not harmed only because the trolley is already headed to them in a case where the bystander would have to topple one other person on a bridge in front of the trolley to stop it. Perhaps Parfit means that the only reason the five need to be aided while the one needs not to be harmed is that the trolley already headed to the five could instead have been headed to the one, or it could have been at a crossroad where the choice would have been between sending it to harm the five and sending it to harm the one. This is not true if we have to topple someone to stop the trolley. In that case, the trolley not already being headed to the five would not mean that it would have instead been going to the one person on the bridge.
21. He here seems to borrow this idea from Judith Thomson given in her "Killing and Letting Die, and the Trolley Problem," though he does not cite her. She says (p. 209): "There is no Principle of Moral Inertia; no prima facie duty to not interfere with existing states of affairs just because they are existing states of affairs."
22. Compare with what Thomson says in "Killing, Letting Die, and the Trolley Problem": "Edward (or Frank) may deflect the trolley if and only if the one has no more claim against the trolley than any of the five has." Her view about either goods (like a health pebble) or bads (like a trolley threat) is that its being headed to someone does not per se give him more claim than others to have the good or less claim not to have the bad. The big difference between what Thomson says in that article and Parfit's view is that Thomson holds that one may redistribute to one person what he has no more claim to avoid than others only by doing something to an item to which he has no greater claim than others. So she thinks, unlike Parfit as we shall see, that we may not redirect the trolley by toppling someone over a bridge because we would then do something to his body over which he has more claim than others in order to

redistribute the trolley threat (which he has no more claim to avoid than others). In later work, she revises these views.

23. In the Loop Case, the trolley is redirected to a track that loops back to the five but the one person not originally threatened is on that very track and stops the looping. In my Returning Trolley Case the person not originally threatened is on another track than the one that loops back toward one of the five originally threatened.
24. I discussed Sending Back Cases in my *Intricate Ethics* (New York: Oxford University Press, 2007), 167–9 and in my *The Trolley Problem Mysteries* (New York: Oxford University Press, 2016). In the latter, I also considered the possibility that someone who had been originally threatened by the trolley might also redirect it away from himself even if it harmed more innocent nonthreatening people who had not previously been harmed. I described this as another case in which someone need not let (himself) die rather than kill but not because someone may do much more harm to others to save himself than he may do to save other people.
25. I pointed this out in *The Trolley Problem Mysteries.* It remains possible that other means besides those permissible to harm the one could permissibly be used by the one to stop anyone from permissibly infringing his rights in order to save the five.
26. Similarly, it can in itself be a morally irrelevant difference whether someone makes five movements with his hand or six. Yet the six but not the five could amount to his hitting someone and this is a morally relevant difference.
27. The original case that Thomson discusses in connection with moral inertia involves a health pebble headed toward one person that a bystander can redirect toward five people. Thomson argues that the pebble may be redirected and the fact that it is already headed to the one gives him no greater claim than the five to the pebble. This is not a crosspoint case in which we must decide to whom to direct the health pebble (and thus whom to aid) in the first instance. Rather it involves interfering with aid that is on its way toward someone when the interference is not caused by someone who has ownership over the pebble. This makes interference closer to harming even if it is morally permissible. Indeed, if the owner of the health pebble had sent it to the one person, others interfering with it would probably be impermissible.
28. I discuss this view in detail in *Morality, Mortality,* vol. 2: *Intricate Ethics, The Trolley Problem Mysteries*, and in Chapter 9 in this volume.
29. Like Parfit (p. 388), I am inclined to think that five lives lost is not a threshold number and that whatever could account for the permissibility of turning the trolley to save five and kill one could account for the permissibility of turning to save two and kill one or to save five and kill four. If we could not account for the latter two cases, I doubt we could account for the original Side Track Case. The permissibility of turning in the latter two cases seems even clearer when the trolley driver would turn the trolley to avoid killing the two or five.
30. An example of this is not being indifferent between whether (i) one harms someone to help someone else or (ii) one does not help someone rather than harm someone else, when the loss to each person would be the same.
31. I discuss this case in more detail in *The Trolley Problem Mysteries* and in Chapter 9 in this volume.

32. For two of my attempts to do this see *Intricate Ethics*, Chapter 5, and Chapter 9 in this volume.
33. Parfit's Bridge Case is the same as the Fat Man Case that Thomson introduced in her "Killing, Letting Die, and the Trolley Problem." I think toppling would be impermissible to save the five even if the one person would suffer only a significantly lesser loss such as paralysis in both legs.
34. Strictly speaking, the means to stop the trolley in Bridge is not the person's death but his being hit by the trolley (which causes his death); hence, stopping the trolley requires his involvement in a way that is foreseeably harmful to him. I shall ignore this fine point as does Parfit. The Means Principle is related to but not the same as the Doctrine of Double Effect (DDE) discussed in Chapter 2. It need not contrast states of mind such as intending and merely foreseeing. Instead, it can refer to something having a required causal role in producing an outcome by contrast to something being a mere side effect having no such causal role.
35. Warren Quinn, whom Parfit criticizes (p. 381), emphasized this. See his "Actions, Intentions, and Consequences: The Doctrine of Double Effect," *Philosophy & Public Affairs* 18, no. 4 (1989): 334–51. In Chapter 2 we considered Ronald Dworkin's attempt to justify the related distinction between doing something intending someone's death versus merely foreseeing it. He thinks the former but not the latter involves seeing something good about someone's death contrary to a person's own view and hence usurps someone's guiding his life by his own values, contrary to what dignity requires.
36. The reduced significance of side effect harm from a new threat in war may be due to the status of those who would be harmed. For example, if they are citizens of the unjust side, they may have to bear greater risk of harm so that their country not be unjust. See my "Failures of Just War Theory," *Ethics* 114, no. 4: 2004, 650–692 (reprinted in my *The Moral Target: Aiming at Right Conduct in War and Other Conflicts* [New York: Oxford University Press, 2012]) for more on this.
37. Which I discuss in *Morality, Mortality*, vol. 2.
38. For more on this see *Intricate Ethics*, *The Trolley Problem Mysteries*, and Chapter 9 in this volume. Parfit considers (p. 377) my view that if it were permissible to kill one person as a mere means to save five, the moral status of all six people would be lower. He wonders why I do not think that one's moral status would also be lower if using means that kill as a side effect were permissible. Given that I have argued that killing in Grenade-type Cases is wrong, I do not rule out that one's moral status would be lower if using such means were permissible. However, see earlier discussion of proposals for differential import of harming as a mere means versus harming as a side effect.
39. It is the mere means to the greater good causing the side effect death that is important, not *when* it causes the side effect death. So it is no better if the mere means causes the one death after it causes the greater good than if there is a different temporal order.
40. I discuss these distinctions and a Principle of Permissible Harm (PPH) based on them in *Morality, Mortality*, vol. 2; *Intricate Ethics*; *The Trolley Problem Mysteries*, and in Chapter 9 in this volume.

41. I discuss this case again in Chapter 9.
42. A similar point was made about Parfit's President Cases: Choosing between alternative means to an end does not involve whatever means one chooses to the end being a causal means to preventing bad effects of the alternative means to the end.
43. Parfit thinks that cases like Grenade and Bridge are "more complicated" (p. 388) than Side Track because they involve other differences that must be shown not to matter morally any more than that the trolley is already headed to some people rather than to others. However, since Parfit thinks that a threat already being headed to people does not create a morally relevant difference between their and others' claims to life, it is surprising that he did not simply argue that its being possible to redirect a threat to another person does not create a morally relevant difference between his claim to life and the claim of those who could be killed only by creating a new threat (as in Grenade or Bridge). Some may think that deontological distinctions in how people come to be killed unfairly prevent correcting for the morally irrelevant luck of being subject to death by a pre-existing rather than a new threat. I think it is true that deontological distinctions often make correcting for mere luck impermissible, but this may be a side effect of morally necessary respect for persons that those distinctions reflect.
44. As the President Cases involve killing in response to an enemy's intended threat in war, perhaps his new principle should not be limited to dealing with unintended threats.
45. This chapter is based on a paper presented at conferences in memory of Derek Parfit at Rutgers and Oxford University as well as a keynote address at the Workshop in Normative Ethics (2019) and as the Jack Smart Memorial Lecture (2019) at the Australian National University. I am grateful for comments to audiences on those occasions as well as to Larry Temkin and members of our Rutgers philosophy graduate class. An earlier, shorter version of this chapter (without discussion of moral inertia) appears as "Parfit on the Irrelevance of Deontological Distinctions," in *Oxford Studies in Normative Ethics*, ed. Mark Timmons (Oxford: Oxford University Press, 2020), 9–31.

# 8
# Duties That Become Supererogatory or Forbidden?

In this chapter, I will first review some relations examined in Chapter 7 between making personal sacrifices, fulfilling personal duties, and promoting the greater good. I will then focus on whether fulfilling certain duties could require us, contrary to the relations described, to make sacrifices ordinarily considered supererogatory to promote the greater good. I will first consider this question with regard to duties to provide aid, some of which are correlative to contractual or promissory rights to be aided. I will then compare these duties with ones not to harm (that are correlative to rights not to be harmed) with which Derek Parfit is concerned. I will then consider whether fulfilling duties not to harm could require us to make sacrifices for the greater good ordinarily considered supererogatory or whether acting for the greater good could instead make sacrifices that are ordinarily dutiful become supererogatory. In this connection I also examine some of Judith Thomson's views on choosing between harm to oneself and harm to others in the Trolley Problem. The chapter concludes by considering Parfit's view that nonconsequentialism can result, incorrectly, in an agent's deontological permission to do harm varying depending on the permissions other agents have to do harm. He attributes this to nonconsequentialism's focus on action for a personal rather than a common aim.

I. First let us review some of what was said in Chapter 7. Recall that Parfit first argues against the deontological principle that not harming is a more stringent duty than aiding. He accepts that there are at least two possible measures of such proposed stringency: (a) The agent is morally required to bear greater costs to avoid causing harm than to aid and (b) not harming takes priority over aiding when these conflict. He also accepts that not harming can be more stringent by the first measure (cost) and yet be less stringent by the second measure (priority). That the measures of cost and priority can come apart in this way was one major point of my article "Supererogation and Obligation" (SO).[1] I there argued that one might, for example, have to bear greater costs to fulfill one's contractual business duty (which is a positive duty correlative to a positive contractual right) than to help save someone's life, yet one might also permissibly give priority to saving someone's life over fulfilling the contractual duty when they conflict. (Call this the Business Case.) This is true, I argued, whether saving someone's life is

*Rights and Their Limits: In Theory, Cases, and Pandemics.* F. M. Kamm, Oxford University Press.
© Oxford University Press 2022. DOI: 10.1093/oso/9780197567739.003.0008

what is a simple "natural" duty done at low cost to oneself or it is supererogatory because of the high cost to oneself.[2] For example, one might miss an important business deadline to jump into shark-infested waters to save someone's life. I argued that this is true even when the person to whom the contractual duty is owed would not be morally obligated to waive it so that someone else may be saved, because of the high cost to him of doing so. Hence, sometimes supererogation takes precedence over obligation (duty).

However, the cases that I used to show how the two measures of stringency can come apart did not involve a choice between saving some and not physically harming someone else. It is the latter sort of case, which involves a negative duty not to harm correlative to a so-called natural, noncontracted negative right not to be harmed, that concerns Parfit. Nevertheless, I did note (what Parfit emphasizes) that not harming being more stringent by the cost measure does not alone show it is more stringent by the priority measure.[3]

Parfit may emphasize the difference between these two measures of stringency because he thinks that rejecting the priority within morality of not harming over aiding does not imply that morality requires one to make great personal sacrifices for purposes of aiding. Though he does not say so, his aim seems to be to avoid the so-called Over-Demandingness Objection to Consequentialism by retaining Common-Sense Morality's nonconsequentialist personal prerogative not to make large personal sacrifices to achieve the greater good, thus making such sacrifices supererogatory.[4] However, he wants to combine this with jettisoning Common-Sense Morality's deontological side constraint on not harming others to achieve the greater good. This would permit those who would not sacrifice themselves for the greater good to try to sacrifice another for its sake. Parfit does not rule out that these positions are compatible with costly self-sacrifices being required and not supererogatory to avoid harming others when only one's own interests and no greater good are at stake.

It might seem that if Parfit were correct that not harming has no priority over aiding, then we should not be required to bear higher personal costs to avoid harming than to aid. But I argued in SO that it is intuitively plausible that aiding to achieve the greater good could sometimes take precedence over positive personal duties such as keeping promises, and yet one may not avoid the personal sacrifices necessary to meet these personal duties even if one is not morally required to make such sacrifices to go beyond minimal morality and achieve the greater good. The personal duties can be weaker relative to going beyond minimal morality to produce the greater good than are my interests, and yet my interests in avoiding personal sacrifices can be weaker relative to these personal duties. Hence, Parfit's applying such a view to negative duties yields the same sort of (at least seeming but explicable) intransitivity that I identified in SO in the case of positive personal duties. To see this, combine his and my original view to get the following set of relations: Avoiding personal sacrifices (S) could take precedence over (>) aiding to produce a greater good (A), or (S > A); such aid to some could take precedence over the negative duty (DN) not to harm someone else as well as over performing a personal positive duty (DP) for someone else, or (A > DPN); and yet not harming someone else as well as performing a personal positive duty for someone else could take precedence over avoiding personal sacrifices, or –(S > DPN).

I call this only a "seeming intransitivity" because different factors account for precedence relations in the different steps; there is no single relation that is shown to be intransitive. That is, the dominance of the personal in the first step is accounted for by limits on personal sacrifice to go beyond minimal requirements of morality such as not harming or keeping promises. The greater good may be able to dominate such minimal duties, but mere personal interests (that do not involve greater good) may have to be sacrificed to achieve minimal moral requirements. It is not because one would be doing an even greater good in fulfilling personal interests that these are dominant over pursuing a great good nor is it because the a personal duty involves a greater good that the duty can dominate personal interests in the conclusion. Hence, the fact that personal interests can take precedence over the greater good and greater good can take precedence over personal duty need not imply that personal interests can take precedence over personal duty.

Suppose that in this system of relations between personal duty, personal sacrifices, and the greater good, there is a case in which one has a duty to make significant personal sacrifices rather than harm someone else and also to fulfill a personal obligation to aid someone. Making personal sacrifices rather than harming someone could come about by either (i) not doing something harmful to someone else that would prevent losses to oneself with which one is already threatened (e.g., one would not throw someone else in front of a threat to prevent one's being hit by it) or (ii) preventing harm to someone else from a threat that one would initially present to him (e.g., one would swerve to avoid running over someone). In (i) but not (ii), if one did not harm someone, one would suffer personal losses independently of trying to prevent harming the other person.

Parfit does not consider whether the personal duty to make such large sacrifices rather than harm another might imply having a duty to make them to achieve the greater good *instead* of harming someone else for this purpose when this is possible.[5] Similarly, I did not consider whether the duty to make such large sacrifices to fulfill a personal positive duty to another might imply having a duty to make them to achieve the greater good without abandoning the person to whom one has the personal positive duty when this is possible. In what follows I will first deal with my omission and then with Parfit's.

II. Consider what I will call the Personal Lifeguard Case: Suppose someone's personal lifeguard has a duty to prevent his client drowning not merely at small cost to himself but even at the cost of his own life. This duty is correlative to the client's contracted positive right to be saved even at such high cost. (I assume it is morally possible to contract for such high sacrifice as bodyguards can be morally required to take a bullet for a client.) I shall assume that the client would have gone in the water even if he had no personal lifeguard and no one else but the actual lifeguard applied for the job. A big wave now threatens to drown the client and also 100 other people at some distance from him. If the lifeguard saves the one person, he cannot save 100, and vice versa. He does not have either a contracted, promissory, or simple natural duty to save the 100 at the cost of his life. I think it is morally permissible for him to save the 100 people and abandon the client whether or not the effort involved in saving them would be as great as, more than, or less than what is morally required to save the client.[6]

I am imagining that the lifeguard is employed to help someone and that is what I mean by his having a contractual duty. However, I am not concerned with the legal permissibility of abandoning his job but with the moral considerations that might override his fulfilling the contracted duties of his job. A revised version of the case could involve a promissory duty correlative to the right that a promise holder has rather than a job-generated duty. In this revised case, we could imagine that someone promises to do for someone else what a private lifeguard would do including taking on the risks and burdens that such a personal lifeguard would take on. Then the question is whether other moral considerations could override the moral (rather than legal) rights and duties generated by the promise.

Given what I have assumed, the lifeguard's failure to aid his client would be a case of letting his client die and not a case of killing him. This is because in not saving him the lifeguard has not made his client worse off with respect to loss of his life than he would have been without the lifeguard's commitment. (We assumed the client would have gone into the water in any case and no one else would have signed on to save him.) Still, in this case, the client does not have a moral duty to waive his right against the lifeguard so that the lifeguard may save the others. The client would also not have a moral duty to sacrifice his life (which he will lose if the lifeguard fails him) to save the 100 other people. Hence, I think we cannot account for (what I will assume is) the permissibility of the lifeguard not saving his client on the grounds that there is no duty still in existence to his client that he does not at least infringe.[7]

However, suppose that if and only if the lifeguard employed a means to save the 100 that costs him his life, he could also save his client. (Call this the Personal Lifeguard Both Case.) Suppose in this case he would *not* be willing to pay this price as a supererogatory sacrifice to save the 100 alone though he would be willing to make a much smaller supererogatory sacrifice to do so. But he would be willing to sacrifice his life as morally required by his client's right were this necessary (which it is not as only small cost is actually needed ) to save his client alone. The question is whether he could no longer permissibly abandon his client to save the 100 at small or minimally supererogatory cost when there is a way for him to also fulfill his duty to his client by saving the 100 at a cost that is as great as but no greater than what could be morally required of him to save his client alone. Must he avoid failing in his duty to his client as he saves the 100 or else not save the 100 and fulfill his duty to his client at a low cost? It may seem that he could permissibly refuse to make the larger sacrifice and just do the minimum necessary to save his client or that he could choose to make the larger sacrifice that will save his client and the 100, but that he may no longer abandon his client.

An alternative view that I shall call Still Abandon Client View is that in Personal Lifeguard Both it is permissible for the lifeguard to abandon his client. Here is a particular defense of it: Saving the 100 lives could be a good enough reason for the lifeguard to leave his client to die as shown by what (we assume) the lifeguard may do when there is no possibility of saving everyone. Furthermore, if he would not save the 100 were he morally required to also save his client at the high cost of his life, the outcome that could have overridden the duty to his client will not come about. It may seem odd to have to sacrifice an outcome that could have overridden the duty just so that he will perform the duty when he is only trying not to lose his life in both fulfilling his duty and saving the 100 whom he had no duty to save at that high cost. (Call this the Oddity Defense.) If the Still Abandon Client View were correct, it would show that in this case a duty to make an otherwise morally required sacrifice for one's client becomes supererogatory.

In this case, saving his client at the high cost of giving up his own life becomes necessary only because the lifeguard chooses to save the 100, which is what it is permissible (and even right) for him to do rather than save his client when they cannot both be accomplished. The cost to him becomes so great *because* he would be saving the 100 though he would not be willing to (and morally need not) pay the cost *in order* to save the 100 alone. By contrast, what if it would actually have been physically necessary for him to give up his life in order to save his client alone had he not chosen to save the 100, and he can now save both at this high cost? In this case the high cost predates his saving the 100. (Call this case Personal Lifeguard Both Pre-Cost.) Then it does indeed seem that he should give up his life to save both at this same cost. (Given that he would have to pay the high cost anyway to save his client, it would be wrong not to also save the 100 at no extra cost.) In this case, it is not true that he needn't save both just because when only one option could be achieved, saving the 100 even at low cost would override the contractual duty he would have been required to perform even at high cost. It seems the difference between Personal Lifeguard Both Pre-Cost and

Personal Lifeguard Both is how the high cost comes to be needed to save his client. In Personal Lifeguard Both Pre-Cost it is independent of, but in Personal Lifeguard Both dependent on, doing the act that could permissibly override the dutiful act to his client if only one of them could be done.

However, there is another difference between the cases to consider. In Personal Lifeguard Both Pre-Cost the high cost to the lifeguard is causally needed to save his client. By contrast, in the Personal Lifeguard Both Case as described, the high cost is causally needed to save the 100 if he is to also save his client in a causally noncostly way. I do not think this is a morally significant difference. After all, there could be a version of the Personal Lifeguard Both Case in which it is only because the lifeguard chooses one noncostly way rather than another to save the 100 that he can also save his client but only at the cost of his life. I think the same question of whether he must do what allows him to also save his client arises as in the Personal Lifeguard Both Pre-Cost Case even though here the high cost would have a causal role in saving his client and not the 100.

So we should consider further whether it could be the difference in how the high cost to save both comes about that is sufficient to make a moral difference to whether the lifeguard may abandon his client. Consider a case called Personal Lifeguard Both Post-Cost: The lifeguard abandons his client, whom he could have saved at a low cost, to save the 100 at the only time this is possible and at low cost when there is no way to help both. His client does not immediately drown and he can still save his client after he saves the 100. However, because he saved the 100 first, saving his client now involves sacrificing his life. In this case, even though the high cost to also save his client arises because of his saving the 100, it may seem that he is morally required to pay the cost. After all, many dutiful or nondutiful but morally worthwhile things we do in life may raise the eventual cost to us of doing our contractual duties at a later time, yet this does not relieve us of the duty to pay the higher costs. If so, how could the fact that the high cost to save his client arises from his saving the 100 be sufficient, as suggested earlier, to morally distinguish Personal Lifeguard Both and Personal Lifeguard Both Pre-Cost?

Perhaps the temporal difference between Personal Lifeguard Both and Personal Lifeguard Both Post-Cost plays a role in justifying the Still Abandon Client View for the former case alone.[8] That is, in both cases the lifeguard's act of saving the 100 results in there being a high cost to him of saving both the 100 and his client, but he must pay that cost at different times in each case: In Personal Lifeguard Both, he would have to pay it concurrent with performing the act that could override his requirement to save his client, whereas that act has already occurred by the time he must pay the high cost in Personal Lifeguard Both Post-Cost. Hence, in Post-Cost there is nothing that overrides his duty to his client at the time he must perform the duty. But this analysis in terms of time does not seem fundamental. Rather, it seems fundamental that in Personal Lifeguard Both the high cost would have to be paid to prevent a bad effect (i.e., the client drowning) that would come about because of doing the very act that justifies that bad effect. (Call this the "Causal" Explanation of the Still Abandon Client View. I put causal in quotes because the bodyguard not being available to save the client when he is saving the 100 does not, I believe, strictly speaking cause the client's drowning. The drowning is caused by the big wave whose deadly effect the lifeguard is not available to prevent.) By contrast, in Personal Lifeguard Both Post-Cost the high cost would not be paid to prevent a bad effect that comes about because of the doing of an act that justifies that bad effect since that act has already been done without leading to the client being drowned. What would "cause" the bad effect is crucial, not merely what causes the high cost to prevent the bad effect (i.e., saving the 100).

Nevertheless, suppose that the lifeguard in Personal Lifeguard Both Post-Cost could foresee the high cost he would be morally required to pay to save his client if he first saved the 100. He might then reasonably refuse to save the 100. Even though saving them would not involve a large sacrifice in itself, he would have to lose his life eventually *because* he saved them. Once again, as emphasized in the Oddity Defense of the Still Abandon Client View, we would lose the good outcome that would have morally overridden the duty to save his client when both could not be done, and this may seem odd. But this Oddity Defense of why Personal Lifeguard Both and Personal Lifeguard Both Post-Cost should be treated as morally alike seems too consequentialist, aiming merely to not undermine achieving the best outcome. By contrast, the "Causal" Explanation of why Personal Lifeguard Both Post-Cost and Personal Lifeguard Both are morally different focuses on whether the high cost would have to be paid to prevent a bad effect (death) that comes about by the doing of the very act that justifies the bad effect. This occurs only in Personal Lifeguard Both. The "Causal" Explanation seems to me a better justification of the Still Abandon Client View.

What if it would take only a bit more effort than the lifeguard is required and prepared to make to save the 100 on their own in order to save both them and his client in another version of Personal Lifeguard Both? The total effort would still be within what could be required of the lifeguard to save his client alone. In this case, I think, the fact that saving the 100 is a good reason for not saving his client when both cannot be done would not relieve him of the duty of also saving his client by paying the higher cost. This is so even if the higher cost and the bad effect of abandoning his client would come about by doing the act that overrides the duty to his client and for which on its own the larger cost would be supererogatory. After all, he will have infringed his client's right in abandoning him to save the 100 (even if he acts permissibly and so does not violate his client's right).[9] This means, I think, that he could wrong his client even if he does not do a wrong act and he should pay some price to avoid such wronging if not the very great one required were he not saving the 100. Not doing so would itself be wrong.

In sum, on the Still Abandon Client View deciding whether the lifeguard morally must pay more to save both parties in Personal Lifeguard Both than to only save the 100 does not involve considering what is the most the lifeguard owes to his client independent of his doing what could override his duty at that time. Rather, deciding involves considering the additional price he would have to pay to avoid the bad effect (client's death) that comes about by the lifeguard doing what could override his duty to his client. If the price is low, he should pay it to also fulfill the duty to his client; it is not supererogatory with respect to his client. However, if the price is high, he needn't pay it. The basic idea (roughly) is that when only his personal interests compete with fulfilling his lifeguard's duty, he cannot refuse to make large sacrifices. But when achieving some greater good that overrides his duty to his client would threaten nonperformance of the duty and also increase the cost of performing the duty (even if not above what would be required for the duty on its own), he should not be required to make the very large sacrifice to also save his client. Paying such a cost to save his client, which in some circumstances is a duty, becomes supererogatory.[10]

However, this is not the same as saying that he needn't save his client at any cost to himself that would justify his not actually bringing about the greater good that overrides his duty. The cost that could justify him in not bringing about the greater good is a supererogatory cost for that purpose. But this cost could be the result of even a small additional cost he would have a duty to bear to also avoid wronging his client. Saving the 100 will not justify refusing to pay the small extra cost to avoid wronging his client the way saving the 100 justified not saving the client when both could not be done. Hence, someone could decide to avoid wrongfully omitting to bear the small extra cost to save both by not saving the 100. Whether this would be a morally wise decision I leave unanswered.

We might represent part of our conclusion (where " > S(PD)" means "causes sacrifices to be needed for personal positive duty") as: Sometimes when we needn't make large personal sacrifices to achieve a great good (S > A, where "S" by itself means "avoiding personal sacrifices"), achieving that great good (i) overrides some personal duty to aid for whose sake we could be morally required to make large personal sacrifices and (ii) achieving the great good also causes the sacrifices to perform that personal duty to go up (i.e., (A > PD) > S(PD)). When this is so, we may avoid the large personal sacrifices rather than perform the personal duty (S > PD). (This contrasts with the conclusion that – (S > PD) in the representation of the seeming intransitivity considered earlier.) Whereas an original aim of discussing the relation between personal sacrifice, personal duty, and achieving the greater good was to show that supererogation may permissibly take precedence over duty, the aim of the current discussion has been to show that what is ordinarily a duty (that takes precedence over avoiding personal sacrifices) can become supererogatory (when avoiding personal sacrifices may permissibly take precedence over performing the act that would otherwise be a duty).[11]

III. We must now consider the case Parfit omitted to deal with, whether we must sacrifice ourself to avoid harming someone else in order to achieve a greater good. However, before doing that it is worth noting some ways in which the Personal Lifeguard Case differs from the cases of interest to Parfit. Personal Lifeguard is a case of (i) letting someone die (a type of not aiding) while (ii) merely foreseeing his death in order to (iii) go and help a far greater number of others (not merely any additional number of people). By contrast, Parfit is interested in cases that involve killing someone (a type of harming) in order to help others. He first tries to undermine the moral significance of the harming/not aiding distinction by arguing that a bystander may save five people by diverting a trolley headed to them when he merely foresees that this will kill one other person. However, we have seen (in Chapter 7) that he goes on to argue that killing as a mere means (as in toppling a fat man from a bridge to stop the trolley) and killing as a side effect of a means to redirecting the trolley (as in using a grenade to redirect the trolley when a part of the grenade kills a bystander) are also permissible to save the five. Furthermore, he thinks we may kill one person in each of these ways to save only two other people from an unintended threat. Presumably he would also think we may kill four people to save five others.

Consider the issue of numbers of people saved. Though I disagree with Parfit's claim that all these ways of killing are morally permissible, I do suspect that if an argument justifies turning the trolley toward one person to save five, it would also justify turning it toward one person to save two people. If the argument could not justify this other act, I do not think it could justify killing one to save as small a number as five. (This is not an instance of a threshold on not harming being reached because of the large number of people needing to be saved.)

Furthermore, suppose it were permissible to turn the trolley to save only five or more. This is still a much lower number of people saved, I think, than would justify the personal lifeguard in our cases leaving his client to die. This would be true even if the lifeguard weren't morally required to do as much to save his client as giving up his life. It would also be true if the personal sacrifice he was required to make to save his client was less than the sacrifice he was required to make not to kill someone when only that person's and his own interests were at stake.

It is standardly thought that the ordinary negative duty not to kill someone is more stringent than even a strong positive duty, as shown by the impermissibility of killing to achieve an end that a positive duty may be abandoned to achieve. For example, the lifeguard may not kill or do what kills his client or anyone else to go and save the 100 people. Yet in a further variant of the

Personal Lifeguard Case, the lifeguard would not be permitted to abandon his contracted positive duty to achieve the good of saving *five* lives though many think achieving this would justify one in killing someone at least by diverting a threat from the five. This is so even though independent of any contract or promise each person is thought to have a so-called natural claim right against everyone that they not kill him. Might this difference between the cases exist because the death of the one in the trolley diversion case would be a result of the five people already being saved when the trolley moves away, but the death of the client would be a result not of the five people already being saved but of what the lifeguard does in order to save them rather than his client?[12] But suppose the five being saved by the personal lifeguard would itself create a barrier that alone prevents him from saving his client. Then the five already being saved would also lead to the death of his client. Yet it would still be *impermissible* for the lifeguard to save the five rather than his client.

The added strength of a positive right due to its being contracted can help explain some of the difference in these cases since being contracted can sometimes also strengthen negative rights. For example, an agreement not to kill the one other person on the side track could help make turning the trolley to save the five impermissible, as Judith Thomson pointed out.[13] This suggests that while duties may be distinguished by whether they are or are not correlative to rights (e.g., duties to give charity are thought not to be correlative to rights as discussed in Chapter 4), duties correlative to rights may be distinguished by whether they are correlative to uncontracted, nonpromissory rights (and so are uncontracted or nonpromissory correlative duties) or correlative to contracted or promissory rights (and so are contracted or promissory correlative duties). (See Figure 8.1.)

Let us now consider some ways of not fulfilling the positive duty in Personal Lifeguard that are analogous to harming as a mere means, which Parfit thinks is permissible in order to bring about a greater good. What if the client's not being saved was not a mere side effect of the lifeguard going to save others or of the others being saved? Suppose his not being saved played a causal role in the others being saved. Here are at least three ways in which this could happen: (a) Only the client's drowning makes available a device the lifeguard needs to swim

Duties

Not correlative to rights

Correlative to rights

uncontracted/nonpromissory right

contracted/promissory right

**Figure 8.1.** Duties

fast enough to save the other people. In this case the client's death is part of the lifeguard's required means to save the others.[14] This is why he cannot save the client and also the 100 and he lets the client drown so the device becomes available. (b) Everything is as in (a) except that he leaves his client to save 70 other nearby people he would not otherwise have saved (since he is prejudiced against them), merely because doing so allows his client to die so that the means he needs to save the 100 is available. (c) The lifeguard can save the 100 people from a big wave merely by swimming toward them when that is incompatible with his saving his client. However, doing this would not protect those people from dying of a second threat that arises because he saves them from the wave (e.g., a shark would then sense their presence and attack). It is only because his client died—a result of the lifeguard abandoning him to save the 100 from the wave—that a device is available to ward off the second threat.

In (c) the lifeguard would (reasonably) not go to save the 100 from drowning unless the second threat could be stopped. Hence, he acts because he foresees that his client will die if he first saves the 100 from the wave. Nevertheless, in this case he does not refrain from saving his client as a means to save the 100 from the wave, which is the first threat from which he must save them if they are to survive. In (b) he does refrain from saving his client as a means to save the 100 from the wave, but this does not make what he does impermissible if, regardless of his reason for leaving his client, saving the 70 people could justify his leaving his client. It is only in case (a) that his not saving his client as a means to save the 100 seems impermissible since there is nothing else brought about without the client's death being a means to it (as in [b]) that justifies his refraining from aiding the client. Hence, I think the lifeguard in (a) may not fail to perform a duty for which he is morally required to pay great costs in order to do something for which he is not morally required to pay great costs. But this is not because of the difference in costs morally required of him; it is because he omits to do his duty in order to bring about the death of his client for the sake of its causal role in saving other people and no other effect of what he does justifies his doing it. By contrast, given Parfit's arguments defending killing as a mere means, he would claim that omitting to aid one's client in (a) to save the 100 people is permissible.

IV. As we have seen, Parfit wants to argue that it is permissible to harm, not merely not to aid, people for the sake of a greater good. In his view, the harm might be a mere causal means to the greater good or a side effect either of a mere causal means to the greater good or of redirecting a threat. He accepts that the permissibility of such harm is theoretically compatible with having a duty to make large personal sacrifices to avoid harming someone when no greater good is at stake and also compatible with not having to make the same personal sacrifices to bring about the greater good that licenses one in harming someone else. However, he did not consider whether one might have a duty to make large personal sacrifices to bring about a greater good rather than harm someone else to a similar degree if one chooses (without obligation) to achieve the greater good. We shall now consider this issue in connection only with redirecting a threat.

1. I have already maintained that there are two measures of stringency and that being morally required to make greater personal sacrifices to avoid harming someone than to produce a greater good does not by itself show that we may not harm that same person to produce that greater good. These claims bear not only on Parfit's discussion of redirecting a threat but also on Judith Thomson's discussion of this issue.

In her "Turning the Trolley,"[15] Thomson argued that a bystander may not turn an out-of-control trolley away from killing five people when it will then kill some other innocent person. (Parfit calls this case Side Track, though Thomson calls it the Bystander Case. Since I am here primarily discussing Parfit's view, I shall use Side Track.) She is here denying that achieving the greater good of saving the five people from the trolley can take precedence over fulfilling a duty not to harm another person (i.e., she is denying that in this case (A > DN)). Part of her argument for this conclusion is that the bystander would not be morally required to turn the trolley away from the five when this will kill the bystander himself. Doing this would even show poor judgment. She is here accepting the claim that avoiding large personal sacrifices can take precedence over bringing about the greater good (i.e., (S > A)). She took this to imply that whether or not the bystander could (or would) turn the trolley away from the five in a way that resulted in his own death, it would be wrong for him to turn the trolley away from the five when it would kill another innocent person without that person's consent (i.e., –(A > DN)). This was because this other person too was not morally required and (by hypothesis) did not agree to turn the trolley on himself (nor did he agree to have it turned on him) to save the five. Hence, she thinks that its being true of the one other person that (S > A) implies that it is true that the bystander may not turn the trolley on the other person (i.e.,–(A > DN)). On similar grounds, Thomson might reject the view that a bystander may redirect the trolley, killing someone for the greater good of saving 100 other people from the trolley. In addition, given that one is not morally required to give up one's leg to save five people from the trolley, it seems her argument (implausibly) implies that a bystander may not redirect the trolley from killing five people toward one person whose leg alone it would remove.[16]

By contrast, Thomson thinks that the trolley driver would kill five people (not merely let them die) if the trolley he started hits them and he has a duty of justice not to kill five. Hence, she thinks, he should turn the out-of-control trolley to the one person because at a given time he has a choice between infringing fewer rather than a greater number of rights not to be killed. She thinks this even though that person also need not volunteer his life to either save the five or prevent the driver from unjustly killing them. Thomson thinks that unlike the driver, the bystander would violate no duty of justice to the five if he does not save them.

It might be argued against Thomson that the fact that someone need not sacrifice himself to achieve a great good doesn't mean that one may not do what leads him to suffer a comparable loss for the sake of the greater good. For example, someone needn't let himself drown if this is needed to save the lives of five people. Yet someone else may permissibly let him drown in order to go save five different people, at least when there is no specific agreement to save him rather than the five. Furthermore, it would be wrong to characterize what is done to the person left to drown as making him be an altruist, giving up his life when one would not give up one's own life to save five people. This is because one does not require him to decide to be abandoned. In general, volunteering to suffer a loss is morally different from suffering the loss due to what someone else does. If this is so, imposing the loss on someone by redirecting the trolley to him without his consent might sometimes be permissible even though the person hit by the trolley is not morally required, does not agree, and would be misguided to give up his life. This could be true even though that person may (I believe) permissibly resist (in certain ways) what is being done to him by, for example, turning the trolley back if he could. Hence, it might be argued that it is permissible for the bystander (not only the trolley driver) to impose the loss on the other person by redirecting the trolley away from the five (i.e., (A > DN)) even though the bystander needn't redirect the trolley to himself when killing himself would be his only way to save the five (i.e., (S > A)).

On the other hand, one might argue against the view that the trolley driver's duty of justice not to kill the five is sufficient to justify his turning the trolley to the one. After all, this duty is not sufficient to justify the driver toppling someone from a bridge in front of the trolley as a mere means to stop it. This is an act that I, unlike Parfit, think is impermissible. (Note that even if the driver but not the bystander were permitted to turn the trolley, determining why the driver may turn the trolley but not topple someone from the bridge to save the five would remain as a Trolley Problem.)

It is not my aim to argue these points in greater detail here.[17] I simply wish to suppose that the bystander is permitted to turn the trolley when it is all he can do to save the five, and inquire whether this implies that when the bystander is able to either turn the trolley on himself or on one other person to save the five, he may instead still impose the loss on the one innocent person. This is the sort of case that Thomson calls Bystander Three-Option Case in her 2008 article because the options for the bystander are to let the five die, redirect the trolley to one other person, or redirect the trolley to himself. It is also the sort of case that

I have claimed Parfit did not consider, namely whether if one will not let the five die, one might have a duty to make large personal sacrifices to bring about the greater good rather than harm someone else to a similar degree to bring about that greater good. Thomson uses the Bystander Three-Option Case as one of her arguments for her claim that the bystander may not redirect the trolley to the one other person even when that is the only way to save the five. She claims that the bystander may not redirect to the one other person if he would not redirect to himself in the Three-Option Case, and if he may not do it when he has this choice between himself and the other person, he may not redirect to the other person even when he does not have the choice to sacrifice himself. By contrast, I am here assuming that when he has no other way to save the five the bystander may redirect to the one, and I want to consider whether he may not do this when he physically could but would not sacrifice himself to save the five. We are assuming (S > A) and (A > DN) are both true and their truth is consistent with –(S > DN) as argued earlier. Then in a three-option case could it be that the bystander may not abandon his negative duty but must sacrifice himself if he chooses (which he need not) to achieve the greater good (as Thomson believes)?

2. An analysis like the first analysis offered for the Personal Lifeguard Both Case suggests that the lifeguard may not impose the loss on the one other person in a three-option case. According to that analysis the lifeguard must perform his duty to his client at the maximal required cost if it is possible to do so while saving the 100. Analogously, it might be said in (what I shall call) the Side Track Both Case that while the bystander needn't turn the trolley to himself when this is the only way to save the five, he may have to turn it to himself rather than turn it from the five toward one other person if he chooses to save the five. On this view the important point is that if the duty not to kill another can take precedence over one's self-interest to the extent that one is required to sacrifice one's life rather than kill another, then if the bystander chooses to save the five (which he needn't at great cost), he would have to sacrifice himself rather than kill the one person instead for that end. This is how he can both save the five and fulfill his duty to pay personal costs rather than kill the other person. This could be true even if we (unlike Thomson) think that the bystander may turn the trolley to an innocent person to save the five when the bystander cannot save the five by turning it toward himself instead of that other person.

If this analysis were correct, it would raise a problem in some cases for a view, to which Parfit is open, that having a duty to sacrifice oneself rather than harm someone else is compatible with not having a duty to sacrifice oneself for the greater good. The problem arises in cases where one could both do one's duty and achieve the greater good if serving self-interest drops out. According to the first analysis of the Personal Lifeguard Both Case, one has to fulfill one's contractual duty at the maximal morally required cost if one chooses to save the 100 (whether or not saving them per se is so costly) since this allows one to also save one's client. In the Side Track Both Case, saving the five people would itself involve making a great personal sacrifice (turning the trolley on oneself). However, one would not make the sacrifice to help them alone but rather to help them without failing in a duty not to harm someone else even at great cost to oneself.

There is an alternative view—call it the Still Harm Another View—of the Side Track Both Case that is similar to the Still Abandon Client View about the Personal Lifeguard Both Case. One defense of this view begins by claiming (contrary to Thomson) that if the bystander's only possible means of saving the five were redirecting the threat toward one other person, it would be permissible (though not required) for him to do so. This is so even though that person would not be morally required to give up his life to save the five (e.g., by diverting the trolley to himself) if this were possible and he would not do so. The next step is to consider the case in which the bystander can both save the five and not harm the one by turning the trolley toward himself instead. This high cost to him would arise because he would be saving the five, something that on its own would (by assumption) override not killing the one other person if no other way of saving the five existed. Because the bystander predictably would not kill himself instead of one other person to save the five, a consequentialist argument for the Still Harm Another View might emphasize that the bystander should not be required to avoid harming the one person at any cost to himself that would justify his not saving the five. But a nonconsequentialist would not think the good of saving the five is always sufficient to relieve the bystander of a duty to make large sacrifices rather than kill someone else (e.g., he may be required to make large sacrifices not to topple someone off the bridge to stop the trolley). To defend the Still Harm Another View, a nonconsequentialist might instead emphasize that a person has a duty to make big sacrifices to prevent himself killing another person when he is not doing something that justifies causing that killing. But if saving the five justifies turning the trolley though it kills another person, there is no need for the bystander to sacrifice his life to prevent the justified killing. This is so even in cases where it is not the bystander's duty but is only morally permissible to turn the trolley.

The following type of case might be raised as an objection to the Still Harm Another View: I should not use my neighbor's car without his permission merely to avoid the sacrifice to me of using my own car (when use wears my car down a bit). I may use his car without his permission if there is no other way to get 100 people who will otherwise die to a hospital. However, suppose my car is available. I cannot still permissibly use my neighbor's car to get the people to a hospital on the ground that I am not merely trying to avoid a personal sacrifice (of wearing my car down). Rather, I am trying to save people and the latter overrides the neighbor's personal claim to his car. I think this is not a good objection to the Still Harm Another View because I assume that in this case both my neighbor and

I have a noncontracted duty to use our car to save the 100 people; it is not supererogatory to do so. I should not interfere with the car to which my neighbor has a right in order to avoid my duty even when my neighbor also would have such a duty. By contrast, in the Side Track Case (we are assuming) I have no duty to sacrifice my life to save the five, though (it is assumed) I am permitted to impose loss of his life on another person by turning the trolley. (This is so even though he too has no duty to sacrifice his life to save the five.)

Something similar to what the Still Harm Another View implies about the Side Track Both Case seems to be true in other cases (though in certain ways they are significantly different from turning the trolley). For example, suppose it is true, as commonly thought, that a strategic bomber in a war (at least on the just side) may sometimes permissibly bomb an opponent's military facility even foreseeing that some noncombatants will be killed as a side effect. One condition that must be met for permissibility is that the deaths are at least proportionate to the military goal.[18] Suppose a bomber goes on a very useful but for him optional bombing mission and it becomes possible for him to redirect the effects of the bombing so that he rather than a proportional number of noncombatants would be killed as a side effect (when there is no shortage of other soldiers to fight if he dies). Is the bomber morally required to do what kills him rather than what kills the noncombatants merely because, were he not engaged in doing what made it permissible for him to cause side effect deaths, he would have to sacrifice his life rather than kill noncombatants as a side effect of his actions? I do not think so. When the need for him to sacrifice his life to prevent harm to others arises from his doing something that is morally permissible despite its causing that harm to others and he has no independent duty to die in order to bomb the facility itself, this great sacrifice is not required.[19]

One way this Bomber Case differs from the Side Track Both Case is that the bomber's means to his goal creates a new threat to noncombatants, while the bystander in Side Track Both redirects a pre-existent threat. It would be particularly significant if even this difference does not alter there being implications for the Bomber Case analogous to those that the Still Harm Another View has for the Side Track Both Cases.[20]

What if in a different version of the Side Track Both Case there was already a high cost that the bystander had to bear so as not to harm the one other person independent of his saving others? For example, suppose the bystander's car is going to crash into the one person and the bystander therefore has a duty to swerve toward a tree in order to avoid killing the person, though by doing this the bystander will himself be killed. It turns out that his swerving will also divert a trolley away from killing five toward killing no one. (Call this case Side Track Both Pre-Cost.) In this case, he may not omit swerving, thus killing the other person, in order to instead do something else that will divert the trolley alone perhaps at a lower cost to himself. Omitting to swerve in this case is not justified merely because in a different hypothetical case if his diverting the trolley from five would kill that one person, he need not swerve his car in a way that will cause his own death if this would save the one person from the trolley. An explanation of the difference in duties is that in the Side Track Both Pre-Cost Case having to pay a large cost rather than harm the one person is not called for to prevent harm that is an effect of saving the five that would justify killing the one.

Similarly, suppose a bomber is going to do something impermissible that will kill some noncombatant bystanders and so he should instead divert in a direction where he will be killed. If he diverts in this way, he will also crash into and destroy a munitions facility. He should not omit to divert from killing these noncombatants if not diverting made it possible for him to bomb the facility in a way that does not itself cause any noncombatant deaths and is low cost to himself. Omitting to divert in this case would not be justified merely because in a different hypothetical case if bombing the facility would kill the same noncombatants as a proportional side effect, he need not bomb the facility in a way that kills him instead of the noncombatants.

Now consider a harming case analogous to Personal Lifeguard Both Post-Cost. A bomber goes on a useful but optional mission to destroy a munitions factory in a just war. Noncombatants whose deaths would have been proportional are surprisingly unhurt. It would ordinarily have been easy for the bomber to avoid harming them on his route back to his home base. However, his successful bombing of the factory caused a defect in his plane and now he would have to sacrifice his life in order not to drop new bombs onto those noncombatants. In this case, the cost to him of not harming the noncombatants goes up only because he did something that would have been permissible even if it had caused the deaths of those noncombatants. However, in the actual case the deaths do not arise in doing the act that would have justified causing that bad effect. Hence, he must sacrifice himself in order not to kill the people. This is so even if his foreseeing this course of events would have led him not to undertake the useful mission, thus undermining achieving best consequences.

There is a possible further analogy between the Still Abandon Client View as applied to the Personal Lifeguard Both Case and the Still Harm Another View as applied to the Side Track Both Case. It concerns what one should do if there is only a small additional cost to oneself beyond what is needed to save the many (the 100 in one case or the 5 in the other) in order to also help the one (by saving the client or by not harming the one other person on the track). The lifeguard has a standing duty to help his client correlative to the client's right. As already noted, it seems to me this could imply that he should pay some additional cost to fulfill the special duty to his client even if he is saving the hundred that overrides and also threatens nonperformance of the duty. The situation may be similar for the bystander in the Side Track Both Case. He has a noncontractual duty to pay high costs rather than harm someone correlative to that person's noncontractual right not to be harmed when it is only the interests of these two people that are at stake. Even if this correlative duty would not be violated when he diverts the trolley to someone rather than to himself to save the five, he may still be infringing the right of the one person not to be harmed and even wrong him in the course of a permissible act.[21] His paying a small additional cost to save the five without harming the one could represent the attempt to avoid even infringing a right.

I have argued that Parfit did not consider the possibility that there is a duty to make large personal sacrifices as a substitute for harming someone else if one chooses to bring about a greater good for others. Similarly, in SO I did not consider the possibility that there is a duty to make large personal sacrifices as a substitute for not fulfilling a positive duty to someone else if one chooses to bring about a greater good for others. However, I have also argued that in many cases there are no such duties to make large personal sacrifices rather than harm someone else or not fulfill a positive duty to her in order to bring about a greater good. Hence, what would otherwise have been one's duty to make large personal sacrifices becomes supererogatory. However, this will only be true when the way in which one would not fulfill the positive duty or harm someone else would be permissible for the sake of the greater good if it were one's only option. Given the assumption that turning the trolley toward the one other person would be permissible if it were one's only choice, in Thomson's Three-Option Case it will be permissible to direct the trolley toward the one other person rather oneself if one chooses to save the five. Suppose Parfit is wrong that harming someone else as a mere means, or as a side effect of a mere means, to a greater good is permissible. Then we would morally have to make the large personal sacrifice rather than do these impermissible things if we choose to bring about the greater good.

V. We have considered whether there is a change in the status of an act—from dutiful to supererogatory—based on whether we may impose or not prevent a loss to someone else. Though Parfit did not consider this issue, he did propose that sometimes there is a change in the status of an act—from permissible to forbidden—in a version of deontology that he rejects (in part because he thinks it involves this change). We will briefly consider whether this change occurs.

Parfit believes that what he calls "common sense" deontology[22] gives each of us agent-relative duties in which the aim makes reference to the agent. For example, X's aim is for him (X) not to kill innocents, and Y's aim is for him (Y) not to kill innocents. By contrast, non-agent-relative consequentialism gives each of us a common aim (e.g., to minimize killings of innocents) that may require us to deal with what Larry Alexander has called "other people's messes" (e.g., kill one person to stop other agents from wrongfully killing five other people).

Parfit tries to move us toward a common-aim view of morality.[23] To do so he takes a step beyond dealing only with cases where there is an unintended threat (e.g., a runaway trolley or a natural disaster) and one agent who must respond to it (like the bystander in the Side Track Case). In some cases he presents in the last part of volume 3 of *On What Matters*, one agent is called on to reduce the intended yet *permissible* harmful acts of other agents who are themselves trying to stop an unintended threat. In these cases, he argues, we should all have a common aim of reducing *permissible* (not impermissible) intended harmful acts. For example, in his Power Plant Case the blowing up of the plant that would kill a million people could be stopped by me only if I intentionally kill one person (who would not otherwise shortly die). Parfit assumes that if there were no other alternative, this killing would be permissible according to so-called threshold deontology, which permits killing someone to stop the deaths of others once the number of people that would otherwise die is beyond a threshold. However, if I do not do this, the only alternative is that someone else will permissibly (according to threshold deontology) kill two innocent people (who would not otherwise shortly die) to stop the plant from blowing up. (Note that in one version of this case, if I refrain from killing a person, he will become one of the two killed by someone else. In a second version, if I do not kill the person, he will not otherwise be killed. I will discuss the second case since I think it is the one Parfit intends and because it may be harder to justify killing a person who would not soon be killed by someone else.) Parfit thinks that the agent-relative aspect of deontology incorrectly implies that I should not kill one person to stop the plant from blowing up since I can count on someone else killing two and my primary responsibility is that I not kill. Thus, an act that was permissible becomes forbidden. This is so even though my killing could prevent someone else from having to permissibly kill two other people instead. He thinks this implication shows that deontology incorrectly draws a moral distinction between what I do and what others do and incorrectly tells me to give priority to my not killing over preventing others from permissibly killing even more people.

I think Parfit's analysis of this case involves a misunderstanding of deontology. Suppose that an act that is (by hypothesis) deontologically permissible or a duty for a particular agent (e.g., killing one person to stop the plant from blowing up) has a better outcome than an alternative act that would be permissible or a duty when done by another agent if the first agent did not act (e.g., killing two people to stop the plant from blowing up). While I do not agree that deontology is based on an agent's special concern for his own acts,[24] I also think there is nothing in an agent-relative analysis of deontology that requires (or even permits) the first agent to "kick" the act type (in this case permissible or dutiful killing) down the road so that another agent does it with a worse outcome (more people are killed). What may lead one to think otherwise is conceiving of the Power Plant Case as one in which I would kill one person merely as a means to prevent someone else from killing two other people, which would be ruled out by deontology. It is true that in the Power Plant Case the numerical difference between my act (resulting in one million minus one being alive) and the other agent's act (resulting in the same one million people minus two others being alive) is one extra life. (In this respect it is like killing one person to save two.) However, my saving one million by killing one does not just save one additional person from death; it saves one million and one. That someone else would have saved the same million if I had not does not imply that the one million are not still under a threat at the time I act and that I don't save those million people. Since my saving those one million can help make my act permissible according to threshold deontology, I also kill one person to save two other people by a permissible act unlike what is true when I merely kill one person to save two others.

This is compatible with it being true according to threshold deontology that because another agent will save those same one million if I do not, I should go and save by innocent means a different group of five people who would not otherwise be saved.[25] This is so at least if saving the different group of people is morally more important than preventing a killing of one additional person by the other agent. What if saving that different group of five people required me to kill someone as a mere means? If it is impermissible to do this, I should instead reduce lives lost by killing one person to save the million rather than allowing another agent to kill two other people to save the million. This would not make sense on the view that in the latter (Power Plant) case I would be killing one person as a mere means to save two others given that it is impermissible for me to kill one person as a mere means to save the group of five others.

The Power Plant Case is unlike cases in which act consequentialists claim that an act *becomes* permissible or a duty because it substitutes for another act done by someone else that would have a worse outcome. (For example, act consequentialists can hold that killing one person would be impermissible were it not done to stop someone else from impermissibly killing more people.) In the Power Plant Case the agent's act that kills one person is (by hypothesis) initially determined to be deontologically permissible independent of considering what the other agent in the case would do, and I do not think it becomes impermissible merely because the alternative is that another agent would act permissibly or dutifully though with worse consequences. Of course, if the consequences were better if another agent acted, then the first agent's act could become impermissible. Furthermore, if the first agent will certainly act permissibly with better consequences, it is the second agent's act with worse consequences that becomes forbidden.

Parfit presents another case involving deception. He imagines that it would be permissible for someone to deceive two people to keep some important secret.

He concludes that it would be permissible for someone else to deceive one person instead, thus achieving the common aim of safeguarding the secret by deceiving as few people as possible. In this case, he does not explicitly say that it would have been permissible for the second agent to deceive one person even if no one else would permissibly deceive two. This leaves it open that the person who would deceive two people has special permission or a duty to deceive (so that the secret is kept) that others lack. If so, it is not true that another agent acquires a permission or duty to deceive only one person merely because this is fewer than would be permissibly deceived by someone else. If the agent who would deceive one person does independently have a permission or duty to deceive, then the agent who deceives fewer may act. If he does so, the other agent may be forbidden to deceive more people.

I conclude that Parfit's cases do not show that what he calls common-sense (threshold) deontology incorrectly forbids an agent to do what is initially judged to be a permissible or dutiful killing for him and shifts the performance of permissible and dutiful killings to others simply because of the differences between the agents. Furthermore, common-sense deontology could correctly change the status of an act of killing some from permissible to forbidden because someone else will achieve the same good by killing fewer people. Common-sense deontology could also be correct in not deriving the permissibility of a type of act for one agent from its permissibility with worse consequences when done by another agent. Hence, at least for the specific acts toward which his remarks were directed, Parfit has not shown that there is a status change from permissible to forbidden according to common-sense deontology.[26]

## Notes

1. *Journal of Philosophy* 82 (1985):118–38. Henceforth SO. A revised version appears as Chapter 15 in *Morality, Mortality*, vol. 2 (New York: Oxford University Press, 1996).
2. I claimed that saving at the high cost to oneself remains supererogatory and not a duty even when one is willing to make the effort. If it became one's duty, one could not refuse to save at the high cost to which one does not object per se when the opportunity, for example, to participate in an important scholarly event comes along if such participation would not override the duty to save at small cost to oneself. Yet I think such participation could override saving at high cost.
3. In SO footnote, p. 125. I said: "Because an act that is less stringently required by one measure may take precedence over another act that is more stringently required by that same measure, proving that negative duties are more stringently required than positive duties in the sense that we must make a greater effort to perform them, does not resolve the problem of whether we may violate a negative duty to perform a positive one. For example, Philippa Foot says that we may not kill one person to

save others, because the duty not to kill is more stringent than the duty to aid (in "The Problem of Abortion and the Doctrine of Double Effect," reprinted in Bonnie Steinbock, ed., *Killing and Letting Die* (Englewood Cliffs, NJ: Prentice-Hall, 1980)). But that greater stringency may mean only that we would *have* to make a greater effort to avoid killing someone than to aid others, and this does not imply that if we *want* to we may not violate a negative duty in order to aid."

4. Such a prerogative is argued for in Samuel Scheffler's *The Rejection of Consequentialism* (Oxford: Oxford University Press, 1982).
5. I am grateful to Ingmar Persson for pressing this point in discussion.
6. This is so even if the act of saving the 100 is not a morally exemplary act due to a bad motive on the part of the bodyguard who saves them. For example, suppose it is only because he hates his client or only because the cost to save the 100 is less than what he would have to pay to save his client that the bodyguard saves the 100. The properties that make doing one act rather than another permissible (e.g., 100 people rather than one will live) can still be present to justify doing the act even if an agent does not do the act for the sake of the properties that justify doing it.
7. Perhaps the number saved should be 1,000 (which is the number I used in SO in discussing a similar case) instead of 100 to make it morally permissible for the lifeguard to abandon his client. I am not concerned with the specific number in this example. I am just seeking a number such that (a) the lifeguard is morally permitted to save them instead of his client while (b) the client has no moral duty to release the lifeguard from saving him so that he may save more people instead. I believe there could be such a number.
8. I am grateful to Casper Hare for discussion about the issue of time.
9. "Violation" refers to impermissible failure of a duty or transgression of a right; "infringing" includes permissible transgression of a duty or right.
10. Suppose the lifeguard was morally required to lose up to two limbs to save his client but had already supererogatorily sacrificed one leg to save the 100. Perhaps he is not still required to sacrifice a leg and an arm to save his client if this is possible. This would turn giving up two limbs for his client, which had been a duty, into a supererogatory act. In this case, what he does for others might affect what he is morally required to do for his client (even in the Post-Cost Case) because the baseline for determining his duty to his client might vary with the physical condition he is already in. This is a different way in which what was previously a duty could become supererogatory. Adrienne Martin has pointed out that by contrast to what I have claimed about the lifeguard, a parent's duty to sacrifice himself to save his child seems to remain in place even if it is his doing what would override that duty that both threatens the abandonment of the child and increases the cost to save her. An explanation is needed if there is this contrast.
11. In the original cases I discussed in SO, I considered the absence of a duty to sacrifice oneself for the greater good, the greater good taking precedence over abandoning a contractual duty, and the duty to sacrifice oneself for some contractual duty as separate cases. In the revised version of SO published in my *Morality, Mortality,* Vol. 2, I considered what would happen when all three options were present at once. I agreed

that the option to avoid large personal sacrifices might drop out when one could either fulfill one's contractual duty at the morally required personal cost or pursue the greater good (supererogatorily) at large cost. The point there was that one should be doing the supererogatory act if one wasn't doing one's duty not simply avoiding personal cost. (I didn't claim that one would have to pursue the greater good rather than the contractual duty even when the cost for each would be the same.) I have said in this chapter that if the high cost actually needed to fulfill one's contractual duty comes about independently of one's pursuing the greater good, then avoiding the cost will still drop out as an option even if it can also do double duty to achieve the greater good. However, what I have said in this chapter also implies that if the high cost to fulfill the contractual duty arises because one is pursuing a greater good that can take precedence over fulfilling the contractual duty, then avoiding at least some of the high personal cost is sometimes still an option.

12. I have suggested such an explanation of the permissibility of turning the trolley. See, for example, my *Intricate Ethics* (New York: Oxford University Press. 2007), *The Trolley Problem Mysteries* (New York: Oxford University Press, 2016) and Chapter 9 in this volume.
13. See her "Killing, Letting Die, and the Trolley Problem," *The Monist* 59, no. 2 (1976): 204–17.
14. There could be a version of the Business Case in which it is because of the loss to the client when a deadline is not met that a device is available to save a life.
15. *Philosophy & Public Affairs* 36, no. 4 (2008): 359–74. I discussed this article of Thomson's in *The Trolley Problem Mysteries,* where I raised points in addition to the ones I raise here. See also Chapters 9, 10, and 11 in this volume for additional discussion of Thomson.
16. These views of Thomson's leave it open whether she would think one may permissibly omit a positive contractual duty to save someone in order to instead save 100 other people.
17. I argued for them, including the distinction between imposing and volunteering, when discussing Thomson's view in *The Trolley Problem Mysteries*. I argue further for the permissibility of a bystander turning the trolley in Chapter 9 in this volume, which is based on but revises views I have defended in *Intricate Ethics* (among other places).
18. I think it is not clear why such bombing is permissible, but I will not discuss that issue here. Notice that the deaths due to the bombing would not be proportionate if just one more person would be saved by blowing up the factory than would be killed by blowing it up, other things equal. One indication that the justification for turning the trolley differs from the justification for strategic bombing is that it may be permissible to turn the trolley to save even two people at the cost of killing one other person.
19. Still, he may have a duty to make smaller sacrifices to avoid killing the noncombatants since he infringes their rights not to be harmed even if he acts permissibly. The noncombatants themselves (or their defenders) may defend themselves against his permissible acts even by killing him, I believe. But this would not be because he would have had to lose his life rather than cause their deaths if he could have. However,

their imposing smaller losses on him to resist his harming them might be justified by his having a duty to make such smaller sacrifices to avoid killing them if he could. (I first discussed this issue in "The Insanity Defense, Innocent Threats, and Limited Alternatives," *Criminal Justice Ethics* 6 [1987]: 61–76.) Notice also that, strictly speaking, bombing in a way that kills noncombatants is not necessary when the pilot could do what substitutes his death for theirs. So it seems to violate the necessity condition that it is said must also be satisfied to make doing what kills noncombatants permissible. However, the bombing may satisfy Seth Lazar's account of the necessity condition if a bombing that kills noncombatants is necessary if we are to give appropriate moral weight to the potential deaths of both combatants and noncombatants. (See Lazar's "Necessity in Self Defense and War," *Philosophy & Public Affairs* 40, no. 1 [2012]: 3–44.)

20. I believe Jeff McMahan would disagree that the bomber does not have to do what kills himself, at least when the noncombatants killed are not morally subject to bearing risks of being killed. (He thinks their being potential beneficiaries of the military action could make them morally subject to bearing risks of being killed. I have suggested that their being citizens of an unjust country could make them morally subject to bear risks of being killed in order that their country stop being unjust.) However, McMahan does emphasize the killing/letting die distinction. So he may think the bomber should, for example, let himself die by being killed by enemy fire that prevents his dropping bombs that kill noncombatants if this does not interfere with his destroying a military facility. (There could be a [hard to imagine] case in which his being attacked warns off noncombatants from his military target as nothing else could.) In this case, unlike mine, the bomber would not face a choice of killing himself or killing the noncombatants but rather letting himself be killed or killing noncombatants. However, I do not think the bomber has a duty to let himself be killed either.

    To justify his position, McMahan emphasizes the duties of some professionals like firefighters to take risks as part of their job. But suppose a firefighter was permitted to redirect a fire from killing ten people to killing only two other persons in a burning building. If he is also able to redirect the fire toward himself when this will kill him alone, must he do so? I do not think he has a professional duty to do this (even when there is no shortage of firefighters) rather than redirect the fire to the two other people. (I think this would also be true of someone who had no duty to fight the fire but volunteered to help.) Sometimes when people would carry out permissible harm to others they do not thereby make themselves liable to self-harm instead. Similarly, suppose the firefighter's mission is to save the ten people and, if necessary to do so, it would be permissible to redirect the fire to two other people instead. However, the wind is about to redirect the fire toward the firefighter instead. His only way to stop that is to immediately redirect the fire toward the two. Given that he is there on a mission to help save the ten, must he let himself be killed by the fire rather than redirect it from ten to two others? I do not think he must let himself be killed.

    These Firefighter Cases, like the Side Track Both Cases, involve redirecting threats not created by the firefighter. Hence, McMahan might want to limit his view to agents like the bomber who create new threats. But suppose the firefighter were permitted to start a flood to put out the fire to the ten, foreseeing the flood would create a deadly threat to two other people instead. (This is like Parfit's Fire and Flood Case in volume 3 of *On What Matters* that I discussed in Chapter 7.) I do not think the firefighter would instead have to create a different flood to save the ten that will kill only him.

To further support his position on the bomber, McMahan also refers to what he says is the accepted view that one may not avoid a lethal threat to oneself by means that will kill someone else even as a side effect. But cases to which he refers involve deciding what one has to suffer rather than harm someone else when the only justification proposed for harming is that one's own interests would otherwise suffer. I have suggested that when a greater good would justify doing what harms another, what one is morally required to suffer rather than harm that person may differ from what one has to suffer rather than harm her when only one's interests are at stake. For McMahan's views to which I refer, see his "The Just Distribution of Harm between Combatants and Noncombatants," *Philosophy & Public Affairs* 38 (2016): 342–79.

21. As noted earlier, "violation" refers to impermissible transgression; "infringes" includes permissible transgression. Some evidence that the right is infringed and not merely "wiped out" is the fact that it would be permissible for the one person toward whom the trolley is turned to turn it back toward the bystander and even the five originally threatened. This is so even though the bystander acts permissibly in turning the trolley and it would not be permissible for the one person to turn a trolley that was originally headed to him (rather than redirected) in a way that will kill the bystander or five other people. I discuss this in *Intricate Ethics, The Trolley Problem Mysteries,* and in Chapters 7 and 9 in this volume.
22. This is what I call nonconsequentialism's deontological component.
23. Allan Gibbard also tries to move us toward a common-aim view of morality as we saw in Chapter 5.
24. I have criticized the view that deontology is based on concern for the agent's point of view in acting in my *Morality, Mortality,* vol. 2. See the chapter entitled "Constraints and You."
25. I thank Shelly Kagan and Larry Temkin for suggesting this last case and for discussion of issues raised in Section V.
26. Earlier versions of this chapter were presented at the Workshop on Rights and Supererogation at MIT (May 2019), at the Australian National University (July 2019), and at Claremont McKenna and Pomona Colleges and a conference in honor of Marshall Cohen at the University of Southern California (both in February 2020). I am grateful to Joe Bowen, my commentator at MIT, and to the audiences on all four occasions for helpful suggestions. I also had helpful discussion with Shelly Kagan, Jeff McMahan, and Larry Temkin, and helpful written comments from Ketan Ramakrishnan. An earlier, shorter version of this chapter appears in J. McMahan et al., ed., *Principles and Persons* (Oxford: Oxford University Press, 2021).

# 9
# Rights and Their Limits: Nonconsequentialism in Light of the Trolley Problem

1. The basic aim of this chapter is to understand Nonconsequentialism's (NC) view of harming (specifically, causing the death of) innocent, nonthreatening people who would not soon die in any case when their being harmed is the result of helping others. (Hence, what is said is limited to discussing interpersonal harm and benefit and may not apply at all to intrapersonal harm and benefit.[1] It is also limited to discussing cases in which everyone involved knows their own and others' positions, such as who would be harmed, who saved, and who would act.) Those who would soon die in any case are people who cannot be saved. Among those who fall outside this class are (a) those who are not under any threats to their life and (b) those who are under a threat to their life that will soon lead to their death but who might still be saved. In Chapter 7 we argued against Parfit's reasons for rejecting some nonconsequentialist (deontological) distinctions. This chapter tries to present a positive position about the content of NC as revealed by the Trolley Problem. NC is ordinarily thought to involve rights against harm for individuals and to hold that not harming is a stronger duty than aiding. Why, then, may a trolley driver redirect his out-of-control trolley so it kills one person on the side track rather than five other people to whom it is headed (Driver Case)? Why may a bystander redirect a trolley so it kills one person rather than omit to save five other people to whom the trolley is headed (Bystander Case)?[2]

The person on the side track falls into class (a) of those unthreatened by dying soon. By contrast, the five toward whom the trolley is headed fall into class (b) of those who face such a threat. Suppose it was possible to redirect the trolley away from the five but it would return toward hitting only one of those toward whom it was originally headed. (This is one option in the Returning Trolley Case described in Chapter 7, the alternative being to turn the trolley toward someone not previously threatened.)[3] In this option someone who would have died if nothing had been done will die of the trolley that would have otherwise killed him, but four others who would have been killed by the trolley will be saved. One question this option raises is whether there is a moral difference between taking it and redirecting in the Driver and Bystander Cases so that it would be morally

*Rights and Their Limits: In Theory, Cases, and Pandemics.* F. M. Kamm, Oxford University Press.
© Oxford University Press 2022. DOI: 10.1093/oso/9780197567739.003.0009

preferable from a NC point of view to kill one of the people who was already under the trolley threat rather than the person on the side track. This might be because the first person would be made no worse off than he would otherwise have been, which is not true of the person on the side track. It seems clear that even those who might think it wrong to turn the trolley in the Bystander Case, thereby killing one rather than letting more die, would not object to a bystander turning the trolley onto the returning track, thereby killing one rather than letting more die. This is true even though when considered as a separate case in which this is the only option, one person would be killed to save only four people, and in the Bystander and Driver Cases, one person would be killed to save all five people. (In the Returning Trolley Case there are options to either turn to a side track or use the returning track, so the one person on the side track would not be killed if the one person already threatened were. Hence, five people would live at the cost of one life whichever option is chosen. However, it isn't right to say one person on the side track is "saved" when someone merely does not kill him, so even in this case killing one of those already under the threat would save only four.) Further, even if it were permissible to redirect from the five to the one on the side track if it were the only option, it might be impermissible for the driver or a bystander to do this if they had the option of using the returning track. Killing someone who was not previously under a threat of dying soon arguably makes a moral difference even by comparison to killing someone who is already under a threat of dying soon but need not die (because there is a way to save him). This is part of the issue of moral inertia (discussed in Chapter 7). In this chapter we will assume there is no option such as is present in the Returning Trolley Case and (unless otherwise noted) that innocent, nonthreatening people whose being harmed is at issue fall into class (a).[4]

Judith Thomson is one of those who came to deny that the bystander may turn the trolley. For example, she argues[5] that if the one person on the track has no duty to turn the trolley to himself to save the five and he has not consented to do this, then the bystander may not turn the trolley away from the five when it will kill that one person without that person's consent. (We discussed this and other aspects of her view in Chapter 8.) Arguing against this view involves, in part, showing that in NC what others may sometimes permissibly do to the one person may go beyond what the person is morally required to do to himself or has agreed to have done to him. This has to be shown even to justify the driver turning the trolley because the one person hit by the driver (even if this only severs his leg) has no duty to turn the trolley on himself or have it turned on him (at this cost) to help the driver avoid killing five others.

However, it not being wrong of someone (in the sense that it is permissible) to do this to the one person is consistent with NC implying that the person is wronged by what is done. (Thomson claimed that the one person's right not to be harmed is infringed even when the trolley that kills him is permissibly redirected.[6]) An indication that he is wronged, I believe, is that he may resist the trolley being sent to him (in both the Bystander and Driver Cases), even by sending it back on whoever turns it to him though this kills that person and interferes with saving the five. (This is one example of what I call a Sending Back Case.)[7] However, some infringements may not be resisted (e.g., in Thomson's example of going through private property to get a child to a hospital, the landowner may not resist). Resistance may only be permissible in some cases where a lot is at stake for the victim of the infringement as is true of the one person on the side track. Suppose the one person who would be killed by the bystander turning the trolley would be wronged by this but the five would not be wronged by the bystander if the bystander did not save them. A desire to avoid infringing someone's rights and wronging him in a way that makes it permissible for that person to send back the trolley may be why it is only permissible and not obligatory for the bystander to turn the trolley. Even if the one person is physically unable to turn the trolley back on the bystander who turns it to him, the fact that the bystander becomes morally liable to such a harm is an indication of how morally "complex" the act of turning the trolley is. This could make it permissible to refrain from redirecting.

By contrast, the desire to avoid wronging the one person in permissibly infringing his right not to be killed might not make it permissible for the driver to not turn the trolley. He may have a duty to turn the trolley since otherwise he would wrong the five in killing them.[8] Furthermore, he too is morally liable to the one person sending back the trolley to him. Hence, a redirector being morally liable to having the trolley sent back to him is not an indication that he has no duty to turn the trolley when there are independent grounds for his having a duty to save the five stemming from his otherwise killing them. There may be a further difference between the bystander and the driver. The bystander may permissibly defend himself against the sent-back trolley by resending it to the one other person. By contrast, suppose the driver, had it been possible, would have had a duty to die to prevent himself from killing the five but when he physically cannot do this, he may turn the trolley on the one person. Then it may be impermissible for him to resist the one person sending back the trolley to him by resending it back to that one person. This is because in sending back the trolley to the driver, the one person imposes a cost on the driver that the driver, not the one person, would have had a duty to pay to save the five.[9]

I will here assume it is permissible to redirect in both Driver and Bystander Cases and focus on how to explain why this is so on nonconsequentialist grounds.

2. My basic view is that it is permissible for the driver or the bystander to turn the trolley in part because it satisfies what these and other cases show to be a (defeasible) requirement of NC, namely that given our actions it is possible

for harm that transgresses a right to be justified (in part or whole) by *what produces it*. If a harm cannot be justified in this way, it cannot (except in extraordinary circumstances) be justified by *what it produces* alone, nor should it be used to help produce other goods. Given our actions, goods that could only be brought about improperly are themselves not justified. I call this the Doctrine of Productive Purity (DPP).[10] It concerns how both good (where this includes reducing harm) and harm may permissibly be brought about and presents what I call a "downstreamish" view about justifying harm.[11] It contrasts with a consequentialist view that harm can be justified by the greater good it produces alone and that production of the greater good is inherently justifiable.

Section 4 describes my view of the DPP in greater detail. The methodology used to uncover the DPP involves considering intuitive judgments about cases. The judgments are used to illustrate and support several summary principles that when synthesized, I suggest, yield the DPP.

However, not all cases that satisfy the DPP will involve permissible harm, and not all cases involving permissible harm will satisfy the DPP. We shall examine cases other than the standard Driver and Bystander that show that satisfying the DPP is neither a sufficient condition nor a necessary condition for permissible harm. These cases demonstrate that we must consider further what produces the harm and what alternatives there are to producing that harm. Section 5 investigates conditions other than the DPP that help make turning the trolley permissible or impermissible, including the Principle of Secondary Permissibility, and how these conditions relate to a moral distinction between killing and letting die. Section 5 also considers what deeper moral ideas underlie or supervene on the DPP, how they relate to our moral idea of persons and their relations to each other, and how the DPP bears on what I call "tree trolley" cases.

3. Before considering my own view further, consider alternative proposals for NC's justification of turning the trolley in the Driver and Bystander Cases.

(a) The Doctrine of Double Effect (DDE) claims that harm that is intended as an end or means can make doing or allowing it impermissible, whereas the same harm when merely foreseen need not make the doing or allowing impermissible. One may turn the trolley because the greater good is intended and the harm to the one person is only foreseen, not intended. By contrast, harm (or at least putting someone in harm's way) would be intended as a means in toppling a fat man from a bridge so that he falls in front of the trolley to stop it from hitting the five.[12] The DDE is what I call a "state of mind" theory that traditionally distinguishes the possible moral permissibility of acts, in part, by whether a harm is actually intended or merely foreseen by the agent who kills (or lets die).[13] Traditionally, it also requires that one intend the greater good that is proportional to the lesser harm.

However, suppose that someone does not intend to save five people from the trolley but rather to do something that will benefit himself which, as a foreseen side effect, both redirects the trolley from the five and harms the one other person on the side track. I think the fact that the greater good is not intended does not make his act impermissible. Further, in what I call the Bad Man Trolley Case, it remains permissible for a bad man to turn the trolley, thus foreseeably saving five people from it, even if he only acts because he intends (as an end or a mere means) to kill the one other person to whom the trolley is redirected. Neither intending the greater good nor not intending the lesser harm seems necessary in order for turning the trolley to be permissible.

Some have proposed a nontraditional version of the DDE. According to this version an act is not ruled out as impermissible if its objective, non-state-of-mind characteristics make it one that it is possible for some agent (even if not the actual one) to reasonably do without intending the harm. This is true of the non-state-of-mind properties of the act that the agent does in the Bad Man Trolley Case (i.e., saving five people and harming one). But I do not think this alternative view of the DDE is correct. First, it seems incorrect to continue focusing on the state of mind of agents in determining permissibility of an act even if they are only possible, not actual, states of mind. This is because deciding which states of mind are reasonably possible for agents is dependent on examining the non-state-of-mind characteristics of the act. Hence, it is these characteristics that are sufficient to determine the permissibility of an act.[14] Second, Christopher Fruge has argued[15] that if merely possible rather than actual states of mind are important for determining permissibility, then possible bad intentions that are consistent with the non-state-of-mind characteristics of an act should also count. Hence, when someone turns the trolley to save five people only foreseeing the death of another person, the non-state-of-mind characteristics of what he does are consistent with the possibility that another agent could intend the death. Furthermore, Fruge notes that if a possible good intention can make an act (characterized by its non-state-of-mind properties) not be impermissible and a possible bad intention can make an act impermissible, the theory can determine that a given act is both not impermissible and impermissible, thus generating a contradiction.

We have been proposing that not intending harm is not a necessary condition on permissibility. Philippa Foot raised a different objection to the DDE. She noted that it is impermissible to use a gas to save five people even if it kills one other person only as a foreseen side effect. (I call this the Gas Case.[16]) Hence, even if in the Driver and Bystander Cases causing the death of the one is only foreseen, this will not be sufficient to show that turning the trolley in those cases can be permissible even if toppling the fat man is impermissible. These two points suggest that the intending/foreseeing harm distinction should not be relied on to help distinguish among permissible and impermissible acts in trolley cases.

(b) Foot claimed that the trolley driver may permissibly turn the trolley, killing one person, because otherwise he would kill a greater number of other people impermissibly since he started the trolley. That it is permissible to kill one to avoid killing more people is a non-state-of-mind theory of permissibility. One problem with her proposal is that it rules out the *bystander* in the Bystander Case turning the trolley since he would only let five die, not kill them. It also raises the question whether a driver who is thrown from the trolley and lands near a switch may use it to turn the trolley. In this Bystanding Driver Case, the driver faces a choice between killing one and letting five die. (This is so even though he would become the killer of the five in virtue of both letting them die and having started the trolley.) Another problem with Foot's proposal is that it incorrectly implies that the driver may topple the fat man from the bridge to stop the trolley or explode a bomb that stops the trolley but as a direct side effect kills one other person (Bomb Case). (Notice that even if the bystander were not permitted to turn the trolley, that the driver may do that but he may not topple the fat man is itself a Trolley Problem that requires explanation.)

Foot's proposal also incorrectly implies that if the driver or bystander had a choice between turning the trolley from the five when it would kill two other people or instead toppling one person from the bridge to stop the trolley, they each should do the latter, thereby reducing the number of people they each kill from two to one. That the driver may not do this is important because it has been suggested that an agent's duty to respect rights is "time relative." That is, it is-not permissible for an agent to *now* transgress one person's right (e.g., not to be toppled from the bridge) to prevent the consequences of the agent's *past* act (e.g., starting the trolley) that would transgress the rights of a greater number of other people to the same extent (i.e., they too would die). However, the driver is not permitted to topple one person when it would be the alternative to, *at the very same time,* turning the trolley toward killing two people. So it can be not only impermissible for him to transgress someone's rights now to prevent the consequences to others of his past transgressive act but also impermissible for him to reduce the number of people whose rights not to be killed he will transgress at one time.[17]

(c) In her earlier work, Thomson suggested that the trolley may be redirected by a bystander because (i) it better distributes an existing threat rather than creating a new threat and (ii) it does not do this by infringing anyone's rights (with the emphasis on the "by").[18] However, consider my Lazy Susan Case[19] in which the five are moved on a swivel table away from a trolley that cannot be redirected and would otherwise hit them. This movement causes rocks to fall, killing another person. I think turning the Lazy Susan is permissible for the same reason as turning the trolley even though it doesn't redistribute an existing threat and creates a new one (falling rocks). In a variant, the Lazy Susan itself becomes a new threat because as it turns it will hit and kill someone standing nearby it.

Furthermore, in a third version of the case, another person is on the other side of the Lazy Susan and as we turn the five away from the trolley he is pushed into it. I think this too is permissible even though it is impermissible to topple the fat man from the bridge into the trolley. All this requires an explanation.

4. My positive proposal for NC (the DPP) is a non-state-of-mind theory for the permissibility of harm that synthesizes principles described in the following several parts. I will present each principle followed by cases that help illustrate and support it. (Note, however, that the order of discovery of a principle is from cases to principle.) While I present the principles separately, it must be understood that no principle should be violated in satisfying another principle and that bringing about more harm without violating any of the principles is wrong if one can bring about less harm without violating any of the principles, other things equal. For example, if bringing about an instance of Principle A involves a violation of Principle E, satisfying Principle A will not result in a permissible act. If turning a trolley from five to two is permissible when it is the only alternative, it may be impermissible when one can turn the trolley toward one person instead.

Principle A. Greater good involving elimination of greater harm may permissibly cause lesser harm. (As noted earlier, this assumes that the way the greater good is brought about does not violate any of the other principles.)

Example: We may permissibly move by nonharmful means the five away from being killed by the trolley and place them in a safe area though their being there moves one other person to his death. (Literally, the harm to the one person is caused only by the first temporal component of the greater good since the greater good is really the five living on sufficiently long after avoiding death by trolley to justify the death of the one. We should not act unless we reasonably expect the occurrence of the greater good, of which the first time period is a component [i.e., not a mere means to further survival]. This is to be understood in all further discussion when we speak of the greater good causing or being caused by something.)

The cases with which we are dealing involve eliminating a greater harm that consists in a greater number of people each suffering the same harm that will, by our action, be inflicted on someone else instead. Hence, "greater good" and "greater harm" should here be understood in this way. Whether and when other types of goods and harms can be greater than a harm they cause and also justify that harm is a question not dealt with in this discussion.[20]

It may still be controversial, for example, that it is permissible to move two people away from a threat when this will kill one other person. Perhaps there must be a greater number than one additional person saved to justify killing another person, especially as the number of people killed gets larger. I shall not discuss this issue in detail here but for the most part accept the simplifying assumption that we are dealing with a greater and lesser number of people.

Principle B. Means that have a noncausal relation to the greater good (e.g., means that in the context actually constitute the greater good) may permissibly (directly or indirectly) cause lesser harm. (This assumes that no other principle is violated in bringing about or employing the means.)

Examples: The movement of the trolley away from the five that is the means of saving them constitutes their being saved given that the trolley is the only threat they face. Alternatively put, the movement of the trolley away from the five has their being saved as its noncausal flip side. That is, the movement and the saving are like two sides of one coin; the one side does not cause the other. Note that the movement of the trolley away is different from what is done to move the trolley away (e.g., harmlessly flip a switch), which has a mere causal relation to the five being saved via causing the trolley to move away. What is done to move the trolley should not violate any other principle.

This movement of the trolley involves its being redirected, making it a direct threat to the one person it kills. By "direct" versus "indirect" I mean that the trolley, not something that is in the environment and affected by the redirected trolley, kills the person. This is not to say that it would be impermissible to redirect the trolley if it would hit a wagon on the track and the wagon killed the one other person. Then the trolley would indirectly kill the one person. If the intervening wagon was not placed there by the agent who turns the trolley, I say it is "independently" in the environment.[21] (Another contrast to the trolley directly killing the one person is the Germ Case, my variant [discussed in note 16] on Foot's Gas Case, in which germs independently [of the agent who releases the gas] in the environment kill someone after their position is affected by the released gas that saves five other people. This is a case in which the gas indirectly causes the death by affecting what is independently in the environment. Using the gas in this case seems permissible even if using the gas that we introduce into the environment when it directly kills the one person would not be permissible.)

Consider how turning the trolley in both the Bystander and Driver Cases compares with what I call the Crosspoint Case, in which someone must direct a trolley in the first instance toward either five people or toward one. In the Crosspoint Case the means that has a noncausal relation to the five not being threatened (i.e., the trolley turning toward the track away from them) constitutes the greater good. This is the same as in the Bystander and Driver Cases where the means that has a noncausal relation to the five not being threatened (i.e., the trolley moving away from them) constitutes the greater good. In the Crosspoint Case the trolley moving toward the other track away form the five, in the circumstances, constitutes the five not being threatened by the trolley, just as the trolley turning away when it was already headed to the five constitutes the five not being threatened by it. But in the Crosspoint Case someone faces a choice between doing an act of tuning the trolley that will kill five or kill one. In the

Driver Case, the choice is between doing an act that will kill one or not turning the trolley and killing five in virtue of the past act of starting the trolley and then refraining from redirecting it. In the Bystander Case, the choice is between doing an act that kills one and letting five people die. Suppose it is permissible in all these cases to do what kills one person (though it may be obligatory only in the Driver and Crosspoint Cases). This would show that some particular differences in how the five would come to die in these three cases are less important than (i) its being means that constitute (not cause) the five's surviving (i.e., the trolley turning away) that eventually causes the one person's death and (ii) that this one person's being threatened, in the circumstances, is the flip side of the five not being threatened.

Suppose the choice in all three cases was between one person and another person (not between one person and five others). Then there may well be a moral distinction between the Crosspoint Case, where an act of killing must be done either way, and the Bystander Case, where avoiding the act of killing may take precedence over not letting one other person die. Even in the Driver Case avoiding the act of killing might take precedence over doing something to prevent one's prior act from making it true that in not turning the trolley one will be killing someone else. Those who see the original Driver Case as involving a straightforward choice between killing one and killing five may not have compared it with a Crosspoint Case, which, I believe, has more claim to being a straightforward case of killing one or killing five.

Notice that in the Crosspoint Case there would be reason to turn the trolley where it will kill one person rather than kill even two other people. I suspect this would be so in the Driver and Bystander Cases as well if they involved a trolley headed to kill two people rather than five people. If this is true, it shows that the permissibility of harming the one person in these cases is not a matter of meeting a threshold in what is called "threshold deontology."[22] That theory implies that rights of people not to be harmed in certain ways (e.g., being toppled from the bridge) hold up to a threshold when the number of those who could be saved is large enough (or another disaster to be avoided is great enough) to override the right. Saving two or even five people seems far from enough to justify killing one other person simply on grounds of threshold deontology. One way to conceive of this difference is as a matter of quality rather than quantity: the limits on the right not to be harmed are more like contours that come from within the right (or a set of them) rather than from something weighty outside these factors. Similarly, consider the right to have a promise kept. Suppose there is a conflict between keeping a promise to person A and keeping the same type of promise to each of persons B and C (e.g., A is far away from where B and C are). Even one additional promise can make it permissible (and even right) to satisfy two promises even though it remains true that because A had a right to have the promise to him kept, it is infringed even when not kept as a consequence of keeping other promises. (However, is it possible that an explanation of a low number of additional people needed to justify infringement is that different ways of coming to kill someone [e.g., by redirection versus toppling] have different thresholds so that five is above the threshold for redirection but two isn't? This would be a different way of understanding the idea of threshold deontology.)

Redirecting the trolley that threatens the five contrasts with what is done in the following Two Trolleys Case: Redirecting a second trolley that threatens no one will push the trolley headed to the five away from them. However, on its way the second trolley kills someone else. Here the trolley that directly kills someone else has a mere causal relation to the greater good since it causes the trolley threatening the five to move away. It is this latter trolley's moving away that constitutes (and so has a noncausal relation to) the five being saved. I think redirecting the second trolley is impermissible.

In the Lazy Susan Case the means of saving the five is the Lazy Susan turning; those five being away from the trolley is merely an aspect of the Lazy Susan turning, not something it causes. Their being away from the trolley constitutes the greater good of their being saved, given that there are no other threats to them. The turning swivel table indirectly kills one other person when it creates a new threat by moving rocks that are already independently in the environment, which then kill him. In a different version of the Lazy Susan Case the turning swivel table would itself be a new threat that directly kills a bystander by banging into him as he stands nearby. If the Lazy Susan moved one other person (seated on the table opposite the five) into the trolley that threatened the five, it would move the one person into a pre-existing threat that kills him. Presenting these new and pre-existing threats to the single person is permissible. An explanation of why is that presenting them is caused by a means to saving the five (the Lazy Susan turning) that has as its aspect (and so has a noncausal relation) to the greater good of the five being saved.[23] When means (like the turning trolley and turning Lazy Susan) have a noncausal relation to the greater good, their causing a death is almost as if the greater good itself (as described by Principle A) caused the death.[24]

In these cases illustrating Principles A and B, the lesser harm seems to be causally downstream from the greater good or means that constitute it. But suppose the Lazy Susan turning just enough to get the five away from the trolley is also enough to push one other person on its opposite side into the trolley. (It's a very small Lazy Susan or the one person is already seated very near the trolley on the other side of it from where the five are.) Is the lesser harm then also an aspect of the means that has the greater good as another aspect? If so, then to be permissible, lesser harm needn't be causally downstream from the greater good or means that have a noncausal relation to the greater good. That might be one reason the view of NC being presented here is only a "downstreamish" theory.

However, this downstreamish theory could still require (among other things) that a harm that has not already been justified by what produces it not have an upstream causal role in producing greater good. By contrast, a harm that is already justified may permissibly have a role in producing goods that are greater or even lesser than it is. For example, suppose turning the trolley away from the five justified the death of one other person it hit. Then there would be no moral problem if his death had the direct effect of interfering with someone else's leg being broken even though this is a lesser good than the harm (death) that caused it. There would also be no moral problem if the toppling in front of the trolley of the man on the bridge that saves five from a trolley came about in the following way: Turning five different people away from another trolley causes the man's toppling. In this case his being toppled to his death is already justified by what produces it according to Principle B and so it can have a mere causal role in bringing about another good of five other people being saved from a different trolley headed to them.

Principle C. What could become the greater good or means that constitute it may permissibly cause lesser harm that stops threats that would interfere with what caused the lesser harm from becoming the greater good. This is so when such threats arise from what could become the greater good itself or what produces it. (A particular instance of this is when what I call a "structural equivalent" of the greater good [or means that constitute a structural equivalent of the greater good] may permissibly cause lesser harm that causally sustains that structural equivalent so that it becomes the greater good.)

Examples: In the Loop Case[25] the trolley turning away from the five will loop back to hit them if and only if it doesn't hit the one person on the other track. His being hit is causally required and sufficient to stop the trolley from looping back and the hit kills him. In this case the greater good of the five surviving or means that constitute it cannot be the cause of the one's death since it is hitting the one (resulting in his death) that helps cause the survival of the five for a significant enough period of time to justify the death of the other person. That is, the one person being hit is essential to ensure that the initial period of the five being free of the first hit of the trolley will be followed by what can reasonably be expected to be a period of survival that justifies killing another person. How can turning in the Loop Case be permissible on my view of NC that involves the DPP?

What causes the one person's being hit and killed is not a mere causal means to the greater good (like the bomb in the Bomb Case or the second trolley in the Second Trolley Case). What causes the death is the moving away of the trolley threat as it faced the five when we first had to act if they were to survive. The turning trolley is also unlike a mere causal means that topples the fat man in Thomson's Fat Man Case whose being hit by the trolley would stop it from hitting the five. Furthermore, it is the initial moving away of the trolley from the five that also causes the new threat of the looping back of the trolley. This means that when we abstract from the threat to them of the looping trolley, the trolley turning away is a means that constitutes what I call the "structural equivalent of the greater good." That is, it constitutes what would be the greater good (the five unthreatened for a sufficiently long time) were it not for the threat of the trolley looping created by turning the trolley. The trolley hitting the one person causally sustains the structural equivalent (i.e., what exists when we turn the trolley away abstracting from the new threat of the looping trolley). It does this by defeating a potential defeater (the looping trolley) of the structural equivalent becoming the greater good (i.e., the five saved for long enough to justify the harm to the one person). This allows the structural equivalent of the greater good to become the greater good itself.

However, recall that the downstreamish theory of NC holds that harms are not justified by what they cause but by what causes them and only already justified harms may play a causal role in producing goods. If the downstreamish theory of NC is correct, turning the trolley in the Loop Case can only be permissible because the harm that the redirected trolley causes is already sufficiently justified by what causes it. This is required for it to be permitted to play its causal role in sustaining the structural equivalent. How this is possible must be due to there being a "justificatory loop" as well as a physical loop. That is, a condition on permissibly causing the harm to the one person is that what causes the harm (the trolley being away from the five) would justify the harm if the five are expected to continue to survive. An effect of the trolley turning is to bring about the five's continued survival by causing a harm that eliminates the looping trolley threat that is also caused by the trolley turning. This may make what causes the harm (namely the trolley turning away from the five that constitutes the structural equivalent of the greater good) capable of justifying that harm.[26]

Even if the harm itself did not defeat the potential defeater of the greater good (i.e., the looping trolley) caused by the trolley moving away, what causes the harm could justify it. To see this, consider the following variation of the Loop Case. Suppose the turning trolley kills the one other person as a mere side effect. Afterward the trolley would still loop back to the five unless it is stopped by a large rock (independently in the environment) sometime after the one person is killed. Is this also a case in which the structural equivalent of the greater good could justify the harm it causes given that the structural equivalent would be sustained by the rock only after the trolley kills the one person? Suppose it is. Then if the lesser harm can be justified when it is caused by only the structural equivalent of the greater good in this variant of the Loop Case, it should be similarly justified in the original Loop Case. If the lesser harm is justified, it could permissibly cause the structural equivalent to be sustained and become the greater good in the original Loop Case.[27]

Further, suppose that in yet another variant of the Loop Case the trolley turning originally would not kill the one person but only break his leg. It is the additional pressure on his body of stopping the trolley from looping that foreseeably would cause his death. In this case lethal harm comes to him only because he stops the trolley from looping. I do not think this makes it impermissible to turn the trolley. To see this, consider: If it is permissible (as we are assuming it is) to turn the trolley in one of the original trolley cases when the trolley itself kills the one person as a side effect, then it is permissible for a further effect of the trolley turning to kill him instead. (This would be so, for example, if the redirected trolley only broke his leg but it also caused an electrical discharge that killed the person.) Now suppose turning in the Loop Case is permissible even if the redirected trolley kills the person when it first hits him. Then turning should also be permissible when the trolley at first only breaks his leg but a further effect of its turning is that it starts to loop and this puts pressure on the person that both stops the looping and kills him.[28]

In evaluating this explanation of why the harm in the Loop Case is sufficiently justified by what causes it, consider how the explanation would draw a moral distinction between the Loop Case and what I call the Tractor Case. In the Tractor Case the five are threatened not only by a trolley but also by a deadly tractor, which is a threat not caused by the trolley turning away (unlike the looping trolley). If we turn the trolley away, it will kill and/or move one other person along a track in front of the tractor, thus stopping it from killing the five. The tractor will kill that one person if he has not already been killed by the trolley. In this case, the structural equivalent of the greater good as I described it earlier does not already exist when we turn the trolley away. This is because abstracting from any effects of our turning the trolley, a deadly threat (the tractor) is still headed to the five people and this state of affairs does not have the structure of the greater good.[29]

In the Tractor Case another threat to the five exists independently of anything we do to get rid of the trolley threat and its elimination (initially and forever) causally requires the single person to be hit. In the Loop Case, there is one threat facing the five, and getting it away from its initial hit on them does not causally require the hit on the other person. But eliminating this initial hit on the five results in the threat of the trolley looping, a type of threat whose elimination requires another effect of the turning trolley, namely the one person's being hit. These differences between the Loop and Tractor Cases are present even though in both we foresee that we will need someone's being hit to play a causal role in bringing about the greater good. Hence, it is not a difference in (foreseeing) the necessity of a causal role for harm to the one person that could make a moral difference between the cases (if there is one). What seems significant is whether the threat to the five that can only be eliminated by the hit exists independently of turning the trolley and what this implies.[30]

To test this hypothesis, we might imagine a second variant of the Tractor Case in which it is the trolley turning away from the five that starts up a deadly tractor toward the five, so this second threat is not independent of the trolley turning. In the original Tractor Case, it is because there is another independent threat that there is no structural equivalent of the greater good when the original trolley threat is dealt with. The additional threat also results in a different role for the extra piece of track that in the Loop Case makes looping possible and in the Tractor Case makes it possible to move the person so as to stop the tractor. In the Loop Case if the extra track did not exist, then the looping threat that needs to be stopped would also not exist and so there would be no causal role for the one person's being hit. In the Tractor Case if the extra track did not exist, then the one person could not be moved along it and the five would die from the tractor. The five in the Tractor Case profit from the extra track in a way the five in Loop do not. However, this last fact is also true in the second version of the Tractor Case in which the tractor threat is caused by turning the trolley. Yet in the latter case the hit on the one is needed to defeat a defeater of the structural equivalent of the greater good (i) when the structural equivalent was produced with no causal role for harm to the one other person (as in the Loop Case) and (ii) means that constitute the structural equivalent produce the defeater (i.e., the tractor threat) that needs defeating. If the differences between the Loop and the first Tractor Case and the similarity between the Loop and the second Tractor Case are morally significant, they show that a structural equivalent of a greater good that needs to be *sustained* by the lesser harm it causes could justify that lesser harm. By contrast, a greater good that needs at least part of it (e.g., the removal of the tractor in the first Tractor Case) to be *produced* in the first instance by a lesser harm that is not already at least initially sufficiently justified (by a structural equivalent that causes it) could not justify that harm.

A challenge to the view presented so far that focuses on a structural equivalent of greater good is raised by a third version of the Tractor Case: Suppose that flipping a switch is a necessary causal means to moving the trolley away from the five but doing this immediately starts up a tractor that threatens the five **before** the trolley starts moving away from them. (This might be because it takes longer for the electrical mechanism to affect the trolley than to affect the tractor.) The trolley's eventually moving away hits the one person and moves him in front of the tractor, saving the five from that second threat. In this case, if we abstract from further effects of the trolley moving away, we no more have the structural equivalent of the greater good (as I defined it earlier) than we have in the original

Tractor Case. This is because the tractor threat to the five in this third Tractor Case is not caused by the trolley moving away but by what causes the trolley moving away (flipping the switch). The tractor threat pre-exists (and continues through) the trolley moving away from its initial hit on the five. Yet intuitively it seems as permissible to turn the trolley in the third Tractor Case as in the Loop Case and for the same reason.

This suggests that while a focus on a structural equivalent of the greater good is sometimes sufficient to justify turning the trolley, it isn't necessary and so doesn't get to the heart of the matter.[31] The difference that remains between the third and first Tractor Cases is that in the third the tractor threat is caused by what we do to turn the trolley from the five. In this case also harm to the one person that is causally necessary to stop the tractor is caused by the trolley moving away. This is different from the harm being caused by the flipping of the switch; that would involve it being caused by a mere causal means to the five being free of the initial trolley hit not by means that has a noncausal relation to that good. (However, it wouldn't matter morally if it was a rock that instead stopped the tractor and, as discussed earlier, harm to the one person was a mere side effect of the trolley turning away from the five.) So a potential defeater (the tractor) of saving the five is caused by doing something to save the five, and the trolley being away from its initial hit on the five causes the lesser harm that defeats the defeater (the tractor) of the five's sufficiently long survival. The existence of the additional threat is not independent of what we must do to stop the first threat, and the trolley being away from its first hit causes something that defuses the additional threat.

In sum, a harm that would be justified by what causes it if no other deadly threats were present (i.e., as the harm would be justified by the trolley turning in the original Trolley Case) is not unjustified if the trolley moving away, or what causes the trolley to move away, from the five causes other deadly threats that the harm is needed to defeat. By contrast, suppose it is impermissible to turn the trolley in the first Tractor Case. Then a harm that would be justified by what causes it if no other deadly threats were present could be unjustified if another deadly threat to the five exists independently (not caused by the trolley moving away or what must be done to make this happen) when the harm caused by the trolley moving away from its initial hit is needed to defeat the other threat.

This pattern of justification may be related to the fact that in the first Tractor Case, the five who independently face a tractor threat would actually be better off by being exposed to the trolley threat than they would have been without it were it permissible to turn the trolley. This is because without the removal of the trolley and the harm to the one to which it leads, they would have been killed by the tractor. Hence, it is appropriate to consider this an "opportunistic" (improving-for-the-five) use of the harm to the one person. By contrast, in the third Tractor Case, the five are no better off by being exposed to the trolley threat and the harm to which the trolley's removal leads than if this had never occurred. This is because without having to remove the trolley, they wouldn't face a tractor threat whose being stopped requires the one to be harmed. They are no better off than they would have been if no threats that needed to be eliminated had arisen. This makes it appropriate to consider this (what I will call) a "constancy" use of the harm to the one person for its use would just keep constant rather than improve the five's condition.[32] This distinction between the first and third Tractor Cases matters even when in both what causes the harm would justify it if no other threats were present and the harm is causally needed in order to satisfy a condition for its justification, namely that the five survive long enough to be a greater good relative to the lesser harm of the one's death

What has been said about these cases can be summed up as Principle C: What could become the greater good (or means that constitute it) may permissibly cause lesser harm that stops threats to its cause from becoming the greater good. This is so when such threats arise from what could become the greater good or what produces it. (A particular instance of this is when what I call a "structural equivalent" of the greater good [or means that constitute a structural equivalent of the greater good] may permissibly cause lesser harm that causally sustains that structural equivalent so that it becomes the greater good.)

When Principle C is satisfied, a harm is "initially sufficiently justified" and so may have its causal role. If harm may permissibly have a causal role in sustaining a structural equivalent or more generally what could become the greater good so it becomes the greater good itself, NC would not require that the lesser harm be causally downstream from the fully accomplished greater good. This is another reason to say that NC is a downstreamish rather than a downstream theory.

Principle C(ii). Consider an alternative non-state-of-mind principle that does not distinguish morally between Loop and Tractor and explains the permissibility of turning in Loop in a somewhat different way. Principle C(ii) says: If lesser harm can be justified as a mere side effect of what could become a greater good on condition that it actually becomes a greater good, then the harm may permissibly play any required causal role to make that condition be satisfied.

On this view, to find out whether what causes the harm in the Loop Case sufficiently justifies the harm for its further causal role in stopping the looping, we should first abstract from all other contextual factors and not just from the further effects of the trolley turning or what causes its turning. (This includes abstracting from whether there are other independent threats like the tractor.) Second, we should consider whether the moving away of one deadly threat (like the trolley) from five people on condition that they would continue to live on can justify the death of the one other person it causes as a mere side effect. We are assuming the answer is yes. The third step is to decide that it is permissible for the one being hit by the trolley to have a causal role in defeating any additional threats to the five, thus satisfying the condition that they will continue to live. In the Loop Case the additional threat (of the looping trolley) will be caused by the trolley turning away from presenting its original threat. In the first Tractor Case the additional threat is independently present. But Principle C(ii) implies that in the latter case we should still ask whether what causes the one person to be moved into the tractor (whether he's dead already or will be killed by the tractor) also justifies this happening to him. The answer, C(ii) implies, is found by first considering whether the trolley moving away from five people, abstracting from all other contextual factors, would justify a mere harmful side effect on the one person on condition the five would continue to survive. We are assuming it would. Of course, the harm can be justified in this way only if other threats can be stopped from shortly killing the five for otherwise they wouldn't continue to survive. Since the additional threats will be defeated in both the Loop and first Tractor Cases, in both cases harm to the one other person helps make true what could justify that harm, namely the good of the five's being saved from the trolley threat on condition of their long-term survival. According to this second view, if the five were already threatened by the tractor, we should be glad that the trolley threat to them also arises since getting rid of it when this involves hitting someone helps us get rid of the other threat to the five.[33] It does not matter whether the additional threat that is defeated is caused by what turns the trolley or its turning rather than something else.

Are there problems with this alternative analysis? Consider, for example, the claim that if harm can be justified as a mere side effect of saving the five from the original trolley hit on the condition of their continuing life, then the harm may permissibly play any required causal role to make that condition be satisfied. Imagine the Cure Case: The trolley is headed to kill five people who will soon be dead from a different threat of organ failure if they do not get organ transplants. However, once the trolley turns away from them and kills one other person, it will be easy to use organs he has willed to anyone who needs them to save the five. In this case the second threat to the five of organ failure is present independently of what turns the trolley or the trolley turning and it would be eliminated by a causal role for the one other person's death. I do not think it is permissible to turn the trolley from the five in this case. If this is correct, why should it be permissible to turn it in the first Tractor Case? (By contrast, consider a variant of the Cure Case in which it is the trolley turning away from killing five healthy people that would [somehow] cause their organs to fail. According to Principle C, that we could easily transplant them with donated the organs from the person killed by the trolley is what could make it morally permissible to turn the trolley. This is because the trolley turning away from the five causes a new threat to them that can be defeated by the harm that the turning also causes.). Even if C(ii) fails, it may still be permissible to turn in the Loop Case if Principle C is correct.

Principle D. A component of a greater good may even directly cause side effect harm that the component alone cannot justify if innocent means (including that component of the greater good or some otherwise already sufficiently justified harm) produces the rest of the greater good and that greater good can justify the side effect harm.

Example: Suppose we could move a trolley headed to kill five people only enough to save one person from being hit by it. The trolley being away from him has a side effect of killing two other people not among the five. The good of saving one person does not justify this greater harm. However, suppose we know that the one person being saved will move the trolley completely away from the remaining four with no other bad effects. Intuitively, the five being saved in this way could justify the bad side effect of killing the two other people. By contrast, the trolley should not be moved from the one person when it will kill two if those very deaths are needed to cause the trolley to move farther away from the remaining four. This is because the continued survival of one person saved could not even initially sufficiently justify the two deaths (the way turning the trolley away from the five in the Loop Case is thought to initially sufficiently justify harm to the one for it to have a causal role). Yet the possibility of such justification is needed for the deaths to play a permissible causal role in producing the rest of the greater good (according to Principle C).

In discussing Principle C we considered a variant of the Loop Case in which the death of the one person is a mere side effect that occurs before a rock stops the looping. Suppose the five being saved from the trolley's initial hit on them when the trolley turns should be conceived as a component of the greater good rather than a structural equivalent of it and a component that does not justify the harm it causes. Then the death of the one that in this case does not play a causal role in producing the rest of the greater good could be justified by Principle D without relying on Principle C. But then the rock case could not be used to support Principle C as a justification of turning the trolley in the original Loop Case, where hitting the one person has a causal role in stopping the looping trolley.

Principle E. A mere causal means to producing a greater good—which is not a component of it but causally upstream from it—may not directly produce a lesser harm, nor may a lesser harm that is not caused by what justifies it be a causal means to producing a greater good. However, mere causal means to producing a greater good may sometimes permissibly produce lesser harm by affecting something that is in the environment independently of what we do.

Examples: In the Bomb Case, a bomb may not be used as a causal means to redirect the trolley from five if the bomb would also kill a bystander, just as a gas may not be used as a causal means to save five people in the Gas Case when it also kills a bystander. Similarly, in the Two Trolleys Case we may not redirect the trolley that will kill the one person. Principle E also rules out as-yet-unjustified harm being a mere causal means to the greater good. The greater good that these mere causal means produce cannot justify the direct lesser harm these means either cause or constitute. Hence, there is a more stringent requirement on mere causal means to the greater good than on components of a greater good, as discussed in Principle D. The components may sometimes permissibly directly cause side effect harm when the greater good of which they are components can justify what the components alone cannot.

It is consistent with Principle E that a completely nonlethal gas may be used when necessary to save the five even if this moves germs independently in the environment but previously safely closeted so that they then kill one other person (in the Germ Case). Similarly, a bomb may be used to move the trolley away from the five even if it will foreseeably move rocks independently in the environment that fall on and kill someone. Acting within an environment we did not create can sometimes (e.g., when trying to bring about a greater good) differ morally from acting so as to add something harmful to an environment. In this case, acting to help some people in an environment that contains an independent entity that will then harm someone increases the permissible range of action. By contrast, in the comparison between the Loop and the original Tractor Case, harming someone when this is needed to help others avoid a threat that is independently in the environment can decrease the range of permissible action.

How should we treat the following Worse than Dead Case (which is a version of the Cure Cases)? The five toward whom the deadly trolley is headed will shortly die of organ failure unless they are supplied with organs. We can eventually acquire these by completely innocent means (e.g., a living donor will volunteer) and operate before the five die. But first we must move the trolley away from them and this will kill another person as a direct side effect. The short time period between the trolley being away from the five and when the five are transplanted would be worse than death for them due to rays being emitted by the redirected trolley.

If it is otherwise permissible to turn the trolley, it is clearly permissible to do so in the Worse than Dead Case since the trolley hitting the five would prevent their surviving by the transplants. But since the trolley moving away constitutes the five being worse off (before they become better off), how can we say that it is the first part of the greater good rather than a mere means to it? If the trolley moving away were a mere means to the greater good, it shouldn't be allowed to directly harm the one person according to Principle E.

In this case the trolley threat moving away is not a mere means to the greater good. It is a means that constitutes the five being alive for a short time, which is the first temporal part of the greater good of their long-term survival even if during it they are worse off than dead.[34] Its badness will be compensated by their eventual survival at a level sufficiently above worse-than-death.

Principle F. Modality enters into all these principles about permissible harm. This is because it only has to be *possible* for the principles to be satisfied given our actions even if sometimes, given our actions, permissible routes to an outcome are preempted by routes that would ordinarily be impermissible.

Examples: Consider Thomson's case of bombing a munitions factory to end a war when this would cause (let us assume) permissible side effect deaths and fear.[35] Suppose we know that the role of destroying munitions to end a war will be preempted by people surrendering out of fear of the side effect deaths. As Thomson notes, bombing the factory to end the war does not become impermissible (though causing death and fear as a means to end the war would be) just because the fear of the side effect deaths is what actually ends the war. This is because bombing the munitions could have ended the war even without the side effect deaths and fear—they were not causally necessary to end the war—and (by assumption) it would be permissible to cause the deaths and fear as mere side effects.[36]

Now consider a trolley case illustrating Principle F. Suppose using the only device that can permissibly turn a trolley away from five people causes vibrations as it heats up. The vibrations foreseeably cause a boulder to loosen and the boulder pushes someone into the path of the trolley. This stops the trolley before our device can turn it away. Using the device does not become impermissible just because it is the person's being hit by the trolley that actually stops it from killing the five. This is because (a) using the device to turn the trolley would have saved the five even if the device hadn't loosened the boulder that pushed the person into the trolley and (b) according to Principle E, it is permissible to use the device to turn the trolley from the five even if it affects something independently in the environment that then causes harm to a person as a side effect. The fact that the side effect causally preempts our means of turning the trolley does not make it impermissible to use the device. This is consistent with its being impermissible to use the device when it physically cannot turn the trolley on its own but is only a means of loosening the boulder so that it pushes someone into the trolley to stop it.[37]

5. (i) I believe the DPP (described in Section 2) captures and synthesizes the principles in Section 4. Principles A and B say that the greater good and means that constitute it can justify the lesser harm they produce (assuming this involves no violation of other principles). Principle E says that harm is not justified alone by the greater good that it (or causal means that have it as a direct side effect) is causally necessary to produce. Suppose we should morally distinguish between (a) producing a greater good and causally sustaining a structural equivalent of it

so that it becomes a greater good, and (b) defeating threats to a greater good that arise from attempting to produce a greater good rather than independently of that. Then the DPP is consistent with Principle C, which allows harms produced in certain ways to help cause the greater goods that justify those harms. Principle D says that mere side effect harms directly caused by a component of a greater good that cannot alone justify them, unlike harms directly caused by mere means, may be justified by the good of which the component is a part. However, such harms cannot play a causal role in producing that greater good and until justified should not have a role in producing other goods.[38]

(ii) What morally significant ideas about persons and their relations to each other may underlie or supervene on the DPP? One suggestion is that sometimes harm to fewer people may permissibly *substitute* for harm to a greater number of other people. People may be substituted for each other when harm not coming to some people is what causes the harm coming to fewer other people, at least when making harm not come to the greater number does not itself violate the DPP (such as would occur if we had to kill someone as a mere means in order to turn the trolley from five to one). In Chapter 8, I argued that a bystander may permissibly kill someone in a way that involves such substitution not only when it is physically impossible for him to save the five by substituting himself but also even when he could substitute himself for the greater number of people. I argued he needn't do so rather than substitute another person to save the five because the large effort normally required not to harm someone is not required when (i) one is trying to achieve a greater good in a way that is assumed to justify harming someone else if nothing else can be done and (ii) one would not be morally required to do what harms oneself if that were the only way to achieve that greater good.[39]

By contrast, causing harm would be impermissible when the relation created between people would not be *substitution* but *subordination*. Subordination is clearest when the death of some is brought about (in a way that doesn't make it the effect of permissible substitution) so that it can be the necessary causal means to there being fewer deaths in others. (For example, we topple the man from the bridge to stop the trolley when his being toppled is not itself an effect justified by some permissible substitution.) How could subordination occur when mere causal means to the greater good have only the direct side effect of killing someone else (as in the Bomb Case or Foot's Gas Case)? Suppose we must send a destructive threat either to one person or to an (unowned) tool (Tool Case). Ordinarily we would send it to the tool. But what if the tool is a required causal means to save five lives? Though the tool is instrumentally important, we should still destroy it rather than kill the one person. While killing the person would not be a causal means to saving the five, he would be subordinated to them if the importance of the tool for saving their lives implied that we should kill him rather than destroy the tool. Something similar may happen if we would use a tool to save five lives though as a direct side effect it will kill someone (as in the Gas and Bomb Cases).[40]

(iii) The Tool Case might also bear on how killing some to save others in accord with the DPP relates to the NC view that not killing is a more stringent duty than not letting die. In discussing Principle B we argued that it was as permissible for the bystander who would otherwise only let the five die to turn the trolley as for the driver who would otherwise kill the five. But now suppose a trolley will kill eight people. A bystander can save them either by (1) redirecting the trolley so that it kills one other person or (2) redirecting the trolley toward an unowned tool that he alone could (and would) use to save five other people from a different deadly threat to which he is also a bystander. Rather than kill the one, it seems the bystander should save the eight by doing what will destroy the tool and so lead to his letting the five die. (I call this the Saving-by-Letting-Die Case.[41])

This is so even though turning the trolley from eight to one satisfies the DPP as much as (if not more than) turning from five to one in the Bystander Case. Furthermore, suppose the driver of the trolley headed to the eight is the only one who could and would use the tool to save five people. It seems that he too should turn the trolley to the tool, even if for him redirecting the trolley would be a choice between killing eight and killing one. (We could call this the Not-Killing-by-Letting Die Case as it involves the driver.) If these judgments about these cases are correct, they show that even if satisfying the DPP were necessary to justify killing innocent, nonthreatening people, it is not sufficient for doing so.

Like the Tool Case, the Saving-by-Letting-Die Case suggests that rather than kill another person, someone should destroy (and so not use) the means that only he could (and would) have used when it is necessary to rescue other people from death. Could the moral direction to let five die rather than kill one in the Saving-by-Letting-Die Case be consistent with it being permissible to kill one rather than let five die in the Bystander Case and with it being permissible for a bystander to kill one person by redirecting a threat away from killing eight others if no other way of saving the eight existed? We could think of this as a new Trolley Problem.

In another version of Saving-by-Letting-Die the bystander is already supererogatorily saving the five people by use of the tool (e.g., his life support machine). If he turns the trolley toward the machine it will terminate his ongoing lifesaving assistance to the five people who then die; he would not merely destroy a tool that he could and would use to save their lives. Yet again it may seem that he should turn the trolley from the eight, terminating the aid he is providing (a form of letting die as opposed to killing), rather than turn the trolley away from the eight and by doing so kill the one other person on the side track. Whether this is consistent with the permissibility of turning the trolley in the Bystander Case is also part of this new Trolley Problem.

One possible argument for the consistency of the conclusions about the Bystander Case and the Saving-by-Letting Die Cases is that in the Saving-by-Letting-Die Cases the five who would die from aid not being started or being terminated either have no right to that aid or have a weaker right to it by comparison to the rights had by the five in the Bystander Case not to be hit by the trolley. This could be so even if in the Bystander Case they do not have this right not to be hit by the trolley against the bystander but only against the driver. In both the Bystander Case and the Saving-by-Letting Die Cases the one other person to whom the trolley would be redirected also has a right not to be hit. The fact that it could be permissible to infringe his right in accord with the DPP does not mean we should do so when there is a better alternative. Suppose that in both the Bystander and the Driver Cases the trolley was headed toward destroying the life support machine to which the driver had supererogatorily attached five people when no one else would have. Then even the driver should not turn the trolley away from terminating aid (a form of letting die)to which those five have no right and toward killing one other person instead thereby infringing his right.

According to this proposal for consistency, the crucial issue is whether the five who would be made worse off by the trolley hitting them would have a right against that being done and whether that right is as stringent as the right of the one person not to be killed. In the Driver and Bystander Cases they have such a right. The driver not the bystander would transgress their rights, but in turning the trolley the bystander still prevents the transgression of their rights. Their rights may be counted against the right of the one person who would be hit if the trolley were redirected. The DPP could then be used to explain the permissibility of redirecting as a way of preventing the five from being killed. Satisfying the DPP will make causing harm permissible if the harm thereby avoided would involve as serious a violation of the rights of each of the five as is involved in the harm to the one.

Thomson argued (2008) that since there was no right of the five against the *bystander* that he would transgress in letting them die but there was a right of the one not to be killed that the bystander would transgress, the bystander should not turn the trolley. By contrast, the proposal we are now examining about the Saving-by-Letting-Die Case suggests that what is crucial is not whether the bystander's letting die would violate the five's right, but whether those who could be saved by the bystander have a stringent right that would be violated in being hit by the trolley. The violation of that right is embedded, so to speak, within the scope of what would happen if the bystander in that case were to let die. Hence, his letting five die *from a killing* as in the Bystander Case could be morally different (i.e., not a required letting die) from his letting five die *from a letting die* as in the Saving-by-Letting-Die case (a required letting die) when the alternative is his killing one other person with a right not to be killed.[42]

Here are some objections to this proposal:[43] First, suppose there were naturally occurring germs in the environment headed toward killing five people. Nothing done by any people caused this to happen. These five people will be harmed by the germs, but their rights would not be violated by the germs or by any person. The proposal for consistency we have been examining would rule out the bystander redirecting the germs to harm one other person since that would transgress the one person's right not to be harmed and not prevent any violation of the rights of five others. If it is permissible for a bystander to redirect the germs, the proposal we have been considering for consistency of killing in the Bystander Case and not killing in the Saving-by-Letting Die Case would be wrong

Second, suppose the five in the Saving-by-Letting-Die Case are themselves about to be killed by a second trolley driver who has lost control of his trolley. Suppose that if the bystander turns the trolley from the eight toward the one on the side track, this will also allow him to interfere with the second trolley hitting the five. In this version of the case, the bystander who wants to save the eight must choose between letting the five have their rights violated or killing the one. According to the proposal for consistency we have been examining, it should be permissible for the bystander to turn the trolley from the eight toward the one rather than let the five be killed if it is permissible to turn the trolley in the original Bystander Case. Suppose one thinks it is consistent with turning the trolley in the Bystander Case to be required to let the five be killed in this new version of the Saving-by-Letting Die Case. Then one will have to reject the proposal for consistency we have been considering, at least as the whole story. One will have to locate some further morally significant difference between the Bystander Case and the Saving-by-Letting-Die Case in its original and revised versions.

Here is a proposal for dealing with the second objection. One possible difference that may affect the application of the DPP to the Saving-by-Letting-Die Cases is that in the Bystander Case the lesser harm is caused by the greater good (or means that constitute the greater good) whose existence justifies that harm. What would cause the harm in the Saving-by-Letting-Die Cases is the trolley being turned from the eight people. But in these cases there is another way to save the eight that does not require us to kill the one person, namely not aiding or stopping aid to the five. So to justify killing the one we need to show that there is no need to use the alternative because aiding the five also makes killing the one permissible. To use the DPP to show that, in the way we show that we may aid the five in the Bystander Case, we would have to show that the greater good of the five being saved (or means that constitute this) causes the lesser harm. But that is not what would happen if we saved the five in the Saving-by-Letting-Die Cases since it is not saving the five that kills the one person but turning the trolley from the eight. That is, it would not be true that the greater good of saving the five (or means that constitute it) that is to justify the harm to the one causes that harm. This difference between the Bystander Case and the Saving-By-Letting-Die Cases might make it consistent to save the five by killing the one in the first case but not in the second ones.

However, to save the five from a deadly threat to them in a Saving-by-Letting-Die Case it would be permissible according to the DPP (were it possible) to redirect the threat to the same one person on the side track that could be hit by redirecting the trolley from the eight. Further, suppose that the alternative to turning the trolley from the eight toward the one involved not saving from a threat a number of people great enough to justify turning a trolley from them to hit one other person. Then in such a case, might it not be permissible to save the eight by turning the trolley from them to the one other person rather than do what will interfere with saving the five? That is, it might be argued that it is permissible to save a group of people (the five in the Saving-By-Letting-Die Case) by saving another group (the eight) in a way that conforms to the DPP so long as the number saved in each group is sufficient to justify the harm to the other person. This would allow us to reject the judgment about the impermissibility of killing the one in the Saving-by-Letting Die Case but it would also go beyond using the DPP alone to justify killing. It would provide a different (but related) reason for the permissibility of killing in the Saving-by-Letting-Die Case than is available for the permissibility of killing in the Bystander Cases. (Even on this proposal it would not be sufficient to determine that one may turn a trolley from a larger group to a smaller group without checking to see what alternatives there are. So the fact that turning from eight to one satisfies the DPP and turning from five to one could satisfy the DPP, were it possible, would not make turning permissible if there was an alternative of turning to an empty track.)

(iv) The Saving-by-Letting-Die Case raised the possibility that satisfying the DPP in turning the trolley from eight to one might not be a sufficient condition for permissibility of harming innocent, nonthreatening people interpersonally. Might there also be problems with applying the DPP in a revised version of the standard Bystander Case? Suppose there is something you didn't know about the trolley headed to the five: It is doing so because it was originally redirected by the same bystander from ten other people it was about to hit. At that time, it could not be sent in a way that would hit the one person toward whom the trolley might now be redirected. Would it still be permissible for the same bystander to turn the trolley from the five to the one other person? If not, then this case (which I call a Tree Trolley Case) would show that the DPP is not a sufficient condition of permissibility.[44]

In tree trolley cases one must take the first branch to reach the second branch in order to do what will minimize harm. The person who would be harmed on the second branch was not originally susceptible to harm on any branch that could have been taken first. Might it be impermissible for a bystander to turn the trolley the second time even though turning it would also satisfy the DPP and reduce the number of people the bystander is responsible for permissibly harming?[45] By contrast, suppose it was possible to turn from the ten to the one initially—a possible first branch—but it would have demanded supererogatory effort from the bystander to do so and he could much more easily turn the trolley in two stages. In this case, I think his turning twice is clearly permissible.

The (supposed) impermissibility in some cases of the bystander turning twice is not merely because the one person becomes susceptible to harm from the trolley only because of what the bystander does to get the trolley away from the original larger group of (ten) people. Suppose the bystander could not redirect the trolley away from the original larger group at all unless he quickly built another track. Unfortunately, this new track would lead to where one other person was immovably positioned and so he would be hit when we redirected the trolley. (Call this the New Track Case.) Though the one person was originally not susceptible to being harmed and would become susceptible only because of something the bystander did, I think that it is permissible to build the track and redirect the trolley.

One thing that distinguishes the New Track Case from the Tree Trolley Case is that in the former it is the ten originally threatened by the trolley who would be saved by building the new track, but it is not they but the five who would be saved by the second turning in the Tree Trolley Case; the ten would already have been saved by the first turning. This raises the question of what the relation of the one person is to the ten. Suppose there were two tracks to which we could redirect the trolley from the ten, on one of which five people would be hit and on the other of which one person would be hit. In this case, whether the one or the five would be hit, they would stand in a substitution relation to the ten. But in the Tree Trolley Case, while the one stands in a substitution relation to the five, he may stand in a subordination relation to the ten. Analogously, suppose there was someone whom it was permissible to topple from the bridge to save five other people (in virtue of promises made or relationships had). If we turn the trolley from the ten to the five, would it then be permissible to topple one person to save the five though it would not have been permissible to topple the one person to save the ten in the first instance? I suspect not if the five would be substituted for the ten as a way of making use of their particular relationship with the one person so that the ten could be saved at the cost of only one life when this would not otherwise have been permissible. If this is so, it suggests the possibility that just because there is a permissible substitution relation between B (five) and A (ten), and a permissible substitution relation between C (one) and B (five), this needn't imply that there is a permissible substitution rather than an impermissible subordinating relation between C (one) and A (ten). So before deciding if a course of action affecting C and B is permissible, we would have to check whether the act that is pairwise permissible between those two individuals is overall impermissible because of its side effect of creating an impermissible pairwise relation between C and A. The creation of a subordinating relation between the ten and the one may account for the sense that something is wrong with turning again in the Tree Trolley Case.

Suppose an error was made by turning from the ten people to eleven? Might it be morally preferable to turn the trolley back to the ten rather than turn it from the eleven toward one other person instead if that one person was and is not susceptible to being harmed by a trolley redirected directly from the ten? Someone coming upon a scene in which this is being done with no knowledge of its history would not understand why the trolley is being sent to the ten rather than to one person who stands in the same substitution relation to the eleven as the ten do.[46]

It is being suggested that given the history in the Tree Trolley Case (in which the same bystander who would turn from five to one already turned the trolley from ten others to those five), it could be impermissible for him to turn the trolley from five to one despite the fact that it is permissible to do so in the original Bystander Case where there is no such history. But suppose the person who had to turn the trolley in the Bystander Case had not previously turned the trolley away from other people. Coming upon the scene of the trolley headed to the five, should what he may do also be a matter of the history of the current situation? Should he consider how likely it is that someone else turned the trolley from ten people to five in order to avoid doing something impermissible in turning the trolley from five to one? The permission to turn the trolley might depend only on a given bystander's own history of previously turning the trolley, not on whether anyone else had done so. If so, the DPP would acquire an "agent-relative" character. That is, turning could become impermissible for an agent given his own prior actions, but it would not become impermissible if someone else had first turned the trolley, for example, from ten to five. However, this agent-relative account is problematic. After all, if the one person is still put in an inappropriate relation to the ten if the trolley is turned twice regardless of who turns the trolley, why shouldn't a bystander refrain from turning the trolley from five to one if he knows that someone else turned the trolley from ten to five when it wasn't possible to turn it toward the one person? And if he doesn't know, should he investigate?

(v) We have been discussing whether satisfying the DPP is not a sufficient condition of permissibility. Now consider how satisfying it might not be a necessary condition for permissibility. This could be because according to Threshold Deontology the DPP might hold up to a threshold on how much good effect (including avoiding bad effect) would be lost if harm that violates the DPP is not done. Satisfying the DPP could also not be a necessary condition on permissibility because of what I call the Principle of Secondary Permissibility (PSP). The PSP claims that an act that would be impermissible considered on its own may be permissible, other things equal, as a substitute for a permissible act that would otherwise have been done and caused more harm to the same person (or caused the same harm to that person but harmed others as well).[47] For example, suppose it is impermissible to topple one person in front of the trolley when this would paralyze the person's legs if this were the only way we have to stop the trolley. Paralyzing someone's legs is less of a harm than each of the people threatened by the trolley would face but it is sufficiently great that causing it by toppling the person to save the five from death should be ruled out by the DPP. However, it is permissible to turn the trolley from the five onto another track where it will kill one person. We are about to do this when we discover that we could also stop the trolley by toppling into the trolley the very person we were about to kill, thus instead only paralyzing his legs. What was impermissible on its own becomes permissible when it is the substitute for the permissible act we would have done. This is not only because it is less bad for the person who will be harmed than what we would otherwise have done. It is important that other things are equal. In particular, it is important in this case that both the killing and the toppling are against the will of the person who will be harmed. It might not be permissible to topple the person against his will if it was, for example, not against his will to be killed.

Here is another example of the DPP being superseded by the PSP: The DPP could rule out using a bomb that will kill someone as a direct side effect in order to turn the trolley. However, suppose that if we turn the trolley to another track by innocent means, two other people on the other track will be killed and one of them is the person who would be killed by our using the bomb. Here if we use the bomb instead, the person who dies is no worse off than he would otherwise be as a result of the permissible act of turning the trolley toward the two people and another life is saved. This makes it permissible to use the bomb that directly kills the one as a side effect. (What if a bystander physically could have permissibly harmed five people by redirecting the trolley to them away from ten but is refraining from doing so because he cannot bring himself to kill five people? Now it turns out that if he topples in front of the trolley only one of those people whom he is refraining from permissibly killing, he can save the ten people. In this case, the person he would kill is not someone who would otherwise have been killed anyway but this is so only because the bystander is refraining from doing what he can currently physically and permissibly do; if he were willing to turn the trolley on the five, then it would be permissible according to the PSP to instead topple the one person into the trolley. It would be an extension of the PSP, that I call the Extended Principle of Secondary Permissibility [EPSP], to permit toppling the person who would not have been killed anyway in this case.[48])

When an act ordinarily impermissible is permissible secondarily because it involves less harm to the same person, it can become wrong to do the act for which it substitutes. So if we are going to do something, we should do the substituted act (though it may be permissible to do neither). The PSP does not imply permission to do the "lesser moral evil" since the substituted act is no longer a moral evil. (I have suggested[49] that there could be a Principle of Secondary Wrong [PSW] in which we should substitute for a wrong act [e.g., unjustifiably killing 100 people] another act that is also wrong but less seriously so [e.g., killing in the same way 50 of the same people], which if it were one's only option would also not be permissible. That it is justifiable to substitute the second act for the first does not mean that the act is permissible and not wrong; it is a lesser moral evil since it does not reduce the harm to potential victims of a permissible act. This is a case in which whatever we do is wrong [though it is not a moral dilemma and it is clear what we should do]. It contrasts with a case in which we avoid doing something wrong [e.g., driving the trolley into five people] by doing something else permissible [and not morally wrong] such as redirecting the trolley that still involves wronging the one person to whom the trolley is redirected by infringing his right.)

(vi) It is also possible that the DPP need not be satisfied in another type of case in which the one person sends back the trolley that is redirected to him. I have already claimed (in Section 1) that he may permissibly send the trolley back to the bystander or driver who permissibly sent it to him. Now we should note that he may also turn back the Lazy Susan, resulting in harm to the five if they are innocent threats to him when someone else turns the Lazy Susan with them on it. That is, suppose a bystander turns five people on the Lazy Susan away from the unstoppable trolley and this hurls the five people into one other person. If they land on him, he will be killed but they will be unharmed. However, these cases do not fall within the purview of the DPP since they do not involve harming innocent, *nonthreatening* people.

By contrast, suppose the one person who would be hit by a permissibly redirected trolley can only send it back toward the agent who sent it to him on the track from which it came. Then it will continue on to kill the five it originally threatened who do not threaten the one person at all. In this case the agent who sent the trolley is not made to pay the cost of saving the five instead of the one person since the five will not be saved. In another case sending the trolley back will not at all harm the agent who sent it but only go directly back to killing the five. This happens as well in a case in which a bystander has *impermissibly* toppled one person onto the track to stop the trolley from reaching the five but before the trolley reaches the one person he is only able to press a switch that redirects the trolley onto another track that also leads to the five. He is essentially resisting what was impermissibly done to him by redirecting the trolley though he foresees it will hit the innocent, nonthreatening five it was originally threatening. (He does not merely move out of the way of the trolley which he cannot do; he causes it to move toward the five when it would otherwise have stopped by hitting him.) If the one person's self-defense is permissible in these Sending Back Cases, it cannot be justified by the DPP because the lesser good of his being saved or means that constitute his being saved cause the greater harm of five being killed. The cases would show that one may permissibly harm other innocent, nonthreatening people in a way that doesn't conform to the DPP. In all three cases, the one person's defense would put the five back in the situation they were originally in by permissibly resisting the means of getting them out of that original situation. In all three cases the five lose only the benefit (i.e., continuing to be alive) of the trolley being redirected whose redirection the one person resists. I believe this is part of what makes it permissible for the one person to resist in all the cases. Suppose that the one person's resistance is only permissible in the third case because the five lose the benefit of impermissible (toppling) rather than permissible means of saving them. This would still be a case in which satisfying the DPP is not necessary in order for someone to permissibly harm other nonthreatening innocent people (when avoiding *lesser* harm is constituted by means that cause *greater* harm).[50]

All this is consistent with it being an impermissible violation of the DPP for the one person to redirect a trolley toward other innocent, nonthreatening persons when the threat was originally headed to him.[51] It is also consistent with it being an impermissible violation of the DPP to resist the threat sent to him by sending the trolley back toward the person who sent it to him or the five originally threatened if this also kills other innocent nonthreatening people as a further side effect. These nonthreatening others would lose life that was not merely the benefit they got from the means that the one person is permissibly resisting.[52]

## Notes

1. Hence, it may be permissible to harm a person for his own greater good when it is not permissible to harm a person for the greater good of others. Recall that nonconsequentialism is standardly thought of as denying that *only* consequences matter in determining what it is morally right to do. It does not deny that consequences can be one of the things that matter. This chapter draws on my *Morality, Mortality,* vol. 2 (New York: Oxford University Press, 1996); *Intricate Ethics* (New York: Oxford University Press, 2007); and *The Trolley Problem Mysteries* (New York: Oxford University Press, 2016), among other work, but also modifies and adds to my previous work.
2. Philippa Foot introduced the Driver Case in her "The Problem of Abortion and the Doctrine of Double Effect," reprinted in her *Virtues and Vices* (Los Angeles: University of California Press, 2003). Judith Thomson introduced the Bystander Case in her "Killing, Letting Die, and the Trolley Problem," *The Monist* 59, no. 2 (1976): 204–17. In that article, Thomson introduced the title "Trolley Problem" to refer to Foot's Driver Case (which Foot contrasted with cases in which a doctor may not take organs from one person, thereby killing him, in order to save five other people and a judge may not have one person executed to save five hostages). Thomson there said (p. 206) of the driver of the trolley (whom she named Edward) and the transplant surgeon (whom she named David): "Why is it that Edward may turn that trolley to save his five, but David may not cut up his healthy specimen to save his five? I like to call this the trolley problem, in honor of Mrs. Foot's example." In her later article, "The Trolley Problem," *Yale Law Journal* 94 (1985), 283–310, she changed her use of the title, applying it to a contrast between her Bystander and Fat Man Cases. I shall return to this point later. I do not think the two different references in Thomson's work for the term "Trolley Problem" had been pointed out before Lecture I in *The Trolley Problem Mysteries.* Note that the Trolley Problem does not depend on redirecting to another track; redirecting to someone on the grass could also be part of a Trolley Problem.
3. We might imagine that the trolley would loop back to hit the one, but if so this case should not be confused with what is known as the Loop Case to be discussed later. In at least one way the Returning Trolley Case is similar to Bernard Williams's case referred to as "Jim and the Indians," which has been much discussed. The similarity is that a bystander is called upon to kill one of a group of people, all of whom will otherwise be killed by someone else if the bystander does not act. (See Williams' chapter in *Utilitarianism: For and Against* [Cambridge: Cambridge University Press, 1973]). Some differences in the Williams case that may be morally significant are that a villain is deliberately threatening to kill the group and Jim would not redirect a threat but present a new threat that will kill the one person.
4. Suppose two of the five would be killed by a returning trolley when that is one's only alternative to letting the five die, thereby killing two to save three others. However, only one person on the side track would be killed in the Returning Trolley Case that also includes that option Suppose it would be permissible to turn the trolley from

hitting two people toward hitting one person on the side track in a Bystander Case. Then it is not clear how one could justify using the returning track in the Returning Trolley Case when there is the option of the side track. If it were preferable to use the returning track in this case, it might argue against the permissibility of turning the trolley from two people to one person in the Bystander Case. Similarly, suppose it would be permissible to turn the trolley from killing thirteen people toward one person on the side track but it is also possible to use the returning track that kills only five of the thirteen. If it is permissible to turn the trolley from five people toward one person on the side track in the Bystander Case, it is not clear how one could justify using the returning track rather than save the additional five plus the eight by turning the trolley toward the one person on the side track. But see discussion of this issue in Chapter 7.

5. In her article "Turning the Trolley," *Philosophy & Public Affairs* 36 (2008): 359–74.
6. See her "The Trolley Problem."
7. See my discussion of such cases in *Intricate Ethics*, 167–69.
8. I discuss the threatened person permissibly resisting the threat redirected to him further in Section 5. I also discussed it in *Intricate Ethics,* 167–69, and in *The Trolley Problem Mysteries,* 32, 85–87. Here is a possible alternative justification for the one person permissibly turning back the trolley: Those who turn it in his direction have a Hohfeldian right in the sense of a power, to which the one person is not immune, to change his moral status from having a right not to be harmed to having no right not to be harmed in this way. Hence, they do not wrong him in making him susceptible to the harm in this way. However, his lacking this immunity does not mean that he has a duty not to resist what others have a rightful power to make happen. (Arthur Applbaum argues in this way about the rights of governments and the rights of disobedient citizens. See his "Legitimacy without the Duty to Obey," *Philosophy & Public Affairs* 38, no. 3 (2010):215–39). I do not think this alternative view of the permission to turn back the trolley is correct because it implies that those who may turn the trolley on the one person have the power to alter his moral status so that he no longer has a right not to be harmed rather than a mere permission to infringe his right.
9. For more on Sending Back Cases see Section 5(vi).
10. The DPP should be understood to be defeasible and so not a necessary condition on permissible interpersonal harm to nonthreatening, innocent people. I discuss this further in Section 5.
11. I believe Jonathan Bennett was the first to describe NC as a "downstream" theory. See his "Morality and Consequences," *The Tanner Lectures on Human Values* (delivered at Oxford University, 1980). I try to distinguish between downstream and downstreamish views later.
12. Thomson introduced this case (referred to as the Fat Man Case) in her "Killing, Letting Die, and the Trolley Problem." Rather than think of it as involving someone pushing the fat man "up close and personal," it is better to think of toppling him with a mechanical device from a distance. This holds constant the distanced, mechanical

cause of death in redirecting a trolley. Intentionally involving someone in a way foreseen to cause his death (which is what may actually happen in toppling the man) would also be ruled out by a somewhat revised DDE. Such a revision to the traditional DDE was proposed by Warren Quinn in his "Actions, Intentions, and Consequences: The Doctrine of Double Effect," reprinted in his *Morality and Action* (Cambridge: Cambridge University Press, 1994).

13. This is different from claiming that an act would be impermissible only if no reasonable agent could do it without intending a harm even if the actual agent intends a harm. I do not think such an interpretation of the DDE is correct as I go on to argue.
14. I made this point in my *Ethics for Enemies* (New York: Oxford University Press, 2011), Chapter 2.
15. In his "Possible Intentions and the Doctrine of Double Effect," *Ethics, Medicine, and Public Health* 8 (2019): 11–17.
16. See her "The Problem of Abortion and the Doctrine of Double Effect." However, consider the following variants on the Gas Case: (1) the five can be saved by a harmless gas but their breathing normally will foreseeably use up all the oxygen available so that one other person dies (Breathing Case); (2) the gas used to save the five is harmless but using it will foreseeably move some germs that were safely closeted so that they kill one other person (Germ Case). I think that it would be permissible to save the five in both these cases. This suggests that doing what foreseeably causes death even in non-trolley-type cases can be permissible more often than Foot may have thought. I will suggest an explanation of this later.
17. This conclusion is in contrast to Thomson's in "The Trolley Problem." I use "transgress" to cover both cases of impermissible violations of rights and cases of permissible infringements of rights.
18. See her "Killing, Letting Die, and the Trolley Problem."
19. A version of the Lazy Susan Case was first introduced in my "Harming Some to Save Others," *Philosophical Studies* 57 (1989): 227–60.
20. Here are some other types of cases: Arguably one person's being saved can justifiably cause someone else's broken leg. However, arguably several people being immensely happy is a greater good than the bad of one person being somewhat miserable. Yet suppose the one person would be worse off being miserable than each of the several people would be if they were not immensely happy. Then the greater good may not justify the lesser harm it causes. This is because we should compare the expected condition of each of the people as individuals (known as pairwise comparison) and give at least some priority to the person who would be worse off if harmed rather than aggregating the benefit to each of those who would be better off even if not helped. In Lecture 2 in *The Trolley Problem Mysteries*, I consider whether someone may avoid a threat originally headed to himself in ways that cause more harm to others if he does so in ways that are like those permitted by the DPP. If he may, I there suggested that we might distinguish two parts to the DPP: (a) *how* harm and good come about and (b) what sort of harm and good come about (i.e., lesser or greater). I will ignore this issue here. However, in Section 5 (vi) I will consider whether someone may cause

more harm to others to prevent a threat redirected from them to him. If he does this by means that satisfy the "how" component of the DPP, the "what" for which he does this will not be the greater good.

21. As I use "independently" in the environment, it is not a matter of how many distinct links there are in a causal chain. Suppose A sets up all the elements in a "Rube Goldberg" device for killing B. The presence of the elements in the chain is not independent of what A does.
22. I made this point in *Morality, Mortality* Vol. 2 and argued that it is how the killing comes to pass that is morally crucial.
23. For ease of presentation, henceforth I will include cases in which the means have the greater good as its aspect under the rubric of cases in which the means constitute the greater good.
24. The following case seems problematic: Suppose the five are on an immovable Lazy Susan with the trolley coming at them. If we rattle the Lazy Susan, this will topple the five on the ground away from the trolley. However, there is another person on the Lazy Susan who would not be hit by the trolley but who would be toppled over a cliff if we rattle the Lazy Susan. Rattling the Lazy Susan seems to be a mere causal means to saving the five, a means that has a direct side effect of killing or putting in harm's way someone else. Yet, I suggest, it seems permissible to rattle the Lazy Susan. By contrast, suppose the five were not on the Lazy Susan but on a railroad track with the trolley coming at them while only the one person was on the Lazy Susan. Then if rattling it would (somehow) move the five away from the trolley but also topple one person off the cliff, it would be impermissible to rattle the Lazy Susan. I think there is this difference in permissibility because (roughly) the five's being on the Lazy Susan is an aspect of the Lazy Susan and changing this aspect of the Lazy Susan just is the five being safe.
25. Introduced by Judith Thomson in "The Trolley Problem."
26. The condition that the greater good is expected to continue must be satisfied to make it permissible to do what kills the one person (i.e., turn the trolley in the first place). This is why it is not sufficient to say about the Loop Case (i) that it is permissible to turn the trolley despite its killing the person (as shown by the original trolley cases) and then point out (ii) that no further harm comes to him if his dead body stops the trolley from looping. This is insufficient because in the original trolley case the five are saved (and have the expectation of continued survival) once the trolley turns away, but without the one person being hit that will not be so in the Loop Case. The Loop Case is also unlike a case in which a harmful effect of what we do stops a threat to a greater good other than the greater good needed to justify the harm's existence by causing it. (For example, suppose that in another variant the trolley turning away from the five caused a death that stopped the trolley from also threatening five different people. Here the harm that causes the second greater good is already justified.)
27. However, we will consider another principle (D) that may also account for this case.
28. The DPP does not base permissibility on an agent's state of mind. A state of mind theory that might be offered to explain the Loop Case is what I call the Doctrine of Triple Effect (DTE). For more on this see my "The Doctrine of Triple Effect and Why

a Rational Agent Need not Intend the Means to his End" (Kamm 2007) and the next endnote. The DTE was also discussed briefly in Chapter 2 in this volume.

29. The DPP does not base permissibility on an agent's state of mind. A state-of-mind theory that might be offered to explain the Loop Case that also justifies turning the trolley in the Tractor Case is the Doctrine of Triple Effect (DTE). It distinguishes between (1) turning the trolley because we know the one's being hit will stop the looping and (2) pushing the fat man in order (with the intention) to stop the trolley. It claims that acting for the purpose of stopping the original hit on the five only because we expect an effect of this (the hitting of the one) to play a causal role in the further survival of the five is different from acting in order to bring about that effect. The former can be permissible even if the latter were not (as the DDE claims). That we do not act in order to hit the one person in the Loop Case is shown by its being consistent with turning the trolley in that case to not do anything separate from what we do to turn the trolley away from its first hit on the five (e.g., give it an extra push) if this were necessary in order that the one be hit. It would also be consistent to remove the one person from the track if this became possible even if the trolley would then loop. Not easily removing him would show an intention that he be hit. In turning the trolley in the Loop Case we need merely act on condition of an expected side effect of our action, not in order to bring it about. The DTE need not distinguish morally between Loop and Tractor if in both cases we decide to turn the trolley only because we foresee the further useful effects of harm to the one person without being willing to do anything merely in order to bring about that harm.
30. Another way of drawing the contrast between Loop and this Tractor Case is in terms of how the five profit from the one person being hit. Suppose we imagine a graph where 0 is being threatened with death and 2 on the y axis is not being threatened. In the Loop Case when the trolley turns away from the five, we can think of them going from 0 to 2 but being at 2 would itself cause them to plummet back down to 0 were it not that hitting the one person inhibits their fall, resulting in their remaining at 2. In the Tractor Case, when the trolley turns away from the five, we can think of them as (at best) being at 1 on the y axis. It is hitting the one that moves them further on to 2 and otherwise they would drop back down to 0. These five profit from the hit in being made better off than they would have been if just the trolley threat had been removed from them. The hit does not merely keep the five in the Tractor Case as they would have been if just the trolley threat had been initially removed.
31. Hence, I am here revising some of my views in earlier work about the role of a structural equivalent.
32. Warren Quinn contrasted opportunistic harm with eliminative harm. See his "Actions, Intentions, and Consequences: The Doctrine of Double Effect." The "constancy" use of harm is not eliminative in Quinn's sense since it doesn't involve harming someone in order to eliminate a threat that he himself presents. The harm to the one with which we are here concerned is useful to eliminate a threat the one does not present.
33. Even on this view it would be wrong to deliberately threaten the five with the trolley once we know that the hit on the one person that results from removing it is our only

way of getting rid of the other threat to the five. We would be threatening the five with the trolley merely in order to hit the one person as a mere means to stop the other threat, there being no other good reason for sending the trolley to the five.

34. A temporal part (or component) of the greater good (e.g., the first five minutes of continued survival) should be distinguished from a person component of the greater good that involves, for example, one of the five being saved for the long term.
35. See her "Self Defense," *Philosophy & Public Affairs* 20 (1991): 283–310. Whether, when, and why such direct side effect harm in war is permissible is an important question since it seems contrary to Principle E. This is so at least if it is the result of the mere means (e.g., bombs) rather than an end (e.g., blowing up of a munitions factory) judged to be a greater good relative to the side effect harm. The permissibility in war of harm that is a direct effect of mere means may have to do with the people harmed having to bear risks as citizens at war. I have discussed this in *The Moral Target: Aiming at Right Conduct in War and Other Conflicts* (New York: Oxford University Press, 2012).
36. Elsewhere I discuss different types of cases, such as the Munitions Grief Case, in which bombing would not be permissible were it not that bad side effects help ward off threats to the continuing success of the bombing. Some of these cases are explained by Principle C. For more on this see *Morality, Mortality*, vol. 2, and *The Moral Target: Aiming at Right Conduct in War and Other Conflicts.*
37. The DPP was presented in Section 2 to capture modality. A nonmodal version is: In NC harm is justified (in part or whole) by what produces it. If a harm is not justified in this way, it cannot be justified (except in extraordinary circumstances) by what it produces alone nor should it be used to help produce other goods. Goods brought about improperly are themselves not justified.
38. I have already said that the DPP is defeasible..
39. For a more detailed defense of this see Chapter 7 in this volume and my "Duties That Become Supererogatory or Forbidden?," in *Principles and Persons: The Legacy of Derek Parfit*, ed. J. McMahan et al. (Oxford: Oxford University Press, 2021).
40. Suppose we had to choose whether to save the tool needed to save five people or save the one other person. Would it be only when someone's right not to be harmed is overridden that subordination occurs if the tool is preferred?The similarity between the case in which we would kill someone rather than destroy the tool needed to save five others and the case in which we would kill one person as a direct effect of a tool that we are using to save five others may become clearer if we suppose that to save the tool we had to use a device that as a direct side effect would kill someone else. We should not do this. Indirect harms of mere means are dealt with differently when harms come about by what we introduce (e.g., our means) having an effect on things in the environment independently of what we do. However, if a greater good is not at stake, the difference between our means directly versus in this way indirectly harming may not be morally relevant. This raises questions about whether subordination of the one to the five is taking place if the permissibility of using the tool that harms by affecting something independently in the environment depends on whether it is useful for the greater good. Further, if using a tool that causes harm by

affecting something independently in the environment can be permissible though we shouldn't save such a tool rather than a person, this raises doubts that the latter type of case bears on using a harmful tool.

41. I introduced it in *The Trolley Problem Mysteries*.
42. It is important to distinguish the bystander or the driver terminating assistance he is providing (a case of letting die) from a case in which someone terminates assistance someone else is providing. For example, suppose the bystander who would turn the trolley from the eight would terminate lifesaving support that someone else was providing the five without either that other person's permission or the five's permission. Then he would, I believe, transgress the rights of the five not to be killed. Then according to the proposal being considered, he might redirect a threat from the eight so that it kills one rather than five. In yet another variant on the Saving-by-Letting-Die Case, suppose person A is trying to interfere with life support that person B is providing to the five people and so A would kill the five if he succeeded. Person C, who is the bystander, is able to stop A by turning the trolley from the eight toward the one (e.g., suppose the noise frightens A off). He faces a choice of turning the trolley from the eight to either kill one or let five be killed by A. If it is permissible for him to turn the trolley in the original Bystander Case in which he kills one rather than let five be killed, then according to the proposal we are considering, it should be permissible for him to turn the trolley away from the eight toward killing one rather than let five be killed.
43. In *The Trolley Problem Mysteries* I accepted the proposal for consistency that we have been examining. I am now raising objections to what I said in that book and offering a new proposal.
44. See *Morality, Mortality,* vol. 2, and *Intricate Ethics,* 144–47, for my earlier discussion of the Tree Trolley Cases, some of which is revised here.
45. Suppose it was the driver who had to turn in the Tree Trolley Case. Could he be permitted to turn twice, given his understandable desire to minimize the number of people he harms, even if the bystander would not be permitted to do that? I argued that he may not topple one person from the bridge in front of the trolley to stop it from hitting the five any more than the bystander may. Hence, an explanation for why it could be permissible for him to do what the bystander may not in the Tree Trolley Case would be needed..
46. Suppose that turning the trolley from the ten to eleven others actually moved a piece of track so that it would now be possible to redirect the trolley from the ten onto the moved track at whose end stands one person. If we send the trolley back from the eleven to the ten, would it be permissible to then turn the trolley toward the one? Would it be permissible to send the trolley back from the eleven to the ten so that we may then turn it toward the one? In these cases, turning the trolley to the eleven is a way of moving a track that will then put the one person in a substitutable relation to the ten. But that is what is done as well in the New Track Case when we build a new track that makes it possible to redirect the trolley in a way that will harm fewer people. If redirecting in the New Track Case is permissible, then so should it be permissible to create a new route from ten to one.
47. I discussed the PSP in *Morality, Mortality,* vol. 2, and in *Intricate Ethics,* 169–73.

48. I discussed the EPSP in *Intricate Ethics*, 171. There I said, "It depends on what we can (in the sense of what it is permissible and within our current capacity to) otherwise do." Hence, it excludes harming someone because in the past but not currently it was permissibleand/or within our capacity to do something else to him.
49. In *Intricate Ethics*, 172.
50. In *Intricate Ethics*, I discussed only the case in which permissible redirecting is resisted. See also endnote 20 earlier on separating parts of the DPP.
51. I consider why even this might be permissible in *The Trolley Problem Mysteries*, Lecture 2.
52. For more on this issue see the references in note 8.

# 10

# The Use and Abuse of the Trolley Problem: Self-Driving Cars, Medical Treatments, and the Distribution of Harm

In this chapter I briefly review cases that are standardly considered trolley problem cases along with standard moral judgments about permissible conduct in these cases. As we have seen in previous chapters, these cases raise many issues about the right not to be harmed and its limits. I then consider the ways in which many standard car driving cases differ as a conceptual matter from standard trolley problem cases with which some compare them. I argue that the cases involving cars raise distinctive moral issues different from the distinctive issues raised by standard trolley problem cases, but they also bear on the right not to be harmed and the duty to bear costs to avoid harming. I further consider how some medical cases differ from some standard trolley cases with which some compare them. Finally, I discuss some moral issues raised by self-driving cars by comparison to trolley problem cases, including the role of those who would produce and program the cars and the liability to harm of pedestrians, drivers, and passengers involved with self-driving cars.

## 1. A Hypothetical Case

I once considered what I called the Ambulance Case.[1] In it, society was to decide ex ante (i.e., in advance of knowing who would be affected one way or another) how a self-driving ambulance should be programmed when it came to a choice between (i) saving people by rushing them to the hospital and harming pedestrians on the route or (ii) letting the potential patients die but harming no pedestrians. I imagined that the ambulance could be made to detect how many people it was carrying and how many pedestrians would be harmed and, to simplify matters, I assumed (as I do here) that the life of each person was at stake and that they were alike in morally relevant respects. One question I considered was whether we should deliberately program our ambulance carrying five people to continue on its route by having the program disable a stopping mechanism when more lives would be lost by its stopping than by running over one person on the road. I argued that even though ex ante (at the time we decide on how to program

*Rights and Their Limits: In Theory, Cases, and Pandemics*. F. M. Kamm, Oxford University Press.
© Oxford University Press 2022. DOI: 10.1093/oso/9780197567739.003.0010

the ambulance) each person in the society would maximize his chances of survival by not allowing the ambulance to stop, it could be wrong to program the ambulance in this way, just as it would be wrong for a driver in control of the ambulance to drive over the one person to get the five to the hospital. Certainly, the fact that only a program, not a person, would disable the stopping mechanism at the time of impact does not remove responsibility for this happening from the people who programmed the ambulance.[2]

## 2. Standard Trolley Cases

Recently, reality has caught up with hypothetical cases like the Ambulance Case in which vehicles can be programmed to move in various ways. One such instance is the design of so-called self-driving cars of which there could be at least two types: (1) those that have no person at all driving them and that operate completely on the program designed for them (call this the Complete Case) and (2) those that have a person driving them but whose program can override or supplement a driver's control at crucial points (e.g., the car will stop despite the driver trying to continue; call this the Partial Case).[3]

Some have thought that the Trolley Problem might help us with the practical problem of creating programs for self-driving cars. To review some of what has been said in previous chapters, in the basic Trolley Case created by Philippa Foot,[4] an out-of-control trolley is headed toward killing five innocent people. To save them, the trolley driver can only turn the trolley to a side track where, he foresees, the trolley will instead kill one other person standing on that track. Judith Thomson's Bystander Case variation involves a bystander, not the driver, deciding whether to turn the trolley (with the same effect) when the driver cannot do so.[5] It is commonly thought that the driver is facing a choice between killing five or killing one. However, it might be argued that if the trolley has gone out of control, independently of any act or omission of his, how he comes to cause the death of the five would be very different from his deliberately turning the trolley when he foresees it will kill someone else. For the bystander it is a choice of letting five die or killing one.[6] In none of these cases is the person who turns the trolley or who is on the trolley at risk of dying. In none of these cases is the person who would be killed by the redirected trolley the cause of its threatening the five or obligated to either give his life or assume a position in which he will be killed as a side effect in order to save the five other people. He would also lose his life by someone else imposing the loss on him, not by his imposing it on himself.

Many have thought that in these cases the driver is morally required and the bystander is at least permitted to do what will minimize the number of people who would be killed by redirecting the trolley and that there is some principle that explains the obligation and permission, respectively. (These cases involve a choice between five or one being killed, but the argument that would justify killing one to save five arguably would also justify redirecting toward any smaller number of people to save a larger number of other people. Indeed, I suspect that if an argument could not justify killing one to save two from the trolley, it could not justify killing one to save five from it.)

By contrast, many think it would be impermissible for the bystander to do what is necessary to save the five people by pushing or toppling someone else from a bridge in front of the trolley so that his body stops it and the trolley kills him (which I will here call the Topple Case).[7] I think it is also impermissible for the driver to do this and for the driver or bystander to detonate a small bomb whose explosion would stop the trolley from hitting the five though a piece of the bomb would fly off, killing an innocent pedestrian (Bomb Case). It is thought that some principle explains why these things are impermissible even though they would also minimize the number of innocent people killed. We could think of the Trolley Problem as trying to explain why killing is permissible in the original Trolley Case and the Bystander Case but not in the Topple and Bomb Cases. This problem is part of the more general debate between act consequentialists, who think it always permissible to bring about the best consequences, and nonconsequentialists, who deny this.

## 3. Other Cases

I have described what philosophers who have discussed the Trolley Problem take to be some standard cases involved in it. (I have limited myself to very basic cases and not the many more complex cases [discussed in Chapter 9] that may not be relevant to the practical issues we will discuss in this chapter.) Let us now consider how these cases compare conceptually with those that have been described as trolley problem cases by others, including by contributors to popular internet sites who aim to acquaint the general public with the Trolley Problem in connection with using ordinary and self-driving cars. At this stage, I am concerned only with conceptual similarities and differences and put to one side moral judgment of the cases. Nevertheless, I am concerned with similarities and differences because they may be morally significant. For one example, Chris Rampolla (who describes himself as "a philosopher by training") says the following in his online article:

> Suppose that you're driving your car in the right hand lane of a one-way street on a winter evening. As you approach a red light at an intersection, you tap the brakes and begin to skid. Ahead of you the left lane is closed and is blocked by

> a concrete barrier in front of a crosswalk. There are no obstructions in the right lane. A pedestrian has legally entered the crosswalk on the right side of the street and is attempting to cross over to the other side. You have just enough time and just enough control of the car to make a decision about which lane to enter but you cannot stop your car. Should you choose to continue on in the right lane, the pedestrian will be struck by the car and will likely die. Should you choose to direct your car into the left lane, the collision of your car with the barrier will save the life of the pedestrian but will very likely kill you, the driver. What do you choose to do? Now ask yourself that same question, except this time consider that your child is in the car and would likely die from an impact with the barrier. Next consider that the pedestrian in the road is also accompanied by a child. Still further, consider that this time your spouse and child are in your car with you and there are three elderly people in the crosswalk. Has your choice changed? More generally, what is the moral thing to do in each of these situations and is there any commonality between them? These are modern versions of a philosophical problem known as The Trolley Problem.[8]

## 3.1. Threats and Nonthreats

Rampolla here describes the Trolley Problem as being instantiated in a case where a driver of a car that cannot be stopped has to decide whether to let the car continue on to (very likely) kill a pedestrian or turn it and (very likely) kill himself.[9] (Henceforth, to simplify, I will assume that whatever choice is made someone will definitely be killed, as is assumed in the standard trolley cases.)[10] But the standard trolley problem cases discussed by philosophers are about whether one may kill some innocent, nonthreatening person so as to either not kill or save other innocent, nonthreatening people from a threat already facing them. These cases do not, as in Rampolla's case, involve someone who is presenting a threat of death to others (the driver) deciding whether to kill innocent, nonthreatening people rather than kill himself. Philosophers might refer to the latter sort of case as an "innocent threat case." Such cases are distinguished by the threatener himself, a bystander, or a potential victim having to decide whether to harm the threatener, who became such despite being innocent of any moral wrongdoing, or allow him to proceed to harm some nonthreatening people.

I am not concerned with legislating the use of the terms "Trolley Problem" and "innocent threat case." I am concerned with the possibility that the difference I have identified between standard trolley cases and the car case in Rampolla's example may be morally significant and that it is wrong to assume without additional argument that a driver who threatens people should weigh his life or have it weighed by others as the lives of innocent, nonthreatening persons should be weighed when one decides which of them will be harmed. To keep this moral issue in mind, I shall distinguish the trolley and innocent threat cases in the ways I have just described (though others may follow a different practice).[11]

There are different types of innocent threat cases that make it clearer why the threatener is considered morally innocent. Robert Nozick described a man unwillingly hurled at you by a third party. The man is headed toward landing safely on you who, however, would be killed by the impact.[12] May you who are the potential victim or a bystander kill the innocent threat to prevent his fall from killing you? In other innocent threat cases (sometimes called cases of minimal responsibility for harm)[13] the threatener is not totally inactive in causing the threat but is not at fault in his actions (e.g., a psychotic killer, a nonnegligent driver whose brakes fail in his well-maintained car). All these cases involve unjustified threats, but might there be other innocent threat cases where a nondeliberate threat is justified? For example, consider a pilot fighting on the just side in a war who unintentionally bombs a military facility that it would have been permissible to intentionally bomb given that it will result in only permissible collateral harm to civilians. In standard just-war theory anyone who presents a threat is considered "noninnocent," but morally speaking one might consider him innocent. May these threatened civilians nevertheless shoot the pilot down to protect themselves (especially if this will not affect the good military effect of his bombing)? In this case it is the pilot who is the threat, for if we could eliminate him and thus his control of the plane, the threat to civilians would stop. However, in cases involving an already out-of-control car it is strictly the vehicle that is the threat; getting rid of the driver may not stop the threat,[14] though doing something to the vehicle that as a side effect will kill the driver will stop the threat. Nevertheless, I think in an extended sense, the driver in such cases is an innocent threat if he was driving the vehicle before he lost control of it.

In a standard innocent threat case, the choice is between the original potential victim(s) being harmed and the threatener being harmed (whether the harm to him would be imposed by the threatener himself or by someone else). Suppose a third option is added so that the threat can be redirected to another nonthreatening victim. Then we could possibly have a combined innocent threat and trolley problem case as I am using these terms. However, if a driver should bear the burden of being harmed rather than his original potential victims, it is unlikely to be permissible for anyone except the new potential victim to decide that the threat should be turned to her, holding losses to all constant. If so, problems distinctive to a standard trolley problem case would not arise.

### 3.2. Imposing Harm versus Having It Imposed

Note also that in the standard trolley cases, the person who decides what to do with the trolley (either the driver or a bystander) is not one of those who might be harmed. Hence, those who stand to be harmed have harm imposed on them by others rather than imposing it on themselves. By contrast, in Rampolla's case the driver faces the option of harming himself.[15] One should not assume without argument that what may be imposed on one is the same as what one has a duty to impose on oneself.

Hence, unlike the standard trolley cases, Rampolla's case involves both the possibility of harm to the threatening driver and the driver having to decide whether to impose the harm on himself. The first factor may make it easier to justify harm to one person; the second factor may make it harder to demand it. Suppose one could show that the driver was permitted to treat himself like any nonthreatening possible victim (which is unlikely). The fact that no such victim would have to redirect the threat away from others to himself would imply that the driver (who is actually the threat) would not have to redirect in a way that kills himself.

In sum, the following are among the cases we have so far distinguished: (1) someone who threatens but cannot be threatened decides on which nonthreateners to impose losses (the standard [driver] Trolley Case); (2) a bystander who cannot be threatened decides whether to impose losses on nonthreateners with no possibility of harming the threatener (the Bystander Case); (3) someone who threatens and can be threatened decides whether to impose losses on himself or his potential nonthreatening victims (an innocent threat case as I use the term); (4) a bystander who cannot be threatened decides whether to impose losses on a threatener or allow losses to be imposed on nonthreatening victims (another innocent threat case).

### 3.3. Passengers and Varied Characteristics

As the quote from Rampolla shows, he also considers cases in which there are people in the threatening vehicle who are simply passengers and who stand to be harmed if the threatening driver himself decides to avoid harming pedestrians. Cases with passengers are unlike the standard trolley cases in which there is no one on the trolley who can be harmed, and it is also a complication of the standard innocent threat cases. If there are passengers in a threatening vehicle, it would be another mistake to assume without argument that they are to be treated as morally equivalent to pedestrians who would be hit by the threat and that their lives should be weighed in the same way as pedestrians.

Some of Rampolla's cases also assign different qualities to the different people who might be harmed (e.g., some are old, some young, some are strangers, some are one's spouse or child).[16] By contrast, the standard trolley and innocent threat cases abstract from such distinctions in order to determine (1) whether one particular factor in the trolley cases, namely differences in how we come to kill people (e.g., by redirection, by toppling, etc.), makes a moral difference and (2) whether in the innocent threat cases the difference between being a threat (albeit morally innocent) rather than, for example, a pedestrian makes one more liable to be harmed. As in science, it has been thought in philosophy that to test for the moral significance of a factor, we should insofar as possible hold other variables constant. Nevertheless, varying additional characteristics to see how they affect one's decisions about sparer cases need not be a methodological mistake since otherwise crucial factors can sometimes be overridden or have their effect altered in changing contexts.

## 3.4. Possible Principles

A final point about Rampolla's discussion is that he describes Foot as supporting a revised version of the Doctrine of Double Effect (DDE) to justify the driver turning the trolley. He says:

> A modern interpretation of the doctrine of double effect was put forth by Philippa Foot in 1967. The problem (at the time) had nothing to do with driving, but instead was one of a number of thought experiments she used to examine the morality of abortion. As an example of double effect, she suggested the following:
>
> "The steering driver faces a conflict of negative duties since it is his duty to avoid injuring five men and also his duty to avoid injuring one. In the circumstances he is not able to avoid both, and it seems clear that he should do the least injury he can. The judge, however, is weighing the duty of not inflicting injury against the duty of bringing aid. He wants to rescue the innocent people threatened with death but can do so only by inflicting injury himself. Since one does not in general have the same duty to help people as to refrain from injuring them, it is not possible to argue to a conclusion about what he should do from the steering driver case."

But it is not true that the distinction Foot draws in this part of her article quoted by Rampolla is a modern interpretation of the DDE. The DDE distinguishes morally between harm that happens as a side effect and harm that is intended. It claims the latter is impermissible even as a means to a greater good while the former at least need not rule out pursuing a greater good. As we have seen (in Chapter 9), Foot proposes an alternative to the DDE that has nothing to do with whether one intends harm (or harm is a means). It focuses on a moral distinction between harming and not aiding even when harm is merely foreseen as a side effect and neither intended nor causally a means. For example, Foot thought that using a gas in surgery to save five people from their illness is ruled out if this gas will also cause someone else's death as a mere foreseen side effect. (I call this the Gas Case.) (Note that her claim that the duty not to harm is stronger than the duty to aid also might rule out turning the trolley in the Bystander Case since the bystander would harm one person as an effect of aiding five.[17])

## 4. New and Old Threats?

Other examples of the problematic use of the Trolley Problem occur in medical ethics discussions. One instance is in the work of Dr. Marya Zilberberg.[18] She correctly identifies a version of the Trolley Problem as reconciling the apparent permissibility of the driver diverting the trolley and the impermissibility of a bystander toppling a person in front of the trolley to stop it even though in both cases five people would be saved from death and one person would be killed. She goes on to compare these cases with the use of mammography, which is said to save eight women who would otherwise have died from cancer for every thousand mammogrammed but to lead to the death of at least one woman who would not otherwise have died (due to false positives). She says about this Mammography Case:

> Well, then we have the trolley problem, don't we? We are potentially sacrificing 1 individual to save 8. And who does the sacrificing is where the variations of the trolley problem come in.... The payer certainly sees this issue as the original formulation of the problem: Why not throw this financial switch to achieve net life savings? But for a clinician who deals with the individual patient this may be akin to pushing her over the bridge toward a potentially fatal event.

The first thing to note is that unlike the driver in the "original formulation of the problem," the payer did not have a role in causing the threat that must be dealt with, which is cancer. Nor is he diverting the cancer that threatens the life of some women toward fewer women. If the threat in question is mammography, the payer is not redirecting it away from many to a smaller number of others. The payer is helping to pay for a new means to help some women (the mammogram), which presents a bad side effect threat to a smaller number of other women who use it. (This is in some ways analogous to using the small bomb to stop the trolley when the bomb would kill another person except that the bomb was never used to possibly help the person it winds up killing, unlike the mammogram.) This also implies that the doctor who orders mammograms that as a side effect harm a woman is not harming a woman as a means to help save eight others, so what the doctor does is not like toppling someone in front of the trolley as a means of stopping it. This is shown by the fact that if mammograms the doctor orders did not cause the harm to one woman as a side effect, this would not reduce mammograms' effectiveness in saving 8 out of 1,000 women; the threat and harm to the one is not needed as a means to save the eight.

An additional aspect of the Mammography Case to which Dr. Zilberberg points is that ex ante each person could be either one of the eight who will be benefited or the one who will be harmed. Hence, she thinks it is important to understand the patient's attitude to risk. And indeed, introducing a means that will unavoidably risk harm as a side effect to each of those who, as far as we know ex ante, also get from that means a greater chance to benefit may be permissible. However, this does not imply that it is permissible to use means that will help others when it is known that the means will as a side effect impose certain death on a particular other person and it is still possible to prevent its doing so by not using the means (as in the Bomb and Gas Cases). This is so even if it is permissible in the Trolley and Bystander Cases to impose certain death on a particular other person when one could still avoid doing so. As already noted, it is one aspect of the Trolley Problem to explain these differences in permissibility.

Not distinguishing between the Trolley Case and cases like Bomb and Gas is also exemplified by some discussions in medical ethics that try to analogize the use of electronic cigarettes to diverting the trolley.[19] That is, many people will die of smoking. Suppose we can reduce their numbers by converting them to use of electronic cigarettes, which are somewhat less bad for them. However, suppose also that as a side effect of this policy a smaller number of other adults who would not have smoked will also take up electronic cigarettes, thus becoming worse off than they would otherwise have been. (This Electronic Cigarette Case is a hypothetical case insofar as it abstracts from real effects, especially on underage users.) This case is not analogous to diverting the trolley away from more people to fewer people for the same reason that the Bomb and Gas Cases are not like diverting the trolley. In this case there is a prior threat (of cigarettes) to many people. If we introduced e-cigarettes as a means to help them, we would not be diverting cigarette use but introducing a new means (e-cigarettes) that would have the side effect of harming (by hypothesis) a smaller number of people who never smoked. We may wonder whether this conceptual difference makes a moral difference, but it is a conceptual difference. It is important to remember that not all cases that involve only foreseeably killing fewer nonthreatening people to save a greater number of other nonthreatening people are like the standard Trolley Case in which diverting a threat seems permissible.

However, it is worth noting that, as described, the Electronic Cigarette Case differs from the Gas and Bomb Cases in at least two significant ways: (1) The e-cigarettes that reduce deaths among cigarette smokers do not directly cause harm to others, as do the bomb and the gas. It is only because an intervening agent takes up smoking e-cigarettes that he may be harmed. Helping those who already smoke cigarettes by getting them to use e-cigarettes at most enables the harm to another new group of people by making available to them the new option of e-cigarettes. (2) The likelihood of death to each of the new e-cigarette smokers is (assumed) less than the likelihood of death to each of the original cigarette smokers. This is so even if there are eventually more deaths due to e-cigarettes than to cigarettes because more rather than the hypothesized fewer new smokers will use them. So unlike the Bomb and Gas Cases in which either five or one will certainly die if the trolley hits them, the probability of death occurring to each of the newly threatened people by e-cigarettes is less than the probability of death occurring to each of the people originally threatened by cigarettes. These two factors may make the grounds that rule out using the bomb and gas inadequate to rule out the introduction of e-cigarettes in the hypothesized circumstances despite their bad side effects.

Here is an implication for self-driving cars of what we have just said about how the Mammography and Electronic Cigarette Cases differ from standard trolley cases: The permissibility of killing some to save others in the standard Trolley Case is relevant to programming cars only if programming is about redirecting the threat that the car itself presents. However, this does not mean that to be morally like the Trolley Case anyone who dies as a result of a threatening car being redirected must also be killed by that very car. For example, suppose that the turning trolley (or car) caused a new threat of a rockslide that killed a pedestrian. Turning the trolley (or car) is still a permissible solution in the trolley-type case because it is the trolley (or car) turning away from the five people that causes the new threat. This is not so when a new threat is introduced as a means to turn the trolley, like the bomb; it is a new threat not caused by redirecting the trolley.[20]

The overall conclusion of considering these discussions that try to make use of the Trolley Problem (in both Sections 3 and 4) is that they often fail to recognize the very distinctions the trolley problem cases are about. These distinctions may or may not be morally significant, but not recognizing them is itself problematic if we want to understand the Trolley Problem.

## 5. Particular Moral Issues in Self-Driving Cars

Though some would disagree, let's assume for the sake of argument that all the judgments I cited in Section 2 about what is commonly thought to be permissible, obligatory, and prohibited in the standard trolley problem cases are correct and that there are principles that justify these judgments.[21] This would imply that we know what morally should or may be done in many cases. If we do not have access to the principles that underlie our judgments, we cannot program the principles into cars, though we might provide rules for what they should do in a variety of cases.[22] However, there may be ways in which cars can "learn" what to do without being programmed with rules or principles. It is said that, like people, machines exposed to various situations can self-learn to make correct choices without following explicit rules or interpreting known principles specific to those cases. These are complex issues about learning that I will not discuss here. For simplicity I will refer to the cars in Complete and Partial Cases as being programmed with principles that lead them to behave properly.[23] My concern here is not how to make self-driving cars behave properly but what the proper way for them to behave is and whether there are substantive moral (rather than merely conceptual) differences between what is morally proper in standard trolley problem cases and in the Complete and Partial Cases.

Here are some issues to consider.[24]

### 5.1. Why Have Self-Driving Cars?

The primary benefit of Complete or Partial cars is that they will prevent deaths by preventing cases in which any person's life is threatened. ("Deaths" will include serious injuries.) Their primary benefit is not merely reducing lives lost once something has gone wrong and at least someone will have to die.

In the trolley problem cases something has already gone wrong since the trolley has gone out of the driver's control with respect to the five and the question is who is to die when someone must die. Hence, the primary issue with which trolley problem and innocent threat cases deal—what to do when someone must die—would arise only when self-driving cars have failed to satisfy the primary reason for having them. If self-driving cars got into dangerous situations more often than cars completely under a driver's control, the fact that they could be programmed to do a better job than a driver of minimizing the harm they would cause would not speak as strongly in their favor. However, if these cars got into life-threatening situations less often than human-driven cars, that they were worse in determining who will die when someone must might not speak very strongly against them.[25]

## 5.2. Do Moral Principles That Apply to Persons Apply to Machines?

It may be said by some that the sorts of moral prohibitions that make it impermissible, for example, to kill one person to save five in the Topple and Bomb Cases are relevant to the conduct of persons but not to machines because the prohibitions are grounded in "the agent's personal point of view" of acting in certain ways and automated cars are not agents that have a personal point of view. This so-called agent-focused view of the ground of prohibition on people harming people has been defended by Thomas Nagel in some of his work.[26] It might also be said that there can be *reasons* to do one thing rather than another only for persons because they can have conscious appreciation of considerations for and against acting in some way, but there are no such "reasons for" machines if they have no conscious appreciation of considerations for and against acting in some way. Another ground for thinking that moral principles that apply to people do not apply to machines is that human persons would have emotional responses to, and struggle emotionally with, killing in some ways and this cost to them should be taken into account in determining what they should do. But machines do not have emotional responses or struggles that should be taken into account in determining what they should do.

Consider objections to these three views in turn. Suppose that the ground of the wrongness of acting in Topple and Bomb is not concern for the agent's personal view of acting in certain ways (or even for the relationships between agent and victim generated by acting in certain ways). Rather, suppose the wrongness is grounded in concern for the potential victim's status as a being who may not be treated in certain ways.[27] Then the potential victim might be treated in ways incompatible with his status as much by a machine as by a person. It is interesting and important that which theory correctly grounds nonconsequentialist prohibitions on harming people in certain ways could be relevant to which principles to use in programming machines. For purposes of this discussion I shall assume that the "victim-focused" account of prohibitions is correct.

Second, reasons for an entity's behaving in a certain way can exist independently of an entity's awareness of this. Certainly there can be a reason for a person not to drink a poisoned liquid though he isn't aware it is poisoned. Could there similarly be a reason for a machine not to kill in Topple if a person's status provides grounds for his not being killed in that way? We could at least say that there is a reason for there not to be entities that would kill someone in this way and people who were aware of these reasons might be morally required to interfere with the machine that would kill in this way. This could be true even if the machine was not designed by people but fell like manna from heaven or grew like a plant.

Third, the fact that machines would not be affected emotionally by their harming others is irrelevant to the permissibility of their movements if the impermissibility of people behaving in comparable ways has nothing to do with the emotional costs to them of doing so. This would be so if the reason for not behaving in that way stems from the status of the potential victim and the emotional costs arise from implicit recognition by agents that they have acted impermissibly. If people could take a pill that made them not react emotionally to their killing in Topple, this would not affect the impermissibility of their so acting. (The absence of emotional effects, however, might make it easier for machines than people to do the right thing when the cost to people of doing so would be great [e.g., their own destruction]. Machines would not have excuses that people might have for not doing the right thing when this involves damage or harm to them. I shall return to this point later.)

Finally, at least some self-driving cars would be programmed in advance to deal with any upcoming situation, while a person driving a car would decide what to do when in the situation. Does this make what the car should do different from what a person should do in the same situation? In the Mammography Case it was said that an ex ante decision to use a diagnostic test in a population could be morally permissible even though we know that it will unavoidably harm someone at a time when we will be unable to help her. But that does not mean that we should decide ex ante to use such a mammogram test instead of one that could detect and interfere with harm it was about to cause. Similarly, that a car will be programmed in advance (unlike a human person) does not mean that it should not be programmed in advance to behave in a situation it is in to avoid harming someone in the way a person should. We should not program a device in advance to topple someone in the Topple Case merely because minimizing deaths would be ex ante in the interests of all if it would be wrong on victim-focused grounds for a person to commit in advance to doing the same thing at a time when she could still avoid doing it.[28]

## 5.3. Programmers and Company Duties

### 5.3.1. Programmers as Bystanders?

Do those who program cars they will not drive occupy a role analogous to that of the bystander in the Bystander Case? One difference between these two agents is that the bystander is dealing with a trolley that is already doubly out of the driver's control: The driver cannot control it as it heads to the five and he lacks the ability to turn it away from the five to the side track. By contrast, the programmer, at least in the Partial Case, is deciding whether to make the car be to some degree beyond a conscious driver's control. The program is designed not merely to recommend a course of action to the driver but to actually compel the car to make certain movements. (In deciding whether to make completely driverless cars, programmers are deciding whether there is to be any person driving at all.)

Prima facie, the Partial Case seems to raise special moral issues not raised by the Complete Case since it involves deliberately limiting the liberty of conscious agents to decide for themselves whether and how to prevent harm they would cause to others. The bystander in the following revised Bystander Case seems more like the programmer in a Partial Case: A bystander sees a trolley that can be stopped from killing five people only if it is turned where it will kill one other person. The driver retains the power to redirect the trolley, but she may or may not actually do this. The bystander presses a switch that takes the power to turn out of the driver's hands and puts it in his own hands. Call this the Intrusive Bystander Case. It raises at least two questions: (1) Is it permissible for a private person like the bystander to transfer power to himself? (2) Should a bystander as willingly take it upon himself to redirect the trolley, thereby killing a person, when it is possible that the driver herself would fulfill her responsibility to redirect if she retained power? (As we shall see, the answer to questions analogous to these is complicated in partial cases by the fact that, unlike what is true in the Trolley and the Bystander Cases, the driver herself might be harmed as a result of a decision. Until further notice, I will assume that in the cases we will consider it is not possible for the driver to be harmed but innocent, nonthreatening people would be harmed.)

The program that takes over in the Partial Case and those who create the program seem like intrusive bystanders. They become less intrusive if the driver has the option of turning the intrusive program on or off when using the car. The latter variant seems most analogous to a variant of the original Trolley Case in which the driver himself relinquishes the power to make a decision in a dangerous situation and hands this power to a bystander.

Ordinarily, it is only governments or their agents that are permitted to act like intrusive bystanders. And ordinarily when government takes on the role of a fully intrusive bystander, it is because it has some duty, not a mere permission, to protect people (e.g., to prevent citizens from harming other citizens). This contrasts with the bystander in the Bystander Case, who is thought to have only a permission rather than a duty to redirect the trolley even when the driver has no power to act.[29] As a private person, perhaps the bystander has no right to deliberately take still-retained power away from a driver without the driver's consent, especially if it is power over his own trolley. (Notice that this is consistent with the bystander permissibly interfering in some other way with the driver's controlling the outcome. For example, suppose the bystander quickly pushes a boulder on the track so that it stops the trolley from hitting the five. When the trolley hits the boulder, the trolley is also diverted toward killing another person. This side effect need not make it impermissible for the bystander to push the boulder.) On the other hand, since the driver is a threat to five people, why is he not liable to having his power over his vehicle be deliberately removed when this cannot harm him and will ensure that appropriate diversion of the threat takes place?

### 5.3.2. Company Agents

Are there additional reasons why programmers have a right and also should be willing to do what intrusive bystanders may possibly not have a right to do or perhaps should not be willing to do? Arguably programmers have such a right and should be willing to act on it because they are agents of a company that is in a distinctive position of producing cars that may cause harm. On one view this distinctive position implies that if car producers can make cars that in morally permissible ways cause fewer casualties, other things equal, they have a duty to the community to do so. This contrasts with a second view, that the company has duties only to the purchasers of its cars and to its stockholders.[30] It also contrasts with a third view that the company has none of these duties and is at liberty to make any sort of car it wants. If potential drivers do not like it, they can refuse to buy it, and if the company wants to stay in business, they will have to change their product.[31] In what follows, I will consider only what the first view may imply.

Unlike the bystander in the Intrusive Bystander Case, programmers are employed by producers who are (in part) analogous to those who made the trolley that malfunctioned and endangered people in the original Trolley Case. Indeed, for them the choice may be closer to killing more or killing fewer people rather than letting more die or killing fewer (as it is for the intrusive bystander). Some may say, "Cars don't kill people, people do," and indeed in partial cases it could be the driver's failure that causes a problem. But even in the latter case, a company might have a duty and also reasonably want their product, other things equal, to cause fewer rather than more deaths at the hands of the driver (e.g., by creating cars that will not start until drivers satisfy an in-car device that tests for alcohol level).

In addition, the company programmer is not intruding after the car has been purchased but ex ante. So he need not be changing what the buyer could expect at the time of purchase about what the car would do in certain situations. This is also unlike the bystander in the Intrusive Bystander Case who would first get involved at the time that redirection is needed. (This difference would be present even if we imagined that the intrusive bystander was the producer of the defective trolley who had not acted on the trolley ex ante to reduce deaths.)

If the company is determining what a car that might threaten people through the car's failure alone should be programmed to do, it seems appropriate that they think of themselves as programming requirements on how the car should move.

This would be comparable to (what many consider) an obligation (not mere permission) of the trolley driver to move the trolley so as to minimize those killed (at least when he would not be harmed). This contrasts with merely providing the car with driver-initiated options for minimizing those killed. Programming requirements seem clearly called for in the Complete Case, where company programmers are deciding what a car that on its own will kill some should be programmed to do so as to kill the fewest in a permissible way.

### 5.3.3. Programmers and Drivers

So far we have considered the role of programmers solely in relation to one possible duty of their company regarding its product, namely to reduce numbers of people killed. Now consider whether and how this duty may combine with some duties specific to drivers. If the original Trolley Case is a guide, then in the Partial Case the driver would have a duty, other things equal, to redirect so as to minimize deaths, at least when the driver is not at risk of harm. Then programmers who are agents of the company might be in a stronger position to program a car ex ante so as to bring about a death-minimizing outcome because that outcome corresponds to one that would result from a driver's doing his duty. However, there could be conflicts between the driver's duties and the company's duties. For example, suppose that if the driver diverts from killing five, the one he will kill is his child. Presumably he does not have a duty to divert and may even have a duty not to divert. A company program to reduce deaths would divert the car. Even though the driver would not actually be responsible for killing his child if the program diverted the car, it seems wrong for the company in programming to ignore a driver's moral permission or duty not to divert even when it is the car that malfunctions. Perhaps cars could be programmed to act on such personal information from a driver once a lie detector device in the car had passed it as reliable. (I will discuss later further relations between companies' and drivers' permissions and duties.[32])

### 5.3.4. Programmers as Drivers

Another difference between company programmers and the bystander is that the latter is assumed not to be involved as either a driver or as a potential victim. But ex ante those who program cars can also reasonably suppose that ex post, when the car will do as it is programmed, they might be one of those involved in a situation in which people are threatened (e.g., either as the driver or one of those outside the car threatened by it). So unlike the bystander, in the Partial Case they could be helping themselves to bring about an outcome they would have a duty to bring about as a driver. They also stand to benefit (or be harmed) from programming decisions they made because the lives saved (or taken) may be their own. This could affect the prudential rationality for them of programming in a morally permissible way even if it does not change the morally permissible or obligatory way in which to program.

## 5.4. Pedestrian Liability

A fourth issue to consider is that in the standard Trolley Cases all the people who might die are thought to be equally innocent, nonthreatening individuals whose actions do not make them deserving of or liable in virtue of their actions to being killed by the trolley. (This is on the continuing assumption that the driver cannot be harmed by any action that helps others.) But suppose five people irresponsibly run in front of a car against a red light. (Call this the Irresponsible Five Case.) This does not make them deserve to be killed, but it might make them liable to being killed rather than one innocent person who would be killed if the car were redirected away from them. Desert and liability are commonly distinguished in the following ways: Giving people what they deserve even if it is something bad is thought to be intrinsically good and proportional to what that person has done. Doing something bad to someone because his actions have made him liable to have it done is consistent with the bad being out of proportion to what he has done, with it being regrettable that the bad thing must be done to him to prevent harm to someone else not liable to bear it, and preferable that there be another way to achieve this good end. This Irresponsible Five Case could be one in which a car program should not minimize the number of people killed because not everything else is equal. This is because the degree of liability to being harmed is a morally relevant difference between the five people and the one other person who would be struck in diversion, making everything not be equal among them.[33]

There might even be a case in which several people are hurled at a stationary car (e.g., by a tornado) and would be killed by impact if the car were not redirected. In this case if they impact the car, harm would come only to them and to no one else. However, it may still be best to treat them as we treat innocent threats to others because their trajectory, for which they are not responsible, causes a problem for them that could be avoided only if the driver diverted the car, thus killing a pedestrian. I suggest that if they could divert themselves at some moderate cost to themselves to prevent the pedestrian's dying through diversion, they should do so. Furthermore, it seems that their responsibility to do this is greater than that of the pedestrian to pay the same cost if this would prevent his own death. This is so even though the five and this pedestrian are equally morally innocent of causing the problem situation. People may simply have a duty at some moderate cost to correct the inappropriate location of their body.[34] If they are unable to do so, their having this duty may make it permissible for others to impose at least the same cost on them. It might also be argued that it is permissible for others to allow the five to be killed by impacting the car rather than have a driver redirect to a nonthreatening pedestrian who would be killed. This is so if costs they could permissibly be made to bear exceed those that are grounded in their personal duties to make moderate sacrifices to avoid harm to others.[35]

If these claims are correct, then a company would have a duty in programming to take account of liability to be harmed and moral susceptibility to have harms imposed. This would be in addition to the company having a duty (other things equal) to minimize lives lost. (For simplicity, I will here include both liability to be harmed and moral susceptibility to have harms imposed under an extended notion of liability to be harmed.) Liability might either constrain reducing numbers killed to some degree or possibly have lexical priority over reducing numbers killed. Hence, it would be important for a programmed car to be able to detect not only the number of people whose lives are at stake but also their degree of liability to be killed. There may be heuristics for "detecting" this. For example, a car could detect if a pedestrian was crossing against a light or if a driver was speeding and take these to indicate degree of liability. Possibly probability of liability based on evidence of past differential liability in different circumstances could be used in a program.[36] If cars could not be programmed to detect relative liability, would it be correct to program them at all? Possibly it would be if cases requiring ability to detect liability were rare enough, if drivers were no better than programmed cars at determining relative liability, or if drivers were no more likely than a programmed car to behave on a correct determination of liability.

## 5.5. Driver Liability

### 5.5.1. Principles

As noted earlier, in the standard trolley cases neither the driver nor any passengers on the trolley are at risk of being killed. So far in discussing moral issues in partial and complete cases I have been assuming this is so as well. Let us now drop the assumption that the driver cannot be killed instead of some pedestrians and consider his liability to be harmed. As explained in Section 3.1, I consider these cases to be innocent threat rather than trolley problem cases.

In the course of her 2008 discussion of the Trolley Problem, Thomson claimed that if a nonculpable driver of a car will kill nonthreatening, innocent pedestrians unless he redirects, he has a duty to do so even if he is the one who will then be killed.[37] If he has this duty, it is not because he deserves to die or is even at fault. Nor is it simply because sacrificing himself will decrease the number of people killed (if it would), for individuals may have a morally sanctioned personal prerogative not to sacrifice themselves for that goal even if social institutions had to pursue it. Thomson does not explicitly say, but she may think the driver's duty (which supersedes his prerogative) arises from his being responsible for setting in motion a car that is about to kill innocent people.

But note that if the driver has this duty to divert at the cost of his own life because he started the car, then he could have this duty even when only one other person (not a greater number) would be killed by him. Indeed, suppose it were possible for two drivers to be responsible for driving the car (or for a passenger giving directions to a driver being jointly responsible with the driver for the car's movements). Then the two of them could have a duty to redirect even if this kills them rather than one innocent pedestrian who would otherwise be hit by their car. So an argument for a driver having a duty to impose the death on himself need not be based on and could conflict with reducing the total number of people killed.

Some may find Thomson's conclusion in her car driver case hard to accept because the driver himself has to do what will kill him. A driver who did not do this would most probably be morally and legally excused. However, excuse is not the same as justification, so he may still have failed to do what was right.[38] Furthermore, it would not be as hard for a bystander or a programmer to do what imposes the loss on the driver by either redirecting the car or programming it to redirect, and if either of those people would redirect him, the grounds for the driver's excuse (namely, its being hard for him to do what will kill him) would be eliminated. In addition, the driver might be liable to have this done to him because he started the car even if he has no duty to divert himself and so is even justified in not diverting himself.

Others may reject these conclusions because they think that innocent pedestrians share the liability to be harmed since they are as causally responsible for an accident as the driver simply by being where the car is going; if they were not there, there would have been no accident. I do not accept this view for it seems that a crucial difference between a driver and an innocent pedestrian is that pedestrians are not entities that can damage or harm others on impact in the way cars can harm pedestrians.[39] I acknowledge that this is a complicated issue and moral conclusions could change depending on how this issue is decided.

Some also think that the driver's liability could depend on her reasons for driving. For example, driving an ambulance to fulfill a duty to save other lives might so strongly justify imposing ordinary risk on others that it reduces a driver's asymmetrical liability to suffer any harm relative to pedestrians.[40] But soldiers may have a duty to fight and yet it is commonly thought they rather than noncombatants (even of the enemy country), who could be considered analogous to innocent pedestrians, should absorb harms in war. It is not my aim in this chapter to settle who among nonrisky, nonnegligent individuals is liable and on what ground. I am primarily concerned to emphasize that wherever it is determined by argument that liability for bearing harm should lie when someone must be harmed, companies that produce Partial cars could have a duty to take that liability into account in designing programs. This could conflict with other prima facie duties they may have to minimize those killed and to protect the driver.

This raises the practical issue that people may seek to buy cars that are programmed to always favor survival of the driver. (This is so even though when they think of themselves as possible pedestrians on other occasions, they might not favor such a program. In a televised discussion with a philosopher about self-driving cars, a Public Broadcasting Service interviewer, thinking of herself as a driver, said that if there is an accident, she wants to be the one to survive. The philosopher interviewed did not respond that this may sometimes not be the morally correct outcome.) Responding to consumer demand, companies might seek to both minimize lives lost and take into account liability to bear harm so long as this applied to everyone besides drivers. Companies would then decline to program so as to achieve the morally correct outcome, in the light of drivers' duties or liability to bear harm, to any greater degree than drivers would ordinarily do on their own.

If one wanted companies to do more than this, one could try to get them to show that all people would come out better if all drivers were held to programs with higher standards (as in solutions to Prisoners' Dilemmas). Alternatively, one might insist on government regulation to ensure moral solutions that take into account drivers' liability to being harmed and to ensure uniformity in the programs installed. No producer should get a business advantage by providing an "immoral" car that does not incorporate at least "minimal morality" regarding numbers of lives saved constrained by appropriate liability considerations simply because providing an immoral car will increase their sales.[41] On the other hand, producers and governments should not require the production of what would also be immoral cars, imposing burdens on drivers to which they are not liable and to which they do not consent, for the sake of always maximizing lives saved despite the liability of pedestrians. However, producers should not necessarily be prohibited from programming altruistic (supererogatory) cars at the request of drivers. These cars would allow drivers to bear burdens beyond both those they owe (which a "strictly dutiful car" could ensure) or that may permissibly be imposed on them without their consent.

Finally, note that it is easier for a driver to buy a car that she knows is programmed to do what will sacrifice her than to actually sacrifice herself; buying such a car is not a way to sacrifice oneself. This is in part because it is uncertain whether one will ever be in a situation where one would be sacrificed by one's programmed car. Combined with an ex ante desire to do what might be one's duty in a tragic case and foreseeing one's lack of courage to do it at high cost, some drivers may actually want to buy a car that is programmed to produce outcomes that track either their duty or liability to bear harms (where these differ). (This is in addition to such drivers considering the possibility that they will at times be pedestrians.)

### 5.5.2. Illustrative Cases

To reinforce these conclusions, consider some cases.

#### *5.5.2.1. Case 1*

Suppose (for the sake of argument) an in-control driver would have a duty to sacrifice himself by diverting rather than kill innocent, nonthreatening pedestrians. Does this imply that company programmers have permission or even an obligation to program a threatening car in the Partial Case to divert from killing more nonthreatening pedestrians to killing fewer driver(s) of the threatening car? It would not be surprising if the driver couldn't be trusted when he is in control of the car to do his (assumed) duty to minimize lives lost when doing so would cost him his life. So without forcing anyone to sacrifice himself, a programmer would arrange for the car to generate an outcome that corresponds to that from the performance of a duty that (arguably) both the producer and the driver have in this case to minimize lives lost even at the driver's expense.

Suppose the driver had no duty to sacrifice himself. He still might be liable to have costs imposed on him by others. Suppose he was no more liable in virtue of driving to bear costs (or high costs) than anyone else. In arranging for the car to divert when this minimizes deaths but kills the driver, the programmers would still treat him no worse than they (or the driver) would treat an innocent pedestrian in diverting to her to minimize innocent pedestrians killed, though that innocent has no duty to sacrifice herself and is not liable to bear harm in virtue of her actions.

#### *5.5.2.2. Case 2*

Suppose a driver would have a duty to divert at the cost of his own life to save pedestrians. Does this imply that the company should program to divert a car from killing fewer (or the same number of) nonthreatening pedestrians in a way that results in the death of more (or the same number of) driver(s) of the threatening car? If programmers did this, they would not act on any producer's duty to minimize lives lost due to its machine. Their disfavoring the driver(s) would have to involve arranging for an outcome because it either corresponds to one that would result if a driver performed his duty to sacrifice himself or involves imposing harm to which the driver is liable even in the absence of his duty. Acting on this consideration would override the producer's other prima facie duty to minimize lives lost since more lives might then be lost. Suppose a company has a duty to take account of liability to bear costs in programming cars. Then if the driver is liable, the company has its own duty to take account of his liability even if this does not minimize lives lost.

*5.5.2.3. Case 3*

Should the company program to prevent the diversion of a threatening car from killing both one innocent, nonthreatening pedestrian and the driver of the car toward killing two innocent, nonthreatening pedestrians? In this case the driver would lose his life in not being diverted rather than in being diverted; his life would be saved by diverting toward more pedestrians. The same number of people would be killed either way.

This case raises the following question: When costs to a driver would be high, could there be a moral difference between (1) a program preventing a driver from increasing the number of pedestrians killed and (2) a program reducing the number of pedestrians a driver kills? Suppose there is such a moral difference, in favor of (1). Then it may be permissible for a program to at least prevent the driver's life being saved by diverting when more pedestrians will be killed (though the same number of people would be killed). This could be so even if the program should not lethally divert the driver in order to prevent his killing these pedestrians. Hence, if he were headed to killing two people but would survive this, such a program would not divert him toward one other pedestrian when he would die. However, the program would prevent his diverting from killing one pedestrian to killing two when he will not survive without the diversion. (If the driver's life had the same moral weight as a pedestrian's, preventing his diversion in the latter case would yield the same outcome as letting one set of two people be killed rather than divert toward killing another set of two people.)

However, suppose the driver would kill two pedestrians and himself if the car is not diverted, and he would be saved but kill two other people if the car is diverted. In this case, if the car is diverted, an additional life (of the driver) would be saved and there would be no increase in the number of pedestrians killed. Even if there is something to be said against killing two other people rather than letting those originally threatened be killed, saving the life of a driver who does not deserve to die seems important enough to justify diversion. (If the driver himself were in control, he could permissibly save his life in this way since he wouldn't be increasing the number of pedestrians killed.)

*5,5.2.4. Case 4*

Should the company program to divert a car from killing more innocent, nonthreatening pedestrians in a way that kills the single driver of the car rather than in an alternative way that kills one different nonthreatening pedestrian? In this case, the car producer's duty to minimize numbers killed would be satisfied either way. Nevertheless, if the driver is liable to bear harm, the producer should arrange for the car to divert in a way that kills the driver rather than in a way that kills a different pedestrian.

The overriding conclusion of the discussion of Cases 1–4 is that even if producers should not bring about outcomes simply because they correspond to the performance of drivers' duties, bringing about the same outcome or even one more burdensome for the driver can sometimes be necessary in order for producers to carry out their own duty to take account of a driver's liability to bear harm.

## 6. Passengers and Other Drivers

In the two standard trolley cases (with a driver or a bystander called on to redirect), the five potential victims and the one to whom the trolley could be redirected are not imagined to be either on the threatening trolley or on another trolley. But programmers for cars recognize that a car can face a collision with other cars and that people initially and potentially threatened might also be in the cars. MIT's Moral Machine website and Rampolla present cases in which if redirection occurs, nondrivers who would be harmed are passengers in the threatening vehicle. I do not think they deal with cases in which those initially threatened are also in vehicles or those potentially threatened are in vehicles other than the initially threatening vehicle. Let us consider a variety of such cases.

### 6.1. Other Drivers

Suppose for the sake of argument that a driver is liable to be sacrificed relative to nonthreatening pedestrians she would otherwise hit simply because she is driving a threatening car. Are drivers in nonthreatening cars also liable to have harm from a threatening car redirected to them rather than to nonthreatening pedestrians? For example, suppose the driver in the car threatening pedestrians cannot prevent harm to them by herself bearing the cost. She or the program running her car can redirect either toward another car with a driver or to another pedestrian. Choosing the car with the driver might be justified by analogizing the case to players in a dangerous game (in this case, car driving) who should when possible confine themselves to injuring one another rather than nonthreatening nonplayers if someone must be injured. If so, cars should be programmed to detect and at least sometimes redirect to other cars rather than to pedestrians even when those cars have drivers and diverting in this way will not minimize deaths. "Playing the game of driving" would then be another source of liability to harm.

When a threatening driver could bear costs to prevent harm to others, additional issues related to liability to bear costs will arise: Should the number of all drivers' lives at stake in a decision, possible fault, or merely who is the initial threatening driver determine programming? Could the programmed car detect and "act" on those factors at least as well as unassisted drivers?

Perhaps in some cases involving multiple vehicles it may be possible to distinguish between something like an offensive and a defensive threat. An "offensive" innocent threat would be presented by the Partial or Complete car that initially nonintentionally and nonnegligently threatens either pedestrians or other drivers. A defensive threat might be presented by a vehicle that has to respond to that initial threat; doing so may result in its threatening either the initial threat, other vehicles, or nonthreatening pedestrians. Even if an offensive threat should be programmed so that its driver is sacrificed rather than another driver to whom he presents a threat, the driver who becomes a defensive threat may be liable to be harmed rather than pedestrians his vehicle might harm. (This is because of his participation in the dangerous practice of driving.)

## 6.2. Passengers

Aside from the drivers of threatening vehicles and even in Complete Cases where drivers are absent, there may be passengers in vehicles.[42] Suppose nondrivers in the threatening vehicle would be killed if the car were redirected from harming nonthreatening pedestrians. Should vehicles that can detect the presence of people inside the car be programmed to count their lives on a par with pedestrians threatened by the vehicle and do what reduces the number of people killed?

People often voluntarily decide to be passengers in a vehicle that they know could potentially threaten pedestrians. Furthermore, the vehicle might not have started at all in the absence of passengers, and passengers may tell vehicles where they want to go if not how to get there. For example, one of the benefits of completely self-driving cars is that they would increase the mobility of blind and paralyzed people. But if such passengers gave a command for the car to start, are they not at least in some ways like the driver who started the trolley that then went beyond his control (even if the passengers never drove the car to begin with)? Suppose such a driver should be given less weight than pedestrians because he is liable to bear costs. Then shouldn't passengers whose directions start a car also be given less weight than pedestrians by a program for Complete cars? However, they differ from the trolley driver in that he did not deliberately set the trolley out of his control; it was a failure of the machine that made it go out of his control. By contrast, those who command the Complete car to start deliberately set the car out of their control. This would seem to make them even more liable to bear costs if something goes wrong. This seems true even though they have a reasonable expectation that the car being out of their control is consistent with its functioning safely, whereas the driver's expectation for a trolley being out of his control is that it will not function safely.

What about voluntary passengers who did not start the car but chose to join those who did start the car? Their joining a dangerous game could provide a ground for some liability to bear costs.[43] Perhaps when a car with seven passengers threatens two pedestrians, each of the seven should count for only a fraction of a person in a calculation of lives lost. However, joining oneself to a car before it actually threatens others is still different from, for example, hopping a ride on what one knows is a vehicle headed to killing pedestrians that should be diverted. In the latter case, the passengers' lives should certainly have reduced weight relative to the lives of pedestrians when deciding whether to divert the vehicle. This is because they knowingly attach themselves to a threat that should have been diverted. If possible, a car should be programmed to detect such morally relevant differences among passengers.

## 6.3. Mere Cars

Do the following conclusions at least seem certain? When a car with a driver and/or passengers threatens a completely empty car, one should allow the empty car to be destroyed rather than kill pedestrians or other drivers and passengers. Also, empty Complete cars should be programmed to "sacrifice themselves" rather than pedestrians or drivers and passengers in other cars even when the latter are causally or (sometimes) even morally responsible for the initial problem. These conclusions seem to follow from the view that lives of persons take precedence over property, at least when there is no intentional wrongdoing by those persons that aims at destruction of the property.

However, what if the empty Complete car is the only one that can be sent to save many other people? I think it (like the ambulance) cannot be allowed to run over even fewer nonthreatening pedestrians in order to avoid its own destruction and continue on its mission. But are those who are morally responsible for being in harm's way for no sufficient reason (like those in the Irresponsible Five Case) liable to being harmed by the car rather than having it destroyed when the car is necessary to save many other lives? In the Irresponsible Five Case the five are liable to being harmed rather than have the car redirected to kill other innocent, nonthreatening pedestrians. This is still morally different from liability to being harmed (which in our cases involves being killed) so that the car can go on to save others, I think.[44]

## Notes

1. F. M. Kamm, *Morality, Mortality*, vol. 2 (New York: Oxford University Press, 1996). I there discussed the Ambulance Case in a chapter concerned with whether ex ante agreements could alter our ordinary moral obligations.
2. Discussion in Chapters 2 and 5 in this volume about the use of, and limits on, ex ante agreements are also relevant to whether and how to program the ambulance.
3. I am assuming that the partial cases involve taking control away from a driver who is not allowed to drive only in certain dangerous situations. Other types of partial cases may involve self-driving cars that turn over control to the driver only in certain dangerous situations. In addition, it is said that self-learning cars need not be programmed. For simplicity's sake, I will speak of cars that decide what to do as acting on a program.
4. Though the case was created by Philippa Foot in "The Problem of Abortion and the Doctrine of Double Effect," in *Virtues and Vices* (Los Angeles: UCLA Press, 1978), 19–33, it was only later called the Trolley Problem by Judith Thomson in her "Killing, Letting Die, and the Trolley Problem," *The Monist* 59, no. 2 (1976): 204–17.
5. See Judith Thomson, "The Trolley Problem," *Yale Law Journal* 94 (1985): 1395–415. In a switch from her 1976 article, Thomson came to apply the term "Trolley Problem" to this case alone, though others did not.
6. In another case, which I call Crosspoint, a bystander must decide whether to turn a trolley that will kill many if it remains at a crossing point toward killing five others on one track or killing one other on a second track. Here the bystander is choosing between letting many die or killing either five or one. This case was discussed in Chapter 9.
7. Such a case involving pushing was also introduced by Thomson and is referred to as the Fat Man Case (or Bridge Case). See her "Killing, Letting Die, and the Trolley Problem."
8. Chris Rampolla, "The Trolley Problem Reimagined: Self-Driving Cars," *Aero*, March 31, 2017. I was directed to this site by a nonphilosopher professor who works on the Trolley Problem and who saw it as popular discussion that provided a good introduction to the problem for the general public.
9. Rampolla actually speaks of the car, not the driver, "striking" the pedestrian and the driver possibly causing a collision that "saves" the pedestrian but will likely "kill" him. Reserving the term "kill" only for the latter effect seems a biased description as does speaking of saving a pedestrian when what is at issue for the driver is not killing him. See Chapter 14 for more on saving versus not killing.
10. The problem of applying results achieved by assuming certainty when real life presents us only with risks is a topic discussed by others. See note 24.
11. Neither a nonphilosopher professor nor a postdoctoral psychologist, each working on the Trolley Problem and both of whom were present when I discussed Rampolla on April 23, 2018, had ever heard of innocent threat cases. Perhaps they would still have realized that different moral problems might be raised by them from those raised by the standard trolley cases. However, as noted in Chapter 6 in this volume, philosopher and psychologist Joshua Greene gave as a real-life example of the Trolley

Problem (when speaking at a Safra Ethics Center conference dinner at Harvard in 2017) a case in which doctors must decide whether to confine a person carrying a contagious disease, thus imposing costs on him, in order to save others from the disease. He reported that doctors were concerned about imposing costs on one person to save others, and he seemed to agree that this was like the concern about turning the trolley on one person to save others. But in the medical case costs would be imposed on the person who presents the threat and doctors should not, I think, be as concerned about imposing a cost on an innocent threat as on an innocent, nonthreatening person as is contemplated in standard trolley problem cases.

12. See Robert Nozick, *Anarchy, State, and Utopia* (New York: Basic Books, 1974). The man who is hurled may benefit from falling on the person he threatens if he would otherwise hit a stone floor and die. Susanne Burri notes this in her "The Toss-Up between a Profiting Innocent Threat and his Victim," *Journal of Political Philosophy* 23, no. 2 (2015): 146–65. By contrast someone who would drive into another person does not benefit from doing that by contrast to driving in the same lane but not hitting someone. Burri notes that in my *Creation and Abortion* (New York: Oxford University Press, 1992) I distinguish between innocent threats who do and do not benefit from being where they threaten another. The former threatening person may lose only the benefit from being an unjustifiable threat when we stop her being a threat.
13. See Saba Bazargan, "Killing Minimally Responsible Threats," *Ethics* 125, no. 1 (2014): 114–36.
14. Though in some cases killing the driver might stop the threat, as when killing him causes his body to fall on a brake that is otherwise inaccessible to him.
15. Prof. Bert Huang refers to a psychological study on trolley problems in which researchers expose subjects to "the actual argument—that no one is obliged to sacrifice his own life to save others, and that it seems immoral to force another to make a sacrifice one would not have to make oneself." B. Huang, "Law and Moral Dilemmas," *Harvard Law Review* 130 (2016): 673. This description suggests that the person who would die from the trolley's impact if it is redirected toward him in the standard cases is made to sacrifice his life. But this ignores the possibility that there is a conceptual (and moral) difference between imposing loss of one's life on oneself (either voluntarily or coerced) and having that loss imposed on one by another.
16. This is also true in many cases presented by the MIT Moral Machine website, http://moralmachine.mit.edu.
17. For objections to Foot's proposal, see Chapter 9 in this volume and my *The Trolley Problem Mysteries* (New York: Oxford University Press, 2016).
18. Marya Zilberberg, "Medicine as the Trolley Problem," *Healthcare, etc.*, July 25, 2012, http://evimedgroup.blogspot.com/2012/07/medicine-as-trolley-problem.html.
19. Bioethicist Nir Eyal once suggested this (much before mounting evidence about the dangers of e-cigarettes). The example used merely as a hypothetical case remains useful for my purposes.
20. The Ambulance Case with which I began this chapter also contrasts with diverting the trolley. Though it involves choosing between saving five (by getting them to the hospital) and killing one, it is not like the Trolley or Bystander Case (which also involves

choosing between saving five and killing one). It may seem that one way of marking the distinction is that unlike the trolley, the ambulance (like the gas or bomb) that would kill the one is a new threat that is not already threatening the five. But the case (presented in the text) in which the diverted trolley causes a new rockslide that kills one person shows why it is not quite right to say that the problem in the Ambulance Case is that a new threat kills the one. It would be better to say the following: It is not to remove a threat that the ambulance itself presents to the five that we would consider having the ambulance continue on killing one other person, and this may make it impermissible to drive the ambulance over the person on the road. However, as we have seen in Chapters 7 and 9, I consider (what I call) the Lazy Susan Case to be morally like the Trolley Case, though it does not involve redirecting a threat from the five. Rather, it involves redirecting people away from a threatening trolley that cannot be redirected. In one version, their being moved will create a new rockslide that kills a bystander. I argued that doing what saves the five but kills the one is as permissible in this case as in the Trolley and Bystander Cases, even though the one person is killed neither by what threatens the five nor by a new threat created by the threat itself moving away from the five. I argued that the Lazy Susan Case is like the Trolley Case because the same principle explains the permissibility of both turning the trolley and turning the Lazy Susan. In my view, this principle (put roughly and far too simply here) is that what kills one other person just is the five being saved. The trolley turning away that kills the one does not merely cause the five to be saved (as the bomb in the Bomb Case would); it constitutes the five being saved. Similarly, the five being moved away from the trolley on the Lazy Susan, which leads to one other person dying, just is the five being saved. For further discussion of this, in addition to Chapter 9, see my *Intricate Ethics* (New York: Oxford University Press, 2007) and *The Trolley Problem Mysteries*. I omit further discussion of Lazy Susan–type cases here since they do not seem pertinent to real-life cases of self-driving cars.

21. I do not in this chapter defend the correctness of these judgments and the principles that justify them (though I said something about this in note 20 and gave more detail in Chapter 9). Thomson herself came to reject her earlier judgment that it is permissible for the bystander to redirect the trolley, thus killing one and saving five. See Judith Thomson, "Turning the Trolley," *Philosophy & Public Affairs* 36 (2008): 359–74, and my discussion of her later view in *The Trolley Problem Mysteries* and more briefly in Chapter 8 in this volume.
22. Principles and rules are commonly distinguished. For example, H. L. A. Hart conceived of the legal system as consisting of rules. By contrast, Ronald Dworkin thought that system fundamentally consisted of principles (such as "not benefiting from one's crime" or "fair play") that required more interpretation than rules and that could ground rules. The principles might also guide us when rules run out or when rules lead to conclusions in particular cases that are inconsistent with grounding principles. In *Morality, Mortality*, vol. 2, I suggested that a computer might be programmed to use the Principle of Permissible Harm (PPH) that I there proposed in order to deal with trolley problems. It might also be programmed to use the Doctrine of Productive Purity (DPP) that is based on the PPH and is described in Chapter 9 in this volume and in an earlier form in *Intricate Ethics*.

23. Fiona Woollard and Will McNeill discuss these issues in their "Driverless Cars" and "Ethics without Algorithms," both unpublished manuscripts.
24. I continue to put to one side the important issues of certainty versus risk of deaths and knowledge of this. In the standard hypothetical trolley cases one assumes certain death for the five if the trolley continues or for someone else if the five are saved. One also assumes knowledge of this by the decision maker. This is not necessarily true in real life. On this problem of applying Trolley Problem reasoning to programming cars see Sven Nyholm and Jilles Smids, "The Ethics of Accident-Algorithms for Self Driving Cars: An Applied Trolley Problem?," *Ethical Theory and Practice* 19, no. 5 (November 2016): 1275–89.
25. Note also that in trolley cases it is because the trolley is no longer under the driver's control in heading to the five (though it is also not self-driving) that a problem initially arises. By contrast, it is because human drivers in cars completely under their control often fail to do the right act that initial life-threatening situations often arise. It is somewhat ironic that (1) cases in which a problem arises in the first instance because a vehicle lacks a driver in control are being looked to (by some) for guidance about what to do (2) when a car's lacking a driver in control is supposed to prevent problems from arising in the first instance.
26. See, for example, Thomas Nagel, *The View from Nowhere* (New York: Oxford University Press, 1986).
27. I argued for such a view in *Morality, Mortality,* vol. 2, among other places.
28. As noted earlier, I considered what people may and may not commit to via ex ante agreements and discussed the Ambulance Case in *Morality, Mortality.* See also Chapters 2 and 5 in this volume about ex ante agreements. I am grateful to Jesse Berthold and Arthur Applbaum for raising questions that led to some of my responses in this section.
29. This may be because the bystander will wrong the one person he kills even if he acts permissibly in doing so and he would not wrong the five by not saving them.
30. Suggested by Larry Temkin.
31. Suggested by Shelly Kagan.
32. We could also consider the role of programmers' duties in relation to possible victims' duties. For example, suppose the five toward whom the car is headed were the parents and guardians of the one person toward whom the car would be diverted. They might have a duty or preference to see to it that the car is not diverted. However, drivers are no more likely to know of such relations between potential victims than programmed cars would, whereas they are likely to know about their own duties and preferences.
33. On the distinction between desert and liability, see Jeff McMahan, *Killing in War* (Oxford: Oxford University Press, 2009). In the Irresponsible Five Case, McMahan would say that the five are liable to the harm because they have "assumed the risk." A crucial issue is whether being liable should be a tiebreaker when all else is equal between potential bearers of a loss or whether it should come with built-in limits on the loss to which one can be liable depending on what makes one more liable than someone else. On the latter view one might be liable to a higher chance of bearing a loss (e.g., 80%) or liable to bearing a loss only up to size x. If someone physically

must bear a certain-to-occur loss or a loss over x, then on this second (built-in limits) view who morally should bear the loss may be determined by giving equal chances. On the first view, being liable wouldn't have such built-in limits and could serve as a tiebreaker that determines on whom the certain-to-occur loss or loss larger than x should be placed. (The number of people who would suffer the loss might also count in determining where the loss should fall.)

34. I discussed some of these issues in my "The Insanity Defense, Innocent Threats, and Limited Alternatives," *Criminal Justice Ethics* 6, no. 1 (1987): 61–76.
35. The permissibility of turning the trolley on one innocent person itself relies on the view that what harm may be imposed on someone exceeds what it is his duty to impose on himself (since he would not have a duty to turn the trolley on himself). But if liability depends on a person's having acted or moved in a certain way, this ground could not account for the permissibility of imposing harm on the one person in the Trolley Case since he hasn't done anything to make himself liable to harm. Furthermore, more people who are liable to have harm imposed on them might sometimes permissibly be harmed to save fewer nonliable people. By contrast, the permissibility of turning the trolley and harming the one nonliable person depends on fewer people overall being harmed.
36. I owe these suggestions for the heuristics to Jeff McMahan, Shelly Kagan, and Larry Temkin.
37. Thomson discusses this case in her "Turning the Trolley," 369.
38. Note that his duty is not necessarily to actively redirect when that would have killed him. There might be a case in which unless he diverts he will continue on in a way that results in his being killed, but if he diverts to save himself he will kill others. Then he might have a duty to refrain from diverting. (I discuss such a case later in the text.)
39. Lauren Lyons emphasized this point. However, there is the difficulty of distinguishing morally between a moving pedestrian who is walking and an innocent hurled at a car. Why would the latter person be liable to bear costs, as I argued earlier, and not the pedestrian if neither directly threatens harm or damage to others?
40. Jeff McMahan holds such a view.
41. Analogously, suppose a college complained that it couldn't attract students if it did not allow some cheating because other schools allowed some cheating and students preferred those schools. The solution is not to give up the correct moral standard but for all schools to agree to enforce the standard. Suppose students would then prefer no education (comparable to people not buying any cars that tracked moral requirements). Suppose this education outcome was bad (as might not be true if as a consequence of not buying cars, people used only public transportation). Then it might be necessary to either require people to get educated (as we already do to some degree) or make education more attractive in some way other than by allowing some cheating.
42. Unlike the Moral Machine website, I shall consider only person passengers, not non-person animal passengers. That website also considers animal pedestrians.
43. It might be said that passengers (and drivers) stand to benefit from using cars and this is what grounds their liability to be harmed rather than pedestrians. In the case

of both passengers and drivers, I do not wish to derive liability to harm from standing to benefit. Even if drivers and passengers did not stand to benefit from using cars, the risk of harm to others from the devices they use is an important reason they might be liable to bear costs when someone must.

44. I am grateful to Matthew Liao for inviting me to write the article on which this chapter is based. That article appears in Matthew Liao, ed., *Ethics and Artificial Intelligence* (New York: Oxford University Press, 2020). I am grateful to him, Shelly Kagan, Jeff McMahan, Larry Temkin, students in my Rutgers philosophy seminars, and audiences at the Edmond J. Safra Ethics Center of Harvard University and at the University of Granada Philosophy Department for comments on earlier versions of this chapter.

# 11
# The Trolley Problem and Economic Policy

Could the moral permissibility that we have discussed in earlier chapters of a bystander turning a runaway trolley from killing five people toward killing one other person instead (when all other things are equal between the people) undermine one moral argument for political libertarianism?[1] This moral argument for political libertarianism is that morally one may not harm some people in order to help others and government action should mirror morality. Libertarianism emphasizes personal freedom, as well as negative rights not to be interfered with and not to be harmed by others (at least in certain ways that do not include competition). Such rights give people directed duties not to interfere with and not to harm others. This view de-emphasizes positive rights to be helped and duties to help others without specific agreements to do so. The type of government it favors is referred to as "the night watchman state," which should only enforce negative rights and their correlative duties. In this chapter, I consider the relevance of the moral permissibility of turning the trolley for political libertarianism and government action by examining Guido Pincione's interesting discussion of this issue[2] on its own and in the light of recent work on the Trolley Problem.

## I. A Proposal for Turning the Trolley

Pincione accepts the moral permissibility of a bystander—not merely the driver of the trolley—turning a trolley from killing five people to killing one other person but rejects the view that it is permissible for someone to take organs from a person, thereby killing him, in order use them to save five other people. Though he contrasts these cases, he would (I assume) also reject the permissibility of a bystander toppling a fat man from a bridge so that his body will stop the trolley from hitting the five but kill him. Hence, turning the trolley would not involve aggression understood as impermissible use of force against another (though it involves force), but the latter two cases would. Explaining why it is permissible to turn in the Bystander Case but not to topple the fat man in the (so-called) Fat Man Case is what Judith Thomson called the Trolley Problem in one of her articles.[3] However these are not the cases to which she first applied the term "trolley problem," contrary to what Pincione says.[4] She first introduced the term in referring to the contrast between the trolley driver permissibly turning his trolley

*Rights and Their Limits: In Theory, Cases, and Pandemics.* F. M. Kamm, Oxford University Press.
© Oxford University Press 2022. DOI: 10.1093/oso/9780197567739.003.0011

from five to one and a doctor impermissibly killing one person to acquire organs with which to save five other patients.[5] These were the cases that Philippa Foot had originally discussed involving the driver rather than a bystander turning the trolley.[6] Let us call the contrast Foot drew TP(1) and the one Pincione discusses TP(2). For Pincione's purposes, it is important to deal with the Bystander Case because he analogizes the government to a bystander,[7] preventing harm to some that is not of its own making by harming others. Pincione does not claim to solve TP(2), but he thinks the solution will roughly have the following two-part form: It will be morally permissible for the bystander to turn the trolley when (a) it is ex ante in the interest of each person potentially threatened that the trolley be turned because this maximizes the chance of each to survive, and (b) the lesser harm (of fewer killed) is caused either by the greater good (of more saved) or means that have the greater good as their "noncausal flipside," in the sense that the five saved *just is* (or is in the circumstances constituted by) the trolley moving away from them. Pincione derives the (a) clause from one of Judith Thomson's discussions of the Trolley Problem.[8] On her understanding, the (a) clause is interpreted so that the ex ante time point is one in which it is to the advantage of each person who will eventually be on the tracks that the trolley is turned from killing five people to killing one. This can occur when at that ex ante time point no one knows (and has no indication) who will be one of the five people or be the one person on the other track. Using this ex ante perspective is one way to argue for the view that sometimes in a conflict situation when everyone cannot survive, there is a reason to do what saves the greater number of people. This conclusion might directly imply that when we must choose whether to *save* one person or save five people, we should save the five. But TP(2) involves a choice between *killing* one and saving five and this raises an additional problem. Clause (b) is meant to help justify a killing. Clause (b) concerns causal structure and makes use of my Principle of Permissible Harm (PPH) (a predecessor to the Principle of Productive Purity discussed in Chapter 9).[9] It assumes that the five surviving would be a greater good relative to the one person on the other track surviving, and the death of this one would be a lesser harm relative to the deaths of the five. But it makes the permissibility of bringing about the greater good and lesser harm depend on how they are brought about given that we will be killing and not merely not saving the one person.

Pincione thinks that when conditions (a) and (b) are satisfied, someone's negative moral right not to be harmed does not stand in the way of helping save a greater number of people. Hence, using the notion of aggression as impermissible use of force, there would be no aggression if the one person were harmed in this way. Since the bystander is typically thought to have a moral permission (but not a duty) to turn the trolley if the government's permission "mirrored" this moral landscape, government would also sometimes have a permission to harm some citizens even by force in order to help other citizens.[10] This seems contrary to a libertarian view of government. On the other hand, the bystander's permission would not show that the government sometimes has a duty to help its citizens by harming others.[11]

## II. Analogizing Government Action to Action in Trolley Cases

Even assuming the adequacy of (a) and (b) to explain the moral permissibility of a bystander turning the trolley, I have several concerns about Pincione's applying this to cases involving government action.

(i) First, he starts with trolley cases that involve killing someone rather than letting others die, but the novel use he wishes to make of these cases concerns governments taxing some to provide financial help for others. It is not clear that conditions like (a) and (b) (modified to apply to nontrolley cases) are required to make helpful action even by ordinary bystanders morally permissible in cases where they do not kill, seriously harm, or use other force on someone to help others. For example, suppose five people would die near a rich man if we did not remove five dollars from his wallet lying next to him though he does not wish to donate the money. (Call this the Rich Man Case.) I think it would be morally permissible to take the money in this case even though it could not be repaid. Whether permissible or not, this would not involve the use of force, so it is not the possibility of aggression occurring that is at issue.

Presumably, taking the money is permissible because the rich man has a moral duty to help that he is not fulfilling, and given the irreversible great harm facing each of those in need, a bystander may impose the cost on him. In this case, condition (b) is not satisfied since the lesser harm to someone (of having his money taken) is a mere causal means to the greater good of five living; the harm to him is not caused by the greater good of five living or by means that have the greater good as a noncausal flipside. Furthermore, in this Rich Man Case condition (a) also might not need to be satisfied because it would be permissible to take the money even if we knew it was not ex ante in the interest of each person to have a policy of harming some to help others. This would be so if we knew who would be rich and that this person was invulnerable to needing help. If government taxation policy to save lives should mirror ordinary interpersonal morality, it might be that the analogy to rely on is the Rich Man Case, not TP(2). Then neither condition (a) nor (b) would play a role in justifying such governmental actions.[12]

Of course, there may be other differences between the Rich Man Case and government taxation policy cases that Pincione discusses, and those differences interfere with the latter mirroring the former. For example, helping people's economic condition can be different from saving their lives, and in at least some cases taxation may be causally useful only to do the former. If it would ordinarily be morally wrong for a bystander to take even five dollars from the rich man's wallet against his wishes to improve five people's economic condition, ordinary morality might not provide a basis for the government doing so. It might then be necessary to rely on conditions like (a) and (b) to justify causing the lesser harm. In addition, even if some people's lives were at stake, much more than five dollars may be causally required to help them and it could be impermissible for a bystander to take that amount. Then the Rich Man Case would also not serve as an analogy for government action in many cases. Suppose that the rich man would have no duty to help due to the size of the cost to him and/or the lesser importance of the good to be achieved (even if its importance were still greater than the cost). Call this the Economic Rich Man Case. Then it might be that imposition of the cost by others should only be done in a way that satisfies conditions like (a) and (b). Such cases in ordinary morality do not involve killing some to save others but still might require the use of conditions like (a) and (b) to justify action as much as permissibly killing in TP(2) does. They might be the appropriate moral analogy for government actions that cannot be analogized to the Rich Man Case.

It is noteworthy that standard trolley problem cases involve the potential of equal harms to each of the people who could be affected. That is, each of the five stands to die as does the one person to whom the trolley would be redirected. It is also assumed that they are in other respects equal, so no one would be worse off in dying than anyone else. To be strictly analogous the economic cases should involve removing an economic threat to each of many that is equal to the threat imposed on others. Such cases involve a "greater threat" to the many only because there are more individuals threatened, not because in a pairwise comparison each of those initially threatened would be harmed to a greater degree than each of those to whom a threat would be redirected. However, we could still imagine nonstandard trolley cases in which the harm imposed in redirecting a threat is less than what each of many would suffer if the trolley were not redirected. For example, suppose redirecting the trolley from killing the five would paralyze both legs of one other person. It is still true that doing so could be permissible while toppling the fat man when this would only paralyze both his legs would be impermissible. Hence, satisfying conditions (a) and (b) could be necessary even if harm to each potential victim is not equal in the economic context too though the harm caused by redirecting is still significant.[13]

One possible remaining difference between the Rich Man and Economic Rich Man Cases on the one hand and government taxation on the other is the government's permission to threaten loss of liberty and use of force if that is necessary to acquire money or property needed to help others. Even if the government, like the bystander in the Rich Man Case, never actually uses force, it might be entitled to do so, unlike that bystander. (However, if conditions [a] and [b] could justify killing someone in TP[2], those conditions might also justify some sort of force being involved in someone's losing money or property, at least if this force itself came about in a way that satisfied conditions like [a] and [b].)

(ii) My second concern about Pincione's discussion stems from my belief that even if it is permissible to turn the trolley in TP(2) (and also TP[1]), it is still permissible for the person to whom it is directed to send it back to the person who permissibly redirects it because the redirector infringed the rights of the one person not to be harmed. I would even say that the permission to redirect suggests that the person to whom the trolley was redirected was wronged though the redirection did not violate but only infringed his rights when the redirector acted permissibly or even dutifully. (In TP[1] it is commonly thought the driver has a duty to kill one other person instead of the five.[14]) Further, I think it is permissible for the one person to send back the trolley from whence it came, even if this means it will then kill the five who were originally threatened. This may be in part because the five would be no worse off than they would have been had the trolley not been redirected, and their salvation comes about by way of a serious albeit permissible infringement. If the one potential victim sent the trolley back, he cannot be accused of aggression against the five or the redirector. The permissibility of his doing this would have to be explained independently of (a). This is because a principle that allowed the one's sending the trolley back would not maximize the ex ante chance of each person to live nor have the greater good as the flipside of the trolley moving away from one person toward killing five. However, if he could only send back the trolley rather than use other means to save himself, other parts of (b) might still be required.[15] Hence, if government and citizen permissions mirrored permissions in TP(2), citizens might sometimes legitimately resist the government's permissible and morally justified attempts to tax them for the good of others. This is a problematic view, I think.[16] Morally permissible resistance by citizens to government actions is usually confined to nonviolent civil disobedience concerning gross injustices, not economic policies and not policies that the government is justified in carrying out. Furthermore, punishment of such resisters would also be legitimate, while punishment of the one person who resists the trolley would not be permissible in TP(2) (or TP[1]).

(iii) My third worry about Pincione's discussion concerns identifying when clause (b) is satisfied.[17] Clause (b) would exclude toppling the fat man from the bridge. Putting aside the possible moral significance of the difference between killing and imposing economic harm—which was part of my first concern—it would seem that taxation of some is a mere causal means to providing benefits to others and so should be prohibited by a clause like (b). However, Pincione considers possible alternative descriptions of a case involving taxation. For example, he says that some might say that "the state can 'redirect' a recession from the potential unemployed to individuals whose extra tax burden will be more than offset by unemployment benefits" to the unemployed.[18] This description at first makes it seem as though the recession is removed as a threat to some and redirected to others. But it isn't really the recession that is directed, as the next clause makes clear; it is the new threat of a tax burden that falls on others. Still, if a recession being removed from some people causes even a new threat to others, a condition like (b) could permit this. (Similarly, [b] would permit the trolley being turned from the five even if it consequently hits a heretofore stationary wagon, moving it so that this new threat of the wagon kills one other person.)

How does the loss to each of those in the recession compare to the new threat to others? If the tax burden is "more than offset by unemployment benefits," then the overall economic condition of each subject to the tax burden could still be better than those who would originally have been hit by the recession and the taxes produce more good in the latter than harm in the former. In this respect the case is not strictly analogous to the equal harm facing each potential victim in TP(2). Nevertheless, as noted earlier, conditions (a) and (b) might be necessary to justify a lesser but significant harm on someone and, furthermore, even if the harm left him better off than those helped to avoid a greater individual harm. Let us assume this is so. However, suppose the causal route to removing the impact of recession from those threatened by it initially were to first impose the tax burden on others as a means to provide unemployment benefits to the first group. Then a condition like (b) would not be satisfied. By contrast to such a route, Pincione says that "if the subsidies could be seen as the flip side of (the enactment of) redistributive measures . . . the PPH would authorize such measures. . . . The fact that a subsidy law makes it constitutionally mandatory for legislators who grant a subsidy to tax the rich mirrors here the fact that turning the trolley . . . makes it causally necessary to kill the one."[19] This way of constructing the analogy makes the imposition of the taxes come after the subsidies have already been legislated, and it is the subsidies that help the poor. In helpful comments on an earlier version of the essay on which this chapter is based Pincione further said:

> Unlike toppling the fat man, the taxes that I imagine in the recession case are causally independent of the greater good, e.g., many unemployed being saved from extreme poverty. This greater good comes before the taxes. Moreover, taxes are not necessary to bring about the greater good: other measures, such as printing money, can do that. The taxes are, as I imagine, "constitutionally mandatory" given the enactment of the subsidies, and this normative necessity as it were, may be taken to mirror the fact that in the Trolley Case the lesser harm is a causal consequence of turning the switch.

It seems to me that subsidies that are legislated and provided (even before taxes are imposed) are still mere causal means to the greater good of people being economically improved. If this is so, and legislating subsidies also causes (by way of legal requirement) taxes to be raised on the rich, then a mere causal means to the greater good would have caused the lesser harm. This would not be a case in which the greater good was the noncausal flipside of (or constituted by) the subsidies or their being legislated. This would make the case analogous to one where the bystander sets a bomb that causes the trolley to move away from the five and the bomb itself causes the death of one other person as a side effect. The PPH would rule out setting the bomb, even though using the bomb would not involve harming someone as a mere means to save the five (as in the Fat Man Case). This is because the PPH only permits means that have the greater good as a noncausal flipside to cause (at least "directly," not by entities independently in the environment) the lesser harm. Discussions of the Trolley Problem often ignore (though not Foot's own discussion in her original paper) that it can be wrong to use a device (like the bomb) that causes the five to be saved and also kills someone else as a causal side effect. Attention is typically focused on the contrast between the trolley turning that kills as a side effect and toppling the fat man, not on the contrast between the trolley turning that kills as a side effect and a device like the bomb that kills someone as a side effect.

However, Pincione himself says, "If the subsidies could be seen as the flip side of (the enactment of) redistributive measures . . . the PPH would authorize such measures." In this picture, the subsidies are not taken to cause the lesser harm of taxes. Rather, the subsidies are seen as the flipside (or aspect) of some redistributive measure that also causes taxes. Still, it is only if the subsidies constitute rather than cause some people's being free of the recession that the redistributive measure that causes taxes would also have a noncausal relation to the greater good. This might be so if people's being granted subsidies itself constituted their being saved from the recession. Suppose this is so. Then the redistributive measure that has the greater good (constituted by subsidies) as a noncausal flipside would also threaten others (via its tax component and the taxes to which it leads). Alternatively, the subsidies would legally trigger taxes and so the greater good constituted by the subsidies would cause the lesser harm. These two conceptions satisfy the PPH.

Suppose one of these conceptions is Pincione's view. Then a comparable case in ordinary morality might not be one in which we redirect the trolley but instead one in which we move five potential victims away from a trolley that cannot be redirected by turning a swivel table on which the five sit so that their moving is an aspect of its moving. In this case, the turning table (or the five on it) dislodges rocks that kill a bystander. This is one version of what I call the Lazy Susan Case.[20] It does indeed seem to me that turning the Lazy Susan also satisfies the PPH expanded to include cases in which the greater good is an aspect of the means of saving the five (i.e., if the five moving away from the trolley is seen as an aspect of the turning table). Would it also be permissible to introduce a Lazy Susan device into the scenario in which a trolley is moving toward the five people, placing the swivel table under them so that they sit on it and then moving them away from the trolley, even though we know rocks dislodged by the turning table will kill someone else? This is a case that is closest to Pincione's conception that we are now considering of a redistributive measure that is introduced and that involves a subsidy that constitutes people being free of a recession when the measure also causes new taxes. Hence, surprisingly, it may be a case in which the bystander introduces and turns the Lazy Susan that helps us see how Pincione could best connect ordinary morality to a justification for state action on subsidies, rather than the Bystander Case in which the trolley itself is redirected. His view is not about redirecting the recession away from people but more about directing people away from the recession. Once we do this, of course, we may also get rid of the recession. If so, it would be as if moving people away from the trolley was also a way to make the trolley disappear.

Despite this attempt to model government action providing subsidies on the Lazy Susan Case, I remain skeptical that it is the right way to conceive of government action in this case. This is primarily because it seems to me that subsidies are not yet the greater good. It is only once people have the actual money in hand and use it, an effect caused by the subsidy law, that we have a greater good. On this view, subsidies cause the greater good; they do not constitute it. If so, then a redistributive measure and/or subsidies in law and even actual subsidies would have a causal rather than a noncausal relation both to the greater good and to the lesser harm of taxes. In this way the redistributive measure would be like a bomb whose explosion both (1) causes the trolley or the Lazy Susan to move and (2) also causes someone's death.[21]

However, suppose that government funds available from some source other than taxation (such as voluntary donations or investment gains) were sufficient to provide subsidies and the government costlessly channeling such subsidies did not violate libertarian principles. Suppose poorer people having and using subsidized income increased their purchasing power (the greater good) and this led to the lesser harm of reduced purchasing power on the part of the rich. This way of causing lesser harm would satisfy a condition like Pincione's (b) and the PPH. Further, suppose the reduced purchasing power of the rich (somehow) caused the government to be able to continue the subsidies to the poor that it would not otherwise have been able to do, and it was only because it was foreseen that this would happen that it made sense to provide the original subsidies. Then the PPH would endorse the permissibility of causing the lesser harm, even though the lesser harm would be a causally necessary means to the continuation of benefits and only their continuation would justify providing the initial benefits and causing the harm to others. This would be an economic analogy to a version of the Trolley Problem known as the Loop Case.[22]

In this discussion, I have been accepting Pincione's working assumption (that he accepts for the sake of argument) that the government is a bystander to an economic recession, not its cause by act or (in an extended sense of "cause") by omission.[23] However, suppose the government caused the recession, were morally responsible for it, and had a special duty to rescue citizens from it. Then the government would not be a bystander as in TP(2) but more like the driver of the trolley headed toward the five in TP(1) or even a fully responsible, negligent trolley driver. In this case, actions to prevent the greater harm that are (arguably) only permissible for a bystander might be obligatory for the government. Nevertheless, a government being responsible for causing, or having an obligation to rescue from, a recession need not imply that it may take actions beyond those permitted to a bystander government. I shall elaborate on this point later.

## III. New Issues

Since 2007 when Pincione published his article, several new questions have arisen regarding the Bystander Case (TP[2]). I will now review two of these, already discussed in Chapters 8 and 9, and their bearing both on Pincione's argument against libertarians and on when harming someone constitutes aggression.

### A. Thomson's Revised View

In her 2008 article "Turning the Trolley," Judith Thomson reversed herself and argued that turning the trolley in TP(2) is not permissible.[24] As we discussed in Chapter 8 she accepted Foot's argument that the negative duty not to kill one person takes precedence over saving the five people threatened by the trolley. This is because, Thomson thinks, the bystander would commit no injustice to the five in not aiding them but would commit an injustice in violating the negative duty not to harm the one. She sought to buttress her position by noting that neither a bystander nor the person he would hit would have a duty to turn the trolley on himself (if he could) rather than let the five die: Doing so would be altruism (though not commendable, she claimed). But, she said, for the bystander to turn the trolley on another person would require that other person to be an altruist.

She sought to support and extend this conclusion by citing cases not involving killing. She said that if someone did not want to contribute to Oxfam, no other person may take money from him and send it to Oxfam. This case, however, involves taking money from someone as a means to aid distant people, whereas TP(2) involves aiding those nearby in immediate need when their being out of need causes harm to someone else. Therefore, a better monetary analogy to the trolley case is saving some people nearby by one's own effort when their being saved results in the loss of some money to someone else. This seems permissible. Despite her new view about TP(2), Thomson accepts the view that the trolley driver faces a choice between killing five people and killing one, and she thinks the negative duty not to unjustly kill five takes precedence over the negative duty not to kill one. This is so even though the one person who would be killed by the driver also need not volunteer to be killed to save the five.

Suppose it were impermissible to redirect in TP(2). Then the threat that Pincione sees to justifying a libertarian state (arising from the moral permissibility of redirecting in TP(2)] might not exist. (It is worth noting that Thomson herself may distinguish between what a government is permitted to do to a person and what another person may do to him. For example, she says, possibly the government may draft for military service but one citizen may not draft another.[25]) My own view is that turning the trolley in TP(2) is permissible and does not violate (though it permissibly infringes) the rights of the person hit by the redirected trolley. If this view is correct, Pincione's grounds for considering its implications for political libertarianism would stand. I think it may sometimes be permissible for a bystander to impose losses on someone that the latter could permissibly decline to altruistically volunteer in order to save others. Unlike Thomson, I do not think that imposing a loss on someone is "requiring him to be an altruist,"[26] since we are not requiring him to turn the trolley on himself (nor is he required to not resist our action, as I argued earlier). One possible reason for thinking that the bystander may permissibly kill one other person rather than let five die is that it would be permissible for the trolley driver to do this. That is, suppose that the driver is thrown from the trolley and lands near the switch that would allow him to divert the trolley still headed to the five. (I call this the Bystanding Driver Case.) Given that he started the trolley, this bystanding driver might become the killer of the five if he does not divert it. Still in this case, at the time he must divert his choice is between letting the five die from a threat he started or killing one other person. It seems permissible and even a duty for him to turn the trolley rather than let the five die. It might be suggested that this is because the bystanding driver's letting the five die, unlike the bystander's doing so, will result in his having treated the five unjustly, since he will have killed the five in virtue of also having started the threat to them. I disagree. First, someone who will become a killer of many if a threat he started continues, still may not be permitted to kill someone else in just any way in order to save the many. For example, I think it would be equally impermissible for the driver, whether on the trolley or standing at the switch, to topple the fat man to stop the trolley as it is for the bystander to do so. I believe this supports the view that it is *how* someone would come to kill one person—for example, as a consequence of a greater good -- that is crucial for the permissibility of killing. This also supports the view that a government's being responsible for causing a recession (rather than being a bystander) or having an obligation to rescue from a recession may not alter what it is permissible for it to do to minimize harm from the recession.

The PPH was an attempt to distinguish some permissible from impermissible ways of killing an innocent nonthreatening person. Further, I think that the importance of the "how" factor in killing suggests that it is not crucial to the permissibility of killing that the alternative is killing (or becoming the killer of) a greater number of people or instead letting them die. It is also not crucial to the permissibility of killing whether an agent becomes responsible for an injustice if he does not act though it may bear on whether it is impermissible for an agent to omit doing what is permissible.

Notice that even if one thought the ordinary bystander is not permitted to kill one person rather than let five die, there would still be a version of the Trolley Problem that involves explaining why the driver may carry out his duty to not kill (or to save) the five by killing someone else in some ways (e.g., by redirecting the trolley) but not in other ways (e.g., toppling the fat man). (Call this TP(3).)[27]

## B. How we fail to save

Now reconsider a different type of challenge that we considered in Chapter 9 to the view that when the alternative to killing one person in TP(2) is letting five die, a bystander is permitted to kill. Suppose a trolley will kill eight people. A bystander can save them either by (1) redirecting the trolley so that it kills one other person or (2) redirecting the trolley toward another road foreseeing that this will destroy the only tool that he alone could (and would) use to save five other people from a different deadly threat to which he is also a bystander. (I call this the Saving-By-Letting-Die Case.) It seems that rather than kill the one, the bystander should save the eight by doing what will lead to his letting the five die.[28] So in this case, when faced with the choice between killing one and letting five die, it seems the bystander should let five die rather than kill one. This conclusion raises a problem for Pincione's view that killing the one will be permissible when (a) the policy that permits it is ex ante in the interest of everyone and (b) the causal structure of killing is consistent with the PPH. For in the Saving-By-Letting-Die Case and other cases like it, it could be ex ante in the interest of all to do what saves the greatest number of people and turning a threat from the larger group of eight toward one person seems to be consistent with (b). Yet it may seem that turning is not permissible in this case when the alternative option is letting a greater number of people (five) die. We considered (in Chapter 9) whether this view about the Saving-by-Letting-Die Case could be consistent with the view that in TP(2) the bystander may turn the trolley toward a different person.

I argued that these conclusions could be consistent. One of the things that the Saving-by-Letting-Die Case could be taken to illustrate is that we should not save the means—here it is the tool—to saving other people from death when saving the means requires us to kill another person, even by redirecting a threat away from eight others toward him. Saving the means seems to be morally different from saving people as in TP(2), which may be done by redirecting a threat to another person.[29] But we also considered a version of Saving-by-Letting Die in which the bystander is already saving the five people with his life support machine. If he turns the trolley down that road it will cut the connection of his machine, terminating his assistance to the five people, and they will die. Here he is terminating assistance rather than merely eliminating a means that would be used to save lives. Yet again it may seem that rather than kill the one person he should let the five die by terminating aid he is providing to them. Is this consistent with turning the trolley in TP(2)? One possibility is that it is consistent if the five who would die from aid being terminated have no right to that aid from the bystander, but the five who would be hit by the trolley in TP(2) have a right not to be hit by it. Suppose the trolley in TP(1) were headed toward killing five people who were attached to the driver's life support machine, which he provided as an act of generosity and whose use he could permissibly terminate. Then on the account for consistency being considered even the driver should not turn the trolley away from those five toward killing one person. On this account, a crucial issue is whether the five made worse off by the trolley sent toward them would have a complaint against that being done to them by the person doing it. Then those complaints have to be considered even by a bystander (when he is not the person against whom they have the complaint) and compared with the complaint of the one person who would be hit.

How does this view relate to Pincione's argument? It would imply that it is only if those who would become unemployed due to a recession would have their rights violated by that threat that a government should remove the threat from them or remove them from the threat although this has the effect of harming others. However, Pincione does not argue that the recession (or how it comes to be) violates rights. By contrast the TP(2) case on which he relies does involve the five having their rights not to be killed violated by the trolley killing them which is something the bystander should take into account.

One objection (presented in Chapter 9) to the argument for consistency we are considering is that such consistency would make it impermissible to redirect a naturally occurring threat from a larger to a smaller group (e.g., germs that cannot violate anyone's rights in the group they initially threaten or a trolley headed to the five as a result of a strong gust of wind). If this objection were correct and it was permissible to redirect a naturally occurring threat, Pincione's use of TP(2) would not require showing that a recession violated the rights of those it initially threatened. However, a different argument for the consistency of TP(2) and not saving the five in the Saving-by-Letting-Die case would be needed (a proposal for which was made in Chapter 9).

A consistency argument that denied the permissibility of turning to harm the one person in the Saving-by-Letting-Die Case would have the following implications for a government's ability to affect an economy's direction. Suppose the government were like a bystander to an economic recession it did not cause as Pincione assumes. and had no duties to relieve it (as a libertarian might hold). It nevertheless chooses to provide economic relief to 8% of the population. Should it do so by (1) redirecting what causes the economic distress to other people who make up 1% of the population and who will be caused to suffer comparable harm or (2) terminating economic assistance it had gone beyond its duty to provide to a different 5% of the population (leaving them in comparable economic distress)? The proposal that one should not harm the one person in the Saving-by-Letting-Die Case implies the government should choose option (2) rather than (1) given that terminating aid involves not aiding rather than harming. This again seems to raise a problem for Pincione's view that harming fewer (in this case the 1%) will be permissible when (a) the policy that permits it is ex ante in the interest of everyone and (b) the causal structure of harming is consistent with the PPH.

However, the alternative proposal for consistency we considered in Chapter 9 claims that turning from eight people to one person (or from 8% to 1% of the population) does not satisfy (b). This is because according to both the PPH and the DPP, the greater good that causes the harm should be the good that justifies it. But we wouldn't need to harm the one person as a consequence of saving the eight if we could use the alternative. Hence, it is avoiding the alternative (i.e., not aiding the five) that would have to justify turning to harm the one person. That means the greater good (saving eight) that causes the lesser harm is not the greater good that justifies it.

Despite not strictly satisfying the DPP or PPH, in Chapter 9 we suggested a way to justify turning the threat to the one person in the Saving-by-Letting Die Case that depends on those principles. Since that proposal does not directly bear on Pincione's claims, I will not repeat it here. However, if it is correct, it could also justify removing a threat to the 8% by harming the 1% rather than discontinuing aid to the 5%.

## Notes

1. The concern here is with "right" libertarianism rather than "left" libertarianism.
2. This chapter is a revision of my "The Trolley Problem and Aggression," *Social Philosophy and Policy* 32(02): 1–17 (Spring 2016). Pincione's article is "The Trolley Problem as a Problem for Libertarians," *Utilitas* 19, no. 4 (2007): 407–29. All references to Pincione are to that article.
3. Judith Thomson, "The Trolley Problem," *Yale Law Journal* 94 (1985): 1395–96.
4. Pincione, "The Trolley Problem as a Problem for Libertarians," 412, footnote 14, says: "Judith Thomson's original statement of the Trolley Problem is in 'The Trolley Problem,' *The Yale Law Journal* 94 (1985): 1395–6."
5. Judith Thomson, "Killing, Letting Die, and the Trolley Problem," *The Monist* 59, no. 2 (1976): 206, where she said of the driver of the trolley (whom she named Edward) and the transplant surgeon (whom she named David): "Why is it that Edward may turn that trolley to save his five, but David may not cut up his healthy specimen to save his five? I like to call this the trolley problem, in honor of Mrs. Foot's example." In her later article, "The Trolley Problem," she changed her use of the title, applying it to a contrast between the Bystander and Fat Man Cases. I do not think it had been noticed that there are two different references in Thomson's work for the term "Trolley Problem" until I pointed it out in my *The Trolley Problem Mysteries* (Oxford: Oxford University Press, 2016). See also my "The Trolley Problem," in *The International Encyclopedia of Ethics* 2nd edition, ed. H. LaFollette et al. (Hoboken, NJ: Wiley Blackwell, 2021).
6. Philippa Foot, "The Problem of Abortion and the Doctrine of Double Effect," *Oxford Review* 5 (1967): 5–15, reprinted in Bonnie Steinbock and Alastair Norcross, eds., *Killing and Letting Die*, 2nd ed. (New York: Fordham University Press, 1994), 266–79. Foot did not refer to the runaway train as a trolley; Thomson introduced that term.
7. See Pincione, "The Trolley Problem as a Problem for Libertarians," 419.
8. Judith Thomson, *The Realm of Rights* (Cambridge, MA: Harvard University Press, 1992).
9. F. M. Kamm, *Morality, Mortality*, vol. 2 (New York: Oxford University Press, 1996). In my *Intricate Ethics* (New York: Oxford University Press, 2007) I modified the PPH (though not the part Pincione makes use of). I called the revision based on it the Doctrine of Productive Purity (DPP). See also Chapter 9 in this book. Sometimes Pincione speaks of the lesser harm being caused by "an act" that has the greater good as its noncausal flipside. (See, e.g., p. 418, where he says: "that the greater number was saved . . . is the flip side of the act [e.g., throwing the switch]." See also pp. 424 and 425.) This is not a correct understanding of my PPH. When we flip a switch that turns the trolley from the five people toward the one other person, our act of flipping the switch both causes the trolley to turn and has a causal relation to the greater good. In my view, it is the turning trolley that has a noncausal relation to the greater good of the five being saved and it is what causes harm to the one person. The act of flipping the switch (and so turning the trolley) is not a means that has the greater good as its noncausal flipside; it has a purely causal relation to the turning of the trolley,

which is the means that has the greater good as its flipside. Furthermore, to be permissible, the act of flipping the switch need not itself have a noncausal relation to the greater good because it itself does not cause harm to someone; the turning trolley does. Throughout, where necessary, I will amend Pincione's wording of the PPH to reflect this correction. The PPH is about harming innocent, nonthreatening people and does not necessarily apply to people who are threatening. Furthermore, what the PPH rules out as impermissible in one context may become permissible in another context through what I call the Principle of Secondary Permissibility. (I first argued for this in *Morality Mortality,* vol. 2.) That is, suppose the only way to save the five from the trolley is to topple the fat man from a bridge when this will paralyze his legs. This is a significant lesser harm to him to which the PPH is also intended to apply, and according to the PPH it is not permissible to do even this to the fat man to save the lives of the five. This is so even though it would be permissible according to the PPH to redirect the trolley when it would kill another person were it the only way to save the five, and being killed is worse than being made paraplegic. The difference in *how* we would bring about the different harms is morally important, according to the PPH. Nevertheless, suppose that as we are about to turn the trolley away from the five, thereby killing one other person, it becomes possible to instead topple this same person in front of the trolley, stopping it and only paralyzing his legs. Doing this would be a substitute for what was the only permissible act to save the five up to that point that we could and would otherwise have done and that would have a worse outcome for him. Given this, it becomes at least permissible to topple this person and probably obligatory to do this rather than turn the trolley that would kill him. For more on this see Chapter 9.

10. Pincione focuses on libertarians who subscribe to what he calls the Libertarian Priority Principle (LPP), which asserts "that the difference in strength between the negative and positive legal duties upheld by a libertarian legal system mirrors the difference in strength between negative and positive moral duties" (p. 409).
11. Pincione suggests (p. 418, footnote 41) that conditions (a) and (b) "arguably generate a duty to save the five in Trolley-like situations." I disagree (especially in the Bystander Case) for reasons discussed in II(ii) later.
12. In his comments on the essay on which this chapter is based Pincione said: "I wrote on pp. 409–410 in my article, 'The fact that, as we will see, the negative moral duty not to take an innocent's life is sometimes outweighed suggests that negative moral duties protecting arguably less valuable things (e.g. the duties that correlate with libertarian rights in external things) are even more frequently outweighed.' It should accordingly be no surprise that a legal system that mirrors ordinary morality authorizes the government to take small amounts of money from some to save others from serious harm, even if my conditions (a) and (b) are not satisfied, as it happens with the Rich Man Case." While we agree on this point, I am still concerned with Pincione's focusing on TP(2) and his attempt (as we shall see later) to show that taxation satisfies conditions (a) and (b).
13. Pincione notes (p. 422) that individual economic benefits to many could be greater than the individual burdens they impose on fewer others. He suggests that this would

make it easier to impose the burden than when killing is at issue. However, it is still possible that the individual economic burden would be too great relative to a larger individual economic benefit to avoid relying on conditions (a) and even (b) to justify bringing about the burden.

14. Thomson drew the distinction between unjustifiable transgressions of rights, which she labeled "violations," and justifiable transgressions of rights to which the label "infringements" could apply. See Judith Thomson, *The Realm of Rights* (Cambridge, MA: Harvard University Press, 1990). In her "The Trolley Problem" Thomson says that it is because the one person's rights have been infringed (even permissibly) that it may be only permissible rather than obligatory for the bystander to turn the trolley given he (unlike the driver) would not violate the rights of the five.
15. For more on these Sending Back Cases see *Intricate Ethics* and Chapter 9 in this volume.
16. However, for an alternative position see Arthur Applbaum's "Legitimacy without the Duty to Obey," *Philosophy & Public Affairs* 38, no. 3 (2010): 215–39.
17. This concern is directed especially to Section IV of Pincione's article.
18. Pincione, "The Trolley Problem as a Problem for Libertarians," 419.
19. Ibid., 423.
20. I discuss it in my *Morality, Mortality*, vol. 2, and Chapter 9 in this volume, among other places.
21. Pincione's own use of the Lazy Susan Case (pp. 423–25) does not involve the subsidy case but rent control. He says the rental control law simultaneously alters the legal rights of tenants and landlords, benefiting the former as it harms the latter. This is like a version of the Lazy Susan Case (which both he and I have presented) in which it is an aspect of the Lazy Susan turning that the five are moved away from a threat and also that the one person on the other side of the Lazy Susan is moved into the same threat. I have used this case to argue that lesser harm need not be causally downstream from greater good in a nonconsequentialist moral theory and so the theory is only "downstreamish." See *Intricate Ethics* and Chapter 9 on this.
22. This case was introduced by Judith Thomson in "The Trolley Problem." It is a case in which harm to someone is causally required to stop a trolley from returning to hit the five once it has been redirected from them. In his article Pincione considers a case he calls Prevented Return that is like Loop (see pp. 425–26). He uses it to argue that libertarians cannot argue against harming some for the sake of others on the grounds that it would involve treating people as mere means. Like Thomson, he thinks that it is permissible to turn the trolley away from the five even though its remaining away requires that it hit (as in Loop) or jam into (as in Prevented Return) the one other person. He also goes on to say (p. 426), "It is difficult to see how a prohibition against using others could be formulated in a way that withstands well-known objections to the doctrine of double effect. . . . The doctrine of double effect leads to the . . . result that diverting the trolley is impermissible in *Prevented Return*." With respect to the last point, I have elsewhere argued (in discussing Loop and a case that I introduced also called Prevented Return) that these cases need not involve intending harm but only acting (to turn the trolley) *because* one will cause harm that will have a useful

further effect of keeping the trolley away. Acting because one will cause useful harm is not, I argued, the same as acting with the intention to cause that harm. If this is correct, turning the trolley in Loop and Prevented Return need not be ruled out by the Doctrine of Double Effect. See my discussion of the because of/in order to distinction in Chapter 9 and in more detail in "The Doctrine of Triple Effect and Why a Rational Agent Need Not Intend the Means to His End," reprinted in my *Intricate Ethics*. I do agree that these cases show that acting only because harm to someone will be causally useful need not make acting impermissible even when the harm is causally required. However, in these cases the harm that will be a means is brought about in a special way, namely as a consequence of turning the trolley away from its initial hit. Here the harm may be seen as the effect of what I call the "structural equivalent" of the greater good, the greater good being the five free of all threats. This structural equivalent causes a fatal hit on one other person that sustains the five being free of threats by preventing the trolley's return. Suppose that this way of bringing about the harm that is a required causal means is permissible. This would not imply that other ways of bringing about harm that is a required causal means are permissible. For example, it would not imply that it is permissible to use mere means to topple the fat man so that his being hit by the trolley can be a mere means of stopping the trolley from its initial hit on the five. For more on this see *Intricate Ethics*, *The Trolley Problem Mysteries*, and Chapter 9 in this volume.

23. Pincione, "The Trolley Problem as a Problem for Libertarians," 419.
24. Judith Thomson, "Turning the Trolley," *Philosophy & Public Affairs* 36 (2008): 259–74.
25. She made this point in her oral response to my first Tanner Lecture at the University of California, Berkeley, March 2013. The two lectures, along with her response and those of Shelly Kagan and Thomas Hurka, are in *The Trolley Problem Mysteries*.
26. Judith Thomson, "Turning the Trolley."
27. I discuss these issues at greater length in *The Trolley Problem Mysteries* and Chapters 8 and 9 in this volume.
28. I introduced and discuss this case in *The Trolley Problem Mysteries* and offer a revised discussion in Chapter 9 in this volume.
29. I discussed this in *Morality, Mortality*, vol. 2.

# PART III

# RIGHTS AND EXTREME CASES

# 12

# Thought Experiments: Art and Ethics

In previous chapters we have considered the use of intuitive judgments about cases in arguing about rights and related issues in moral philosophy. But the use of intuitive judgments about cases is not limited to moral philosophy. In this chapter I consider its use in aesthetics and how this compares with its use in moral philosophy. In the first section of the chapter, I consider Arthur Danto's use of a particular thought experiment to support his theory of art and Richard Wollheim's discussion of it. In the second section, I consider a comparable thought experiment about conceptual issues in ethics. I then review how ethics employs thought experiments to determine the permissibility of acts and consider whether thought experiments could comparably be used to determine the merit of artworks. I finally consider how Danto's discussion of torture, an ethical issue concerning human rights that we will consider again in the next chapter, compares with Wollheim's way of challenging Danto's views about art.

## I. Conceptual Issues About Art: Danto versus Wollheim

A. Among the contributions for which Danto is known is his "Gallery of Indiscernibles."[1] It includes a set of imagined red canvases that cannot be distinguished from one another on perceptual grounds. This, presumably, is not due to the limits of perception but because they are identical with respect to perceptual properties. However, they have different descriptions, which include (1) a painting of people drowning in the Red Sea, (2) a landscape of Red Square, (3) a minimalist painting (perhaps "homage to the red square" by Josef Albers), (4) a canvas stretched and painted red by Giorgione that he never used for a painting, and (5) a stretched red canvas that "an egalitarian" artist finds and submits as art and that is accepted as such. There are other indiscernible items described by Danto outside of this set, such as (6) a canvas painted red by a child and (7) the product of a puff of red paint "miraculously" (and accidentally) forming another indiscernible canvas.

These imagined red canvases involve at least two representational artworks ([1] and [2]). These two canvases have different subjects but cannot be distinguished

*Rights and Their Limits: In Theory, Cases, and Pandemics.* F. M. Kamm, Oxford University Press.
© Oxford University Press 2022. DOI: 10.1093/oso/9780197567739.003.0012

perceptually; they could be perceptually mistaken for each other. There are also artworks that could be mistaken for things that are not artworks (e.g., [1] and [4] could be mistaken for each other). The items in this thought experiment could be raised as counterexamples to the claim that (a) different artworks must be perceptually distinguishable, and (b) artworks can be distinguished from nonartworks by perceivable properties (introduced by artists). If these two general claims were shown to be false by the "red" counterexamples, there would be at least some artworks that are not artworks because of their perceptual properties alone. Assume we could create comparable indiscernibles with other perceptual properties that other artworks have (e.g., fuzzy blue halos). If the items in these further thought experiments were also successful counterexamples to claims (a) and (b), they would go a long way to showing that perceptual properties are never sufficient to distinguish between what is an artwork and what is not.

B. Richard Wollheim has counterargued[2] that something like (a) and (b) could be "general truths" rather than necessary truths. The general truths, he thinks, are that "objects . . . made with the broad intention of being works of art will stand out from objects . . . not made with such an intention and works of art . . . made with different specific intentions will stand out from one another" (p. 35). So the fact that (5) could be accepted as an artwork does not function as a counterexample to a necessary condition on art, and that a certain assumption can be transgressed in a particular case (or particular cases) does not show it could be universally transgressed. In addition, (i) Wollheim suggests that it might not be possible to accept (5) as a work of art if the general truths he describes did not hold (which seems to imply that it is necessary that certain truths hold at least generally if [5] is to be a work of art), and (ii) he claims it is important that we would only "reluctantly" (p. 34) accept this atypical item as an artwork.

Consider Wollheim's claim about reluctance. Once the barrier is breached and one atypical item is recognized as art, it may become increasingly easy to recognize other atypical entities as works of art. This shows that one might have to distinguish the particular content of general truths from the suggestion that atypical works of art depend on works of art generally having the properties they lack. If many once-atypical items get admitted to the "art world," it may no longer be true that the same general truths hold, and while the formerly general truths may have been necessary at one point for the then-atypical item to be art, they will no longer be necessary for other items to be art (since the others may be judged relative to the "new normal"). I will later return to Wollheim's views to ask how they relate to possible positions in ethics.

## II. Ethics and Indiscernibles

A. In this section, I consider how some thought experiments in moral philosophy do and do not resemble Danto's gallery of indiscernibles. Danto was concerned with conceptual issues (e.g., what is and is not an artwork). Perhaps the strictly comparable issue in ethics would distinguish between events subject to moral evaluation (part of the "moral world") and perceptibly identical events that are not subject to moral evaluation (not part of the "moral world"). For example, an act (e.g., moving one's hand in a particular way) might fall into the first class, while an identical bodily movement due to a twitch would fall into the second class. (However, acts taken to interfere with twitches would be part of the moral world.) This is what is called the issue of the scope of morality. Given that what distinguishes the act from the twitch is not a perceptible property, we know that there will be perceptually indiscernible events that do and do not belong in the scope of morality.

However, within the realm of events subject to moral evaluation, there are also conceptual issues related to indiscernibles. For example, there has been discussion of what behavior is a killing rather than a letting die. Some of these discussions make use of "galleries [hospitals?] of indiscernibles," comparable to Danto's gallery for art. Here is a well-known case: Someone is attached to a life support machine. If the person's doctor unplugs him, it is said by many to be a case of terminating treatment that constitutes a letting die. By contrast, if the person's "greedy nephew" unplugs him, in a "perceptually indiscernible" way with perceptually indiscernible consequences (the uncle dies), it is said by many to be a killing.

Though it is imagined that the doctor and the nephew engage in the same exact bodily movements, this is not necessary in order for the issue to arise of whether the two acts are of the same type (a killing or a letting die). This is because no one would take seriously the idea that, for example, a difference in the curve made by the doctor's hand from the curve made by the nephew's hand could be relevant to whether one act was a letting die and the other a killing. The same could be true of Danto's examples. Suppose that each of his red canvases had a slightly different tiny dot in its right corner. The canvases could then be perceptually discernible, but it would not be any easier to determine by perceptual means what was an artwork from what was not. However, once one decides (by reference to nonperceptual factors such as "aboutness," etc.) which canvases are artworks, the dots could help avoid confusing the artwork with the nonartwork.

It has been argued that factors not perceptible in the action of unplugging the life support machine (such as who owns the life support machine, who has the right to control the machine, etc.) could account for the physically identical act (and consequences) of pulling the plug being either a killing or a letting die.

For example, if a doctor exercising legitimate control over the machine attaches someone to it and then while still retaining legitimate control over its use unplugs the person, he could be letting the man die in withdrawing life support as much as he would be letting him die if he did not start the life support machine to begin with. By contrast, if the nephew pulls the plug on the machine, assuming that he has no right to decide whether to let others use it, he will have interfered with a machine he has no right to control when this results in someone's death. This may make what he does a killing. The view that factors not perceptible in an act can determine whether the act is a killing or a letting die is analogous to Danto's view that something not perceptible in a physical object can determine whether something is or is not art.

B. Note that some other factors imperceptible in an act may not be relevant to whether the doctor and the nephew kill or let die. For example, if the doctor is greedy and intends the patient's death for his own interests and against the patient's interests, this needn't mean that he kills rather than lets die. It may only mean that he impermissibly lets die. If the nephew is not greedy but correctly thinks his uncle would be better off dead and acts for his sake, this needn't mean that he lets die rather than kills, though it might make his killing permissible. One implication of this is that conceptual issues in ethics can be distinguished from judgments about permissibility and impermissibility; it is a mistake to determine that pulling the plug is a killing merely because it is impermissible or that it cannot be a killing merely because it is permissible. Similarly, the merit of an artwork is not relevant to deciding if it is an artwork. For example, item (5) in Danto's list may be an artwork and yet be a very bad or meritless one.

The most famous thought experiments in ethics are not concerned with determining into which conceptual category an act falls, but with whether an act is permissible and why. For example, many variations on the Trolley Problem that we have considered in past chapters are thought experiments about *whether* and *why* it is permissible for a bystander to turn the trolley away from five people toward killing someone else when he could instead let the five die, given that he had nothing to do with creating the threat to the five. In philosophy of art, a question comparable to whether an act is permissible is *whether* what has been determined to be an artwork is at least minimally good. A second question is *why* the minimally good work of art is good. Other thought experiments in ethics are concerned with whether an act of one type is morally equivalent to or morally different from an act of another type and why. A famous example is whether killing is per se morally worse than letting die per se. The comparable question in philosophy of art might be whether one type of artwork (e.g., still life) has less merit per se than another type (e.g., landscape) and why.

None of Danto's thought experiments that I have described is concerned with these comparable questions about the merit of works of art. Hence, use of thought experiments in ethics is often unlike the use of thought experiments in Danto's work. One question is whether thought experiments could be used in art to deal with questions of merit as they are used in ethics to deal with (im)permissibility or moral (in)equivalence and the reasons for it. Another question is how the use of these thought experiments in ethics bears on the issue raised by Wollheim of what a particular case can tell us about a general claim. Let us consider the second question first.

To determine if killing in itself (per se) is morally worse than letting die per se, the philosopher James Rachels asks us to imagine two different cases in which all factors are held constant except that one is a killing and the other a letting die. In the letting die case, someone who planned to drown a child sees him drowning in a bathtub. He does not rescue him because he intends the child's death in order to inherit his money. In the killing case, someone holds a child in a bathtub under the water, drowning him, because he intends the child's death in order to inherit his money.[3] Rachels thinks that the killing case is not morally worse than the letting die case and from this he concludes that killing is not per se morally worse than letting die per se.

Much has struck philosophers as problematic about Rachels' discussion. I shall discuss only one point that will inform my discussion of the Danto/Wollheim debate. If it were true that a particular *case* of killing is morally equivalent to a particular case of letting die (and it is not clear this is so in Rachels' cases), one could not conclude from this that killing *per se* is never morally different from letting die *per se*. The claim that (a) there is a per se moral difference between killing and letting die is not the same as the claim that (b) in every case killing will make some moral difference that letting die does not. One could show that (b) is not true by a set of particular cases without undermining the per se moral difference claim in (a). Only one set of cases in which a killing and a letting die differ morally when all other factors are held constant is needed to defeat the claim that killing and letting die are per se morally equivalent, but one cannot establish a universal claim of per se equivalence on the basis of just one set of cases in which killing and letting die do not differ morally when all other factors are held constant. There might be a per se moral difference that does not show up sometimes because even if the cases are equalized for all factors besides the ones whose moral significance we are testing, the particular equalized factors in the case might "silence" or override a per se moral difference between the factors we are testing. For example, if someone has competently requested that one end his life, it may not make a moral difference whether one does so by killing him or letting him die. Or if someone has been legally sentenced to death, it may not matter whether officials authorized to see that he is dead do so by letting him die or by killing him. But these cases where a killing and a letting die are morally equivalent do not show that per se one type of act has no factors that could make it morally different from the other that would account for moral differences in other sets of equalized cases.

This claim—that the moral character of different acts could differ per se while some cases involving the different acts are morally equivalent—brings to mind Wollheim's remarks on Danto's gallery of indiscernibles. The fact that in some cases it is impossible to distinguish an artwork perceptually from a nonartwork does not show that there is no per se conceptual difference based on perceptual properties between an artwork and a nonartwork. Given what I said about killing and letting die, it might be suggested that there is some factor in some cases that is overriding or "silencing" the role of perceptual factors that still make a per se difference between art and nonart that might show up in other cases.[4]

Now let us consider the first question: whether thought experiments could be used in art to deal with questions of merit as they are used in ethics to deal with (im)permissibility or moral (in)equivalence and the reasons for it. Could thought experiments be used in art to determine whether some works of art are at least minimally good or why one is worse (or better) than another? It seems unlikely that the method of thought experiments I have described will settle questions of merit and relative merit in art. This may be because in morality there are thought to be factors that weigh in the direction of permissibility or impermissibility or, other things equal, make an act morally worse than another. This is one reason thought experiments can be good predictors of how one should deal with real-life cases in morality. But there do not seem to be comparable factors that weigh in the direction of one artwork being good or better than another. That we correctly admire the blue in one good artwork does not mean that the same blue in another artwork will weigh in favor of its being good. Perhaps properties at a very high level of generality, such as effective composition or dynamism, could lead us to think that an artwork would be better than another. Even this seems unlikely. The goodness of an artwork does not seem to be predictable from a list of its qualities in the way the permissibility of an act is.

Those who think there are basic principles or even rules that account for moral rightness and wrongness have an explanation of this phenomenon. They contrast principles and rules in morality with the absence of principles and rules for the production and appreciation of great and even good works of art. This was supposed to be the mistake made by academicians in art who tried to codify rules where "genius" was supposedly required instead.[5] But those who reject the adequacy of basic principles or rules in morality can also use hypothetical cases to judge whether an actual case would involve right or wrong conduct. This is true even when interaction effects between factors make a factor that would ordinarily render an act wrong be silenced or overridden by another factor, as this can happen in a hypothetical case too. It is still possible that being involved in an actual case (not just hearing about it) can make one aware of additional factors that one did not but should have built into a hypothetical case. But building that factor into a hypothetical is just as good as witnessing an act in reality for purposes of rendering judgment. Instantiation in art seems much more crucial and limits the predictive adequacy of an imagined artwork for the merit of the actual artwork.

But perhaps this is true only when nonartists consider hypothetical qualities (even at a high level of generality) of artworks. Is it possible that (as some have thought) an artist can know that characteristics she thinks (or "sees" with the mind's eye) will make for a good artwork once instantiated? And perhaps matters are different for conceptual art than for other art forms? These are questions I merely raise but do not answer.

## III. Danto on Ethics by Comparison to Art

A. Surprisingly, in his own discussion of the permissibility of certain acts of killing and harming, Danto seems to have adopted a view similar to the one Wollheim adopted about Danto's indiscernibles. Consider the following excerpt from Danto's consideration of whether assassination could ever be morally permissible:[6]

> Because he was a monster, Hitler may be considered too extreme a case upon which to base a philosophical analysis of assassination. Consider torture. . . . I am utterly opposed to the use of torture, but I suppose cases can be imagined, along Dostoevskian lines, in which one's stand against torture might be weakened because it is a dramatically lesser evil. Suppose a man has, but refuses to divulge, information which would save millions of innocent lives. . . . I do not know what I would say if torture were proposed. There is no morality for extreme situations and it is a mistake to argue from extreme cases to routine ones. In any event, it is not true that torture in the extreme case is justified. Patterns of justification cannot be designed for extreme cases; it is not that torture is justified, but that under such wild circumstances "right" and "wrong" do not apply. It is, thus, no justification of cannibalism that cases are available in which cannibalism seemed the only alternative to an agonizing death. I could understand a man who resisted the opportunity to survive, and I could understand a man who yielded. Extreme cases warp the concept of a policy, and Hitler's seems precisely to be an extreme case. No argument from it is available, not even if one could secure the assent of every moral person that the killing of Hitler would have been a dramatically lesser evil than the deaths of millions of people directly traceable to his policies. I do not say a way cannot be paved from the extreme case to the practice. . . . All I am saying is that a way *has to be paved*, that

> the inference from the extreme case to the routine is fallacious without supplementary defense and then the supplementary defense eliminates the relevance of the extreme paradigm. . . . Is assassination, therefore, never justifiable, or at best not unjustifiable because of the moral structurelessness of the extreme case? Is it "beyond good and evil" only when the intended victim is a monster like Hitler?. . . Routinization of assassination is . . . consistent only with the devaluation of all values. . . . Accordingly, it can only be consistently [sic] with any true system of values that assassination is exceptional and hence extreme.[7]

I think that this quoted position about right and wrong action has echoes of what Wollheim says about the conceptual issue of art versus nonart. Consider the case of the egalitarian artist who exhibits the found red canvas ([5] in my list earlier of Danto's indiscernibles): (i) A Wollheimian might say (applying Danto's words about assassination to [5]) that this is an extreme case, "and it is a mistake to argue from extreme cases to routine ones. . . . [I]nference from the extreme case to the routine is fallacious without supplementary defense and then the supplementary defense eliminates the relevance of the extreme paradigm" (to determining what is art). (ii) Wollheim thinks it is revealing that "art" might be applied to (5) with a degree of reluctance or indecision that Danto ignores. However, Danto takes note of indecision in the case of the permissibility of torture or cannibalism. Of extreme case he says, "I could understand a man who resisted . . . and one who yielded." Wollheim might use the same words to describe his response to whether (5) is art. (iii) Wollheim might say of (5) (using Danto's words about torture), "it is not that one is justified in saying . . . [(5) is art] . . . but that under such wild circumstances 'right and 'wrong' do not apply." (iv) Wollheim might say that a concept of art for ordinary cases derived from concluding that (5) is art "is then consistent only with the devaluation of values" (or concepts, in the case of art); "accordingly it can only be consistently [sic] with any true system of values or concepts) that (5) "is exceptional and hence extreme."

B. Is Danto right in what he says (seemingly à la Wollheim) about assassination, cannibalism, and torture? I do not think so. Here are some reasons that pertain to torture.[8]

(i) The fact that one could be reluctant to think that torture is sometimes morally permissible, or that one could understand both the person who said it was and the one who said it wasn't, does not mean that torture isn't in fact sometimes permissible (e.g., all things considered justified).

(ii) The fact that a type of act that is usually wrong would be done in circumstances where the consequences of its not being done would be extremely bad does not mean that the act is now "beyond good and evil." Thomas Nagel thinks that cases like one of those Danto imagines, in which we would torture an innocent in order to save millions of other lives, are "moral blind alleys" in which no matter what we do (torture or not), we act wrongly.[9] But doing an all things considered *wrong* act no matter what we do would obviously not mean that the whole issue was beyond right and wrong (or good and evil). Another way in which the torture of an innocent could be not beyond good and evil is if it is *not wrong*. This is implied by what is known as "threshold deontology": deontological side constraints (such as duties to not harm innocents correlative to their right not to be harmed) may *permissibly* be overridden in some cases when the consequences are bad enough. (Notice that this is different from a threshold above which the innocent's right not to be harmed no longer exists at all.) Though I do not think that this "dramatically lesser evil" argument is the best way to morally analyze all cases of torture, it may be the way to analyze the so-called Dostoevskian one that Danto mentions in which an innocent who has no responsibility for the threat facing the world must be tortured or killed to save millions. This view should be, I believe, compatible with "wronging" the innocent person in the course of acting permissibly and so not doing a wrong act. A sign of his being wronged is that the innocent person may permissibly resist the torture in self-defense. This is a sign that we are trying to impose a greater loss on him than he is required to bear or tolerate for the sake of preventing the greater evil, even if our doing this is not wrong. It is also a sign that his right does not merely disappear above the threshold.[10]

(iii) In cases where the person to be tortured is morally responsible for the threat, there could be other grounds for permissibility than that torturing him is a "dramatically lesser evil" done to prevent the threat coming to fruition. For example, Danto describes someone who is refusing to give information that he has that could save many people. This person might not have started the threat facing them; however, he is letting them die when he could easily save them (and so may have what is called "negative responsibility" for the event). However, if letting die is morally less serious than killing, he might lack sufficient responsibility for the threat to justify torturing him to prevent it. By contrast, suppose the very person who presented the threat to the world (e.g., Hitler) was the person who would have to be tortured to stop the threat from coming to fruition. The argument for the moral permissibility of torturing him is not that it is the dramatically lesser evil, but that Hitler's wrong act makes him responsible for the threat and so he is liable to be harmed in order to save his victims. Call this the Responsibility Argument. I think it may succeed.

The Responsibility Argument need not be restricted to cases involving a potential enormous loss to many in the world. Consider "ordinary" cases in which a villain threatens to kill one other person (e.g., he has set a bomb that will go off unless we torture him for the information to stop it). I agree with Danto that we should not rely on the extreme case to argue about the ordinary case. However, this can imply that we should not rely on the extreme case of potential enormous loss to many to argue about torture when we can use the ordinary cases, and it could be correct to use the same type of Responsibility Argument in trying to justify torture in the ordinary case as in the extreme case. That is, it might be that in order to save his potential victim once he has finished setting his bomb, the villain could be liable to suffer at least the sorts of harms that it would be permissible to impose on him while he is establishing his threat in order to stop him from doing so.[11] Using the Responsibility Argument to justify sometimes torturing in such nonextreme cases might not signify "the devaluation of value."[12]

## Notes

1. See Arthur Danto, *Transfiguration of the Commonplace* (Cambridge, MA: Harvard University Press, 1981).
2. See Richard Wollheim, "Danto's Gallery of Indiscernibles," in *Danto and His Critics*, 2nd ed., ed. Mark Rollins (Hoboken, NJ: Wiley-Blackwell, 2012), 30–39.
3. These cases are based on ones by James Rachels in "Active and Passive Euthanasia," *New England Journal of Medicine* 292 (1975): 78–80. Rachels imagined that the person who lets the child drown was also prepared to kill him. I am not sure that is a factor that should be equalized in both cases.
4. It is also possible that it is because killing and letting die differ morally per se that a particular killing is morally equivalent to a particular letting die. This can be true when a particular conceptual property that makes letting die less serious than killing gets "exported" to a particular killing case and makes the killing in that case less serious than killing in other cases. (For more on this see my *Morality, Mortality*, vol. 2. [New York: Oxford University Press, 1996].) This is analogous to Wollheim's claim that it is because as a general matter perceptual differences are important in distinguishing art from nonart that in some cases it is not perceptual differences that distinguish art from nonart.
5. Kant emphasized that the judgment of taste could be sound though it was ruleless.
6. Arthur Danto, "A Logical Portrait of the Assassin," *Social Research* 42, no. 3 (1974): 426–38.
7. Oddly, Danto goes on to say that despite assassination's "categorical extremity," it is not really "beyond good and evil" and it is not true "that nothing morally useful can be said about political assassination" (Danto, "A Logical Portrait of the Assassin," 434–35).
8. Some of what I say here is based on my discussion of torture in *Ethics for Enemies: Terror, Torture, and War* (New York: Oxford University Press, 2011). I continue the discussion of torture in Chapter 13.
9. See p. 74 of Thomas Nagel's "War and Massacre," in *Mortal Questions* (Cambridge: Cambridge University Press, 2012), 53–74.

10. See my discussion of another such case in my *The Trolley Problem Mysteries* (New York: Oxford University Press, 2016) and Chapter 9 in this volume.
11. See *Ethics for Enemies* and Chapter 13 in this volume for additional steps in the argument.
12. This chapter is a longer version of a chapter of the same name in ed. J. Gilmore and L.Goehr *A Companion to Arthur C. Danto* (Hoboken, NJ: Wiley-Blackwell, 2022).

# 13
# The Torture Puzzle

Torture is among acts that clearly raise issues of moral rights violation. In Chapter 12 we briefly considered Arthur Danto's views about torture in connection with deciding about extreme versus ordinary cases of potential harm. In that chapter, "extreme" was used to refer to averting deaths of very many innocent, nonthreatening people whereas "ordinary" was used to refer to averting death of even one such person. However, torture itself even in the "ordinary" case might be considered an extreme means even if the consequences of not using it are not extreme. In that sense, this chapter is generally about extreme cases in discussing whether and why torture could be a violation of moral rights, morally wrong the person to whom it is done, and be morally impermissible.[1]

## 1. Some Conceptual Issues

A. In this section, we will try to develop a clearer understanding of what torture is and will consider differences among various legal and philosophical conceptions of torture.

There are several different legal definitions of torture. One is from the United Nations Convention against Torture and Other Cruel, Inhumane, or Degrading Treatment or Punishment (CAT). It says torture is

> any act by which severe pain or suffering, whether physical or mental, is intentionally inflicted on a person for such purposes as obtaining from him or a third person information, punishing him for an act he or a third person has committed or is suspected of having committed, or intimidating or coercing him or a third person, or for any other reason based on discrimination of any kind, when such pain or suffering is inflicted by or at the instigation or with the consent of a public official or other person acting in an official capacity. It does not include pain or suffering arising only from, inherent in, or incidental to lawful sanctions.

This definition first points to what is imposed on a person, then for what purpose, and then by whom. Here are some things to consider about this definition: (1) It does not specifically say that the person does not consent to the treatment or

*Rights and Their Limits: In Theory, Cases, and Pandemics*. F. M. Kamm, Oxford University Press.
© Oxford University Press 2022. DOI: 10.1093/oso/9780197567739.003.0013

that it is against his interests. Both these ordinarily seem important to torture. However, suppose someone who had wanted, but was unable, to divulge information requested that he be made to suffer because only that would trigger his memories. Could not what was done to him still be torture even though he requested such treatment? (2) The definition is limited to torturing persons and so it makes it impossible to torture an animal. (3) The definition excludes the possibility that someone might be tortured by an ordinary person, not someone in an official capacity. (4) The definition makes it impossible to be tortured if there is no additional purpose (such as getting information) beyond inflicting mental or physical suffering as an end in itself. Yet the latter could certainly be torture. (5) The definition enumerates various specific purposes for inflicting suffering on someone, such as getting information. But some have argued that there is a unifying, antecedent purpose to torture that is a means to achieving other purposes, namely "breaking someone's will."[2] However, torture might be imposed simply to make someone act from self-interest, getting him to change his behavior so that the imposed suffering will stop. This suggests that attempting to break someone's will need not be a component of all torture. (6) This definition allows that severe mental suffering inflicted on one person to coerce or obtain information from another person is torture. It is clear that the definition claims that the first person would be tortured, but would the other person also be tortured? If witnessing the first person's suffering caused the other person to also mentally suffer, then this could be his being tortured. This could even be accomplished without torturing the first person but merely, for example, showing a film to the second person of a fictional staging of the first person being tortured. (7) It is important to see that, according to the CAT, pain and suffering inherent to a sanction is not torture if the sanction is lawful. This is problematic if it implies that it would be consistent with the CAT to simply pass a law permitting torture as punishment for torture to be legally permissible.

A second definition of torture is present in the U.S. Torture Statute (USTS): "An act committed by a person acting under the color of law specifically intended to inflict severe physical or mental pain or suffering other than pain or suffering incidental to lawful sanction, upon another person within his custody or physical control." The USTS further specifies "severe mental pain or suffering" as "the prolonged mental harm caused by or resulting from, among other things, the threat of imminent death and intentional infliction of physical pain and suffering."

A crucial addition to the CAT in the USTS is that torture requires that a person be in the custody *or* physical control of the person inflicting the pain or suffering. According to this statute, it is conceptually possible to torture someone who is not in custody but over whom one nevertheless has physical control, but it is conceptually impossible to torture someone who is not in custody and also not under physical control (e.g., when he is at liberty, engaged in battle, or has some ability, however small, to defend himself). As a conceptual matter, this may be a problematic result. Note also that being in custody is consistent with someone being a threat, for example, by acquiring a weapon. If inflicting pain upon someone in this situation to get him to drop his weapon should not be considered torture, intentionally imposing suffering "under the color of law" on someone in custody would not suffice for an act to be torture.

By contrast to the USTS, the CAT allows that torture can occur to someone not in custody and not in the physical control of those who would impose pain and suffering. It might therefore allow that fighting a threatening person with pain could be torture, at least if its aim is to coerce or intimidate that person, for example, to drop his weapon. However, it may rule this out if the pain inflicted on an unjustly threatening person is inherent to a "lawful sanction." The USTS also differs from the CAT in (i) not speaking of various purposes for which pain and suffering are imposed and (ii) not speaking of pain "inherent in" but only "incidental to" an act as not undermining an act's status as a lawful sanction.

The U.S. Military Commission Act of 2009, the War Crimes Act, and the Torture Victims Protection Act add to the USTS the requirement that specific purposes like those described in the CAT be the aim of causing pain or suffering.[3]

By contrast to the USTS's emphasis on someone being in custody or under physical control, the philosopher Henry Shue characterizes standard torture as involving the infliction of severe distress on someone who presents no threat *and* is defenseless.[4] (Notice that person B could present a threat to person A while being defenseless to person C's attack on him to stop his threat. If fighting B with severe pain in this circumstance would not be torture, it is because he is a threat although defenseless to the attack on him. If, as suggested earlier, inflicting severe distress on someone who can mount only a weak defense could still count as torture, then someone's defenselessness is neither necessary nor sufficient [e.g., if he is a threat to someone other than the person in relation to whom he has no defense] for torture to occur.) Shue (p. 458) thinks that sometimes the ability to reveal information that would make torture stop is a form of defense that could be had even by those who are physically under another's control; such people are not, therefore, strictly defenseless. Thus, on Shue's view, someone could satisfy a *strengthened* USTS condition for being tortured—being made to suffer while in custody *and* under physical control—but not count as being tortured because he is not defenseless if he could reveal information that would stop the suffering.[5]

By contrast to Shue, philosopher David Sussman believes that when someone in custody refuses to reveal information that would both stop a threat he has started and stop torture of himself, he is continuing his threat, not merely refusing to defend himself against those who would torture him.[6] On this view, someone in custody and under physical control might still be presenting a threat and so, on Shue's view of torture, imposing suffering on him would not be torture.

The views we have so far discussed do not focus only on the type of pain and suffering being imposed; some also consider their purposes and by whom and when (e.g., in custody or under physical control) they are imposed. Hence, these views narrow the application of "torture" (e.g., one cannot torture an animal to get a confession). David Sussman's characterization (which is not a definition) further narrows the application of "torture." He says: "At minimum, torture involves the deliberate infliction of great pain or some other intensely distressing affective state . . . on an unwilling person for purposes the person does not and could not reasonably be expected to share."[7] But he adds:

> [Torture] seems to require that its perpetrators and victims be placed in a distinctive kind of social setting and relationship to one another. Victims of torture must be, and must realize themselves to be, completely at the mercy of their tormentors. . . .[T]he victim takes her tormentor to be someone who can do anything he wants to her. . . . [T]he torturer confronts no moral or legal impediments stemming from the victim's will. . . . [A] victim might know that her torturers operate under some significant restrictions. . . . [T]he victim's grounds for such beliefs . . . come from how these torturers choose to present themselves. . . . Typically a torture victim has no independent way of corroborating.[8]

Sussman adds that interrogational torture has a distinctive wrong-making characteristic not had, for example, by imposing pain and suffering on someone as punishment or to get someone else (not the person tortured) to reveal information. Unlike the CAT, he does not accept that such impositions are torture; he calls them "ordeals." The distinctive characteristic they lack is trying to control someone's agency—getting him to do something—by affecting his body (or mind, presumably). This might involve getting the person to decide to act differently to stop the suffering or his will being "taken over" by the torturer for whom he acts. Hence, on Sussman's view, imposing distress on someone when the distress interferes with that person completing a freely chosen act (as when electric shocking someone for a long time causes him involuntarily to stop acting) or causes him to involuntarily drop information he is holding onto is not torture. In addition, Sussman's conception implies that governments would not be engaged in torture if they are known by all, through sources independent of the torturer, to abide by court-imposed limits on what they will do so that victims know they are not completely at the mercy of their tormentors.[9] Sussman's view, I believe, is too narrow a conception of torture and is morally problematic because it allows too many to incorrectly escape the charge of torturing.

Our discussion so far shows that there are different conceptions of torture that do not overlap and also have problematic features.

B. Now consider a Bomb Threat Case: A is not in custody or under anyone's physical control. He is a morally responsible and informed agent who has deliberately set and is directing a bomb to impermissibly kill B. The bomb will shortly kill B if nothing is done to stop it from being directed to him. If and only if the police repeatedly shock A for an hour, causing him intense pain as he is directing his bomb, can they save B. (I will call cases like this one where an identifiable victim must be saved Rescue Type Cases.) We can imagine five different cases each involving only one of the following different ways of using the shocks: (a) to stop A's act of directing the bomb by interfering with the act, (b) to get him to stop his act, (c) to get him to give information needed by others to stop his act, (d) to get him to inadvertently reveal information needed by others to stop his act (e.g., by involuntarily dropping information he holds), and (e) to stop his act from harming B by, for example, eliciting movements or sounds from A that make a protective screen drop around B. Categories (b) and (c) could include getting him to decide to stop his act or to give information in order to stop the shocks or his will being "broken" by the shocks. Category (a), by contrast, would bypass his will by physically interfering with his act. Similarly, category (d) would bypass his will by physically interfering with him so that he reveals information. In category (e) we cannot stop A's act but can use pain in A to, for example, (i) cause involuntary movements or sounds of his (bypassing his will) or (ii) get him to decide to move (affecting his will) when (i) or (ii) would cause a protective screen to drop around B.

In the Bomb Threat Case, A is actively threatening someone and police defend the person from A's threat during A's act. With the possible exception of the CAT, most of the preceding conceptions of torture would not count this as torture, not because it is not painful enough but because it occurs while someone is at liberty and doing something wrong. But my own view is that in an ordinary, everyday sense of torture, police would be torturing A because of the pain and suffering they cause him to stop his harming his victim. Those who disagree might claim that this is only a case of fighting with pain by using a sublethal weapon.

Regardless of whether this case involves torture, it shows something important: For at least some (and possibly all) cases that satisfy the preceding conceptions of torture we have considered (such as pain and suffering inflicted on a captive *after* he has set and directed a bomb to a location where it will kill someone to get him to stop it from killing his intended victim), we can imagine a hypothetical case in which someone is in the midst of actively threatening his victim, and the same pain or suffering would be imposed on him during his act. This could be done when he is not in custody or under physical control by public officials for some of the same specific purposes (e.g., getting information, getting him to act) with the same general purpose of saving a victim he threatens.

In the documents discussed, conduct characterized as torture in addition to imposing pain involves imposing prolonged standing or stress positions, sleep deprivation, denial of medical treatment, food deprivation, or exposure to excessive auditory stimulation.[10] We could imagine variants of the Bomb Threat Case involving each or all of these means applied to someone during his threatening act for purposes of saving his victim. Because inflicting severe suffering by any of these means on someone during his act may not be considered torture according to at least some of those documents' conceptions of torture, let us call doing this "torture*" by contrast to "torture." Here are two important questions:

*Question 1*: Is torturing* A in the Bomb Threat Case, in any or all of its variants involving the (a)–(e) methods with the purposes I have described, morally permissible to prevent his harming B?

*Question 2*: Suppose such torture* of A is permissible. Now imagine Bomb Threat Post-Act Case (which is also a Rescue Type Case of a known victim): It is known that the bomb was already set and directed by A and is about to kill B. In an ordinary sense of action (which does not include A's merely refraining from stopping his bomb), it is post-A's act.[11] We can imagine two further variants of this case. In Variant (1), A is not in custody but police can observe him from a distance near his bomb. He presents no threat to others since he will soon be captured but before then B stands to die from the bomb. By means of a mechanical device from a distance, police can impose the same pain and suffering as in the Bomb Threat Case. In Variant (2), A is in custody. In both variants officials (like police) are able to impose the same pain and suffering as in the Bomb Threat Case when it is necessary and sufficient to save B from A's bomb. Some of the ways in which this is done are analogous to what is done in the Bomb Threat Case, but they cannot involve stopping his act since it is already over. They might involve getting him to decide to stop the bomb, or give information to stop it, or inadvertently reveal information needed for others to stop the bomb (analogous to [b], [c], or [d]), or make movements or sounds needed to drop a protective screen around B (analogous to [e]). A is defenseless against the pain and suffering in that he is susceptible to it and cannot retaliate. One or both of the post-act variant cases do seem to involve torture as understood by the legal statutes. Since it was permissible to torture* A in the Bomb Threat Case (the presupposition of asking Question 2), is it morally permissible to torture him in these cases? Figuring out the answers to both Questions 1 and 2 is what I call the Torture Puzzle.

In asking and answering Questions 1 and 2 (and thus dealing with the Torture Puzzle), we should be concerned with whether, in virtue of their inherent properties and independent of considering further societal consequences or a moral obligation to obey any existing laws, torture* and torture in our imagined cases are morally permissible. To do this we could imagine that the public officials in our example are dealing with a unique situation not already covered by legal rules and that will not set a legal precedent for any future situation.[12] Hence, this is a nonconsequentialist moral inquiry. Furthermore, in deciding on moral permissibility we shall focus on whether we would mistreat the person tortured* or tortured (a victim-focused approach); this is in part because it is unclear that we would morally mistreat ourselves (an agent-focused approach) in torturing* or torturing if we are not doing something wrong to someone else to begin with. (However, we shall reconsider this issue briefly in Section 4. A later.)

The general argumentative strategy is to consider a case involving torture* that is in some ways similar to a case of torture and see whether conclusions about it should imply similar conclusions in a torture case. This is an instance of analogical reasoning in which we consider a (possibly) less controversial case in order to help us decide about a more controversial one.[13] I am considering imaginary not "real-life" examples of torture* and torture because real-life cases are often very complicated and so make it harder to locate what specific factors could make actions permissible or impermissible. One may attribute the impermissibility of torture to a factor that in a real-life case always accompanies the factor that actually makes torture impermissible, and it is only in a hypothetical case that one can separate the two factors. (However, this also means that getting the right answer to what makes torture impermissible by using hypothetical cases may not lead us to alter any judgments about its impermissibility in real-life cases; it just helps us give the right reason for the same judgment.) Real-life cases may also involve the most extreme versions of torture and so don't help us decide about less extreme versions.

What if, given the specific content I have assigned to torture* in my discussion, the answer to Question 1 was "no"? Then we could revise the content of torture* and ask the two questions again. The aim is to see if there is a least bad type of treatment that would still be considered torture* and torture and yet yields "yes" answers to Questions 1 and 2. If there is, we would know that not all torture is morally impermissible. If initial answers were "yes", we could test to see if more severe forms of torture* and torture could be morally permissible.

It is a mistake to think we can avoid the normative issue of whether torture is always impermissible by defining it as morally impermissible as a conceptual matter. This might be like saying something cannot be a killing unless it is morally impermissible, which would imply that there could be no killings in self-defense when the self-defensive acts were permissible. Might we treat "torture" the way we treat "murder" if the latter is defined as impermissible killing? But then we would still have to decide what ways of treating persons have the descriptive properties of torture that ground its always being impermissible and what ways of treating persons have descriptive properties (close to those of torture) that do not ground a judgment of torture because those ways of treating persons are not always impermissible. This would be another way to pursue the normative issue. I will pursue the normative issue by taking "torture" to be a descriptive term that doesn't conceptually imply that torture is always impermissible and then consider whether torture is always impermissible as a normative issue separate from the conceptual issue.

## 2. Normative Issues in Rescue Cases

A. With respect to Question 1, intuitively it does seem permissible to engage in at least some torture* against A by methods (a), (d), and (e[i]), which bypass his will. It would even be permissible to intentionally kill him if this were necessary and sufficient to save his victim. Indeed, it seems permissible to do these things to him not because we override for some important purpose his moral rights not to be killed or tortured* but because given what he is trying to do either these rights by their nature do not cover him or he has forfeited some of them relative to preventing the harm to his victim.[14] Perhaps we might sometimes permissibly override the rights of a morally innocent, nonthreatening person who fully retains his rights. (The sort of Dostoevskian Case that Danto imagines, discussed in Chapter 12, would involve overriding a right.) But we may owe him some compensation for doing this not owed to A since we infringe the innocent person's right albeit permissibly. This is an indication that A has no right not to be harmed in the circumstances when he is harmed to protect his potential victim (I discuss overriding further later on in Section 4.)

Being tortured* seems better for A than being killed. However, I believe we should not determine whether this is so simply by considering A's forthcoming life overall if he is not killed but tortured* and seeing if the negative period for him of torture* is less than the good for him in living on. This is because it would sometimes not be unreasonable, out of concern for one's well-being, to refuse to go through a period of life that is bad enough even though it is the only way to get a period of life whose good outweighs the bad.[15] This could also make it not unreasonable for others to refuse to impose such a bad period on someone for the sake of not imposing death. Nevertheless, some of what can be described as torture* (such as the hour of shocking that is done in our case) falls outside the class of things it would not be unreasonable for reasons of one's well-being to refuse to go through for the sake of avoiding immediate death and living on for a significant time. Furthermore, we can assume that both such torture* and being killed when imposed on him by others are contrary to A's will. (Hence, it is not that we substitute something that is better for the person contrary to his will when what is worse for him is something he chooses for himself.)

Perhaps it still could be wrong to torture* rather than kill A if doing so was more disrespectful of A than killing him. It is for this reason, I think, that some might object to using methods (b), (c), and (e[ii]) in torture*, which affect someone's will in getting him to do something, even if this does not involve breaking his will but just getting him to make a prudential decision to avoid pain by protecting B. I agree that these methods are morally different from bypassing someone's will by shocking to interfere with his act or causing involuntary motions (such as bring down the protective screen in [e(i)]). But what should we do if our only alternatives were to kill A or else use methods (b), (c), or (e[ii]) in torture* given the unalterable aim of saving B? I do not think we should choose to kill A. This means that given the unalterable aim of saving B, it is not absolutely impermissible to use methods (b), (c), or (e[ii]) on him. Furthermore, it is commonly thought to be morally permissible for police to threaten to kill someone like A while he threatens B in order to coerce him into stopping his attack. This is preferable to merely killing him right away even though it is an attempt to affect his will. It is also commonly thought to be morally permissible for police to use nonlethal physical force on someone like A to get him to decide to drop his weapon (e.g., painfully squeezing his fingers until he decides to drop his weapon). Doing this might also be preferable to using greater physical force to simply take away his weapon from him. Ruling out coercion, intimidation, and physical force in order to affect someone's will would rule out such morally permissible police action.[16]

To make the issue of disrespect clearer, consider another case: An aggressor is threatening to kill someone. Police can stop her in only two ways. One is to kill her from a distance. The second involves getting the aggressor away from her victim and closer to where she can be captured without injuring her. The only way to do this involves shouting insulting remarks at the aggressor so that she becomes justifiably angry and moves toward attacking the insulter instead of her original victim. Arguably, the second way to save her victim is more disrespectful of the aggressor than simply killing her even though it does not greatly reduce her well-being. It is manipulative and makes use of her reasonable susceptibilities, in addition to involving insulting verbal content. Yet, I suggest, it is morally permissible because not killing her takes priority over not being disrespectful, given the unalterable aim of saving her victim. I think the same could be true in the Bomb Threat Case were it true that torture* using methods (b), (c), and (e[ii]) is more disrespectful than the only alternative of killing. However, it is possible that A's right to be treated respectfully is always fully in force and cannot be forfeited (unlike other rights) but only overridden. Hence, something like requesting forgiveness would not be inappropriate even if it were for his own good that we treat him in ways (b), (c), and (e[ii]) rather than killing him given the unalterable aim of saving his victim.

Suppose we are physically unable to kill A, so torturing* him does not improve on a fate he would otherwise have actually suffered. Torturing* A by methods (a), (d), or (e[i]) still seems proportionate to preventing the harm he will otherwise do to B and so permissible. Torturing* A in these ways is permissible because he is responsible for causing the large threat to B and so is liable to being tortured* by others to avert that threat. (In Chapter 12 I referred to this as the Responsibility Argument.) If someone must suffer a loss, it should be A, not B. Indeed, A even seems to owe it to his victim to bear the costs involved in any of (a), (d), or (e[i]) rather than harm him.[17]

What about method (b), (c), or (e[ii])? Suppose that for his own sake we could permissibly do any of them to A rather than kill him but now we are unable to kill him. Would he also have a better fate if he were simply prevented from killing B? Certainly yes if he were going to be subsequently executed for doing so. But what if being tortured* is better for him only in the sense of his having lived a better life in which he does not do a seriously morally wrong act? Even if this case should emphasize saving B rather than helping A have a better life, it could still be true that we can achieve our goal of helping B because we are also doing what makes even A's life better. My own view is that even if (b), (c), or (e[ii]) were simply an infringement of A's right to be treated respectfully with no benefit for him, it is permissible to do any of them in order to prevent him from killing B. If we could permissibly use (b), (c), or (e[ii]) on him for his own good (e.g., rather than kill him), his special responsibility not to reduce the good of his victim (by killing him) could also justify us in using (b), (c), or (e[ii]) on him.[18] Similarly, we might permissibly shout insulting remarks if this will get him away from killing B even though we are unable to physically harm A as an alternative way to stop his attack on B. Suppose (b), (c), or (e[ii]) were permissible infringements of respectful treatment to which he still had a right, he might be owed an apology, unlike what is true of using methods (a), (d), or (e[i]).

B. To consider Question 2, recall that we know with certainty that A has activated and directed the bomb that would kill B and he need not actively do anything further to kill B. Since A is no longer engaged in harmful actions, Question 2 is about torture even if Question 1 is not about torture. To save B, officials must torture A (shock him painfully for an hour) either to get him to give or to inadvertently drop information to stop the bomb, or to make him stop it himself, or to make uncontrollable movements or take deliberate action to trigger a device (like an impenetrable screen) that will protect B against the bomb's effects. Does our answer to Question 1 and the way of reaching it lead us to a conclusion about Question 2?

Consider Variant 1 of the Bomb Threat Post-Act Case (introduced earlier) in which A has not yet been captured. Suppose torturing* A would have been permissible only because it is better for A than permissibly killing A, but killing A post-act is impermissible even to stop harm to B. Then the permissibility of torturing* would not bear on the permissibility of torturing A.[19] However, torture* seemed permissible even if it were physically impossible to kill A and so torturing* would not substitute for killing. If this is so, then even if killing A post-act were impermissible, this would not rule out torturing him in the ways described in our case to save B.

It might be argued that torturing A in these ways after his act in Variant 1 is permissible because A is deliberately refraining from doing what could stop the bomb from going off. It has been noted that Shue's position implies that torture would be impermissible if A were defenseless and not a threat. In Variant 1 he is not a threat despite not being under physical control but he may not be defenseless if he could avoid torture by stopping the bomb or giving information to do so. Because A is not under control and not defenseless, perhaps Shue would agree that it is permissible to torture A if doing this would cause him to either fall on the bomb switch, thereby stopping the bomb, or fall on a switch that sets off the protective shield. In Sussman's view, as we saw, A's refraining from stopping the bomb constitutes his continuing to be a threat and so on this ground Sussman might also justify torture (as we, not he, have characterized it) to stop the bomb or protect B with the screen in Variant 1.

However, there could be cases in which A was not refraining from stopping his bomb in Variant 1. For example, he might become paralyzed after setting the bomb or lack information that only his co-conspirator has about how to stop the bomb or protect B from its effects. Then on Shue's view A would be defenseless and on Sussman's view he would not be continuing to present a threat. Nevertheless, the question could still arise whether torturing A in the same way as torturing* when torturing would cause involuntary movements from A that stopped the bomb or dropped the shield is permissible due to A's responsibility for the threat to B and what A owes (or may be done to him) on account of this. The question could also arise as to whether shocking A for an hour was permissible to elicit responses from his co-conspirator who had knowledge of defusing the bomb. (A comparable question could have arisen with torture* if during their joint act, torture* of A would not stop A's act or the bomb's effect but it would stop his co-conspirator's act and that was sufficient to stop the bomb's being directed.)

If permissible torturing* had implications for permissible torturing in our cases, should permissible killing during A's act have implications for permissible killing of A post-act in Variant 1 for some of the same purposes? Furthermore, suppose mildly tasing A for only a minute during his act is not torturing* and is permissible to get A to stop his threat to B by any or all of the causal routes described in (a)–(e). If permissible torturing* had implications for permissible torture in Variant 1, then should permissible tasing of A during his act have implications for permissible tasing of him post-act in Variant 1 if this is the only way to save B? (Neither of these questions is Question 2 but related to it.)

On the one hand, it seems that if some of what may permissibly be done to A during his act has straightforward implications for the post-act case in Variant 1, the permissibility of intrusions greater than torture* (e.g., death) and also less than torture* (tasing) should have implications for the permissibility of these after A has acted in Variant 1. On the other hand, if such nontorture acts would be impermissible post-act, even though their counterparts would be permissible during A's act, then this implies that deliberate harmful intrusion upon someone's body (or in controlling his mind) post-act is morally problematic whether or not the intrusion is torture. If post-act tasing and killing were morally impermissible (as they are currently viewed), this suggests that the focus on torture per se might be misleading. There seems to be a broader issue of the relation between violability in general of the agent during his act and after it even in Variant 1.

C. Our analysis so far suggests two new questions 3 and 4 that may help us answer Question 2 about Variant 1 (and also eventually about Variant 2). Whereas our discussion in Section B focused on possible reasons torture is no different from torture*, these new questions focus on locating differences between them. Trying to find reasons that torture* and torture are either morally alike or morally different are both part of what I have called the Torture Puzzle.

Question 3: Are there morally significant differences between our torture* and torture cases that make imposing this harm (and others) on perpetrators impermissible post-act although it is permissible during their action?

Question 4: Could these differences, if any, be consistent with the permissibility of some types of post-act harm but not other types?

One might try to justify an asymmetry between harm during- and post-act in this way: The types of threats involved in permissible torture* would themselves be ways to stop the threat if they didn't succeed in getting A to stop the threat to B. For example, killing A would stop his threat to B and so the threat to kill A (considered a form of mental torture*) involves an actual alternative that could be used to stop the threat to B even if the threat to A doesn't succeed. But many of the things involved in torture (i.e., post act) would not succeed in eliminating the threat independent of their role in getting A to stop the threat. For example, killing A wouldn't stop the threat to B if the threat of killing A (considered a form of mental torture) did not succeed. This proposal for justifying an asymmetry doesn't succeed. Here is why. First, we can imagine cases in which permissible torture*, such as prolonged painful twisting of A's leg, would not itself succeed in stopping the bomb threat to B if it didn't succeed in prompting an act from A. So the threat to twist A's leg would not involve threatening to do what is an alternative way of stopping his threat to B. Second, killing A post act could stop the threat to B if the threat of killing A (said to be a form of torture) didn't succeed. This is so, for example, if his dead body would fall on the switch that turns off the bomb. There could also be a case in which shocking A would elicit movements from him that stop his bomb, so repeatedly threatening to shock him (which could be considered a form of mental torture) would also involve threatening a form of torture (shocking) that is an alternative way of stopping his threat if he doesn't stop it.

A related proposal for an asymmetry between during- and post-act is that presenting a threat of death to A during his act threatens to do something to him that it is actually permissible to do (kill him) to stop his attack on B. But presenting a threat of death to A post-act to get him to defuse his bomb threatens to do something to him that we would not actually do because it is (assumed to be) morally impermissible to do it. Hence, it is only in the post-act case that we are telling a lie to A. However, it is hard to believe that what makes it wrong to threaten death in this case is that it involves telling a lie when other sorts of lies committed by officials would be morally permitted to get A to stop his bomb (e.g., that he will receive a reward). This account also assumes something that itself has to be defended, that killing would not be permissible post-act when it is permissible during the act.

Here is another way of attempting to justify an asymmetry between torture* and torture: Torture* is permissible because it involves stopping or getting A to stop his act. Torture is impermissible because it cannot stop or make A stop his act, which has already occurred. A related proposal is that torture* is permissible because it does not involve harmfully using A as a mere means to opportunistically help B; instead, it involves harmfully using A to eliminate A's own threatening act.[20] The problem with these proposals is that, as we've already seen, torture* seemed to be permissible if it did not stop or get A to stop his act and instead used pain to A as a mere means to protect B by getting a screen to drop around him. When we do this, we harmfully use A as he acts without eliminating his act to help B relative to his prospect of death as A acts. So this seems to be a crucial case.

However, even if torture* in this case benefits B, it only puts him in the condition he would have been in if A had not been present at the time we torture* him. This is because A's absence at that time would have eliminated the threat to B in our case; hence, we do not require A' s involvement (his absence would do as well) in order to help B.[21] By contrast, in Bomb Threat Post-Act Cases torturing A to drop a screen around B uses A to provide a benefit that puts B in a better condition than he would be in if A were not involved, given that B would not survive if A were not still present after setting and directing the bomb so that we could harm him.[22] This seems to make torturing A by contrast to torturing* A purely opportunistic as we require his involvement to help B. But is this difference morally significant if torturing A only puts B in the condition he would have been in if A had not presented his threat at all? Furthermore, suppose (in a hyper-unrealistic hypothetical) that while A is present at the time officials torture him to drop the screen had he been elsewhere, he would have inadvertently done something that dropped the screen long distance. Then torturing A would not put B in a better condition than he would have been in had A not been present for us to torture him. Could this difference alone make torturing A to drop the screen permissible when it would not be otherwise? I don't see why it should.

Some may think that whether we interfere with an act (as might occur in torture*) is important because it need not involve us making someone suffer in order to affect his will, trying to get him to do something. When there is no act with which to interfere, it may be thought that we have no alternative but to cause suffering in order to affect someone's will (e.g., get him to decide to do something). One problem with this view is that we can harm someone after his act to make him fall on a switch that stops the bomb or causes his involuntary movements that triggers the protective shield, bypassing his will. In addition, as we have seen, during-act torture* (e.g., painful twisting of limbs or death threats) can also be done to affect someone's will and yet that seems permissible. Suppose one refuses to permit torture in order to affect someone's will post-act in Variant 1 yet thinks torture* using methods (b), (c), or (e[ii]) involves *permissibly* affecting someone's will in the Bomb Threat Case (e.g., to get A to stop directing the bomb). Then we will need another explanation of the during- and post-act moral difference.

Another proposed answer to Question 3 is that torture involves doing something to A to aid B, whereas torture* involves preventing A from harming B. Many think that one can be required to bear greater costs to avoid harming someone than one must bear to aid someone. In response, it could be noted that the moral difference between preventing harm and providing aid collapses in some cases. We have already seen that is true when torture* is required not to stop a harmful act but to provide a screen to protect B from harm. Further, if someone has begun a process that will harm another, in virtue of starting the threat and not saving his victim from it, he will wind up harming someone rather than merely not aiding him. Hence, arguably, the costs he morally must bear to save someone from his harmful act are the same as he is required to bear not to act. Even if saving the victim requires the agent to bear losses beyond those he has a duty to impose upon himself, he may still be liable to others imposing the greater loss on him.

However, sometimes the losses to which one is liable even during a harmful act to save one's victim seem to vary depending on factors such as one's location. Consider a driver who through no fault or negligence is inadvertently speeding up his car when he thinks he is braking. His car careers toward a pedestrian. Suppose the only way to save the pedestrian is for the police to shoot the driver, which will cause a screen to drop and shield the pedestrian. Arguably, the driver may be shot, especially if the harm to him would be far less than the harm that would come to his victim if nothing is done. But suppose the driver is thrown from the car as it continues speeding toward the pedestrian due to what the driver has already done. It seems impermissible for police to shoot him on the sidelines even if the lesser harm to him would drop a screen between his car and the pedestrian.[23] (Call these the Car Cases.)

The Car Cases are importantly different from the Bomb Threat Cases. The driver, although responsible for starting the car, is not at fault, whereas A is. Still, suppose there is a morally relevant difference between harming the driver when he is part of the threat and harming him when he is on the sideline. Then something like that difference, between engaging in as opposed to having engaged in a threatening act, might exist in the Bomb Threat Cases. This is so despite A's being at fault for the threatening act and even subsequently refusing to voluntarily, at low cost to him, interfere with the harm. In both Bomb Threat Cases, A's culpability might discount the force of the difference noted in the Car Cases, but it could still account for some variation in what may be done to A during his act and post-act. This sort of account would imply an answer to Question 4: Some imposition on A's body could be morally permissible post-act—this might include some torture (given that an hour of pain by shocking or being in a stress position for many hours is considered torture)—but not the full range that was permissible during his act.

Caspar Hare, for one, denies that harming a villain post-act is morally different from harming him during his act.[24] He imagines that a villain directed a trolley toward several people who will die if it hits them. The only way to save them is to topple the villain from the bridge where he stands so that he lands in front of the trolley, stopping it but being killed by it. We might even (as Hare suggests) imagine that we have to hold the villain on the tracks to ensure he is hit and killed for the five to be saved. He thinks that doing these things would be morally permissible (presumably by officials or bystanders).

In Hare's case, which also involves the villain not in custody, I believe the person responsible for the threat is post-act made to be a shield from that threat for those he threatened. A similar arrangement would occur in the Bomb Threat Post-Act Case Variant 1 if officials could move A so that he blocks his bomb's effect on B and is killed (or suffers in ways comparable to torture). (Call this the Bomb Threat Post-Act Shield Case.) In both this case and Hare's, the villain is moved against his will (e.g., the trolley or bomb is not merely redirected away from his victim and to him) and he is the victim of his own threat. Using the villain as a shield does seem morally permissible in both cases.

However, would matters differ morally if Hare's villain had to be thrown in front of a different moving trolley from the one he started in order to save his victims (as Hare further imagines)? Would matters differ morally if the villain had to be shot to stop the trolley he started so that in this particular way we create a different threat to him from the one he started? It is such cases that should be compared with Bomb Threat Post-Act Case Variant 1 since in that case officials do use a different threat to harm A than the one he created to B.

D. Now consider Variant 2 of the Bomb Threat Post-Act Case. Everything is the same as in Variant 1 except that A is in custody (either captured or surrendered) and under control. Other officials in addition to police bear responsibility for his condition. Does this imply that it is morally impermissible to torture him in any of the ways it would have been permissible to torture* him or torture him in Variant 1 in order to save B from A's bomb, which is about to go off? To avoid the issue of violating legal rules already set up for such situations, continue to imagine there are as yet no rules for a first-time situation. We are considering the issue only as a matter of noninstitutional morality.

Suppose those who hold someone in custody had a moral responsibility to maintain his welfare at a "normal" level until he is put on trial. Then it would be impermissible to redirect A's bomb away from B when it is foreseen it will harm A in his place of custody even if A had previously set the bomb to harm B in the very place A knew he would be held in custody (believing he would there be immune to harm). But I think redirection would be morally permissible if it were necessary and sufficient to save B. Furthermore, it also seems morally permissible to move A while in custody between his bomb and B so that he is made into a shield for B against A's own threat, especially if the harm would be no greater than what is involved in torture*. Hence, from a moral point of view, being in custody per se should not ensure someone's not being harmed to protect his victim. If this is so, it is not clear why being in custody and under the control of authorities should distinguish what may permissibly be done to A in Variant 2 of the Bomb Threat Post-Act Case from what may be done to him in Variant 1. (Suppose someone were in custody and under control of authorities after having been tried and found guilty for setting and directing the bomb to B but [unrealistically] before B was killed. This would seem to make it even easier to justify harming him to save B than in Variant 1.)

Ensuring good treatment in custody may be a way of securing the surrender of wrongdoers who might otherwise remain free to harm others. This is a reason not to harm in custody at least those who surrender even if some torture might be permissible outside of custody. However, this is not the sort of moral reason inherent to harming in custody with which our inquiry is concerned. It is a consequentialist consideration, since it points to a further morally significant bad effect of torturing in custody (namely wrongdoers not being willing to surrender).

E. Regardless of the answers to Questions 1–4, our discussion shows that the issues crucial to whether torture is permissible may often differ from what is commonly thought. For example, it is commonly thought that it is crucial that in torture cases (a) a type of harm is to be done to someone that should never be done to anyone, at least without his consent; (b) this harm is morally distinctive in terms of the strength of the objection it merits relative to other types of harm that do not involve torture; and (c) many lives of potential victims are at stake. But in our cases, none of these issues is crucial. With regard to (a), torture harms the subject in the same way and without his consent as does torture*, and yet torture* is sometimes permissible. So (a) alone cannot explain the impermissibility of torture. With regard to (b), objectors to some types of torture involved in our Bomb Threat Cases would probably also object to painlessly killing someone, painlessly removing a pellet with information on defusing the bomb from his ear when this causes deafness, or briefly tasing to elicit nonvoluntary information- revealing movements all post-act. Suppose the objections merited by these nontorture post-act bodily invasions were at least as strong as objections merited by the types of torture that do not involve affecting someone's will. Then (b) would not be a crucial reason for the impermissibility of some types of torture per se. Suppose we do not unintuitively narrow the notion of torture to its worst or will-affecting forms, and yet still conceptually distinguish torture from other harms (e.g., brief tasing). We may find that prohibitions on each of these impositions post-act to prevent harm to victims may have to be rethought. With regard to (c), in our Bomb Threat Case it would have been permissible to torture* the perpetrator to save only one victim. If torture were no less permissible than torture*, saving even one victim from his perpetrator could justify some torture. Then (c) would not be necessary for torture to be permissible. Rather, in our cases what seems crucial is (1) moral responsibility for the impermissible threat by the agent who would be tortured* or tortured, (2) required use of the torture* or torture to stop the harm to his victim, (3) the proportionality of the torture* or torture to the harm to be stopped, (4) (possibly) whether the harm in torture* or torture is intended to affect someone's will or bypasses it, and (5) (possibly) whether harm is imposed during an agent's act (torture*) or after the agent's act (torture). When these factors are relevant to deciding whether and why there is a difference between torture* and torture, considering them is an attempt to answer the Torture Puzzle.

F. Another normative issue is how the moral status of torture should affect its legal status. A law would cover many possible cases of torture, not just one unique case such as we considered in trying to decide about torture's inherent moral status. Some think that torture should always be legally prohibited because it is always inherently morally wrong.[25] However, this could not be a sound argument for outlawing all forms of torture if torture were not inherently morally wrong in some of our cases. A different argument would be needed (such as I suggested for not torturing in custody in order to encourage surrenders).

Some think that legalizing any type of torture would lead to an uncontrollable "culture of torture" because regulation would be difficult and there would be a slippery slope to instances of torture that are in themselves morally wrong.[26] This argument may be correct, but it does not affect the possibility that not all cases of torture are inherently morally wrong. Furthermore, does this argument also apply to torture*? For example, when a perpetrator is in the act (or engaging in the process that results in the act) of severely harming or killing someone else, should it be illegal for officials to deprive the perpetrator of food and sleep for many hours, shocking him for an hour, or keeping him in stress positions, and the like if doing these things are the only way to stop or get him (in a will-affecting way) to stop harm to his victim(s)? If not, then we need to know why we think that torture* can be regulated so that a culture of torture* does not develop while denying the same with respect to torture for the purpose of preventing harm to a perpetrator's victims.

Law enforcement officials commonly shoot at or physically coerce people into dropping their weapons. This has sometimes resulted, or threatened to result, in a culture of police brutality. Yet the answer to this is commonly thought to be regulation (or elimination of some types) of police violence in defense or protection of others—not its complete elimination. Might we apply the same logic to post-act harms done for the same purpose? For example, suppose police are required to wear cameras to monitor their harmful behavior during a perpetrator's act when their harm aims to stop harm to his victim. Then could their post-act physical harm for the same purpose be similarly monitored?

G. Our hypothetical cases of torture* and torture so far have involved officials being certain of who the perpetrator is, what he would deliberately do, and what harm to his victim will ensue if nothing is done. It was also certain that torturing or torturing* him was necessary and sufficient (given other innocent things that may be done) to stop the imminent harm to his victim. We could vary these conditions in several ways (holding constant from our earlier cases what torture* and torture involve). Here are some examples.

(i) Suppose officials remain certain of who the culpable perpetrator is and what will happen if they do not intervene. They know torture (which occurs post-act) is necessary to stop the harm to his victim, but they do not know that it will actually save her. For example, any information revealed by shocks may come too late. Presumably, it would be permissible to torture* or otherwise harm (to the limits we have imagined) such a perpetrator during his act even if officials were not certain that this would stop harm to his victim but they thought it was sufficiently likely to do so. It is not clear how low the probabilities of success must be for it to become impermissible to torture* or otherwise harm the active perpetrator in this way; at minimum these things should not be done if it is certain no good for the victim will come of it.[27] If torture and torture* were equally permissible, the same would hold for torture. Hence, suppose it is certain who the culpable perpetrator is, that he will kill his victim if officials do not intervene, and his being tortured is necessary to save his victim. Then that torturing the perpetrator is not very effective at stopping the harm (which is often pointed to in arguing against torture) may not rule out its permissibility if there is a sufficient chance that it will avert the perpetrator's harm and no other more effective means is available.

(ii) What if we are not sure that torture* of a known culpable perpetrator is necessary to prevent the harm? If torture* is more harmful and disrespectful than some other mechanisms, they should be used instead of torture* when the probability of saving the victim is the same (or increases). If torture* had implications for torture, the same would be true of torture. But this suggests that we know torture* or torture is not necessary. If we are actually unsure and can try the other mechanisms without foregoing the chance to do what turns out to be necessary, we should try the other mechanisms first. It would be very important to know the probability of its being necessary to torture* or torture if trying alternatives meant we would have to forego torture* or torture.

What if the fruition of a harmful act is not imminent? Does this mean torture* would not be necessary? Not if the harm will definitely come about in the further future (e.g., a year) unless we torture* or torture now in order to avert that later harm. If imminence per se is important only because it correlates with necessity of acting (because delay eliminates opportunity to prevent harm), then we should sometimes deal with imminent and more remote threats similarly.[28]

(iii) What if officials are not certain that the person they would torture* or torture is an agent whose deliberate actions will kill someone? It might nevertheless be reasonable for them to believe that they are dealing with such actions relative to evidence they have and that is all the evidence it is reasonable to require them to have. For example, they might not be certain that the agent pointing a gun at someone has a real (rather than a toy) gun or that he is able to hit his target. But if it would be farfetched to doubt the evidence of danger, it might be permissible to torture* the agent to stop or get him to stop what is reasonably believed to be his harmful act. If torture* has implications for the permissibility of torture, torture to stop harm might be permissible even if it turned out that, contrary to grounds for reasonable belief, the person tortured did not present a threat.[29]

## 3. Normative Issues in Prevention Cases

In our Bomb Threat Cases so far discussed there is an identifiable person B who will definitely be harmed if we do not rescue him. I called these Rescue Type Cases. However, many cases in which torture of a perpetrator can be imagined to be necessary and useful to save his victim are cases in which harm will definitely come to someone if we do not torture, but at the time we would need to torture* or torture a perpetrator the person whom the perpetrator will harm is one among many, each of whom has only a small risk of being harmed by the perpetrator. Call these Prevention Type Cases (said to involve "statistical deaths"). For example, suppose a terrorist puts a bomb somewhere in a large city. It has only a very small chance of killing any given person in the city but given the large number of people in the city it is certain that if nothing is done someone will be killed by the perpetrator's bomb (City Case). In such a case, we need to *prevent* there being someone who will be threatened whom we will not be able to rescue once the bomb is about to kill him. *If* it were permissible to torture* or torture a perpetrator in our earlier rescue cases, would this imply that it is permissible to torture* or torture (holding constant with our earlier cases what doing this involves) a perpetrator in prevention cases at a time when the risk to any person of being the victim is small but we know someone will die if we do not intervene?

Some think that Rescue Type Cases and Prevention Type Cases are not morally equivalent because we have a stronger duty to protect someone whom we know is certain to die than to protect someone who, as far as we know at the time we must act, has only a small chance of being the one person who will die. This view emphasizes that what is morally important is what we owe to each person as an individual (not aggregated with others) given her known risk of dying. (As such, this view might be associated with a certain sort of contractualist moral theory and theories that emphasize distributing rather than concentrating risk.[30]) However, some also think that it is compatible with this view to weigh the number who would certainly die in deciding what to do if many people will die in the group whose members each have only a small chance of dying. There being a moral difference between rescue and prevention cases might imply that even if torture* and torture of a perpetrator were permissible when there is someone (or many) needing to be rescued, it might not be permissible to do the same to prevent comparable harm certainly befalling even somewhat more people in Prevention Type Cases.

To decide if the difference between rescue and prevention cases bears on the permissibility of torture* and torture in cases involving a deliberate wrongdoer, recall that what distinguished the types was a difference in the probability of harm to any given innocent person at the time when we would have to torture* or torture the wrongdoer. So consider the Old Gun Case in which a villain deliberately aims at someone a very old gun that is known to have only a small chance of killing anyone.[31] This is like a rescue case insofar as there is an identifiable potential victim. However, he has the same small risk of dying that each person in a prevention case has, although, unlike the prevention cases that I have imagined, there is a strong possibility that no one will die from the gun going off. Because this case involves someone who deliberately imposes a risk of death on someone else, I believe it might be permissible to torture* the threatener if this were necessary and useful to eliminate any possibility of the gun killing his victim. Then why should not torture* also be permissible in prevention cases like the City Case where there is the same small risk of death to each of many people, especially if someone (or several) of the many will certainly be killed? Suppose the permissibility of torture* bears on the permissibility of at least some types of torture. Then torturing a perpetrator who has already finished setting up a threat that will go off in order to prevent the harm to victim(s) in a prevention case might be morally permissible.

In sum, perhaps one should be careful in moving directly from considering torture* and torture in rescue cases like the Bomb Threat cases to considering the use of these means in prevention cases like City.[32] Nevertheless, if a perpetrator's wrongdoing causes a threat in prevention cases from which someone is certain to die, then the significance of the rescue/prevention difference to the permissibility of torture* or torture may be reduced.

## 4. Normative Issues in Other Types of Cases (Including Punishment)

There could be other types of people whose being tortured could save lives in addition to a perpetrator whose being tortured will save his own victim from the harm he would impose. Assume (only for the sake of argument) that in the latter type of case (which we have been discussing) some torture of types (a)–(e) could be morally permissible. Then we should decide about the moral permissibility of torturing in the same way these other types of people. Consider six categories:

A. Innocent, nonthreatening people who would not soon die anyway might be useful in preventing a perpetrator's harm (e.g., because if they are tortured a perpetrator will give information needed to save his victim). Prima facie, such people are not liable to being tortured to save victims whom they would not have a duty to rescue at the cost of undergoing torture. Hence, one should place greater weight on not torturing such an innocent, nonthreatening person to get a perpetrator to give information than on rescuing the perpetrator's innocent victims. The inviolability of the innocent, nonthreatening person stands in the way of his being used to save other victims even from acts seriously disrespectful of their inviolability.[33] Suppose someone is only withholding information it would be easy to give that would save a victim. Arguably, he is doing something morally wrong and so is not completely innocent. His failing in the duty to aid at low cost might make him liable to having greater costs imposed on him to save others. Nevertheless, if there is a moral distinction between killing people and even wrongly letting a perpetrator's victims die, this person may not be committing a serious enough wrong for him to be liable to being tortured to save others.

However, suppose the number of people that could be saved grows to millions (e.g., stopping a nuclear bomb that will explode in a large city) but only if information needed to stop a threat is obtained from an innocent person (safely not in that city). Presumably if the cost were low, the person would have a duty to provide the information but suppose he refuses to do so because he is threatened with death. Would it be permissible to use torture that either bypasses or affects his will to get the information? Such a scenario is like Danto's considered in Chapter 12 and the ticking time bomb cases involving the possible deaths of millions (though they involve torture of a perpetrator). According to what is known as threshold deontology, the inviolability of even an innocent, nonthreatening person who will not soon die anyway can reach its limit when there are extraordinary bad consequences of not harming him.[34] One interpretation of this claim is that above the threshold the person no longer has a right not to be harmed. This should be distinguished from an alternative interpretation according to which his right can be overridden by the extraordinary bad consequences of not harming him. If either interpretation of this view were true, it might justify some type of torture of those in category (A). However, only the second interpretation leaves it open that even if harming the person to avoid extraordinary bad consequences were morally permissible and not a *violation* of rights (defined as wrong), it could still *infringe* the rights of the innocent, nonthreatening person. This is because he has not forfeited the right not to be harmed in virtue of anything he has done or become liable to harm because of any threatening role in which he finds himself. Indeed, even if overriding his right were not morally wrong, it could *wrong* the person to whom it is done. This could be shown by the fact that he would do no wrong and have a justification based on his right not to be tortured if he resists being treated in this way. (Such resistance would be wrong if he had no right beyond the threshold that could be infringed [as the first interpretation of threshold deontology implies]. Resistance could also be wrong if someone had a duty to permit the torture [e.g., so that the perpetrator will divulge information to prevent the enormous harm] or if someone had forfeited his right not to be tortured in virtue of trying to harm others.) Possibly this is a case in which an agent called on to torture this innocent person might permissibly refuse to do so even though it would be permissible and not wrong for him to do so. He might refuse because he would be doing what he knows his victim would have a moral right to resist his doing (for the reasons given) even if the victim is not able to resist.[35]

B. There are people who are suspected on statistical grounds of being involved in or knowing about plots to harm others (e.g., suspected because they are young, male, and unemployed), not because there is information relating them in particular to a threat (e.g., some eyewitnesses saw them plant a bomb). Is it any more permissible to torture such people than ordinary nonthreatening innocents to save victims just because there is a greater probability of finding among them a perpetrator or someone who knows about one? A person whom statistical evidence indicates may only know more about a threat than most innocents should be treated even less badly than those in category (A) whom we know have information they refuse to give. Hence, it is only the chance of finding (by way of torture) a perpetrator whose being tortured could help a victim that could be at issue. What if the statistical evidence was so good that it made the probability of torturing a nonperpetrator miniscule? Would this case differ morally from torturing someone whom it is not certain but only reasonable to believe is a perpetrator on the basis of eyewitnesses? It has been argued that there are important moral differences between (i) using and acting on statistical evidence about wrongdoing as opposed to (ii) using and acting on evidence that is causally generated by the wrongdoing itself (such as eyewitness evidence).[36] If these arguments are correct, they would bear on the impermissibility of torturing those in category (B).

C. There are people who belong to a group with a member known to be a guilty perpetrator. Some of these people are responsible for ideologically supporting the threatening goals of a perpetrator but not actually performing or providing material support for particular threatening acts. Is being such a group member a wrong sufficient to make one liable to being tortured to prevent the harm done by a fellow member? It is usually thought that one has a moral (and in liberal democracies a legal) right to hold and associate with others holding immoral beliefs if one does not engage in or materially support harm against others. (This may involve a moral right to do what is morally wrong.) Hence, it does not seem that a person in category (C) does what makes him especially liable to be tortured to stop someone else's harmful conduct or protect that perpetrator's victim.

D. There are people who unsuccessfully attempted to harm in the same way as a current perpetrator either that perpetrator's current target or someone else. These people did something morally impermissible—attempt to harm someone in a morally impermissible way. Suppose A attempted and failed to kill B, who will now be killed by C unless A is tortured. The following is such a case (based on Jeff McMahan's Attempter Case[37]): Aware that several villains independently plan to kill you, the police provide protection. On one occasion, a villain confronts you in an alley and fires all his bullets at you but fails to hit you. A second, independent villain is preparing to kill you from behind a narrow basement window. The police cannot accurately fire through the window; they can save you only by wounding the first villain, causing him to slump in front of the window so as to block the second villain's line of fire and stop him from shooting. Reasoning analogous to that involved in a particular theory of punishment (such as that proposed by Victor Tadros[38]) might justify using the first attempter to stop the second attack for which he is not responsible.

First, consider the reasoning applied to punishment: (i) Consider what it would be morally permissible to do to a perpetrator to stop or get him to stop harming his victim before we know his attempt at harming would fail; call this amount x. (ii) The permissible punishment for a mere attempt would be less than x (i.e., x – n). (iii) Suppose a justification for punishment (which is always post-act) were the wrongdoer's being liable for protecting his attempted victim from future attacks by deterring others from attacking him. (iv) Then a known wrongdoer might permissibly also have cost x – n imposed on him as punishment to stop, or prevent harm from, an actual ongoing attack by someone else on the same person he attempted to victimize.[39] (v) If torture fell within x – n, it could be permissible to impose it on the attempter as punishment to stop someone else's attack on the person he had attempted to victimize. If this argument were correct, it would justify some torture as punishment if undertaken to rescue certain particular people.

However, punishment is applied after a public trial in a legitimate court system. That would not yet have occurred in the Attempter Case and so it might be argued that a theory of punishment does not have implications for this case. I agree that the reasoning to justify harming A to save someone he tried to harm from a similar harm caused by C could at most be analogous to the argument we have considered for punishment. Further, if either the theory of punishment or the analogy to it here relied on is not correct, then we would not have provided a justification for torturing someone in category (D) either as or before punishment.

For the sake of argument, suppose this justification of some torture (or other post-act harm) as either punishment or for use in Attempter-like Cases succeeded. What if the person who currently needs protection from a threat is not the same person whom the past attempter had threatened? One possibility is to make use of an "exchange of debts among victims" mechanism also suggested by Tadros in his theory of punishment. That is, suppose attempter A owes x – n assistance to save person B (whom he attempted to victimize) from C's attack but C is attacking D not B. Even an innocent person like B has a duty to rescue D at small cost to himself. Hence, following Tadros, it might be suggested that B has a duty to transfer protective services A owes him to D. If such transfer were permissible, and some torture fell within x – n, then some torture of attempter A might be justified to rescue someone (such as D) whom he had never attempted to harm. An objection to this conclusion is that it is not generally true that strenuous services owed by A to B may permissibly be transferred by B to D merely because doing this is easy for B. (For example, offspring may not transfer not-needed services their parents owe them to a friend who needs the services.)

E. There are people who are now threatening, or have set up a device that now threatens, someone but whose being tortured (in one of the ways we have discussed) would be useful only in preventing threats to someone else. This category might involve a perpetrator whose own current victim can only be saved by authorities torturing another perpetrator when this second perpetrator's victim can only be saved by authorities torturing the first perpetrator. Assume for the sake of argument that a perpetrator would be liable to some torture (i.e., post-act) to save his own current victim. Then in the current case, the perpetrators would each be liable to being tortured to some degree to save those they did not threaten because this is a necessary, indirect means to each saving the person he did threaten. That is, A and C should be treated as though they had exchanged duties to their respective victims in order to ultimately fulfill duties to their respective victims. However, what if no one is able to help the first perpetrator's victim? It might be argued that this victim has a duty to transfer his right to be helped by the first perpetrator (given it does this victim no good) to the potential victim of the second perpetrator. This transfer proposal raises the same concerns voiced in regard to its use in category (D).

In discussing whether it is permissible to torture those in categories (A)–(E), we considered rescues of particular individuals. In particular, in the transfer of a protective debt from one victim to another, we considered cases in which there is a second victim who needs to be rescued from certain death. But many cases in which it would be useful to harm a wrongdoer to save people other than his victim are Prevention Type Cases. Hence, our previous discussion suggests that we should consider whether torture* or torture of those in each of the categories could be justified on the ground that lives will certainly be saved by eliminating the small chance that each of many people has of being someone who will be killed. For example, if punishment is used for deterrence, there is not usually an individual whose would-be attacker is deterred from harming him due to a transfer from one person to another of a claim to protective services from the person who is being punished. Rather, each of a great number of people is spared a small chance that he will be someone who is criminally attacked.

F. There are people from whom we seek confessions of wrongdoing. It is sometimes argued that confessions to wrongdoing elicited by torture are worthless because individuals will falsely admit to a crime merely to stop the torture. This may be true. However, suppose we knew that the innocent would never falsely confess and the guilty would always tell the truth in response to torture. There would still be reason not to torture to acquire confessions if this would result in our having tortured innocents who had a right not to be tortured. In addition, suppose only saving victims from threats could justify some torture of their perpetrators. Then unless confessions helped to do this (perhaps by leading to deserved punishment that was also necessary for deterrence that would in the future protect someone's attempted victim), even torture that got confessions only from actual perpetrators would not be justified.

In sum, in this section we have raised doubts about the moral permissibility of any type of torture in cases that do not involve a perpetrator suffering for the sake of preventing harm due to his own act to his own victim.[40]

## Notes

1. These three objections are not necessarily overlapping, as we shall see.
2. See Seamus Miller's *Terrorism and Counter-terrorism* (Oxford: Blackwell, 2009).
3. Descriptions of the CAT, the USTS, and other acts can be found in *The Report of the Constitution Project's Task Force on Detainee Treatment*, Appendix 1.
4. In his "Torture," *Philosophy & Public Affairs* 7 (1978): 124–43. I discuss Shue's views further in my *Ethics for Enemies: Terror, Torture, and War* (Oxford University Press, 2011), Chapter 1.
5. However, Shue thinks that someone who truly believes he "must" pursue his cause is psychologically incapable of giving up that cause and the information that would betray it. So he remains defenseless even when a mercenary is not defenseless. I think psychological commitment is not enough to make one defenseless in this way.
6. David Sussman, "What's Wrong with Torture," *Philosophy & Public Affairs* 3 (2004): 1–33. He rejects Shue's view that a perpetrator's commitment to his cause makes it more than one can ask that he stop refraining from ending his threat and give information that would stop his suffering from torture.
7. Note this adds the absence of consent by, and it being against the interests or goals of, the person tortured, which I noted was absent in earlier descriptions. It also implies that there could be no torture if one had requested the suffering necessary to achieve goals to which one could reasonably consent (by contrast to one's having consented to be tortured).
8. Sussman, "What's Wrong with Torture," 5–8. Given the source and the inability to corroborate independently, it seems odd to say the victim might really "know."
9. For a more complete discussion of Sussman's views, see *Ethics for Enemies*, Chapter 1 (which is also the basis for Sections 3–6 of the following discussion).
10. As described in The Report of the Constitution Project Task Force on Detainee Treatment, Appendix 1.
11. If refraining involved continuing to act, many cases that are now thought to involve torture would involve torture*. Refraining (which involves a decision to let the bombing occur) might show that the bomber's intentions have not changed (though he might refrain for other reasons). It is not clear that constancy of intention matters morally. If one would be liable to be harmed post-act were there constancy of intention, one might also be liable to be harmed to save one's victim regardless of one's current rejection of one's past wrong act of threatening.
12. This is referred to as extrainstitutional morality.
13. A famous example in philosophy is Judith Thomson's consideration of the violinist case to try to draw implications for some cases of abortion. See her "A Defense of

Abortion," *Philosophy & Public Affairs* 1 (1): 1971, 47–66. I have defended the use of analogy in my "Theory and Analogy in the Law," *Arizona State Law Review* 29 (1997): 405–26, reprinted in part in my *Bioethical Prescriptions* (New York: Oxford University Press, 2013). See also Chapter 3 in this volume.

14. A's having forfeited his right not to be harmed in order to save B is not the same as his deserving to be harmed for this purpose. If there were some harmless way to save B, that would be morally preferable. By contrast, if someone deserves to be harmed (even for a particular purpose), there is something good about his being harmed that should not be avoided.
15. I argue for this in Chapter 2 of my *Almost Over: Aging, Dying, Dead* (New York: Oxford University Press, 2020) among other places.
16. This a one reason why the CAT's condemnation of coercion and intimidation with threats of death seems too broad (given that it doesn't restrict itself to dealing with cases in which someone is in custody), unless it would include police threatening A with death to stop his directing a threat to B in the Bomb Threat Case as falling under "lawful sanction." (If so, such a threat could be legal elsewhere.)
17. I consider how someone may be liable to our imposing losses on him that he would not have to self-impose and does not owe to another in my *The Trolley Problem Mysteries* (New York: Oxford University Press, 2016) and Chapter 9 in this volume.
18. This needn't mean that whatever it is permissible to do to A against his will to avoid harming him even more could also be done to him against his will to prevent his harming B more.
19. Except possibly if killing A during his act when torture* was not physically possible was replaced with torture post-act in A's own interests, given there would still be time post-act to save B.
20. These distinctions derive from those drawn by Warren Quinn between opportunistic and eliminative agency in his "Actions, Intentions, and Consequences: The Doctrine of Double Effect," reprinted in his *Morality and Action* (Cambridge: Cambridge University Press, 1994).
21. However, that the victim's situation does not get better than if the person we need to torture were not present is consistent with agency still being opportunistic rather than eliminative, as the following case helps show: A villain threatens Joe only because he wants to impress innocent Jane standing nearby. If Jane were not there, the villain wouldn't threaten Joe. Jane cannot get away, and the only way to save Joe is to shoot Jane in the leg to cause a screen to drop around Joe. The benefit obtained from using Jane does not make the situation better than if Jane were not there. Yet shooting her would involve opportunistic agency (and possibly be impermissible since she is not the one threatening Joe).
22. This contrast between the during- and post-act use of A to bring down the screen around B was pointed out by Kristi Olson.
23. Things might be different if the bystanding driver were at fault for refusing to do something low cost to him to stop the car.
24. In his "Torture—Does Timing Matter?," which is his commentary on *Ethics for Enemies*, in *Journal of Moral Philosophy*, 11 (4) (July 2014): 385–94.

25. See Charles and Gregory Fried, *Because It Is Wrong* (New York: W. W. Norton & Company, 2010).
26. See, for example, Jeremy Waldron's "Torture and Positive Law: Jurisprudence for the White House," *Columbia Law Review* 105, no. 6 (October 2005): 1681–750.
27. Possible exceptions are discussed later in Part IV.
28. David Luban made this point in his "Preventive War," *Philosophy & Public Affairs* 32, no. 3 (June 2004): 207–48.
29. The use of "permissible" in this analysis depends on an evidence-relative rather than fact-relative sense of the term.
30. Johann Frick makes these points in his "Treatment and Prevention of HIV/AIDS and the Question of Identified vs. Statistical Lives," in *Identified Versus Statistical Lives: An Interdisciplinary Perspective*, ed. Glenn Cohen, Norman Daniels, and Nir Eyal (New York: Oxford University Press, 2015). Frick uses the case (that I somewhat modify) of giving flu protection to make his point clearer: We would not give a flu shot to someone when we know at the time we give it to him that he will have a rare negative reaction and die of it. Suppose the only way to protect many people from the flu were to use an antiviral spray over them. We should not use it when we know we will cause the death of this one person who cannot be separated out of the group. However, Frick argues, we may permissibly use the flu spray on everyone even though we are certain that someone would die from it when, as far as we know at the time we spray, each person has only a small chance of being the one who will die. I try to make a similar point in reverse by considering that we each would take an aspirin for a headache though we know there is a small chance each has of dying of it and that in a large enough group someone will die. Nevertheless, suppose we find the person who is dying and can save him with all the available aspirin. Then we should give him the aspirin even if others go without headache relief (and even if each thus has a small risk of dying). See my *Intricate Ethics* (New York: Oxford University Press, 2007), 36–7. I make the same point in the Chocolate Bar Case in Chapter 5 in this volume. Michael Otsuka presents the contrasting view to Frick's, that only the number of people who will die is relevant. See his "Risking Life and Limb" in *Identified and Statistical Lives*.
31. A similar case is presented by Charles Fried for other purposes in his *Right and Wrong* (Cambridge, MA: Harvard University Press, 1978).
32. Something similar seems true when justifying punishment. For example, Victor Tadros (in his *The Ends of Harm* [Oxford: Oxford University Press, 2011]) seems to move from considering (i) what may permissibly be done to a perpetrator when there is a victim of his who faces certain death unless we act to (ii) conclusions about what may permissibly be done to a perpetrator as punishment to deter future crime and thus save people. In the latter cases, at the time we punish, each person has only a small risk of being some (other) perpetrator's future victim. We will return to this issue later.
33. In *Morality, Mortality*, vol. 2 (New York: Oxford University Press, 1996).I discuss inviolability of innocent, nonthreatening people. I am not here considering those who are morally innocent but nevertheless present a threat.
34. We briefly considered threshold deontology in Chapters 7, 8, and 9.

35. For discussion of this issue as it may arise in the Trolley Problem (e.g., if a bystander is permitted but not obligated to redirect a trolley) see my *Intricate Ethics* (Oxford University Press, 2007), *The Trolley Problem Mysteries*, and Chapter 9 in this volume.
36. See Judith Thomson, "Liability and Individualized Evidence," *Law and Contemporary Problems* 49, no. 3 (1986): 199–211 and Laurence Tribe, "Trial by Mathematics: Precision and Ritual in the Legal Process," *Harvard Law Review* 84, no. 6 (1971):1329–93.
37. McMahan's original case is in his "The Basis of Moral Liability to Defensive Killing," *Philosophical Issues* 15 (2005): 386–405.
38. In his *The Ends of Harm*. I use his approach as illustration without necessarily endorsing it or implying that Tadros would justify torture.
39. Steps i-iii follow Tadros's analysis. Step iv (a move from deterring attacks to interfering with them) is my extension of Tadros's approach.
40. For comments on earlier versions of this chapter I am grateful to Shelly Kagan, Seth Lazar, Jeff McMahan, Liam Murphy, Thomas Nagel, Kristi Olson, Samuel Scheffler, Larry Temkin, Jeremy Waldron, and Ben Zipursky. I am also grateful for comments from audience members at Bowdoin College, Northwestern University, and New York University Law School where an earlier version of this chapter and its predecessor were presented. This chapter is a revised version of my "Torture: Rescue, Prevention, and Punishment," in the *Oxford Handbook of Ethics of War*, ed. Seth Lazar and Helen Frowe (New York: Oxford University Press, 2018). The first part of both that article and this chapter is based on Chapter 1 in my *Terror, Torture, and War* (Oxford: Oxford University Press, 2011).

# 14

# Rights and Aggregation in a Pandemic

**After (Others') COVID**
I have lost the ability to smell the truth
I can no longer hear the sun
I used to be able to taste reasons but no more
I can only touch dreams
And see through walls
My sense of sense is gone
My hopes have grown apart

In the United States many ordinary citizens and even political officials on the political right objected to wearing masks intended to prevent the spread of the airborne COVID-19 virus during the pandemic, which began in 2020.[1] They refused to do so even when mask wearing was mandated; they judged government mandates as illegitimate. They claimed that their personal liberty was being violated when they were not allowed to decide for themselves whether to wear a mask in public spaces and businesses. They also refused when asked to do so to "help save" others.

One of my aims in this chapter is to show that even a type of view that places great weight on personal liberty would not support some of these objections to wearing masks as a matter of interpersonal morality (aside from government mandates). A second aim of this chapter is to consider objections raised by some economists (not necessarily on the political right) to requiring lockdowns to prevent the spread of the COVID-19 virus. This will involve comparing different ways of aggregating harms and benefits. Ultimately, the chapter will show the connection between the arguments that can justify the use of masks and the arguments about how we should aggregate harms and benefits of lockdowns, thus tying together the two parts of the chapter.[2]

## I. Masks

A. **Not Harming vs. Saving**. Speaking generally, libertarian philosophical views (of which there are many types)[3] emphasize personal freedom to do or not do things, as well as negative moral rights not to be interfered with and not to be

*Rights and Their Limits: In Theory, Cases, and Pandemics*. F. M. Kamm, Oxford University Press.
© Oxford University Press 2022. DOI: 10.1093/oso/9780197567739.003.0014

harmed by others.[4] In this respect they seem to align with the views of the citizens who objected to wearing masks. However, libertarian views emphasize that such rights give people correlative moral duties not to interfere with and not to harm others who also have rights not to be interfered with. Hence, these views imply that one's liberty can be limited (at least) by others' moral rights not to be harmed or interfered with by what one does. Speaking generally, libertarian views de-emphasize positive moral rights to be helped and positive moral duties to help others, at least without specific agreements to do so.[5] This too seems to cohere with the views of citizens who refused to wear masks when asked to do so to "help save" others. The type of government that libertarian views of moral rights support is one that should enforce negative rights and their correlative duties even if it should not legislate and enforce positive rights to be aided.[6]

Because of the ways in which the citizens' objections dovetail with some of what is characteristic of libertarian views, I will refer to their views as "libertarian-like." I will also speak of the citizens as being libertarian-like. Unlike the libertarian views as described, the mistake the citizens make is not to realize that their libertarian-like views when properly understood should also commit them to a moral concern not to interfere with others and what this implies.[7]

Many who argued for wearing masks during the COVID-19 pandemic spoke in terms of how many lives would be "saved" by doing so. There are problems with this "help save others" reasoning, both from a libertarian perspective and outside of it. It suggests that we would benefit others in the way someone who saves a drowning person benefits him. It may even suggest that those who need saving have a positive moral right to be saved. But, as noted, libertarians and libertarian-like citizens may deny that there are positive duties to aid and moral rights to be aided. They may also oppose laws that give people legal positive duties to help strangers even at low cost. To characterize wearing a mask as benefiting others may feed a source of their resistance.

However, when we wear a mask to prevent the spread of illness, we do not benefit someone by making him better off than he would otherwise be as when we save someone who would otherwise die without our help. Rather, we prevent ourselves from harming him by making him worse off than he would otherwise be (as when we refrain from pushing someone into deep water).[8] This is because in the case of COVID-19 (at least until 2022), the general public was asked to wear masks (e.g., cloth) that primarily helped prevent the wearer from transmitting the virus to others rather than masks (e.g., N95) that would have significantly protected the wearer as well. This failure to recognize the conceptual distinction between benefiting others and not harming them was not limited to those with libertarian or libertarian-like views.[9] The pervasiveness of this misperception was illustrated by a popular message analogizing sacrifices Americans were asked to make for the sake of others during COVID-19 to the sacrifices made by the "greatest generation" who fought in World War II. But Americans who fought in World War II were benefiting Americans whom they did not threaten with harm; the point of many COVID-19-era sacrifices was to avoid harming others.[10]

Assume (for the sake of argument) that the following were true: one (i) had the virus, (ii) would certainly spread it to others by not wearing a mask around them (because wearing the mask is necessary to prevent the spread), (iii) would (a) cause serious harm (b) to those who have not waived their right not to be infected, (iv) would significantly reduce infection spread by wearing the mask, and (v) would not harm oneself by wearing it.[11] Then one could violate the negative moral rights of others not to be harmed if one did not wear the mask. Hence, even on a libertarian-like view one could lose one's right not to wear a mask because the mask would stop one from first harmfully interfering with others.

Note that one could violate the negative moral right of others not to be harmed even if one did not intend to do so. Consider how this could be so when conditions (i)–(v) hold:

First, one would be a threat in virtue of spreading a disease and that is a capacity that one has prior to refraining from wearing a mask. One might spread the virus simply by breathing, an automatic behavior that one can avoid only at the cost of dying. Wearing a mask stops (at least to a significant degree) one's being a threat without requiring that one not breathe. If one doesn't wear it, one remains a threat. That omission is a failure to interfere with the condition of one's body that makes one a threat.

Second, as discussed in Chapter 10, sometimes individuals can be what is known as "innocent threats" to others even when they have no control over, and so are not at fault in, their presenting a threat. Recall a classic example, introduced by philosopher Robert Nozick,[12] in which a man will survive being hurled at someone whom he will kill when he lands on him. We can imagine that he was hurled either by a villain or by a tornado. Another example might be the person who spreads a virus he did not willingly acquire simply by breathing when he cannot avoid breathing except at the cost to him of death.[13]

There is debate among philosophers about whether the hurled man who has no control over his trajectory would violate the negative moral rights of the person who would be his victim. Some think he would because if he lands on the other person, he would be where he has no right to be and cause harm he has no right to cause. Others think this man would no more violate the rights of his victim than a rock would. However, it is clear that if at small cost to himself the man could divert himself away from harming the person toward whom he is hurled, he should do so, and if he doesn't he would then violate his victim's right not to be harmed. Sometimes we are required to do something to avoid being a threat to others even if we were not responsible for or at fault in becoming a threat. If we don't do this, then we would violate their right not to be harmed by us even if we do not intend the harm. Further, I have argued, if the person being hurled cannot or will not divert himself, we may divert him at least at small cost to him (in part because of his duty to divert if he could).[14] Similarly, it might be argued that if someone were an innocent threat in doing no more than breathing, he might not violate someone's negative right in doing so. However, if there were a low-cost option to him to avoid harming them and he did not exercise it—for example, he did not wear a mask when he could (given our earlier assumptions)—he would violate negative rights. If he could not or would not put on a mask, then someone else (who was authorized) might permissibly put it on him even against his will, in part because of his own duty to do so.

What if the person with the virus who would spread it by breathing was at home but then voluntarily goes out and into the presence of other people? Even though he performs a self controlling act, he still might be classified as a morally innocent threat, for example, if he is a child who has no awareness of his being a threat. Nevertheless, it would be morally permissible for others to mask him even against his will.

Third, suppose a responsible adult who knows (or is morally responsible for knowing) the threat he presents in having the virus voluntarily goes outside among other people he knows (or is responsible for knowing) are susceptible to the virus. Assuming there was no great threat to him in remaining at home, he would no longer be a morally innocent threat. He would violate the right not to be harmed of those who become infected by him even independently of his violating their right in failing to wear a mask. In the case of someone who knows he has a dangerous virus that would certainly infect others and certainly do them serious harm (the assumptions of our current discussion), libertarian views imply that he would have a moral duty either to stay at home or to wear a mask to avoid harming others. (Similarly, a driver might have a moral duty to divert his car at minimal cost to himself to avoid foreseeably harming someone else.) This duty would be present even if only one other person would be harmed by the virus. In this case being prevented from presenting a certain and serious threat to others overrides one's right to free movement and noninterference. Furthermore, because one is not an innocent threat but a morally responsible one, the costs that could be imposed to prevent one's transmitting the disease might be greater. Hence, others (who are authorized) would be morally permitted to mask someone if he failed to mask himself or even to isolate him against his will if necessary.[15]

If libertarians believe, and libertarian-like citizens should believe, that there is a moral duty not to violate others' moral right not to be harmed, they should emphasize mask wearing by those who are definite threats (and meet other conditions described earlier).[16] However, some libertarians actually emphasized virus testing, contact tracing, and isolating the infected in order to discover and limit the freedom of those who are threats.[17] Their arguments contrasted testing and isolating the infected with general lockdowns on the grounds that the latter would reduce the freedom of many who present no threat. Many might be in lockdown either because they have some chance of being someone who presents a threat but have not been identified or because they are being required to prevent themselves from being infected. If the latter, this might be for their own good (a form of paternalistic interference with freedom) or to stamp out the virus and new mutations of it by preventing people from being infected. We shall consider the issues of merely possible threats and paternalism later. In the meantime, it is worth noting that requiring that many be tested also involves the possibility of imposing on those who do not in fact present a threat because they will test negative. For this reason, I believe, required testing (an imposition on one's body) is not as easy to justify from a libertarian perspective as requiring masking or limitations on the freedom of those who are known to present a certain and serious threat.

What if someone A will certainly spread the virus to someone else B who will be asymptomatic and not personally harmed but who will in turn certainly seriously harm others by infecting them? A will turn B into a threat (either innocent or not). Suppose we knew that this would occur by both persons voluntarily being among others but only A could be masked or isolated. Is there a foreseeable rights violation committed by A that could justify these constraints on him? There is a common view that an agent is not responsible for harm if it comes about through an intervening agent's act (at least when there is no agreement between the agents to cause harm) and in this case the harm comes about by way of intervening agent B. However, suppose there is a right not to be made into a threat by having one's body altered by infection. Then there could be a violation of B's negative right by A and grounds for some constraints on A even if B does not become ill. If B were only an innocent, nonresponsible threat, those who would eventually be harmed by him could at least have a right against A that B not be made into a threat to them. Similarly, those who would be harmed by the man hurled at them by another person in Nozick's example have a claim against that other person that he not do the hurling. In what follows, I will focus on cases of harm that do not involve intervening agents like B.

B. **Risk.** What if it is not certain that one has the virus, will spread it, and will harm others? Some (e.g., Nicholas Kristof, *The New York Times*, July 1, 2020) have argued that in such a case going out without a mask is like driving a car drunk. This car driver has at least an increased risk of harming others by drinking alcohol and so violating their right not to be harmed. (There is debate over whether she violates their right merely in creating the risk of harm even if no harm comes to pass.) Hence, Kristof argues, someone has a moral responsibility (which those on the political right who emphasize personal responsibility should endorse) to avoid drinking if she drives. Similarly (he thinks) one has a moral responsibility not to go out among others without a mask during a pandemic (a responsibility those on the political right should also encourage).

I do not think the drunk driver is a successful analogy to going out without a mask in a viral pandemic spread by airborne transmission. In the driver's case a person presents (and let us assume knows she presents) a risk of harming[18] others just in driving a car. If she is drunk, the risk goes up. It is clear (I believe) that the person should reduce the risk she presents by not drinking. We can think of driving a car as analogous to having the virus when car and virus each are dangerous entities and present some risk of harming people. Wearing a mask can be equated to not drinking when driving only if the mask wearer has the virus. But in a pandemic many individuals might be required (either morally or by government) to wear masks who may present no threat because they do not have the virus. Not knowing whether someone actually has the virus and yet requiring them to wear a mask might seem like not knowing whether someone is actually driving a car at the time we require them not to drink.[19]

However, we know that in a large group of people there will be some who will have the virus (by the so-called law of large numbers) and those people have a high risk or even certainty of infecting and harming other people. If testing is not widespread, with results timely and sufficiently definitive, we won't know who these spreaders are. (In the U.S. prior to 2022, testing was not adequate. Further, as noted earlier, required and repeated testing of everyone, even self-testing, could also be a greater interference that some libertarians and libertarian-like citizens might oppose even if they would accept as justified interfering with someone who is a known and certain threat.) Suppose only one individual had a small chance of being someone who harbored the dangerous virus and presented a certain or highly probable threat of infecting others. Then requiring him to wear a mask might be inconsistent with libertarian or libertarian-like views since the chance of anyone being harmed by him is low. But when there are many people who have even a very small chance of being someone who presents a certain or highly probable threat, we know (by the law of large numbers) that some among them *will* present such a threat, and that it is certain that some people will be harmed. Because libertarians and libertarian-like citizens focus on individual rights, it may seem inconsistent with their views to require each person to take precautions on account of his being a member of a group, some of whose members will present a threat and harm others. However, requiring the precaution is not "guilt by association" since the individual in being a part of the group might be the one of many who will present a certain or highly probable threat and thus still bear the individual responsibility to prevent the harm that will occur. (I assume that this Group-Based Argument for requiring everyone to wear a mask applies only when enough people do not wear masks voluntarily, for their doing this can bring down the risk that unmasked individuals will cause disease to a level that might be inconsistent with universal masking requirements.)[20] Whether such a Group-Based Argument can be used to justify imposing a greater burden than mask wearing when there is uncertainty about any given individual that he will present a threat (though it is certain someone will) may depend on how much uncertainty there is, how much more effective in preventing serious illness that greater burden is, and how great the additional burden is.[21]

This argument also raises the issue (discussed in Chapter 13 when discussing Prevention Type Cases) about uncertainty that any given individual will be one of those threatened (not only one of those who threatens). That is, though we may know with certainty that many will be harmed if people do not wear masks, in a large population the probability that any given person is one of those who will be harmed may still be small. If this factor and not only the total number of those harmed is morally relevant, it could also play a role in deciding whether there is a moral duty to accept burdens greater than wearing a mask.

C. **Paternalism.** Libertarians object to interfering with personal freedom against a person's will even for his own good. I assume that libertarian-like citizens would similarly object. However, given that the masks recommended before 2022 for use by the general public during the COVID-19 pandemic did not provide much protection for the person wearing them, it seems inapt to call arguments made before 2022 for requiring them paternalistic.[22] Yet during that time period some who encouraged wearing masks compared requiring them to requiring seat belts,[23] which do protect the person who wears them and whose being morally required might be argued for on paternalistic grounds. If libertarians and libertarian-like citizens are likely to be opposed to these arguments, is the analogy to requiring seat belts of any use in discussions with them?

There may be nonpaternalistic reasons for a moral duty to wear seat belts (as well as for seat belt laws). For example, suppose medical costs for those in car accidents are often borne by the general public through emergency room care and public health insurance. This is a public burden that libertarians and libertarian-like citizens may oppose, but given that they cannot change laws that license publicly financed health care, they might want to reduce the burden. Then requiring some to wear seat belts could be justified as a way to reduce people from burdening the health care system. If wearing masks would have reduced numbers of COVID-19 patients and thus also reduced the burden on health care systems, libertarians and libertarian-like citizens might see the merit in a nonpaternalistic understanding of the seat belt analogy to wearing masks. However, requiring masks (unlike seat belts) would also interfere with some people who would not be presenting a risk of burdening the system since those without the virus could not cause infections (but those driving cars could cause harm). The justification for nevertheless requiring the masks could be similar to that given previously: namely, they are members of a group, some of whom will cause harm that burdens the health care system; they might be one of those who will cause harm; we do not have an adequate way of identifying those who are threats; and wearing a mask is not a great burden for most people.

The argument for mask wearing that appeals to the libertarian or libertarian-like objection to bearing (public health care) costs is different from an argument that appeals to an objection to violating another's right not to be harmed by infecting them with COVID-19. Furthermore, it might not provide a similar justification for a requirement to wear masks whenever this would reduce the economic burden of health care. For example, suppose people not wearing masks leave some individuals in the community depressed simply because seeing attractive masks would lift spirits. Suppose the depressed seek publicly provided psychiatric help whose cost has to be borne by others. Wearing the masks would help relieve the community of this economic medical burden. However, wearing masks would then be an act of assistance to those susceptible to depression and to the community, the sort of duty to aid to which libertarians and the libertarian-like might object. In the depression case, unlike the case of wearing a mask to prevent spreading COVID-19, not wearing the mask would not worsen the condition of others (by transmitting the virus) when they would then require costly medical services; it would just not improve their condition.

An appeal to wear masks to prevent the spread of COVID-19 because people being healthy would help the economy (as was suggested by Goldman Sachs) also emphasizes the positive economic effects of not infecting people rather than objecting to the violation of a right not to be infected. But again, there could not be a requirement to wear a mask on a libertarian or libertarian-like view whenever this would be necessary to help the economy. Suppose the economy would tank if people did not buy masks that only enhanced facial beauty. Buying such masks to maintain or raise up the economy would be considered offering aid rather than not harming. Even if one had previously kept the economy strong by buying the masks, ceasing to boost the economy is not a case of harming it or the people who would benefit from a good economy. Rather, it is more like discontinuance of aid that one did not have to provide to begin with, and so ceasing to provide more benefit than one had already provided.[24] The linchpin for a mask requirement from a libertarian or libertarian-like point of view should be that infecting or risking infection in others could violate a negative right not to be harmed, and it is that harm that causes the economic problems of burdening the health care system. We return to the issue of paternalism in the following section.

D. **Self-reliant self-defense**. Libertarian-like citizens in the United States are advocates of an individual right to self-defense as shown by their support of the Second Amendment right to bear arms and even "stand your ground" laws.

Suppose they are personally opposed to there being a moral or legal requirement to wear masks that primarily protect others but see others who do not wear masks as threatening them with infection. They are not permitted to attack those they think present a threat without proof of this. Rather than retreat to a safe distance, self-defense against a COVID-19 threat can be provided by N95 masks or other devices that provide superior protection for the wearer. This suggests that libertarians and the libertarian-like might support ramping up production of such devices for the general public, not just for health care workers, in support of the general right to self-defense. Even if they opposed a paternalistic requirement to wear such masks, they might be motivated to engage in self-defense by using them, not needing others to reciprocate.[25]

Furthermore, suppose there are N95 masks that are easy to wear and can protect the wearer from the virus but some people refuse to wear them. This is a purely self-affecting decision, subject to a libertarian or libertarian-like bar on paternalistic interference, only if people absorb the cost of getting the virus by not infecting others. Possibly this also implies not seeking medical care whose provision puts medical personnel at risk of infection and raises health care costs. If refusing to defend oneself leads to harming others in this way, anti-paternalism may not be an adequate basis for refusing a moral requirement to wear self-protective masks. So there is a reason to prevent oneself from getting infected that also relates to the duty not to harm others.[26]

Those who do not deny that there is a moral (or do not oppose a governmental) requirement to wear masks that primarily prevent harm to others but are simply faced with many other people who will not wear them might also favor using N95 masks or other devices that provide increased protection for the wearer. They too would support ramping up production of them for the general population for reasons of self-defense.

The possibility of strong self-defense (by use of N95 masks or vaccines) would give lie to the claim that "no one is safe until everyone is safe." Those who seek to encourage people to help others worldwide avoid COVID-19 often make this claim in order to appeal to helpers' self-interest in being safe. But potential helpers having excellent means of self-defense would reduce the effectiveness of this appeal. Presumably libertarians and libertarian-like citizens would oppose limiting their right to engage in self-defense merely in order to keep it being in their self-interest to help others.[27] Those who recognize a strong moral duty to aid would, of course, not need to be motivated to help by self-interest.

Some have suggested that in order not to limit the free movement of those who would or might spread the virus, susceptible people should in self-defense either isolate themselves or keep their distance. For example, as reported in contemporary news, a woman who tested positive for COVID-19 refused quarantine and said that those who were afraid of her going out should stay at home to avoid her rather than requiring her to stay at home to avoid them. (We shall consider this issue further when we discuss lockdowns.) Here it is worth considering the response that no one's freedom of movement is limited by wearing a mask and it is rather the people who must self-isolate when others will not wear masks who lose the freedom to move (in the absence of access to and use of self-protective masks). However, such a response focuses only on who would bear the greater cost (the isolater or the mask wearer). It ignores a fundamental asymmetry that is of importance in libertarian views as to who should bear a cost (even if the costs were equal) for if there is a right not to be harmed, there is a correlative duty on the part of others not to harm even at some cost to themselves (as argued earlier). If costs should instead fall solely on the person who would be harmed to avoid being harmed, there would be no duty not to harm or right not to be harmed. This is contrary to libertarian views and contrary to a correct understanding of libertarian-like views I have been arguing. There would only be a right to prevent oneself from being harmed (though not a duty to do so). Furthermore, as noted previously, libertarian-like citizens typically support so-called stand-your-ground laws, which do not require someone in public to retreat from a threat. The burden on keeping one's distance is placed on those who do or even well might present the threat.[28] Even if those who self-isolate thus avoid exposure to a virus, they would have to self-isolate for a much longer time if others continue to spread infection in the community by not wearing masks. (It has been pointed out that there are at least two different goals in dealing with COVID-19: eliminating the virus from the community and protecting vulnerable populations from it. Masks can help with both. Eliminating the virus might be said to fall under providing assistance rather than avoiding harm to others but being a breeding ground for the virus seems to be another way to harm others, as discussed in endnote 9.)

However, sometimes a person's susceptibility to a threat does imply their responsibility for self-defense rather than a threatener's responsibility for limiting the threat he presents. Suppose someone is a hemophiliac who (hypothetically) would bleed to death if someone bumped into him on the street, an interaction that is not at all out of the ordinary and would be harmless to most people. In this case, it is the person who is unusually susceptible who should (arguably) bear the cost of self-defense. This might require his wearing protective clothing or self-isolating. There might be no fault in the threatener not taking precautions, thus resulting in the potential victim having to self-defend. (Similarly, the immunosuppressed typically wear masks protecting them from many others who do not wear other-protecting masks in public.) Even in cases where the potential victim is not unusually susceptible, suppose the cost of his self-protecting is lower than or equal to the cost to each of many unintentional potential threateners of eliminating their threat. For example, suppose a potential victim wearing a self-protective N95 mask could eliminate the need for many symptom-free people with the virus to wear a mask that primarily protected others and the cost per person of wearing a self- or other-protecting mask was the same. Then it could be morally reasonable to require the lesser total cost. However, libertarians who set a limit to the value of freedom at the point where it harms others might disagree that the burden should fall on those threatened.[29]

There is another group that could become susceptible to the virus whose self-defending by retreat from the threat is controversial. These are health care workers who could help those who are infected. Suppose that if they did not help they would not become infected and would be infected if they helped. They do not bear moral responsibility for their own infection if they have a duty to help. The duty could arise from an oath to maintain standards of the profession, or alternatively the duty could be owed to sick people correlative to their right to health care. In the latter case, the question is whether at least some of the people who could be treated have forfeited (or weakened) their right to treatment when they could endanger their caretakers.[30] Those who are morally responsible for becoming threats such as those who did not take easy measures to prevent their becoming threats, might be among those who have forfeited (or weakened) their rights to be treated by those they threaten.[31] Suppose this is so and the health care provider's duty to help stemmed not from a professional code but from people's right to health care. Then some health professionals might argue self-defense in not helping someone who's right to health care has been forfeited or weakened as much as a mere bystander might argue self-defense in not helping an infected person who had no right against the bystander to be helped. The possibility of forfeiture (or weakening) should be recognized as a possible implication of emphasizing a right to health care as the basis for a professional's duty to treat.

## II. Lockdowns

How should we weigh the economic costs (determined independently of any libertarian or libertarian-like views) of keeping the economy shut down via lockdowns versus the lives lost by reopening it when a deadly virus is still actively spreading? And how might libertarian and libertarian-like views about moral rights that we have examined so far bear on answering this question? We will begin with a discussion of aggregation of costs and benefits that is completely independent of commitment to libertarian or libertarian-like views and only later, in (D), turn to the relevance of these views.

A. **Simple Aggregation.** Speaking on PBS Evening News Hour (June 18, 2020), economist Nick Bloom calculated that the experience of being shut in and suffering economic trauma due to a lockdown could result in the loss of a year of life for a person. Bloom added up all the years of life that would be lost given the loss of forty million jobs in three months of economic distress and came up with forty million life-years lost. His aim was to translate economic losses due to a lockdown into the language of life lost. The question is how that translation helps us compare a closed economy to deaths caused by opening up the economy.

Bloom did not go so far as to compare this total number of life-years lost with actual deaths from the virus. Indeed, the tenor of the discussion of which he was a part was that people especially vulnerable to the virus (who also might transmit it) should stay at home for their own safety, while less vulnerable people could avoid the cost to them in terms of life-years lost by not being in lockdown and opening up the economy. This is a version of the view that those who would cause but are not susceptible to illness should be free (to open up the economy) and those who would be harmed by them (but also, it should be added, benefit from an open economy) have a right (if not a duty) to isolate in self-defense. (Bloom seems to assume that one could know in advance whether or not one is susceptible to serious harm from COVID-19. I shall proceed on this assumption but reconsider it in [E] later.)

Some might be tempted to go further and conclude that the large total of (forty million) life-years lost outweighs the deaths of individual people. But in translating economic loss into life-years lost, we must not lose sight of the fact that if forty million people each lose one year of life, no one of those people will suffer a loss as great as someone who, for example, dies at the age of forty and thereby loses an additional thirty years of his life. It is a mistake in what is called "moral mathematics" to always aggregate small losses to many people and morally equate the total to a large loss to a single person. How a total is distributed across separate persons is thought to be morally very important by nonconsequentialists. For example, if thirty people die at age seventy rather than at seventy-one, it would be wrong to think of the summation of those one-year losses as morally equal to the complete loss of life to someone at age forty if he could otherwise have lived to seventy even though in both scenarios thirty life-years are lost. (In this case, the loss of thirty life-years to one person not only has more significant impact on him than the loss of one year has on others, but he will die having had a much shorter life than any of those who die at seventy.)

It is interesting to note that while Bloom offered a figure of one life-year lost per forty million people, he did not mention that this might be an average per-person figure. Hence, it is possible that some of the individuals on whom the average is based suffered more and others less than a one-year loss.[32] Indeed, some people may have died losing many years of life as a result of a lockdown (as in reports of teenagers taking their own lives). If this were so, Bloom would weaken his own case for avoiding lockdowns by using an average figure since it conceals possible losses to many individuals due to lockdowns that are as great as (or even greater than) the deaths due to COVID-19 that lockdowns are intended to prevent. In that case, we wouldn't be interpersonally aggregating loss of a year of life in many but rather counting the deaths due to lockdowns.[33] Then we might balance those deaths caused by lockdowns against those due to the absence of lockdowns. This would avoid the issue of aggregating many smaller losses and equating them to larger losses to individuals.[34]

I will discuss this issue further later. But first consider an even more extreme version of interpersonal aggregation of smaller losses. Suppose someone calculated that each one of 1.2 million people would lose a month of life due to closing the economy. That would mean a total of 100,000 years of life lost. But no person will suffer more than a month of lost life. Even more grotesquely, someone might use this kind of interpersonal aggregation to calculate how many months there are in an average lifetime and then figure out how many "lifetimes" would be lost even though no single person of the 1.2 million people would lose a lifetime—indeed, none would lose more than a month of life. I have been told that this method was once used to argue that lower speed limits that made many people waste more minutes in traffic "cost lives," once the minutes were added up to form units of minutes in an average life and those lives lost could be weighed against lives saved from more traffic accidents that would occur at higher speeds.

This last case especially raises another factor missing from Bloom's discussion: that those who are in lockdown, like those who are told to slow down in traffic, might otherwise harm other people. From a libertarian perspective, imposing the cost has a different role in such a context from what it would have if the cost was imposed merely to benefit people who would otherwise lose their lives. We shall return to deal with this issue in (D) after first examining the question of aggregation independently of it.

B. **Balancing, Pairwise Comparison, and Relevance.**

(1) Is there an alternative to always aggregating smaller losses interpersonally to weigh them against larger individual losses, and what is the justification for it? In what follows, we will first consider two alternative procedures for deciding on what smaller losses to individuals it would be morally appropriate to aggregate when the issue is which people an impartial agent should aid when he cannot help everyone.

Suppose a health care provider, government, or other impartial agent responsible for helping people in a social system must ration scarce resources (such as ventilators) and is trying to decide whom to help when not everyone can be helped. (This case involves deciding whom to help when people face a loss that the impartial agent does not cause. This is different from the impartial agent deciding whether to impose a situation on some [such as a lockdown] that will cause the loss. We shall return to that case later.) How might they reason?[35] To start at the most basic level, the agent could permit counting the numbers of lives that can be saved assuming for the sake of argument that everyone would lose as much if not helped and gain as much from being saved.[36] But this needn't be seen as producing the best outcome by summing up a large group of people who could be saved if one thing was done and weighing them against a smaller group of other people who could be saved if something else was done. Rather, it might be seen as a way to treat each person fairly by using the method I call "balancing," which compares a person in one group against his equal and opposite in the other group. At a certain point there will be some people in the larger group who are not balanced by those in the other group and they should determine which group will be helped. Giving a smaller and larger group an equal chance to be helped would ignore the presence of the additional members of the larger group.[37] What if the same number would die if not treated in two completely different groups but in the larger group there was one additional person who could also be helped to have his sore throat cured? Should the fact that he could be helped as well only if we helped the larger group serve as a tiebreaker? Even though the good we could do would then be greater, I think his sore throat cure is an "irrelevant utility" (or irrelevant good). Because it is such a small good, it seems disrespectful to people whose lives are at stake in the smaller group to deprive each one of them of the 50% chance to survive he would have if we used some random-decision procedure to decide which group to help.[38] This depends on recognizing at least two things. First, even though the same number of lives would be saved whatever we do and from an impartial perspective it doesn't matter whose lives are saved, from the perspective of each person it matters that he rather than someone else survive and so that he not be deprived of the 50% chance of being saved. Even from an impartial perspective, an allocator should take into account such a morally permissible degree of preference for oneself. (I refer to taking account of the personal (or subjective) view from the impartial (or objective) view as "sobjectivity.") Second, it depends on recognizing that even on many nonconsequentialist views one would have a moral duty to suffer a sore throat in order to save someone's life, and also in order to provide someone with a large equal chance to survive even in a case where the same number of people will survive no matter what is done. (This may not be true, however, on the libertarian and libertarian-like views we have been considering.[39])

However, what if the additional person whom we could help if we saved one group of lives would otherwise lose his leg? Arguably, preventing such an additional loss could be a tiebreaker and so not be an irrelevant good in this context. This is so even though in a pairwise comparison of life and leg, one life should be saved rather than the leg on its own. Indeed, I would say that the loss of a leg to someone pales in comparison with the loss of a life to someone else. One way of putting this point is that from an impartial perspective, loss of a leg is not "relevant to" loss of a life. So something (like loss of a leg) not being an "irrelevant good" in the choice of whose life to save need not mean that it is a loss that is "relevant to" the greater loss on its own.[40] This is consistent with it being an implication of nonconsequentialism that one does not have a duty to lose one's leg even to produce the greater good of saving someone else's life, let alone to give someone a large equal chance to have his life saved. (Doing so may be a morally worthy supererogatory act.) What if the extra person on one side could have his three fingers saved along with one person whose life was at stake? I think the loss of three fingers is also something that it would not be someone's duty to sacrifice to save someone's life, let alone to give someone a large equal chance at life when someone will be saved in any case. Yet, I think an impartial allocator should view saving the three fingers as an irrelevant good and give an equal chance to be saved to each person who stands to lose a life.[41]

Now consider cases involving losses like those mentioned in section II (A)'s discussion of simple aggregation. Suppose an impartial agent must decide whether to save one person for a significant period of life or save a great many people from each suffering a sore throat (no one of whom needs to have his life saved). In this case, if we pairwise compare each person who would suffer a sore throat with someone who will die, we should decide to save the life rather than cure the sore throat in each of many people (other things equal, including cost). (No sore throat that is pairwise compared with the life at stake for someone else balances that greater loss. So not all pairwise comparison involves balancing of equal losses on opposing sides.) In addition, as noted previously, it might be argued that a person has a moral duty to go through a sore throat in order to save someone's life (though libertarians might disagree). If each of the people who had a sore throat had a moral duty to suffer it to save a life, then in the view of an impartial aider no number of cures for sore throats should count against saving the life of the person.[42] They would all be irrelevant goods because they occur in separate persons who, when compared pairwise with the person who would die, should not be treated. It is no counterargument to this conclusion to imagine that some of those who are not saved from their sore throat will eventually die because their sore throat was not treated. This would not be an argument in favor of interpersonally aggregating the small benefit of a sore throat that is assumed to present no risk of developing into a fatal condition. It would be an argument in favor of considering the number of people who would die if the sore throats were not treated and balancing them against the one person who currently needs his life saved.[43]

But what if the choice was saving someone's life or saving many people from each losing a leg? One view is that since in a pairwise comparison someone's losing a leg is not anywhere near as bad as someone's losing a life, and in that sense is not "relevant to" someone's losing a life, an impartial agent should save the person's life rather than any number of individuals' legs. This is so even if no one has a moral duty to sacrifice his leg to save someone else's life. The same might be true in the case in which each of many would lose three fingers. This would mean that an impartial aider cannot decide what lesser losses to each of many may or may not be aggregated merely by seeing what loss it would be morally permissible for someone to refuse to suffer in order to save a life.[44]

However, it is possible that there could be cases in which no individual in a large group would "win" or "tie" a pairwise comparison with someone else in a smaller group yet those in the large group should be helped. For example, suppose one person will die and another person would be totally paralyzed. Other things equal, in a pairwise choice we should help the first person when we cannot help both. (Unlike slight differences that are morally irrelevant in comparing each of two people—e.g., one will live ten minutes longer than the other—the difference between death and total paralysis could count morally in a one-on-one choice of whom to help.) However, it is still possible that it is morally right to save 100 people from total paralysis rather than one person from death when we cannot do both. If this is true, it shows that the lesser loss is "relevant to" what is at stake for the person who would be worst off, and counting the number of people who will be helped avoid the relevant loss could be morally appropriate.[45]

It is only after pairwise comparison of losses to determine the relevance of a lesser loss to the worst loss that would be suffered (and how much benefit would occur if it were avoided) that we should consider how many people would suffer that relevant lesser loss by comparison to how many would suffer the greater loss. Then the government or health care provider could determine if helping the first set of people supersedes saving the lives of others.[46]

A partially contrasting view is offered by Alex Voorhoeve, who accepts my view that if someone has a moral duty to suffer a loss to save a life, then an impartial aider should not aggregate any number of those losses in each of many people to decide whether to help them rather than save a life for a significant additional time.[47] However, he also thinks that if an individual would suffer a loss he would not have a duty to suffer to, for example, save a life, then (i) each of those losses is "relevant to" the loss of a life, giving some claim to be aided and (ii) an impartial aider may aggregate those lesser losses and (iii) then get the sum of the claims to be aided weighted by the strength of the claims. (His notion of "relevant to" is general and applies in situations where loss of life is not at stake.) If there are a sufficient number of people with the weaker claims, it could be morally right to help them rather than the person whose life could be saved.[48] Voorhoeve's sense of "relevant to" is different from the one I employed earlier. (I denied that any loss that one would not have a duty to make to prevent someone else's loss would be a loss that was relevant to someone else's loss and should be interpersonally aggregated by an impartial agent for purposes of choosing whom to aid.) He defends his view by arguing that we should be able to reach unanimity on not pressing a claim to have one's sore throat treated when saving someone else's life is at stake. This is an implication of having a duty to suffer such a loss to save a life. However, he argues, there need be no unanimity on not pressing a claim to avoid some larger lesser losses (e.g., loss of a limb). For example, each could permissibly refuse to suffer such a loss for another's benefit and on this ground insist on being counted in a decision on whether to prevent a group of such lesser losses or save someone else's life. A concern about this view is that it is not clear why what someone has no duty to lose in order to save another's life should determine what an impartial aider should do in deciding whom to aid. After all, no one is being asked to volunteer to suffer a loss of what is his when an impartial aider decides whom he will assist with society's resources. Not helping some people avoid a loss in order to help someone else is not the same as requiring the other people to each help someone else. The outcome may be the same in both scenarios (e.g., each of the many suffers the loss of his limb), but it is important in nonconsequentialist theory how the loss comes to be suffered.

(2) Now using just the figures from Bloom's example, consider a case in which an impartial allocator of aid must decide whether to help forty million people each of whom would lose a year of life or fewer people who would each die and thereby (assume) lose many more years of life. On the first alternative to simple aggregation, this would involve comparing types of losses: would any among the forty million suffer a type of loss that is as (or nearly as) great as the type of loss suffered by each of a smaller group of people who would die of COVID-19 when they would otherwise have lived much longer.[49] If there are no such people, then the impartial provider should help the people who would lose more in dying (assuming they can get a significant benefit if saved) rather than each of the many who would suffer a lesser loss (and be better off even with that loss, e.g., dying at seventy) than the person who would die (e.g., at forty). On this version of the view, when the question is whom to help, the moral idea is to *give some priority to those who will be worse off* if not helped (and be helped significantly). Once we know who will be worse off and benefit significantly, arguably we should help the greatest number of these people, other things equal. So numbers of people who can be helped need not be irrelevant, for example, when it is a choice between saving 100 people who would otherwise die at forty and be helped significantly versus saving a group of 50 different such people.

On the views of pairwise comparison that we considered, there are cases in which no individual in a large group would "win" or "tie" in a pairwise comparison with someone else in smaller group yet those in the large group should be helped. The question then is what loss to each individual is relevant to the loss of the worst-off person who would benefit significantly and how many individuals would suffer that relevant loss. On one view I presented, even loss of a leg does not seem relevant to death, so no matter how many would suffer that problem (other things equal), we should save a person from death rather than many from each losing a leg. In the case of death from COVID-19 we would have to consider whether an individual's losses from lockdown (e.g., losing a year of life or losing one's business) are relevant to deaths from COVID. It is only after pairwise comparison of these losses to determine relevance to the loss that the worse-off person would suffer and how he would benefit from help that we should consider how many people would suffer that relevant loss by comparison to how many would suffer the greater loss. Then the impartial health care provider could determine if helping the first set of people supersedes saving the lives of others.[50] At noted previously, if Bloom's figure of one life-year lost per forty million people is an average per person, it is possible that some of the individuals on whom the average is based suffered more and others less than a one-year loss. From the point of view of the procedure of pairwise comparison, by using an average figure that conceals possible greater losses to certain individuals, economists weaken their own case for avoiding lockdowns.

As we have seen, Voorhoeve offers a different view of what "relevant to" means; it applies to any loss that someone does not have a duty to suffer to prevent a greater loss, for example, death. If one would not have to suffer loss of a leg, loss of a year of life, or loss of one's business to save one person's life, these lesser losses are relevant to death that causes a large loss of life-years. On this view what remains is to consider the number of such people who would suffer the lesser losses and aggregate them to see if they should outweigh the number of deaths from the point of view of an impartial allocator of assistance. (This is *not* the same as claiming that in the lockdown context in which Bloom discusses these losses, we should aggregate. We will return to this issue later.)

C. **Whose Death Is Worse and Whether It Matters.** If starting with some version of pairwise comparison rather than general interpersonal aggregation is sometimes a better way to think morally, how should we decide who will be worse off? (This question bears on all the views of pairwise comparison I have considered for it is part of deciding whose claim to aid is stronger.) Consider the death of a single person and the expected number of years that person would lose if he dies and have if he is saved. Some think that we can determine how *bad* a death would be for the person who dies (even if death involves his future permanent nonexistence) on the basis of expected years of (adequate) life that a person would lose out on if he were not saved.[51] Thus, a death is worse—a greater harm—if more years of expected life are lost. This is a version of a view known as Deprivationism. Suppose, for example, we must ration a resource such as a drug or ventilator. Some think that medical personnel should save the person who, assuming equal chances and costs of achieving survival, would live the longest after treatment. Typically, this will mean saving the younger person: The idea is that it is worse for that person to die now because he has more (expected) years of life to lose and, therefore, would suffer a greater harm. A March 2020 report in *The New England Journal of Medicine* on the pandemic in Italy described doctors there considering rationing so as to save younger rather than older people because more life-years could be expected from saving a younger person. (Consider a possibly worrisome implication of Deprivationsim for a given person [i.e., intrapersonally]. Suppose most people now live to 80 and could not live beyond 120. However, we can ensure most people's survival to a good life of 150 years by altering them. This alteration also makes it possible for them to live to 500 years, though few live that long. Then most will be deprived by death of a realistic possibility of 350 more years. This is more than we are currently realistically deprived of yet all people will die having had a better, longer life than currently. In this case, it seems Deprivationism might imply that alteration leads each to suffer a worse death [since each loses out on more realistically possible life-years]. Yet contrary to this conclusion, it seems that it would be worse to die at 80 when there is no realistic possibility of much more life than to die at 150 when there is a realistic possibility of much more life.)

It is understandable that a given person would want to have more years of life to live rather than fewer years of life (assuming adequate quality of life), which would be an *intra*personal choice. However, given that he has no choice but to live fewer additional years rather than more when the alternative is death, he would probably care as much for the fewer additional years as for the greater number. If we have an *inter*personal choice to make between a person who would live for more additional years of life and someone who would live for fewer, is denying a lesser benefit to someone else clearly the better choice (other things equal) when each person wants to be the one to go on living?

Suppose the cost to produce the lesser or the greater benefit is the same and each person who stands to benefit is equal in all other respects (including age). Those who support cost-effectiveness analysis may see this as a situation in which we would spend as much to buy fewer years of life if we do not save the person who will live longer. But for whom is this bad if we are concerned with each person who wants to be the one to live rather than the instrumental value to society of extra years of life? It is important to distinguish lack of cost effectiveness in this case from a second case in which the cost to produce the same (or lesser) benefit in one person is more expensive than to produce the same (or greater benefit) in someone else. In this second case, there may be an opportunity cost in spending the extra money to produce the same or lesser benefit because that money could otherwise be used to help other people besides the two people whose benefit is initially in question. Suppose the extra benefit that could be produced in another person with the extra money is no greater than the extra benefit that would be produced if we saved a person who would live longer than another person in our first case. It could still be more important to distribute a benefit of a few extra years of life to a third person than to produce that additional benefit when it is concentrated in the same person who would already be benefited significantly in avoiding death for a few years even if he didn't get the additional years of life. Simple cost-effectiveness analysis does not capture the moral distinction between the first and second cases.

Regardless of our ultimate position on the policy of saving younger rather than older people, we should understand that an argument for the morality of saving younger people need not be based on pairwise comparisons of life-years expected from point of treatment. An alternative argument focuses on the fact that the older person will have had more life-years even if he dies than the younger person will have had if she dies. On this view, if the younger person is not helped, she would wind up being the worst off person in having had less time alive. Hence, if we should give some priority to helping the worst off person, it could be most reasonable to save her (assuming there is some significant benefit to her) rather than the older person who, even if not saved, would still be better off than the not-helped younger person. I call this approach Willhavehadism.[52] One way of putting this point is that it is morally more valuable (all else equal) to provide a benefit to someone who will have had less of that good thing.[53] This way of thinking captures our intuitive thought that often the death of a younger person is worst. But this need not be because he is harmed more by a greater loss of future life, but because by the time he dies he will have had less of the good of life.[54]

The Willhavehadist way of making pairwise comparisons can conflict with a focus on future years of life. For example, if doctors think in terms of helping people based on expected life-years, they might decide to help a sixty-year-old whose life would be extended twenty years by treatment in preference to a thirty-year-old whose life would be extended only ten years by treatment in virtue of a pre-existing condition. By contrast, concern for helping the person who will have had the fewer life-years if he dies would favor helping the younger person because he will have had only thirty years of life if he dies (and he can be helped significantly), whereas the older person will have had sixty life-years even if he is not helped. The death of this younger person is worse not because he loses out on more years than the older person but because he will not have lived very long.[55]

Taking into account either years of additional life from the point of treatment or years of life that will have been lived by time of death may conflict with the idea of a right to health care or such a right had in order to achieve what are called "fair innings" or "a complete life" (in the sense of having had an opportunity for all of life's important phases). If there were such rights, the fact that some people would achieve more life in the future if treated or others would have already gotten more of what they had a right to have might be irrelevant. (Analogously, those who will exercise more of their right to free speech are not entitled to have greater protection of their right than others, and those who will have already exercised more of their right to free speech are not entitled to less protection of their right than others.)

D. **Imposing Lesser Losses and Rights.** Now let us return to the particular issue of lockdowns, showing how our initial discussion of libertarian and libertarian-like rights combines with our discussion of aggregation. Suppose (for the sake of argument) that an impartial agent of a health care system should use pairwise comparison in any of the ways we have considered when deciding whom to help and whether to aggregate losses to individuals. As we have seen, this is consistent with the libertarian and libertarian-like views (and up to a point with any nonconsequentialist view[56]) that no one of the individuals whom Bloom estimates would lose a year of life has a duty to suffer that loss to save the lives of those who would each be worse off than he were he not to help them. Nor does a sixty-year-old who can live to eighty have a duty to die so that a thirty-year-old may live to forty, forty-five, or eighty. What an impartial agent deciding on or carrying out a policy of allocating scarce resources should do need not be the same as what someone has a personal duty to do to help others. A doctor should save someone's life rather than someone else's leg, other things equal, but that does not mean that a person has to give up his leg, or a medicine that he has a right to control that would save his leg, in order to save someone else's life. On libertarian and libertarian-like views (and up to a point on any nonconsequentialist moral view), requiring a person to do so would be a violation of his rights to control his own body and important property.

This can bear on how we should view interpersonal aggregation of smaller losses (that on some views are not relevant to the greater loss of another) when an impartial government or health official is deciding whether to *harm* some people for the sake of helping others rather than merely deciding *not to help* some people for the sake of helping others. For example, suppose there were a noncommunicable disease that causes death at an early age in those who have it and it could be cured by other people doing what causes each of them to lose one year of their life. Suppose also, as libertarian or libertarian-like views might imply, that a person does not have a duty to give up a year of his life (so that he will die at seventy rather than at seventy-one) to save others from dying at a young age, thus losing many more years of their life. Requiring that each of those who can help do so would be a violation of each one's moral right not to aid in this way and of his negative right not to be imposed on in this way for the sake of helping others. Further, the more people who would be required to do this, the greater the number of people whose rights would be violated. Violation of one right would be serious, but violating many would be more serious, with no diminishing significance to further violations.[57] In this case, aggregating the smaller losses to each of many people to weigh against the lives lost would not be unreasonable because each of the smaller losses would, by hypothesis, involve a violation of a right.

Hence, suppose one views either a government-imposed lockdown or a moral duty to remain in lockdown as involving such violation of the rights of many for the sake of saving some others' lives. Suppose also that libertarians and libertarian-like citizens view the lockdown as involving a paternalistic violation of the rights of even those saved. Then pairwise comparison of the size of losses (or how badly off people wind up being) would *not* be a better way of deciding what should be done than aggregating the smaller losses to many people. When Bloom pointed to the number of people who would lose a year of life if there were a lockdown, he did not go on to say that this would involve many rights violations (and as an economist he may not think it would be important to do so). However, the role of interpersonally aggregating smaller losses to some in an argument in favor of opening an economy when this will result in many others dying could depend, from a libertarian and libertarian-like point of view (and up to a certain point from any nonconsequentialist point of view), on whether or not the lesser losses to many involved imposing losses on them that violate their rights not to suffer such losses in order to save other people's lives.

Crucially, however, whether these rights violations occur could depend on whether those who are placed in lockdown would harm or be at significant risk of harming others if they were not in lockdown. This is another factor to which Bloom does not attend. Whether rights are violated in a morally required or government-imposed lockdown could also depend on whether being in lockdown and eventually losing a year of life to prevent harm is a burden proportional to the harm that one might otherwise cause. This might depend on how great the harm to others would be and how great the risk is of harming others.

Hence, the sort of arguments I have already given for a moral requirement even from a libertarian or libertarian-like point of view to wear a mask to prevent harm to others might also justify the greater imposition of a lockdown. Recall that the arguments I gave in I(A) and I(B) applied to cases of certain harm but also to each person possibly being someone who will cause the harm that is certain to come about. If these arguments applied to lockdowns, then there would be no moral rights violations in morally requiring a lockdown since it would prevent some from violating the negative rights of others not to be harmed.

Then pairwise comparison of lesser and greater losses to different people might again be relevant but in a different way than for an impartial agent who is deciding whom to help when allocating scarce resources. This is because it is necessary to determine proportionality between the harm prevented and the loss imposed on those who would or might cause the harm in order to prevent it and because this proportionality condition can sometimes be met even if a *greater* loss is imposed on someone to prevent his causing a lesser loss to someone else. For example, consider cases not involving a COVID-19 lockdown: One might permissibly kill someone if that were necessary to stop him from certainly paralyzing another person's legs even if he were not intentionally seeking to cause the harm that was a side effect of what he was doing. Hence, it is not always crucial that someone who would do serious harm suffer only an equal or lesser loss in being prevented from doing so. Furthermore, one might even permissibly kill several people if that were necessary to stop them from certainly paralyzing one other person's legs even if they were not intentionally seeking to cause the harm. In such a case, it would be wrong to interpersonally aggregate the losses to all those who would be prevented from harming someone in order to determine the permissibility of preventing the harm they would do.

However, what of cases where it is not certain that the actor(s) will cause any harm to occur? As the risk of harming someone seriously goes down, imposing only a lesser loss and on fewer people to prevent even a greater harm may be reasonable. As the harm that would occur (certainly or only possibly) itself becomes less serious (e.g., because the illness caused by someone never results in death due to therapies available), imposing only a lesser loss and on fewer people to prevent the harm also seems reasonable. These are all complicated issues about proportionate response to threats (especially when those who present them are morally innocent) that bear on whether people's rights have been violated by having out-of-proportion losses imposed on them to prevent the threat they do or may present.

Recent discussions by economists about the harms and benefits of lockdowns seem to ignore these points about preventing those in lockdown from harming others. For example, while supporting the use of lockdowns, Prof. Olga Yakusheva expressed concern that their associated costs are not shouldered "only by those who benefit from a lockdown" but by those who do not benefit (since they are not vulnerable to the risk the lockdown is designed to prevent). Similarly, Prof. Jay Bhattacharya's discussion of costs and benefits of COVID-19 lockdowns characterized the lockdowns as efforts to protect the vulnerable that cause "collateral damage" to others less susceptible to the virus.[58] However, contrary to these claims, it is not problematic if costs are borne by those who do not benefit if the costs prevent those who bear them from causing harm. Indeed, the use of the term "benefit" is inappropriate if it is meant to describe what happens to their potential victims when those in lockdown are merely prevented from harming them. It is true, however, that when a third party (like the state) interferes with one party harming another, that third party can be said to benefit the person who would otherwise be harmed. For example, if someone shoots at an aggressor to prevent harm to his intended victim, there is no moral problem with the potential victim benefiting from the third party's action and the aggressor bearing costs but not benefiting. When costs prevent some from (even unintentionally) spreading an illness, it is not necessary that the costs benefit them. This could be especially true if it is through first failing to pay a much smaller cost (e.g., wearing a mask) to prevent their causing harm that they then must bear the greater costs of a lockdown.

"Collateral damage" is a term in just-war theory describing the unintended harmful effects to nonthreatening civilians of hitting a permissible military target. Bhattacharya's applying it to harm to those who are in lockdown though they are not among the most vulnerable to COVID-19 is inapt in at least two ways. First, the lockdown of these people is not a mere side effect; it is an intended means to an end (protecting the vulnerable and/or stamping out the virus). This need not mean that the damage to them is intended, but intending to involve someone in a lockdown foreseeing that harm (e.g., economic loss or loss of a year of life) will come to them is still unlike merely foreseeing the involvement of others (as occurs with collateral harm in war).[59] This could make lockdowns morally more problematic than collateral damage in war were it not that the lockdown is intended to stop those who may threaten others with disease and create an environment in which new variants of a disease could develop. By contrast, innocent civilians in war are not threats. An analysis is not satisfactory if it does not consider the moral significance of the possible harmful causal role of those who pay a cost and the fact that the "benefit" to others is only a matter of interfering with that causal role.[60]

In sum, from libertarian and libertarian-like (as well as generally nonconsequentialist) moral perspectives: (1) Pairwise comparison of losses rather than simple interpersonal aggregation may be the correct method to use when an impartial agent is deciding among eligible people whom to aid. Numbers of people and the losses they would suffer could count only once losses are at the same level or are relevant to the level of the most seriously affected (assuming they would significantly benefit from help). (2) If there are rights violations in imposing lesser losses on some for the sake of merely aiding others, aggregation of these losses and wrongs may be appropriate in objecting to the imposition. However, it may not even be necessary as a single rights violation might be sufficient. (3) If losses would be imposed on those who would (or might be one of those who would) otherwise violate the rights of others not to be harmed, simple aggregation of losses to them would be inappropriate. But pairwise comparison should be done to determine proportionality in costs imposed to prevent the threat. This could yield different results from pairwise comparison in the case of allocating scarce resources (as in [1]). If proportionality is violated, considering the number of people who suffer the out-of-proportion imposed losses could be appropriate in objecting to the imposition. We see that concluding whether it is morally wrong from a libertarian or libertarian-like perspective to interpersonally aggregate smaller losses requires first deciding whether or not the loss is being permissibly imposed on someone to prevent his violating others' right not to be harmed.

E. **Intrapersonal Risk.** This discussion has been based on Bloom's assumption that (i) those who would be seriously harmed by COVID-19 and (ii) those who would be harmed overall by lockdowns are different groups of people. However, suppose people were not sure whether they would be seriously harmed by COVID-19 or rather be asymptomatic but harm others. (Of course, those who could be seriously harmed could also harm others who are susceptible to serious harm, and there could be some who neither are susceptible to serious harm nor pose a threat of such harm to others.) Then it could be a matter of *intrapersonal* rationality whether, for example, to risk dying from COVID-19 shortly or risk eventually losing a year of life due to a lockdown. If there were a marker for only a small risk of dying from COVID-19 (e.g., being under thirty), it might make sense to take the risk. In the absence of such a marker, it seems reasonable to choose to eventually lose a year. It might nevertheless be objectionably paternalistic to enforce the lockdown for this reason alone on those who reject it. However, it would remain true that those who are unlikely to be seriously harmed by COVID-19 or who choose to risk such harm to themselves could infect others, and this could be a reason to prevent them from acting in their own best interests or by their own lights. An exception could be to their interacting only with those who agreed to be put at risk.[61] Suppose some people choose to take these risks. Then if they become ill with COVID-19, they may have weakened their claim to scarce health care and if they die, this may some times be viewed less as a tragedy than as losing out in a lottery they chose to enter. It is preferable to avoid the need for a lockdown altogether and still reduce everyone's risk of dying by following public health practices, such as social distancing, wearing masks that prevent transmission but are also highly protective of the wearer, and when possible using vaccines.

## Notes

1. Those who objected included members of the general public who refused to wear masks when going to supermarkets or restaurants and also public officials (e.g., Senator Rand Paul). This chapter is a reorganized and expanded version of my article "Moral Reasoning in a Pandemic," *The Boston Review*, July 8, 2020. I am grateful to Joshua Cohen for helpful editorial and philosophical suggestions on that article. The poem that begins this chapter is my own. Earlier versions of this chapter were presented to a graduate class at Rutgers University; as the Keynote Lecture at the NYU Bioethics and Moral Theory Conference, November 2020; and at the Colloquium on Ethical and Legal Philosophy at Warwick University, March 2021. I am grateful for comments I received from Matthew Liao, Adam Lerner, Alex Guerrero, Tom Parr, Andrew Williams,

Francesca Minerva, Victor Tadros, and students in the graduate class. There are many rights relevant to a pandemic (e.g., such as to health insurance, unemployment insurance, etc.) not discussed in this chapter. This chapter was written relatively early in the COVID-19 pandemic and only minor revisions were possible thereafter. My more recent work on rights in a pandemic is "Handling Future Pandemics: Harming, Not Aiding, and Liberty," forthcoming in ed. J. Savulescu et al., *Pandemic Ethics: From COVID-19 to Disease X* (Oxford: Oxford University Press, 2023) and "Health Policy and Innocent Threats: Some Issues in Abortion and Pandemics," for a *Social Philosophy and Policy* workshop on Health Policy, May 18–20, 2023.

2. This chapter was conceived and for the most part written prior to the development of vaccines against COVID-19, but many of the points that are made about the use of masks apply to the use of vaccines. I discuss issues that arose after vaccines in my "Handling Future Pandemics: Harming, Not Aiding, and Liberty". That paper also discusses aggregation in relation to choosing between cancelling therapies for non-life-threatening conditions and providing lifesaving therapies in a pandemic.
3. My aim here is not to consider the details of any particular libertarian view. Rather, I will characterize, in a rough way that will be sufficient for my purposes, some elements of a recognizable nonconsequentialist moral form of libertarianism. That is, it is not a version of libertarianism that would trade off one person's liberty in order to maximize liberty overall. It is also not a form of political libertarianism that focuses only on correct government action.
4. Negative rights to noninterference could also apply to not interfering to benefit someone against his will and so rule out paternalism.
5. I use "positive" here to mean duties to do something rather than refrain from doing something. I am not using the term to distinguish positive (i.e., legislated) law from natural law. In focusing on moral rights and duties, I am also assuming that these can exist without being legislated and are discovered by reasoning rather than by investigating what the positive law is.
6. The focus on moral rights and the duties correlative to rights distinguishes my discussion of libertarian moral views from a discussion about what morally ought to be done. For example, there may be many things one morally ought to do, that it would even be morally wrong not to do, and that nevertheless do not involve failing to do what others have a right against one to do. For example, if one morally ought to give someone the time of day when he asks for it, that need not mean he has a right against one to be told the time. Even if we act wrongly in not telling the time, we may not wrong the person who asked if he had no right to be told.
7. My discussion of libertarian-like citizens is limited to those in the United States.
8. Not all cases in which we make someone worse off than they would otherwise be involve harming (even if harming involves making someone worse off in this way). For example, suppose we begin to aid someone by means to which he has no right when no one else would have aided him. Then we discontinue this assistance. The person is worse off than he would have been if we hadn't discontinued assistance. Nevertheless, this is a case of not benefiting him more than we had already benefited him, not a case of harming him.

9. Once vaccines against COVID-19 were introduced, some who refused to take the vaccine were described as harming others (rather than not saving them) because herd immunity would not be achieved or variants of the virus would be allowed to develop that would reduce protection afforded by vaccines. But just as wearing a mask that prevents transmission is not properly described as saving lives, refusing to get a vaccine may not be properly described as harming. This is because helping to produce herd immunity seems to be a way of helping others as shown by the fact that if someone who is vaccinated stays at home rather than interfacing with others, they do not contribute to herd immunity but they do not thereby harm others. Allowing new variants of a virus to develop is a more complicated case since it could be about helping to defeat a threat of the virus rather than harming people by threatening them with the virus. However, it might also be seen as a way of preventing one's body from being a location where a variant develops that would threaten the efficacy of current vaccines. If so, this would raise the issue of whether taking a vaccine (that also helps the person taking it) is beyond what one could have a duty to do to avoid becoming a threat.
10. So it is wrong to analogize what citizens are called on to do in wearing a mask to what soldiers were called on to do in wars, as an op ed writer did in *The New York Times* (May 31, 2021, available at https://www.nytimes.com/2021/05/30/opinion/memorial-day-covid-national-service.html). Governor Cuomo's statement (in his last daily briefing of 2020 on the pandemic to New Yorkers) failed to draw a different distinction, between sources of motivation. He said that wearing a mask is an act of love because we wear a mask to protect someone else, who wears a mask to protect us. However, wearing a mask can be motivated by a duty not to harm rather than by love. It could also be motivated by the self-interested desire to contribute to reciprocal behavior from which one will ultimately benefit. Furthermore, unlike not harming others, love cannot be legally or morally required.
11. When could someone have been said, as a matter of morality, to have waived his right not to be infected? On a libertarian view, assuming informed consent, he could simply announce that others are permitted to infect him though infection would cause him significant harm. Those attending President Trump's rallies were required to waive their legal rights to sue the Trump campaign if they did become infected, but this did not amount to a waiver of their rights against individuals in a rally who might infect them. In New York City many in the ultra-Orthodox Jewish communities refused to wear masks, and these communities had higher positive test results for COVID-19 than other areas in the city. The adults were said to have been informed of scientific evidence in favor of wearing masks but did not accept this evidence. They may have believed they would not be infected in the absence of a mask, but this is not a waiver of their right not to be infected or exposed to risk of infection. It is, however, the voluntary assumption by adults of risk about which they have been informed (even if they do not believe the warning). Putting to one side the children who might be involved, the people who might infect them are other members of their community who share their views about masks and with whom they voluntarily associate. If such adults only interacted with each other, it seems there would be no rights

violations if some infected others even without an explicit waiver on the part of the person infected. Libertarians and other anti-paternalists might have no problem with allowing people to risk themselves. Problems arise if members of this group enter into other communities and if there are either moral or legal problems with "ghettoizing" them to prevent the spread of the virus to those outside these communities. Harm that befalls people who have assumed risk for reasons of their own convenience also seems less tragic than harm that befalls people who have been trying to protect themselves from harm or have to expose themselves for reasons of duty or need. This could justifiably affect one's attitude to even large numbers of deaths from COVID-19 in the United States.

12. In his *Anarchy, State, and Utopia* (New York: Basic Books, 1974).
13. The man who is hurled may benefit from falling on the person he threatens if he would otherwise hit a stone floor and die. Susanne Burri notes this in her "The Toss-Up between a Profiting Innocent Threat and his Victim," *Journal of Political Philosophy* 23, no. 2 (2015): 146–65. By contrast someone who breathes out the virus on someone does not benefit from doing that by contrast to breathing out but not on someone. Burri notes that in my *Creation and Abortion* (New York: Oxford University Press, 1992) I distinguish between a threatening person who does and does not benefit from being where she threatens another. The former threatening person may lose only the benefit from being an unjustifiable threat when we stop her being a threat.
14. See my "The Insanity Defense, Innocent Threats, and Limited Alternatives," *Criminal Justice Ethics* 6, no. 1 (1987): 61–76.
15. How much cost innocent threats or morally responsible threats could be required to bear to avoid harming others is an issue I will discuss later. I continue to assume that wearing a mask and even quarantining oneself is not beyond what could be morally required of, and even imposed on a spreader when the threat presented is certain and serious.
16. In other work I consider whether this is also true about using safe vaccines against a virus. I consider the threat of transmitting disease in the absence of a vaccine. Separate from transmission, I also consider the threat to others of one's body being a location where mutation of a virus can occur, given that a variant could undermine the usefulness of currently available vaccines. See my "Handling Future Pandemics: Harming, Not Aiding, and Liberty."
17. See "A Pro-Freedom Approach to Infectious Disease" at the Ayn Rand Institute website: https://newideal.aynrand.org/pandemic-response/.
18. Throughout I will assume a subjective probability view of risk. That is, even if it is objectively true in a deterministic universe that a particular car driver will not harm anyone, it can only be reasonable for those who are not omniscient to believe she does present a risk.
19. Sometimes the same probability may be assigned to (1) someone being a person who will definitely infect others (or run over someone) as would be assigned to (2) someone known to be infected (or known to be driving) being at risk of infecting others (or running over someone). Nevertheless, the causal story is different: In (1) the risk arises from someone possibly having the virus (or possibly driving the

car) and in (2) the risk arises from the probability of someone who has the virus infecting others (or the probability of someone who is driving hitting someone). The fact that some people who were asked to wear masks do not have the virus makes not wearing masks in public also unlike not smoking cigarettes in public (to which Mayor Gelber of Miami compared it). This is because each smoker can contribute in a small way to the cumulative harm done to others, but someone without the virus would not contribute to cumulative harm to others. Yet he would be one of those who could be required to wear a mask.

20. There may be fairness issues raised by some not having to wear masks if enough others do so as they may be seen as free-riding on those others. The Group-Based Argument differs from an argument based on the risk that any given individual will infect others insofar as the Group-Based Argument involves the certainty that someone (though it is not known who) will infect others. So the requirement to wear a mask is not based just on the risk of infecting others but also on the certainty that infection will occur. There is an interesting parallel between (1) the case where there is a small probability of any one person being a threat but given the number of people, it is certain that someone will be a threat and (2) the case in which there is a small probability that someone will be a victim of a virus but given the large number of people susceptible to it, it is certain that someone will be a victim. In the latter case, it has been argued that we should save someone who is certain to die rather than prevent even some additional deaths that would result from the small chance of death that each of many people has at the time we must decide what to do. See N. Daniels, "Reasonable Disagreement about Identified vs. Statistical Victims," *Hastings Center Report*, May 2014, and J. Frick, "Treatment versus Prevention in the Fight against HIV/AIDS and the Problem of Identified versus Statistical Lives," in *Identified versus Statistical Lives: An Interdisciplinary Perspective*, ed. Glenn Cohen et al. (New York: Oxford University Press, 2015)). Analogously, it might be said that if there were a conflict with doing both, we should act against the person whom we know, at the time we must decide what to do, will certainly harm someone else rather than against each of the people in a group who has a small chance of being someone who will harm even more people. If this is so, what shall we say in a situation where there is no such conflict? It seems the cost imposed on each of the people who has a chance of (nonintentionally) harming someone should be less than the cost imposed on someone whom we know will certainly harm someone even if the same number of people will be victimized by someone in the group as by the single individual.
21. Could we not just do an expected utility calculation for each individual and translate the small possibility that they will cause a large harm into the certainty that they will cause a small harm? Then we might require each person to wear the mask to avoid certainly causing this small harm (e.g., a cold or a scratch). (I owe this suggestion to William Gildea.) My concern with this approach is that if we think that each person is wearing a mask so that, for example, each will not certainly give someone a cold or a scratch, we will not think it urgent that they do wear a mask. This is by contrast to emphasizing the certainty that some (even if fewer) will suffer the greater harm of death even if it is not certain who will cause that death.

22. Revised data available during the pandemic led the U.S. Centers for Disease Control and Prevention (CDC) to accept that the masks it recommended at that time for the general public do provide some protection for the wearer. However, during much of the time when wearing those masks was recommended, the emphasis was on each mask wearer, thereby protecting others. It is on this basis that I here consider the issue of paternalism. The public's confusion on this issue at a time when the CDC claimed mask wearing was primarily needed to prevent transmission to others might be exemplified by former New Jersey governor Chris Christie's expressed belief that he got COVID-19 by "letting down his guard" in not wearing a mask at a large event at the White House. But if his wearing a mask only protected others, his not wearing it would not have lowered his defense against the virus.
23. For example, the governor of Kentucky. See https://www.wlwt.com/article/beshear-compares-wearing-a-mask-to-wearing-a-seat-belt/33302787.
24. See also note 8.
25. Apparently, any mask can be made more protective for the person wearing it without increasing risk to him by inserting a HEPA filter into the mask. If this information were broadly known, it might have increased people's willingness to wear masks.
26. Later we consider health care professionals themselves taking self-defensive measures.
27. I discuss this issue further in "Handling Future Pandemics: Harming, Not Aiding, and Liberty."
28. Scholars of law and economics, such as Richard Posner, have argued (on the basis of the Coase Theorem) that we should decide where rights lie by finding out who would pay more to get what they want, the person who would be harmed (in order to avoid being harmed) or the person who would harm (in order to be free to do what harms). In the case of COVID-19 it might well be that the person who would be harmed would be willing to pay a lot to avoid infection and the person who would have to wear a mask would pay much less to avoid wearing one. It's not clear that libertarian or libertarian-like views cohere with this way of deciding where rights lie, however.
29. We shall consider some of these issues in greater detail in the section on lockdowns later.
30. Even if the right to health care were a human right, this does not imply that it is not subject to being forfeited (or weakened) so long as one is a human person. After all, there is a human right to liberty (it has been argued), but someone may lose that right and be incarcerated as punishment if he commits a crime.
31. Determining whether someone, B, is morally responsible for becoming someone who could infect health care workers is complicated by the fact that those, like A, who had the primary duty to wear masks but did not do so could bear primary responsibility for infecting B. Why should B suffer the loss of a right to health care when he is in part a victim? If there were easy ways to avoid maskless persons (e.g., social distancing, wearing a self-protective mask, etc.), then responsibility for becoming infected might still be borne in part by the infected person. Unlike the case of the innocent man hurled at others whose right not to be harmed is (arguably) overridden in order to save his victim, patients are ordinarily thought not to lose their right to treatment

regardless of how they came to be sick. However, this may ordinarily be true because personal protective equipment (PPE) is available to the doctors that protects them against infection. But the issue I am discussing arises when there is no such PPE available.

32. Daniel Hausman emphasized this point to me.
33. In response to my argument in *The Boston Review* against Bloom a colleague wrote to me: "It strikes me that you and Bloom are talking past one another. He is speaking in statistical life terms, where we do his calculus all the time. E.g., If we taxed the whole population in such a way as to provide better healthcare for a much smaller number of the most fragile, we could avoid some premature deaths, but then the taxed would perhaps forgo some voluntary medical procedures that could be life preserving or forgo recreational activities (or healthier but more expensive diets) that are similar. In a statistical sense, it would be better not to do the tax. But it's a comparison in a statistical sense; there are no identified lives in the balance, where we are commonly irrational (in this statistical sense)." Notice that this response suggests that more lives would ultimately be saved if we did not save the smaller number who would currently die. It really is another way of *not* interpersonally aggregating smaller losses to weigh the sum against greater individual losses to others, so it is *not* a defense of Bloom's original presentation that I criticized. My colleague's response sees the issues as (1) preventing deaths in identified persons now by contrast to (2) preventing deaths in unidentified persons (3) who would die later due to absence of some care that could be provided now. My objection to Bloom did not rest on these distinctions. Though I do not necessarily think relying on these distinctions is irrational, I will not discuss them here. See note 20 for some references on this topic.
34. In a Princeton Center for Human Values online colloquium on December 7, 2020, Prof. Olga Yakusheva reported on her research whose aim was to compare deaths averted by lockdowns and deaths caused by lockdowns. I assume her research did not involve aggregating life-years to create "lives." She estimated that many more deaths were averted than were caused (1.5 million versus 96,000). Sometime later statistics were released by the U.S. government claiming that on account of the pandemic in the United States up to that point average life expectancy for Whites had dropped one year from seventy-eight years, three years for Blacks from seventy-two, and two years for Latinx from eighty-two. (This may have included losses due to both deaths and lockdowns.) Blacks lost the most and wound up with the least given their lower starting point. It was surprising that though Latinx people lost more than Whites, they still wound up better than both Whites and Blacks in terms of longevity given their higher starting point than either other group. After initial news reports, emphasis was put on their loss rather on the fact that they were still more long lived.
35. The reasoning I describe in what follows (including the cases involving sore throat, leg, and three fingers) is based on my "Equal Treatment and Equal Chances," *Philosophy & Public Affairs* 14 (1985): 177–94; "The Choice Between People, 'Common Sense' Morality, and Doctors," *Bioethics* 1 (1987): 255–71; and *Morality, Mortality*, vol. 1 (New York: Oxford University Press, 1993), Chapters 5–10. A summary of the latter is available in my "Nonconsequentialism," in *Blackwell's Guide to Ethical Theory*

(Malden, MA and Hoboken, NJ: Wiley Blackwell, 2000 and 2013) and reprinted in my *Intricate Ethics* (New York: Oxford University Press, 2007). A yet shorter presentation is in my "Health and Equity," reprinted in my *Bioethical Prescriptions* (New York: Oxford University Press, 2013). The discussion of aggregation when an impartial aider must decide whom to help is relevant to the question of whether to delay or deny non-lifesaving therapies to many in order to provide lifesaving therapies to a fewer number of people. The need for such a choice arose in the COVID-19 pandemic when hospitals could not treat everyone. I discuss this issue in "Handling Future Pandemics: Harming, Not Aiding, and Liberty".

36. There has been much debate about whether numbers of people count since John Taurek published his article, "Should the Numbers Count?," *Philosophy & Public Affairs* 6, no. 4 (1977): 293–316.
37. Giving chances in proportion to the numbers of people in each group would not ignore the additional people. One would have to argue why balancing rather than proportional chances was the correct method to use. I discuss these issues in more detail in "Equal Treatment and Equal Chances"; *Morality, Mortality*, vol. 1; and other works cited in note 35.
38. Suppose we were certain that on which side the person in need of a sore throat cure was located was random. Then "where the sore throat is" could function as the random decision procedure. We might also select among random decision procedures (e.g., fair coins) on the basis of whether one of the coins was magical and so when flipped would cause a sore throat cure.
39. In "Nonconsequentialism" (reprinted in *Intricate Ethics*) I wrote (pp. 34–35): "According to nonconsequentialists, each of us who is otherwise fine has a duty to suffer (at least) a relatively minimal loss (e.g., a sore throat) in order to save another person's life. So long as suffering the small loss is a duty for any given person, no number of the small losses can be aggregated to outweigh saving the life. Further, if it matters to each person from his partial point of view that his be the life saved in a conflict situation, we each also have a duty to suffer a minimal loss in order to give someone else a significant chance at life. So long as suffering the small loss in order to give someone a significant chance at life is a duty for any given person, no number of the smaller losses can be aggregated and combined with another's life to outweigh someone's significant chance to live." I discuss different ways in which one could come to have the sore throat and how this bears on the duty to suffer it in "Handling Future Pandemics: Harming, Not Aiding, and Liberty."
40. This is how I used "relevant to" in previous work. I also think it is the use intended by Thomas Scanlon in his *What We Owe to Each Other* (Cambridge, MA: Harvard University Press, 1999). Would it be appropriate to say that in my view the leg is "relevant to" giving an equal 50% chance to each person whose life is at stake? (I owe this question to Daniel Hausman.) That would mean that giving each an equal chance to live could be morally less important than preventing someone from losing his leg. If this would imply that no one would have his life saved, it would be wrong. However, not losing the leg could be said to be "relevant to" giving a person a large equal chance to survive so long as someone does survive.

41. This is one objection I raised in *Morality, Mortality*, vol. 1, Chapter 9, to the first proposal I offered for determining what makes an extra good relevant in a choice between people's lives. The first proposal implied that if one did *not* have a duty to suffer a loss to save a life or give someone a 50% chance at life, then it was relevant to making a choice between people. For a short discussion of this issue see *Intricate Ethics*, 34–35.
42. Note that in this case the decision that someone has a duty to suffer the sore throat to save someone's life must take into account that other people will also be doing this. This requires that one person could not decline to make his sacrifice when it is still necessary on the ground that many will already being doing their duty.
43. Daniel Hausman has argued (in unpublished material) that if some of the sore throats will develop into a fatal condition if not tested for strep throat, then in being tested each of many people with a sore throat would receive a very small benefit of a reduced risk of dying. He argues that if only a few of the sore throats would develop into a fatal disease, this benefit to each is even smaller than curing a sore throat that will not turn fatal. Yet, given that some people will be saved from death in having their sore throats tested, at least as a matter of public policy, we should test many people rather than invest in a program that would save one person's life. Hence, Hausman concludes, we should also have a policy that would save many from a sore throat rather than a policy that would save one person from death. The objection to this argument is that it does not show that we should interpersonally aggregate small benefits *that stay small, so its conclusion about mere sore throats does not follow*. Rather, it shows that when deaths will result from not testing the sore throats, we should balance saving several people from death rather than one person, a conclusion for which I have already argued. The objection to Hausman's example is the same raised to my colleague's argument in note 33. It is also the same issue I raised when discussing in II (A) whether Bloom's figure of loss of a life-year per person due to lockdowns is an average, so that it may conceal loss of many years of life to some of the people on whom the average is based.
44. Presumably someone would be willing to run a small risk of death in order to avoid losing his own leg. If one has a much greater chance of being one of those who will lose a leg than of being the person who will die, it might be argued that one should similarly take that chance of dying. On this use of ex ante reasoning behind a veil of ignorance see the discussion in Chapter 5.
45. Suppose saving someone from partial paralysis was relevant to saving someone else from total paralysis and so saving many from partial paralysis rather than a few from total paralysis could be morally appropriate. This does not mean saving from partial paralysis is relevant to what total paralysis is relevant to (namely, saving even fewer from death). What if all three options are present at once? My view is that we may save those with total paralysis but not save those from partial paralysis even if we would do so were only these two options available. Though we do not act on the option of saving from death, it should nevertheless rule out what is not relevant to it (partial paralysis) being chosen. Notice that this remains true if only two options are present because we decided not to save someone in order to save more from total paralysis

and the person has already died. This is due to "path dependence": We come to the situation of having only two options because we decided not to save someone's life and so what is not relevant to saving a life is not something we should do. It would be wrong to let someone die and then turn our back on the reason that we did that (i.e., to save some from total paralysis). This is so even if, had we come to the situation of having the two options in a different way, saving many from partial paralysis should be preferred to saving fewer from total paralysis. See "Health and Equity," p. 370.

46. I discuss these issues in greater detail in, among other places, my *Morality, Mortality*, vol. 1, and "Health and Equity."
47. See his "How Should We Aggregate Competing Claims?," *Ethics* 125, no. 1 (2014): 64–87. Voorhoeve footnotes my previous work in this and some other connections (though he does not always identify the work in his text).
48. Voorhoeve does not discuss the case in which the choice is between one person and another person plus someone who needs a sore throat cured. Possibly he would think that the sum of weighted claims implies that we should save the two people. Suppose he thought that there was a duty to suffer a sore throat to give someone a 50% chance of life even when someone will be saved whether or not this is done. Then he could say the sore throat was an irrelevant good in this case as well.
49. By "nearly as much" I here mean to signal that some differences between even two competitors for a resource would be morally irrelevant. (This makes use of the notion of an irrelevant good in addition to the irrelevance of a third person's small loss in choosing between the two people whose lives are at stake. See *Morality, Mortality*, vol. 1, for more on this.) For example, suppose each of two people would suffer the loss of twenty years but one of them would lose an extra ten minutes. The ten minutes should not mean the two would not suffer comparable losses.
50. I discuss these issues in greater detail in, among other places, *Morality, Mortality*, vol. 1, and "Health and Equity."
51. Some would also consider the specific quality of those years. This results in multiplying years of life by quality, yielding the QALY measurement. I shall ignore quality judgments but use "adequate" to cover many types of years of life. I discuss the QALY measurement in other work such as "Aggregation, Allocating Scarce Resources, and Discrimination against the Disabled," reprinted in my *Bioethical Prescriptions* (New York: Oxford University Press, 2013).
52. I compare Deprivationism and Willhavehadism (as well as other views about the badness of death) most recently in my "The Badness of Death and What to Do about It (if Anything)," in eds. E. Gamlund and C. Solberg, *Saving People from the Harm of Death* (New York: Oxford University Press, 2019, 146–62) and as revised in my *Almost Over: Aging, Dying, Dead* (New York: Oxford University Press, 2020). It is very important for those who are prioritarians to decide whether they will use Deprivationism or Willhavehadism to decide how badly off someone will be if not helped. Willhavehadism explains (in the example given earlier in the text) why it is better to live to 150 rather than 80 even if one thereby loses out on more realistically possible life-years than one gains; one will have had more life before one dies.

53. An alternative way of making this point involves comparing the individuals among whom a choice must be made and giving priority to helping the person who will have had less if not helped.
54. In October 2020 *The New York Times* reported on a study that claimed that millions of life-years had been lost to COVID-19 in the United States. The study did emphasize that even though fewer young people than older people had died, life-years lost per person through younger deaths were greater than life-years lost per person due to older people dying. Nevertheless, the importance (as reported) of this fact to the study seemed to be to emphasize the impact on the total life-years lost when younger people died. This is different from emphasizing that each young individual suffered a greater loss than each of the older people or that each young person died having had less of the good of life than each older person. There was some concern about this study that their figure of life-years lost was inflated because the study had not taken account of the fact that many of those who died of COVID-19 had underlying health conditions that would have reduced the number of life-years they would have lived in any case. While this may be true, it is worth noting that on a Willhavehadist view, the deaths of people with pre-existing conditions might be worse for each of them than the death of someone who lost out on more years of life because the former will die having had fewer years of life than the latter.

    In the case of those who will have lived longer, more people may be affected when they die (e.g., grandchildren as well as children, though probably not parents). But before we add those other people's losses into the pairwise calculation, we have to consider whether the loss to them is as or almost as serious as the loss to people who actually die. Even if it would be much worse for each of those affected by someone else's death if they instead also died, being affected with lifelong damage might be as serious as loss of some years of life in those who died.
55. Suppose we apply the idea of diminishing marginal utility (DMU) to each additional life-year one gets. This can bring closer the results of focusing on future life-years lost and focusing on what someone will have had by the time of death. So, it might be said, due to DMU, giving twenty additional years of life to someone who has already had sixty years is really like giving ten years to a thirty-year-old. If that were so, the benefit given to the sixty-year-old by extending his life twenty years would really be less than the benefit given to the thirty-year-old in saving his life for an additional twelve years. Then even a view focused on maximizing future benefit from a treatment could often recommend saving the younger person who will get fewer years of life than the sixty-year-old. Two concerns about this approach are that (1) it is not clear that there is much or how much DMU of years of life, at least when we focus on the utility provided to the individuals who would otherwise die rather than on the instrumental utility of those years of life to the community, and (2) the point of focusing on the person who will have had the least by the time he dies is that the moral value of giving even a smaller benefit to that person could be greater than the moral value of giving even a greater benefit to someone else. Hence, suppose a sixty-year-old could live another forty years but due to DMU this is no more than a twenty-year period given to a thirty-year-old. It could still have greater moral value to give fifteen years to the

thirty-year-old than the already DMU-adjusted twenty years to the sixty-year-old. For more on these issues see my "The Badness of Death and What to Do about It (If Anything)."

An example within life involves having to decide whether to help (a) someone who will lose a million dollars and be left with many thousands or (b) someone who will lose thousands and be left with nothing. Though the first would lose more (even assuming DMU) than the second person, it would be reasonable to help the second person because he would be worse off if not helped. Nevertheless, one might give only some priority rather than absolute priority to the person who would be worse off if not helped. Suppose the person who will have had more by the time of death stands to gain much more if saved than the person who will have had less by the time of death. In *Morality, Mortality,* Volume 1 (New York: Oxford University Press, 1993), I suggested assigning multiplicative factors in accord with how badly off the worst off person would be by the time of death and using those factors to give extra weight to whatever good the worst off person stands to gain. Despite giving priority to him in this way, he may lose out on help in favor of a person who would be better off even if not helped.

56. That is, one would not have to be a libertarian or conservative to agree. Many nonconsequentialist views that deny that one has a duty to produce the best outcome allow that one has a morally sanctioned prerogative not to make such large sacrifices even to produce impartially considered better outcomes. By "up to a point" I mean to refer to the possibility that nonconsequentialist prerogatives have a threshold, as it has been suggested that nonconsequentialist negative rights have a threshold. See Chapters 9 and 13 in this volume on the idea of a threshold on rights. See also Judith Thomson's *The Realm of Rights* (Cambridge, MA: Harvard University Press, 1990).
57. That is, in this case I claim we can aggregate the number of rights violated when many individuals would each have his right violated. In threshold deontology, justifying overriding each would require the same additional amount of good to be achieved. This is unlike a view that claims that once there is a breach of a right, each additional subsequent breach requires less to override it. This might be because, for example, the first infringement of a right to free speech is a watershed and further infringements are not significant in the way the first is.
58. Their remarks were made in the colloquium already cited in note 35.
59. Warren Quinn is one of those who distinguish between intending harm, merely foreseeing harm, and intending involvement foreseeing harm. See his "Actions, Intentions, and Consequences: The Doctrine of Double Effect," *Philosophy & Public Affairs* 18, no. 4 (1989): 334–51.
60. Some in the medical community have, I believe, made similar mistakes in attempting to use the Trolley Problem to discuss imposing and lifting lockdowns in a pandemic. In one such attempt, the mistake occurs when those in lockdown are compared to five people toward whom a trolley is headed. I discuss this in my "Health Policy and Innocent Threats: Some Issues in Abortion and Pandemics".
61. We discussed such a case earlier in note 11.

# 15
# Harms, Wrongs, and Meaning in a Pandemic

When the number of people who died of COVID-19 in the United States reached 500,000 in February 2021 special notice was taken of this great tragedy. As a way of helping people appreciate how enormous an event this was, some commentators thought it would help to compare it to other events that involved a similar number of people losing their lives. For example, it was compared to all the United States lives lost on the battlefield in World Wars 1 and II and the Vietnam War (or World War II, the Korean War, and Vietnam). Such comparisons raise questions concerning the dimensions of comparison besides numbers, some of which are about degrees of harm, wrong, and meaningfulness, which are considered in this chapter. (Since the focus in the comparison was on the number of soldiers who died rather than on the number of other people affected by their deaths, this discussion will also focus on the people in the United States who die in a pandemic rather than on those in society affected by their deaths.)

1. **Harms.** As has been discussed in earlier chapters, harms and wrongs should be distinguished. Harms have to do (roughly) with how much worse off people are made relative to either how they were or would otherwise have been. Wrongs involve violations (and even permissible infringements) of persons' rights. These rights give others duties owed to those persons, and when there is a failure to perform the duty the right bearer may be wronged. Harms can occur without wrongs (as when a storm destroys one's property) and wrongs can occur without harms (as when we interfere with someone's privacy even as we benefit him). Wronging should also be distinguished from doing something wrong; it can be wrong not to be generous, but that does not mean that one will have wronged the people to whom one has failed to be generous (for one has not denied them that to which they had a right).

Suppose COVID-19 was the cause of 500,000 people dying just as they were about to die of a multiplicity of other conditions. Presumably, we would not consider this pandemic as serious as the one that began in 2020 because COVID-19 would in that case not rob people of much, if any, life they would otherwise have had. This suggests that one thing that is missing in the comparison of number of deaths is consideration of what harm befell those who lost their lives and what this implies about the badness of their deaths for them. Most deaths in the wars

*Rights and Their Limits: In Theory, Cases, and Pandemics.* F. M. Kamm, Oxford University Press.
© Oxford University Press 2022. DOI: 10.1093/oso/9780197567739.003.0015

mentioned were of young, healthy soldiers, each of whom could have been expected to otherwise live much longer and who also died at a young age having had few years of life.[1] They were greatly harmed by their deaths in part because it made them much worse off than they (probably) would otherwise have been in terms of having lived much longer lives. By contrast, it has been said that as of the time when the 500,000 mark was reached, 81% of all deaths due to COVID-19 occurred in people sixty-five or older who died, for the most part, losing out on fewer future life-years per person than each of the soldiers who died. Arguably, a pandemic would have caused much more harm to the people who died in it if it had targeted mostly otherwise young and healthy people.[2] As discussed in Chapter 14, another way of considering how bad someone's death is for him is to consider how many years of acceptable life he will have had by the time he dies. Someone who dies in old age will have had more years of life than someone who dies when young, and in this sense his death would be less bad for him. This could be true even if the young person would not lose out on as many future years of life as the older person. Even if we reserve the term "harm" for how much good one is caused to lose out on, we might say that the young soldier is caused to lose out on having had a long life, whereas this is not something the old person loses out on. Of course, this does not mean that the deaths in older people from COVID-19 were not tragic and terrible. It just means that the deaths of some are worse than the deaths of others in virtue of differences in what each person stands to lose or not have had (without this implying that they do not have equal moral status as persons).

Another comparison made (by a television journalist) to the 500,000 deaths from COVID-19 was the disappearance of the entire population of Sacramento, California. This comparison as well ignores the fact that many in that population would have lost out on more years of life or would have died having had fewer years of life than those who died of COVID-19 by the time of the 500,000 mark. People with some pre-existing conditions (such as diabetes and obesity) are said to have accounted for 78% of COVID-19 hospitalizations and at one point 20% of those hospitalized died. Like the elderly who die, those with pre-existing conditions might have lived fewer future years of life than healthy people even if COVID-19 had not killed them, but they are likely to die having had fewer years of life by the time they die than the elderly will have had. In this way their deaths are as bad for them as for the young soldier.

There is another distinction to be drawn. That is between *death* (understood to be the permanent end of someone's existence) and *dying* (which is the process that leads to death [when death is not sudden]). A comparison of deaths is different from a comparison of dyings. It is entirely possible that those who died from COVID have been harmed by the process of dying more than if they had died at the same time from other diseases or more than soldiers in wars were harmed by their process of dying. Indeed, if death ends the badness of someone's dying, it can be relatively better for them because it helps them avoid continuing life that may be worse than death because of the dying process. This need not mean that their deaths do not harm them since what could be a lesser harm by comparison to a greater harm would still be a harm. However, we should still consider whether the harms from the process of dying from COVID-19 are as significant for the person harmed as a soldier's dying young having had few years of life or losing out on many years of good future life even if his dying process is less bad.

2. **Wrongs.** Were U.S. soldiers who died in the wars mentioned not only harmed but wronged? They usually died because they were intentionally killed by soldiers on the opposing side. Those who died of COVID-19 were not intentionally killed by others. Does this mean soldiers who died were wronged but not those who died of COVID? Suppose the U.S. soldiers fought on the just side and were killed by those on the unjust side. On the traditional view of jus in bello (justice in carrying out the war), it is thought that soldiers are not wronged by the opponent soldiers (even on the unjust side) who intentionally kill them. This is because there is said to be an equal legal and moral right on the part of each side's soldiers to kill soldiers on the other side in combat. (The traditional view is described and defended by Michael Walzer in his *Just and Unjust Wars*.[3] Objections to this view are due most recently to Jeff McMahan in his *Killing in War*.[4]) They could be wronged by those who kill them if this killing is what is known as a war crime (e.g., intentionally killing captured soldiers), but it is not war crimes that constitute most deaths of soldiers in wars.

Consider other issues related to whether soldiers were wronged. If they volunteered for service or were legitimately sent to defend their country or its principles in a just war, then they would not be wronged in how they initially came to be exposed to being killed. They would have been wronged by the leaders of their own country if the war violated conditions of jus ad bellum (justice in starting war). This could happen, for example, if the war was unnecessary or futile—which would make their deaths unnecessary and avoidable—even if the war's goals were just. Even if such injustice was not present and (as we assumed) they were fighting on the just side, they could still be wronged by leaders on the unjust side who began or continued to fight an unjust war in which U.S. soldiers died. They could also be wronged if they were unnecessarily exposed to risk of death by poor decisions by their military commanders in deploying them in the war, though it is commonly held that the U.S. military takes avoiding harm to its own soldiers very seriously.

When the cause of one's death is a disease due to nature, one is not wronged by nature or the disease. We have no rights against nature or diseases per se; they do not have duties to us not to harm us that they violate. However, if diseases are due to some people's negligent or unreasonably risky behavior (let alone intentional wrongdoing), then those who die of the disease may be wronged by those people. This includes those in national and international organizations who fail in their responsibility for early warnings and containment of spreading disease. Wronging can also come about by a reasonably avoidable failure to provide assistance or resources to which people have a right. If the absence of medical testing, inadequate production and provision of the best protective equipment (e.g., N95 masks), and failure to provide available treatments are due to negligence, deaths that result may involve wronging.

In addition, when individuals can transmit disease to others, the failure to use simple measures that would prevent such transmission (such as use of masks or safe vaccines if available) can violate others' right not to be harmed and so wrong those people. In an interview Drew Faust claimed that "the sense of mastery over nature" has been seriously challenged by the pandemic. In what sense might this be true? At the time prior to the development of vaccines, science could not provide a simple shot that would prevent the disease without interfering with people's "normal" routines. But that does not mean that there were no means available to people to "master the disease." For example, it was said that when all people who interact use masks (even below the N95 grade), transmission of COVID-19 (at least in its early forms) could be reduced by 96%. The problem is that this means of mastery of the disease requires individuals to be responsible for altering their conduct away from what it had mostly been previously.

However, wronging by those who fail to easily contain or prevent transmission of COVID-19 would occur only if it is reasonable to expect them to know about the means to contain or prevent its transmission. They may not know because those responsible for acquiring such knowledge in the first instance have not yet discovered it. For example, suppose it is true that eating raw papayas actually prevents death from COVID-19, but there is no reason for anyone to believe this is true at the current time. Then the deaths from COVID-19 could have easily been avoided, but no one was wronged in the failure to provide raw papayas to the public. Those responsible for acquiring and transmitting knowledge may or may not be at fault in not yet knowing, but if they are at fault they may have wronged those whose deaths from the disease could have been prevented. Similarly, those who were at a certain time informed about the efficacy of using masks and yet did not prevent their transmitting disease by using them may have wronged some of those who died from COVID-19 by violating their right not to be harmed.

The seriousness of a wrong can be a function of the harm that is done; that is why though one can wrong someone by kicking them as well as by killing them, it is a more serious wrong to kill someone than to kick someone. So the earlier discussion of the varying harm of death to different people can bear on how serious a wrong may have been done to those who died from COVID-19. However, one could seriously wrong someone by violating an important moral right even if this does the person little or no harm (e.g., intentionally killing someone against his will even when the person has only a few days to live).

On the whole, it is possible that there may have been more wronging *by U.S. entities and persons* of many who died of COVID-19 than of U.S. soldiers who died in wars in the twentieth century even if the latter group were harmed to a greater degree than those who died of COVID-19 and were wronged by non-U.S. entities that engaged in unjust wars. This is so if the U.S. role in the wars was not unjust and if the care of political and military leaders, as well as fellow soldiers, to see to it that soldiers did not die unnecessarily was greater than the care by U.S. federal and state governments and individual U.S. citizens to see to it that their actions did not cause U.S. citizens to die unnecessarily from COVID-19.

On the other hand, suppose many of those who died of COVID-19 bear some moral responsibility for becoming infected when the alternative was remaining uninfected. For example, they may have exposed themselves to risk for no adequate reason (e.g., going to parties where they knew others would not be masked) or have agreed mutually to risk exposing each other. These victims of COVID-19 may be at least partially responsible for their own deaths and so their complaint at being wronged is not very strong even when others failed in their duty not to harm them. These people are unlike soldiers (and essential workers) who exposed themselves to risk as a matter of duty. Many ordinary U.S. citizens may have let each other and themselves down, which probably cannot be said of U.S. soldiers in past wars. There would also be a special contrast in that those soldiers were protecting U.S. citizens from harm that others would have imposed on them, thereby benefiting U.S. citizens. By contrast, not only did some of those who wronged U.S. citizens harm them, but even those who prevented themselves from harming others did not thereby benefit them since not making someone worse off is not (in general) the same as improving their condition.[5]

3. **Meaning.** Soldiers in at least some of the wars in the twentieth century may have believed and had good reason to believe that they would die for a worthy cause and that their risking their death was necessary to achieve the worthy cause. In this sense, their sacrifice at least seemed meaningful to them. Suppose at least some of the wars were in fact for a worthy cause that was great enough to justify many deaths and killings, and there was no other less bad way to achieve that cause. Then whether or not their sacrifice would have seemed meaningful to those who died, their deaths could have actually been meaningful. It is whether their deaths were meaningful (as an objective matter) rather than whether soldiers (merely) felt that they would be (as a subjective matter) that is most important. However, some wars may have failed either the subjective or objective test.

Many who died from COVID-19 could not be said to have risked or sacrificed their lives for some important, justifying purpose that was either subjectively or objectively meaningful. Their deaths were unnecessary not only in the sense that they were avoidable but also in the sense that they were not needed to achieve some justifying purpose that those who died could reasonably accept as making their deaths meaningful. Exceptions might include someone who voluntarily and supererogatorily (i.e., beyond the call of duty) participated in a challenge trial (in which she was injected with COVID-19 in order to see if a vaccine would protect her) and died from that COVID-19 injection. Essential workers did not intentionally expose themselves to risk of death in this way and their death would not provide the useful information about the lack of efficacy of a vaccine. Rather, they deliberately accepted the foreseen risk of death from COVID-19 in order to perform their essential duties or to provide income for their families. From a subjective and objective point of view the risk all these people took and their ensuing deaths might have been meaningful if the risk was worth the good that could only have been brought about by their supererogatory or dutiful actions. We can sometimes make it true after the fact that people "did not die in vain" by arranging for their deaths to have some instrumentally valuable role, such as teaching us how not to repeat past mistakes. However, this is not the same as that role providing a justifying purpose for their death or risk of it from the perspective of those who died (either subjectively or objectively).

In sum, my aim here is not to render an overall judgment on the relative seriousness of deaths in COVID-19 by comparison to military deaths in U.S. wars in the twentieth century. I am just concerned to emphasize that the meaninglessness, reasonable avoidability, and wronging involved in many deaths are factors in addition to the degree of harm to, and number of, those who died that should be considered in evaluating and comparing different deaths. Some deaths are worse harms than others for those who die, and there are different ways of thinking of the harm. Some deaths are wrongs, and some are meaningless. The number of deaths counts, but it is not all that counts.[6]

## Notes

1. Focusing on the loss of future life-years is a mark of Deprivationism as an account of the badness of death for the person who dies. Focusing on how many life-years one will have had is a mark of Willhavehadism as an account of the badness of death for the person who dies. On these two theories see Chapter 14 in this volume and my "The Badness of Death and What to Do about It (if Anything) in my *Almost Over: Aging, Dying, Dead* (New York: Oxford University Press, 2020).

2. In the summer of 2021 the Delta variant was seriously harming young children. This chapter was conceived prior to that change. Nevertheless, it still remains true (in 2022) that far fewer young people are seriously affected by COVID-19 than older people.
3. New York: Basic Books, 1977.
4. Oxford: Oxford University Press, 2009.
5. The contrast between not harming and benefiting was emphasized in connection with the pandemic that started in 2020 in Chapter 14.
6. This chapter is a revised version of my article "Harms, Wrongs, and Meaning in a Pandemic," *The Philosophers' Magazine,* June 3, 2021. https://www.philosophersmag.com/essays/246-harms-wrongs-and-meaning-in-a-pandemic

APPENDIX 1

# Claiming and Waiving Rights

## Claiming a Right

In having a right to something, do we acquire a right to demand that we be accorded that thing?[1] In my "Rights Beyond Interests"[2] (p. 94) I said:

> Rights are most often thought of either as claims to something or as a protected option to act . . . . (By "claim" I do not mean that anyone does [or is even permitted to] engage in the act of claiming but only that someone is entitled to something).[3]

I do not think that having a right necessarily implies that one has a right to engage in the act of claiming it—one form of which might be demanding it—if it was not respected. I think that a right does not necessarily entail a right to demand it even though the right gives rise to, or is equivalent to, a directed duty. That is, to have the right implies that someone else has a duty owed to you in particular as the right holder. Here is the sort of example I had in mind when I said that a demand right might not come along with a right involving a directed duty: A child might have a right against her parent for generous economic support and the parent would have a directed duty to the child to provide it. But, in virtue of the child/parent relationship, the child might have no standing to demand the support or rebuke the parent if he does not provide it. (The child might assert [state] that she has a right without this being an assertion of her right.) I don't think this is an "institutional case," in which some rights having directed duties may be explicitly specified as disjointed from the standing to demand, or merely a case in which the child has a standing to demand but it would be morally wrong for her to act on it. Furthermore, some third party, perhaps the child's godparent, could have the right to demand that the child receive what she had by right from the parent even though the godparent was not owed anything from the parent. The child would be wronged if she did not get that to which she had a right, she could justifiably resent the parent and lose trust in him on account of his failing in his duty to her, and it would be to her that the parent owes an apology or recompense. These characteristics would distinguish a parent's failure to conform with a directed duty owed to his child from the parent merely doing something wrong with regard to his child.

Another example might involve a person who does not have the standing to even address someone else—let alone demand anything. This might be a person who has forfeited such standing in virtue of having failed in his directed duties to the other person. I do not see why such a person could not nevertheless have a right that gives that other person a directed duty to him. For example, suppose every person has a right not to be lied to by others. If one person repeatedly lies to another person without excuse or justification, she still has a right not to be lied to by that other person. Yet she would not be in a position to object if she were lied to by that other person or demand that the other person not lie to her on account of her right.[4]

It also seems to me that one could have a right to something that someone else had a directed duty to one to provide and yet whether one had standing to enforce one's right would be a separate matter.

Another way in which a directed duty would not in fact give the bearer the standing to demand is if there had been a specific agreement to this effect. But in this case, it is because the right to demand was assumed to be part of the right that there would have to be a specific agreement to detach it. This is not the sort of case I had in mind, but it is still a case in which someone could have a right to performance of a directed duty. Yet it would be wrong to conclude without further investigation that they also had the standing to demand.

Now consider this issue specifically with respect to a theory of rights that isn't about serving interests but rather about respecting a person's status. I do not think such a theory is any different in not necessarily involving a right to demand performance of a directed duty. The example of the child and parent may suggest that it is only when one's status is not equal to that of the individual who owes one the duty that there is no right to demand. If this were true, then rights that were a reflection of one's high status might come along with the right to demand the directed duty. However, I don't think that this is necessarily so. Qualitative differences between people that were not a mark of greater or lesser status might still interfere with having the standing to demand. Indeed, respect for sufficiently high moral status held equally by all parties might, by its nature, rule out anyone having the standing to rebuke or demand things of those who failed in their directed duties and so wronged others.

Could all this be consistent with someone who was promised something sometimes having standing to demand it when the cost to her of nonperformance is high, while someone else who was not similarly promised had no standing to demand performance though the cost to her of nonperformance was just as high? I think this is possible. A right that had a directed duty as its correlative could fail to generate standing to demand on its own and yet in conjunction with another factor, such as high cost of nonperformance avoidable in no other way, it might generate standing to demand. I would consider this an instance of what I call contextual interaction.

Even if all that I have said is not wholly wrong, I think there are infelicities in the way I put my point in my earlier work. For example, in the passage quoted earlier, I said that even if a right is a claim, that does not mean that anyone actually claims or is even permitted to claim. This seems consistent with accepting that no one may actually engage in a demand and still have the standing to demand. Further, one could agree that no one is permitted to demand in the sense of morally permitted since it could be morally wrong to act on the standing to demand even if one has it. It would have been better to say that the right (or standing) to actively claim is not necessarily part of having a right that someone perform their directed duty that they owe to the right bearer. Another infelicity is my having said in arguing for directed duties that in their absence "you have no more (or less) ground for complaint . . . than anyone else" (*Intricate Ethics* 244). This was infelicitous if I also wanted to argue that your failing to get what is owed to you need not give you more standing to actively complain than anyone else.

Margaret Gilbert proposes a theory of demand rights according to which they arise through a joint commitment that gives someone a directed duty to the right bearer.[5] She finds it useful to think (following Feinberg) that as a result of the joint commitment the right bearer "owns" the dutiful act and because of this can demand it (e.g., p. 71). But for reasons similar to the ones I pointed to earlier, I don't see why owning something in itself gives one the standing to actively demand the thing if it is not given or to rebuke the person who wrongs one in not giving it. Her joint commitment account also leaves one wondering if there are *in rem* rights that give everyone a directed duty to you (e.g., not to kill you) that do not come about by way of joint commitments. As I understand it, she denies that there are. She claims that if you want someone to have a directed duty to you not to kill you, you should have an agreement with that person not to kill you. By contrast, I think that such an agreement is mostly a redundancy. (Perhaps in a forced-choice situation a person with whom you had an agreement that you not kill him has a stronger claim against your killing him than a person with whom you did not have the agreement, other things equal.)

In sum, it seems to me that there can be rights with directed duties in the absence of demand rights, that there can be rights with directed duties independent of joint commitments, and that rights stemming from joint commitments need not involve demand rights.

## Waiving a Right

Gilbert also denies that a right holder has standing to unilaterally waive (or even cancel) the right against someone. (However, she thinks he may waive a right he has to demand or rebuke [p. 178]). She says, "In the case of demand-rights grounded in a joint commitment a given right holder has the power to free the right's addressee of his obligation if and only if the addressee . . . has expressed his willingness to contribute to its rescission" (p. 178). According to Gilbert, a right from a promise is a demand right due to a joint commitment: there is no promise unless the potential right holder accepts the offer of a promise (pp. 108–11).[6] Further, suppose that I say to the promisor that I no longer want him to meet me for dinner after I had him promise to do so. On Gilbert's view, even if there is no additional burden to him, I am not able to free him of his obligation if he does not agree. (At one point, she describes him as saying to me that though I may have waived my right, I still have it and he is acting because of this. Presumably Gilbert's view also rules out my unilaterally giving up (alienating) my right.) She also says that I have an ancillary obligation not to act in ways that prevent the promisor from fulfilling his promise (p. 144). Hence, if I cannot unilaterally relieve him of his obligation and he does not agree, it seems I have acquired an obligation to him to meet him as a mere result of having accepted his promise to meet me. Relieving me of this ancillary obligation presumably will also require both of us agreeing, since if his promise to me is still in place, he will not have the standing to unilaterally waive his right to my ancillary duty to him.

This does not seem right to me. A commitment to me may result from something we do with each other and in that sense be a joint commitment. But I think it is a mistake to think it eliminates my standing to unilaterally rescind both his obligation to me (assuming there is no additional burden to him) and any ancillary obligations I would have to him had he continued to have an obligation to me. Gilbert cites cases as intuitive support for her views. But does a case in which someone insists on carrying out an obligation to meet me for dinner when I have waived my right that he do so provide intuitive support for the view that he has a right to consent to rescission? I don't think so.

## Notes

1. This appendix is based on my "A Note on Margaret Gilbert's *Rights and Demands*," *Law and Philosophy* 40 (2021): 89–95.
2. Originally published as "Rights," in *Oxford Handbook of Jurisprudence and Philosophy of Law*, ed. Jules Coleman, Kenneth Himma, and Scott Shapiro (Oxford: Oxford University Press, 2002), 476–613; subsequently reprinted as "Rights beyond Interests" in my *Intricate Ethics: Rights, Responsibilities and Permissible Harm* (Oxford: Oxford University Press, 2007), Chapter 8.
3. "Rights beyond Interests," p. 237.
4. Examples of this sort, in which someone retains a right but not a right to complain about violation of the first right, are employed by G.A. Cohen, "Casting the First Stone: Who Can, and Who Cannot, Condemn the Terrorists," *Royal Institute of Philosophy Supplement* 58 (2006): 113–36, and Johann Frick, "What We Owe to Hypocrites: Contractualism and the Speaker Relativity of Justification," *Philosophy & Public Affairs* 44, no. 4 (2017): 223–65.
5. In her *Rights and Demands* (Oxford: Oxford University Press, 2018).
6. This leads her to think (p. 110) that campaign promises that are not literally accepted by anyone are not full-fledged promises. Both the first President Bush (with respect to no new taxes) and President Trump (with respect to a wall between the United States and Mexico) appear to have viewed things differently.

APPENDIX 2

# The Moral Rights and Status of Animals: Considering Some Arguments

I. (A) I begin with consideration of Tom Regan's views in his *The Case for Animal Rights* (Los Angeles: University of California Press, 1984). Regan focuses on animals who "have a life" in the sense that they pursue goals and have a continuing self over time. (This need not involve self-consciousness or continuity of interests in his view.) He thinks all animals who reach this level (including humans) have equal moral status, which gives them equal inherent value. We have direct duties to these animals in the sense that just in virtue of their own properties we should treat them in certain ways. He also accepts the Hohfeldian view of claims rights that implies that they really amount to "directed duties"' that are owed to those who have the rights. On this ground he concludes that those to whom we have direct duties have rights (see pp. 150–154). Unlike Hohfeld, he is not concerned with legal rights but with moral rights that can exist independently of being legally recognized.

My concern with this argument of Regan's for animal rights is that there should be a distinction drawn between direct duties and directed duties. For example, there may be (or we can imagine that there are) animals who have very short lives and no goals but who are sentient and capable of experiencing pain. In virtue of the latter, presumably, we have a pro tanto direct duty (just in virtue of what they are) not to cause them pain. But such animals, even on Regan's view, would not have a self to whom one can owe such treatment, and so we would not have directed duties to them, and so they would not have rights (if these are understood as the correlatives of directed duties). Regan fails to see that there is no clear route from direct duties to directed duties and rights.

(B) With respect to the animals "who have a life," Regan accepts a non-species-relative view of value with which to evaluate the goods and bads in their life. On this ground he concludes that while they all have equal moral status, in virtue of their different capacities they stand to gain or lose different goods, that can differ in value, in living or losing their lives. For example, if an average dog dies, it will lose out on fewer important goods than an average human person will lose if he dies. Regan says that he does not want to deny that a human's life is better than a dog's life because of what it can contain. This is why the dog's death is less bad than an average human person's death, not because it is the death of a being that counts less in its own right. (This view of the badness of a death is based on the Deprivationist account that the badness of death depends on how much one is deprived of if one dies.)

Regan seems to combine these views with a nonconsequentialist view that we may not always impose a lesser loss on a being such as a dog with equal moral status just in order to save the life of another being who would get more good out of its life than the dog would lose. A possible exception to this is presented by his case in which a dog and a human person are both already under a threat of death. Regan thinks that if both are under threat of drowning on a raft that cannot sustain both of them, it is the dog not the person who should be thrown overboard in order to save at least one of them. However, this view seems to also imply that if two human people are on the raft the one who will have less good in his future life should be thrown over even if he will lose a lot more than a dog would. A morally preferred alternative might be to give each person an equal chance. If so, this suggests either that there is some difference in moral status between a dog and a person or that the difference in future good between two persons can never be as great as that between a dog and a person. Regan (and also Korsgaard in her book discussed in II later) seems to distinguish the previous case in which both dog and person are subject to a pre-existing threat from one in which the dog is not threatened. In the latter case, he as well as Korsgaard argue that one may not create a threat to the dog to save the life of the person (so this rules out harmful scientific use of a healthy dog in medical research). However, extrapolating from the raft case, they might agree to use a dog who is dying from a disease to save a person dying from a disease rather than let both die even when the alternative is available of using the person to save the dog or giving each an equal chance of being saved by using the other.

Regan also accepts that it is morally correct to save a greater number of beings rather than a smaller number of other beings each of whom stands to suffer a comparable loss when not all can be saved (other things equal). I will call this the Minimal Aggregation Thesis.

II. (A) Christine Korsgaard's arguments in her *Fellow Creatures* (Oxford: Oxford University Press, 2018) focus, like Regan's, on beings "with a life" who pursue goals and have a self that persists through time. However, she is not arguing for animals' moral rights since she thinks the notion of rights should be reserved for legal rights. Yet, in many ways her views are much more radical that Regan's.

First, she rejects the view (with one possible exception discussed later in [B]) that there are objective, interspecies judgments of the value of various pursuits and achievements in a life. She thinks that it is not true that the goods possible in the life of a human person are better than those possible in the life of a pig. Indeed, she says that she is denying that it is better to be a human person than a pig. In her view, something is valuable if it is valued by some creature and then it is only valuable to or for that creature; it is not that something is (or is to be) valued because it is antecedently, objectively valuable. Poetry may be valuable to people but it is not valuable to pigs and so, she claims, it is not inherently, nonrelatively (objectively) valuable. However, she does say that a creature can mistakenly value things; these are the things that are contrary to its good (e.g., not conducive to that kind of being's health and survival). This suggests that even in her system there is a standard for what is valuable for a being that is independent of what the being values and that the value of that valuable thing is tied to the survival and well-being of an individual (not a species). If this is so, it raises the further question of how it could be reasonable (as it seems it could be) for a creature to sacrifice its own well-being and survival for other things.

(B) Korsgaard's second radical position is based on her dominant view that value stems from valuing: It is only if something is valuable from the point of view of every creature that it has what she calls "absolute value." For example, she claims the life of a person would be more valuable absolutely than the life of other creatures only if every creature valued that person's life more than its own. This way of deciding what is more valuable conflicts with the possibility of recognizing that something is more valuable (or important) to *you* than something else is even while you recognize that the second thing is objectively more valuable or important. For example, ordinarily one thinks it is consistent for person A (i) to think that having his leg saved is more important from his personal point of view than having person B's life saved and yet (ii) to recognize that having B's life saved is more important from an impartial point of view than having A's leg saved.

If this common view is correct, why does it have to be a condition on something's being "absolutely" more valuable or important than something else that it be more valuable or important to each creature from its personal point of view? On the other hand, claiming that something is "absolutely" valuable or important if it is valuable or important to every creature, as Korsgaard holds, conflicts with the view that it is conceptually possible that all creatures can mistakenly value something that in fact lacks value. This view, of course, assumes we can conceptually distinguish between what is universally valued and what is worth being universally valued (i.e., what is objectively valuable), but Korsgaard's dominant view implies we cannot draw this distinction.

Despite introducing the idea of "absolute value" as what is valuable to all, Korsgaard subsequently makes it a linchpin of her argument for the moral status of animals (in Chapter 5) that they no less than persons take what is good for them to be "absolutely good" and persons do so on no better grounds than animals. It is not clear how this is consistent with her original notion of "absolute" unless she is claiming that all these beings are making a mistake. It is also not clear how it is consistent with her view that a person but not an animal can subject instincts and desires to evaluation, only endorsing and pursuing them if they are consistent with the ends of others—thus not taking what is good for one as "absolutely good." Indeed, she thinks the fact that people can take the ends of others into account when deciding what to do means only they and not animals are capable of acting according to what she thinks is truly the correct way of interacting with others. It is odd that she does not view this as a capability that speaks to the superiority of persons even if it doesn't imply that persons should be favored relative to other beings. Further, shouldn't her argument for animals' moral worth be based on what such persons discover to be the correct way to treat creatures who have ends rather than her actual argument, namely that persons' grounds for claiming their good has absolute value is no better than animals' grounds for doing so?

(C) Korsgaard's third radical claim is that death can be equally bad for each creature insofar as it loses everything it has (even if this is very little). This could be true intraspecies (so on her view death could be as bad for a pig that will lose little of what is good for pigs if it dies as for a pig that will lose much). A bird that has a very short life span and so will lose very little could have as bad a death as a creature that loses twenty years of its life. Furthermore, she also rejects the Minimal Aggregation Thesis and so would see no reason to save five rabbits from death rather than one other rabbit when all could not be saved.

(D) These theses seem to be the basis for Korsgaard's views about the relative worth of animals and human persons (even though she very sensitively distinguishes between the way animals and persons function). Rejecting the theses would undermine her particular way of defending the moral importance of animals. To accept her theses, we would have to accept the view that saving a chicken is no less important than saving a dog or a human being and it is only (as she says) species solidarity that might justify us in saving the human being.

III. (A) Shelly Kagan in his *Counting Animals: More or Less* (Oxford: Oxford University Press, 2019) denies that moral status is an all-or-nothing matter among creatures. He notes that even Regan (and we can add Korsgaard) focuses on animals with more complex capacities and this itself suggests that it is hard to assign the same moral status to all animals. Kagan also distinguishes descriptively between nonperson animals and persons on the basis of their capacities in almost exactly the way that Korsgaard does. However, like Regan and unlike Korsgaard, he accepts that there can be objective judgments of the value of capacities and contents of different beings' lives. Unlike Regan, he thinks the same capacities that give beings access to better contents that make life better for them also determine the degree of moral status of the being. He gives special weight to degrees of autonomy and moral self-governance that a being has as important to determining moral status. (In this regard, he seems more of a Kantian than Korsgaard, although he allows that capacities one could have had or that one has the potential to have also can play a role in determining the level of one's current moral status.)

(B) Kagan also thinks that even noncomplex beings have minimal moral status and, bypassing any proof of rights such as Regan attempts, he speaks of them as having rights to certain forms of treatment. He thinks this means that we can wrong them—not merely do the wrong thing with respect to them—if we do not treat them properly. So a fly could have a pro tanto right not to be swatted on his view. Despite this easy introduction of rights, Kagan speaks mostly in terms of the moral value of outcomes. However, he thinks this could be translated into the language of claims to be treated in certain ways.

(C) An important component of Kagan's view is that a given achievement or good (which could be common among different species) has greater moral value when it occurs in the life of a being who has greater moral status. So relieving the pain of a dog could have less moral value than relieving the same degree of pain in a human being (independent of considering any difference in further effects of the pain and its relief). Put in other terms, it could make the stringency of the dog's claim to be relieved of its pain less than the stringency of the human being's claim to be relieved of the same pain. Kagan defends the plausibility of this view by comparing it to the idea of a given pain having different moral value when it occurs in the life of someone who deserves the pain rather than someone who doesn't deserve it or in the life of someone who is already very badly off as opposed to someone who is doing well (a prioritarian view).

(D) A concern Kagan has about his own theory is what he calls the Problem of Normal Variation: Human persons differ in the capacities that he thinks give rise to moral status and this should result in there being variation in the moral status of different people. Given epistemological limitations, we may not be able to accurately capture the moral variations that track minor differences. However, an implication of Kagan's view is that a person who clearly has dementia has a lower moral status than a person who clearly does not have dementia and in this case there is no epistemological barrier to acting on the moral difference. But suppose the person with dementia retains the ability to enjoy music or select his preferred meal (known as task-relative competence). Kagan's view implies that this person's right to choose his music or dinner is weaker than the right to do these things of a human being without dementia; even if the desire of the person with dementia is as strong, it is had by a being of lower moral status and so morally counts for less. It may be either that Kagan is wrong about the moral status of these individuals differing or that differing moral status does not affect the moral value of otherwise equal experiences or satisfaction of desires in beings.[1]

## Notes

1. I am grateful to Alex Guerrero for comments on this appendix.

# Index

www.ingramcontent.com/pod-product-compliance
Lightning Source LLC
Chambersburg PA
CBHW071250180926
51613CB00002B/193
* 9 7 8 0 1 9 7 5 6 7 7 3 9 *